A Naturalist's Guide

MATAGORDA ISLAND

Wayne H. McAlister and Martha K. McAlister

UNIVERSITY OF TEXAS PRESS   AUSTIN

Requests for permission to reproduce material from this work should
be sent to Permissions, University of Texas Press, Box 7819, Austin,
TX 78713-7819.

☉ The paper used in this publication meets the minimum
requirements of American National Standard for Information
Sciences—Permanence of Paper for Printed Library Materials,
ANSI Z39.48-1984.

Library of Congress Cataloging-in-Publication Data

McAlister, Wayne H.
    Matagorda Island : a naturalist's guide / Wayne H. McAlister
and Martha K. McAlister.
       p.   cm.
    Includes bibliographical references and index.
    ISBN 0-292-75150-8. — ISBN 0-292-75151-6 (pbk.)
    1. Natural history—Texas—Matagorda Island.   2. Matagorda
Island (Tex.)—Description and travel.   3. Natural history—
Texas—Matagorda Island—Guidebooks.   I. McAlister, Martha K.
II. Title.
QH105.T4M38   1993
508.764'121—dc20   92-13024
                                                        CIP

Contents

Photo section following page 6

Preface and Acknowledgments

This guidebook, written with an ecological theme, not only names the common plants and animals but also emphasizes their interrelationships. It is intended to orient, to inform, and, hopefully, to excite the routine visitor to Matagorda Island. It should be of interest also to professionals, teachers, and students. Relationships among animals mostly involve who-eats-whom; among plants it means how to compete for scarce resources and tolerate environmental extremes. For both, it implies getting there and hanging on through good times and bad. But wind, water, and sand are as important as the biota itself for an understanding of the origin and continual adjustment of the ecosystem of this barrier island. We attempt to bring these living and nonliving elements together and suggest how a visitor can observe and enjoy them.

The book is intended to supplement, not to substitute for, the many well-illustrated field guides that are available. It is anticipated that all the birders who visit Matagorda will bring their Peterson, beachcombers their Andrews, and wildflower enthusiasts, their Ajilvsgi. These and many others are available in paperback at any well-stocked bookstore. We have listed some of our favorites in the bibliography.

The text will be most useful if it is read before your visit so you can plan and know what to watch for. Most readers, and especially first-time visitors, will benefit from Chapters 1, 2, and 4. If you are a cultural history buff, you should enjoy Chapter 3. The remaining chapters cover specific groups; after you read those that interest you, at least scan the others—you might become interested in something you didn't even know existed on the island.

The appendices are mostly for those with specialized interests:

1. Information about Matagorda Lighthouse, including a historical chronology.
2. Complete list of flowering plants, with their Latin names.
3. List of eighty common wildflowers by color.
4. Audubon Christmas bird count for three years.
5. Invertebrate list, necessarily incomplete, but including the Latin name of each creature mentioned in the text.

Matagorda Island has come into the public domain at an opportune time. The public is becoming environmentally aware and people are interested in visiting the island and in helping guide its destiny. Although management of the area is still in early stages—some political decisions are yet to be made—and interpretative programs are hardly begun, a guidebook seemed an early priority for promoting awareness and enjoyment of Matagorda Island. We hope you agree.

We owe many favors for the completion of this guidebook.

Brent Giezentanner, manager of the Aransas National Wildlife Refuge, gave us access to the island, encouragement, and unfailing interest. Other members of the U.S. Fish and Wildlife Service (USFWS) who assisted us in many ways include Jim Clark, Claude Lard, Mark Koepsel, Chris Pease, Ken Schwindt, Tom Stehn, Mickey Harris, Norman von Huevel, James Shelton, and Martha Talbot.

Ronny Gallagher, superintendent of the Matagorda Island State Park, permitted access to the island and was unstintingly accommodating. Other members of the Texas Parks and Wildlife Department (TPWD) who helped us were Dennis Brown, Luke Thompson, Sam Vinson, David Riskind, Raymond Neck, and Catrina Martin.

Neal and Diane Lillard, of the Texas Nature Conservancy, extended us gracious hospitality at the Wynne lodge.

Among the many others who contributed their expertise, suggestions, and encouragement were Linda Hetsel, Joe Hawes, and Arthur Barr.

Matagorda Island

Introduction

It's sunrise in Port O'Connor and you're off on a boat ride to the north end of Matagorda Island! Heading south along the Gulf Intracoastal Waterway, you must keep alert for fishing boats zooming off in all directions and give to a ponderous barge the right of way its unwavering course demands. On your left, Blackberry Island, studded with mesquites and capped by drifts of white sand, is sprinkled with soon-to-fade yellow saucers: last night's bloom of beach evening primroses. Until this quarter-mile strip was isolated by the dredging out of the waterway in 1939, it was the edge of the mainland. Though a few cattle graze here, the deep piles of dredge spoil look like wind-blown dunes, and desolate Blackberry Island already provides a nice contrast to the congestion of the mainland.

As the jumble of docks and machinery on the right bank thins, you pick up speed and run straight until, at marker #1, you leave the waterway and veer east through Ferry Channel Cut at the southern tip of Blackberry Island. Plunging into the openness of Espíritu Santo Bay, you keep the green channel markers on your port side and open the throttle in anticipation and sheer exuberance.

The mundane land draws back until there is only water, sky, and the prow of the boat, suffusing you with a sense of separation and remoteness. You feel your own meagerness, and a tweak of vulnerability, but also the exhilaration of detachment and liberation and the growing tingle of adventure.

The rushing air, snatching away all speech quieter than a shout directly in an ear, makes conversation difficult. After awhile it becomes too much of a distraction anyway, and you surrender to the white noise of the engine and the silence of your thoughts. Even as you are encompassed by space, you are ignored by time. The past left on the shore; the future still out of sight; a hypnotic sequence of wave crests, each identical to the last, suspends you in the present, moving but immovable, lacking even the desire to seek a fixed frame of reference. In this mood, the 4-mile journey across the bay becomes a dimensionless, abstract excursion in unconsidered self-absorption.

The watery approach, geographically necessary, is a psychologically vital part of your island expedition. While the body is propelled to its destination, the mind is swept out, the sense organs purged, and the muscles toned. By the end of the trip, you should be in the proper spirit to submit to the spell of Matagorda Island.

There are harbingers along the way to ward off a complete trance: magnificent frigatebirds and brown pelicans sitting humped atop guano-stained posts and platforms; laughing gulls and Caspian terns patrolling the edges of the wake; a passage through a silent constellation of cabbagehead jellyfish or the sight of dark dorsal fins of porpoises passing by. At the very least, an occasional striped mullet will flash silver above the waves in a show of piscine exhilaration. Out over the Gulf, the day's boon of cumulonimbus clouds boils up into a pastel cordillera, seared through here and there by shafts of sunlight. And there is always the taste of the salt spray, the cloying stickiness of the wet breeze, and the earliest warning that bare skin will burn, lips chap, and eyeballs ache unless they are protected from the raw edges of this fervent environment.

At another time of the year, the same trip may achieve its purpose with a different array of preliminaries. Among the muddy wintry waves pushed into jagged whitecaps by an unimpeded north wind, common loons and bufflehead ducks toss complacently—a juxtaposition bound to impress you with the difference between how cold it is and how cold it feels. A dark sky engenders somber thoughts; the thin, trailing funnel of a distant waterspout brings mixed thrill and anxiety; a drenching thunderstorm, direct from the sky to you, demands abject capitulation.

A cluster of white squares materializes from the darker smudge on the horizon, grows, and becomes buildings. Away to your left, the graceful silhouette of the lighthouse is etched against the northeastern horizon. A thin white strip to your right is a low ridge of oystershell along the island's margin. An abrupt bump on the dock brings you finally out of your reverie, and you gain the island on slightly wobbly legs, already in some measure a different person than when your jaunt began, and a prime subject for the magic of Matagorda.

You know that "No man is an island," but can you agree with an ecological corollary: "No island is an island"? Certainly there is land surrounded by water, but the boundary between the two is much less discrete than it seems. The edges are smudged by the crash and backwash of every breaker, continually breached by the onshore breeze, redesigned by storms, and rendered nearly meaningless by the constant exchange of matter and energy among the creatures that haunt the water, ply the air, and inhabit the sand.

This is no metaphorical island, then, but a fragile yet resilient ecosystem, an exquisite concatenation of time, sunshine, sky, sea, wind, sand, supremely adapted living inhabitants—and for awhile, you. Every ingredient, it seems, has come together at the right moment and place and in the correct proportion, and you are a significant part of the mix. Without you, all of the rest is meaningless, dumb, without value. The ecosystem needs to be comprehended just as you need to comprehend it. Together, there is a synergism: you become a more enlightened and self-satisfied person, the island a more revealing and revered place. Help perpetuate the opportunity. Pass the word, above all to your children.

CHAPTER 1

Matagorda Island

Location

The barrier islands of Texas are near the southern end of a great chain of low sandy bars that intermittently fringes the Atlantic and Gulf coasts from Long Island, New York, to La Pesca, Mexico. Over half of the state's 367 miles of Gulf coastline are on its principal barrier islands: Galveston, Matagorda, St. Joseph, Mustang, and Padre. These islands share a common geological history and topographic appearance but, because of slight differences in natural forces and considerable differences in human access and exploitation, each island has its own personality.

Matagorda Island, second from the east of the state's five barrier islands, lies 5 miles off the central Texas coast in Calhoun County, centered at about 96°20′ west longitude and 28°20′ north latitude. It is 45 air miles northeast of Corpus Christi and 120 air miles southwest of Houston. Pass Cavallo separates the island's north end from Matagorda Peninsula, and Cedar Bayou cuts the south end from St. Joseph Island. Matagorda is separated from the mainland by five shallow bays in which oyster reefs, live and dead, and islets of oystershell and dredge spoil are common. Fringing the north end of the island and emptying directly into Pass Cavallo, Matagorda Bay receives fresh-water discharge from the Lavaca/Navidad rivers; a current engineering project will reinstate a natural connection to the Colorado River. The other bays are part of the San Antonio/Guadalupe estuary. Nearly midway down Matagorda Island a series of shell islets called the First Chain stretches toward the mainland to separate Espíritu Santo Bay from San Antonio Bay. To the south, the Second Chain marks the division between San Antonio and Ayers bays. Finally, Mesquite Bay is bounded by Ayers Reef and the Third Chain.

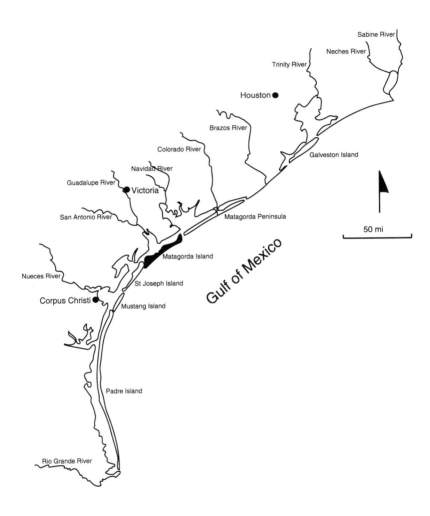

Map 1. Texas barrier islands and major drainage basins.

A coppice dune, captured by sea oats and Gulf croton and riddled with the burrows of ghost crabs, symbolizes the fragile beauty of Matagorda Island.

Third-order Fresnel lens installed in Matagorda Lighthouse in 1873. With only minor repairs, this durable collage of thick glass lenses and prisms survived the wrath of numerous hurricanes, the bumbling of a drunken air corpsman who managed to climb inside, and the vicissitudes of time. Removed from the lighthouse in 1977, the lens is currently on display in the Calhoun County Museum in Port Lavaca.

Matagorda Lighthouse and the cemetery. The view is from the east. The lighthouse was relocated to this site from the north perimeter of the island in 1873. The trees are saltcedars. Note the Spanish daggers growing among the tombstones.

The sand dunes and backbeach communities. Pioneering goat-foot
morning glory trails across the windswept backbeach. Gulf croton
has captured coppice dunes in the central area. In the background the
primary sand dunes are darkened by gulfdune paspalum and capped
with the waving seedheads of sea oats.

On August 5, 1981, this gantry withstood the abortive explosion of *Percheron*, the first of two attempts to launch a private spacecraft from Matagorda Island. This structure is located beside the main road on the south end of Matagorda Island, about 8 miles north of Cedar Bayou. The gantry for the second (and successful) launch was dismantled.

Shelter sites at the Army Hole campground near the main dock and Visitors' Center on the north end of Matagorda Island.

Barrier flat community in the vicinity of the lighthouse (center). The view is south, down the island's main axis. In the background to the left, longitudinal bands of vegetation (dark swale and pale ridge) are evident. The barrier flat meets the tidal flat along the right edge of the photograph. An extensive growth of saltcedars partly surrounds the lighthouse. The road in the foreground runs north toward the J-Hook.

The Wynne lodge. Originally built by Clint Murchison, subsequently enjoyed by the Toddie Lee Wynne family, today it is owned by the federal government and leased to the Texas Nature Conservancy. The building is located on a sandy upland about 4 miles north of Cedar Bayou on the south end of Matagorda Island. This view from the east shows the long, screened veranda (right-hand section) where guests enjoy the onshore breeze from the Gulf of Mexico.

Tidal flat community. The tide is in, covering the soft, dark sediment
and flooding a low marsh, which is an extensive mixed stand of maritime saltwort and perennial glasswort. The several tidal inlets provide
marsh access for marine fish and invertebrates. Everything from wading birds to fiddler crabs congregates along these waterways to tap
their bounty.

When a sand dune is isolated on the barrier flat behind the main dune ridge, it quickly becomes stabilized by a thick cover of vegetation. This secondary dune supports a variety of grasses, herbs, and, in the foreground, a clump of Texas prickly pear. Badgers and coyotes often excavate their dens at the base of secondary dunes, and birds of prey perch on the peaks.

Shells of common bivalves (clams) from Matagorda's beach: (1) blood ark (*Anadara ovalis*); (2) transverse ark (*Anadara transversa*); (3) incongruous ark (*Anadara brasiliana*); (4) ponderous ark (*Noetia ponderosa*); (5) mossy ark (*Arca imbricata*); (6) giant Atlantic cockle (*Dinocardium robustum*); (7) brown rangia (*Rangia flexuosa*); (8) disk (*Dosinia discus*); (9) sawtooth pen (*Atrina serrata*); (10) alternate tellin (*Tellina alternata*); (11) Clench's chione (*Chione clenchi*); (12) channeled duck clam (*Raeta plicatella*); (13) coquina clam (*Donax variabilis*); (14) yellow cockle (*Trachycardium muricatum*); and (15) Atlantic surf clam (*Spisula solidissima*). Scale is 2 inches long.

Shells of common univalves (snails) from Matagorda's beach: (1) lightning whelk (*Busycon contrarium*); (2) common sundial (*Architectonica granulata*); (3) scotch bonnet (*Phalium granulatum*); (4) common baby's ear (*Sinum perspectivum*); (5) Atlantic moon snail (*Polinices duplicatus*); (6) pear whelk (*Busycon spiratum*); (7) Salle's auger (*Hastula salleana*); (8) purple storm snail (*Janthina janthina*); (9) lettered olive (*Oliva sayana*); and (10) apple murex (*Murex pomum*). Scale is 2 inches long.

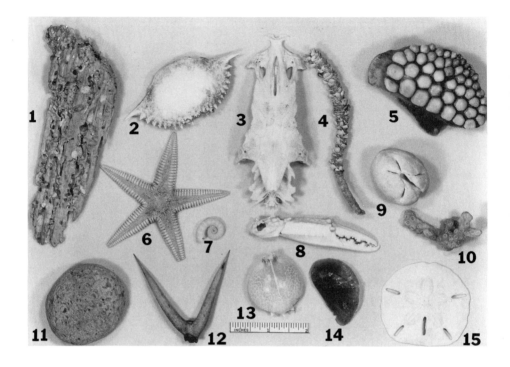

Sea wrack from Matagorda's beach: (1) wood riddled by burrowing clams (*Martesia sp.*); (2) the carapace of a speckled crab (*Arenaeus cribrarius*); (3) the skull of a gafftopsail catfish (*Bagre marinus*); (4) the tube of a plume worm (*Diopatra cuprae*); (5) pebble teeth from the throat of a black drum (*Pogonias cromis*); (6) a two-spined starfish (*Astropecten duplicatus*); (7) the internal shell of a pelagic squid (*Spirula spirula*); (8) the cheliped of a speckled crab (*Arenaeus cribrarius*); (9) the internal skeleton of a heart urchin (*Moira atropos*); (10) an ivory bush coral (*Oculina sp.*); (11) pumice (volcanic glass); (12) thorns from a bull's horn acacia (*Acacia cornigera*); (13) the carapace of a purse crab (*Persephona aguilonaris*); (14) the operculum from a lightning whelk (*Busycon contrarium*); and (15) a sand dollar, the internal skeleton of a keyhole urchin (*Mellita quinquiesperforata*). Scale is 2 inches long.

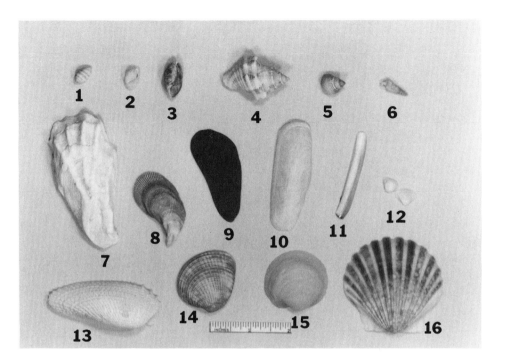

Shells of common molluscs from Matagorda's bay side: (1) saltmarsh snail (*Melampus bidentatus*); (2) elegant paper bubble (*Haminoea antillarum*); (3) striate bubble (*Bulla striata*); (4) rock shell (*Stramonita haemostoma*); (5) marsh periwinkle (*Littorina irrorata*); (6) plicate horn shell (*Cerithidea pliculosa*); (7) eastern oyster (*Crassostrea virginica*); (8) hooked mussel (*Ischadium recurvum*); (9) ribbed mussel (*Geukensia demissus*); (10) razor clam (*Tagelus plebius*); (11) jackknife clam (*Ensis minor*); (12) dwarf surf clam (*Mulinia lateralis*); (13) angel wing (*Cyrtopleura costata*); (14) cross-barred venus (*Chione cancellata*); (15) thick lucine (*Phacoides pectinatus*); and (16) bay scallop (*Argopecten irradians*). Scale is 2 inches long.

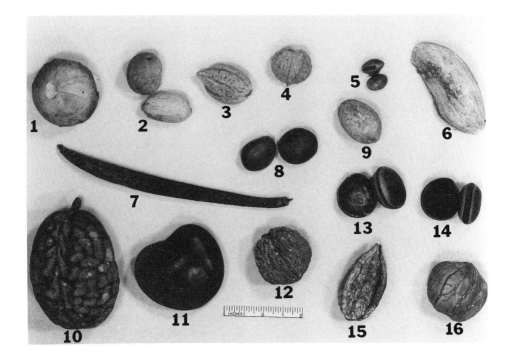

Common seabeans from the beach on Matagorda Island: (1) sea coconut (*Manicaria saccifera*); (2) cocoid palms (*Acrocomia spp.* above &
Maximiliana caribaea below); (3) country almond (*Terminalia catappa*);
(4) water hickory (*Carya aquatica*); (5) bay bean (*Canavalia sp.*);
(6) mango (*Mangifera indica*); (7) red mangrove (*Rhizophora mangle*);
(8) nickernut (*Caesalpinia sp.*); (9) pecan (*Carya illinoensis*); (10) Donovan's brain (*Andira galeottiana*); (11) sea heart (*Entada gigas*); (12) black
walnut (*Juglans nigra*); (13) sea purse (*Dioclea sp.*); (14) true seabean
(*Mucuna sp.*); (15) white walnut (*Juglans cinerea*); and (16) Jamaican
walnut (*Juglans jamaicensis*). Scale is 2 inches long.

Setting

The mainland adjacent to Matagorda Island currently is not heavily developed. The Port O'Connor peninsula across from the northern half of the island is largely sandy grazing land, with the unincorporated community of Port O'Connor on its tip and Port Lavaca 18 miles further inland. Victoria (population 50,000+) is about 50 miles to the northwest. The southern half of the island lies across San Antonio Bay from Blackjack Peninsula, a unit of the Aransas National Wildlife Refuge.

The island is not as disjunct from the bustle of the world as it seems. The Coastal Bend lies at the center of that 6 percent of the state where 33 percent of the people and industry occur, and local growth is on the upswing. Agriculture, the petrochemical industry, commercial and recreational fisheries, and tourism constitute the backbone of the local economy. Heavy barge traffic plies the Gulf Intracoastal Waterway, which hugs the coastline and transects San Antonio and Matagorda bays. Deep-draft cargo vessels enter Matagorda Bay via the Matagorda Ship Channel and there is talk of a major deepwater port in the vicinity. Portions of the bays have sediments laced with industrial toxins. Tons of human debris annually accumulate on the Gulf beaches. Like virtually every other stretch of Gulf coastline, Matagorda Island lies in an area where the overall quality of the environment is in increasing jeopardy.

The barrier islands form the distinctive gulf-side edge of the Gulf Prairies and Marshes vegetation zone. The prairie, parallel to the shoreline and extending inland about 40 miles, is a flat, poorly drained expanse of medium-high grasses dissected by sluggish rivers and sloughs. Mottes of scrubby live oaks dot the sandy uplands and wind-sculpted forests crouch along the streams. Near the coast, the grasses blend first into damp meadows of rushes and sedges rimmed with rattlepods, and finally into swamplands choked with cattails and bulrushes. On increasingly saline uplands, rank clumps of Gulf Coast cordgrass reign.

Where the stream deltas turn brackish, a dense but narrow band of salt-marsh vegetation begins, pushes to the edges of the soft mud flats, and skips across the tops of the spoil islands (heaps of sediment dredged out of bay channels). The open bays have no emergent plants, but shallows support luxuriant submerged gardens of marine "grasses." The maze of protected coves on the backside of Matagorda Island has extensive salt marshes, and the sandy nucleus of the island nurtures a distinctive plant cover.

A barrier island, though a discrete land mass, is also an integral part of an ecosystem—a ramifying and interrelated set of living and nonliving elements that collectively produce the natural environment. This only-partly-understood relationship extends as far as we care to probe: from the island itself to its living inhabitants, and on to the climate, the Gulf of Mexico, the passes, the bays, and the local rivers and their inland watersheds. It is not only the position but the very presence of a barrier island that renders it such a critical part of the ecosystem; its ecological roles are suggested by its name. A "barrier" creates a shallow shoreside lagoon and protects it from all but the stormiest moods of the ocean.

Where fresh water comes in, a lagoon becomes a highly productive estuary. The rivers pour in sediment-laden water, continuously replenishing a nutritious broth and creating a gradient in salinity from fresh through brackish to marine. By absorbing and diverting the energy of the Gulf, a barrier allows the accretion of a rich river delta with mud flats, algal crusts, oyster reefs, submerged grass beds, and fringing marshes. The passes play their part as outlets for floods and storms that flush the bays, and as portals for sea creatures seeking a place to spawn, mature, catch prey, or take up permanent residence. So, an estuary becomes a seething reservoir of wildlife that passes water-borne detritus up through bacteria, widgeon grass, crustacea, molluscs, and worms on to fish, birds, raccoons, and humans. Because of its location and alignment, Matagorda Island stimulated the formation of the Guadalupe/San Antonio estuary, one of the eight major estuaries along the Texas coast.

Physiography

Matagorda Island is 38 miles long and varies in width from ¾ mile at Cedar Point near the center to over 4 miles at the ancient flood-tide delta near the Wynne lodge at the south end and at the active delta of Pass Cavallo on the north end. In contrast to the smooth Gulf shoreline, the back side is some 80 miles of irregularly contorted bay shore. The island encompasses nearly 57,000 acres, making it a distant second to Padre and twice the size of neighboring St. Joseph.

In general appearance Matagorda is a typical Gulf barrier island, with a straight, high-energy Gulf shoreline edging a broad sandy beach that extends to a prominent line of sand dunes about 15 feet high. The interior, essentially flat with occasional isolated clusters of interior dunes, grades into the much-dissected backshore of the lagoon. Its long axis and main physiographic zones are aligned parallel to the sea and every surface feature is profiled by the prevailing on-

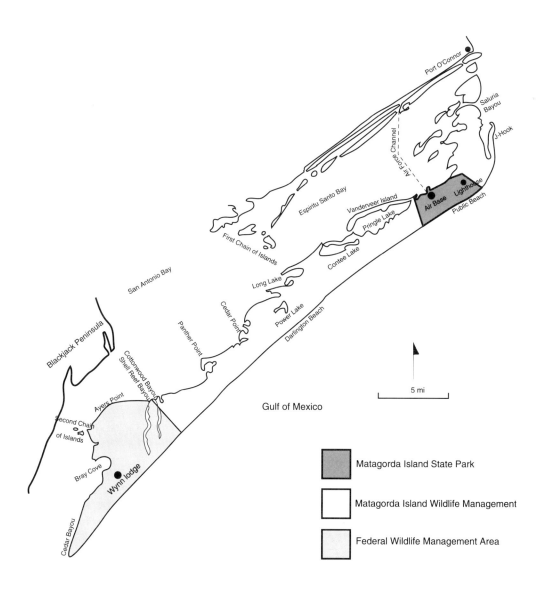

Map 2. Matagorda Island landmarks.

shore wind. The midrib of Matagorda Island lies east-northeast by west-southwest, so the ends should be designated east and west, but we have bowed to tradition and refer to them as the north end, with the state park, and the south end, with the Wynne lodge.

Most of the surface of the island is 5 to 8 feet above sea level, but washover channels may be below sea level until they fill with sand, and the dune chain, which averages 10 to 15 feet high, has taller crests at 20 to 25 feet. One exceptional dune near Cedar Bayou is over 40 feet high. The most picturesque dunes occur where irregularities cause excessive deposition of sand by the longshore current—at the public beach south of Pass Cavallo and just north of Cedar Bayou on the southern end of the island. The alignment of the strong south-bound offshore current sweeps sand past the midsection of the island, and here, lacking a significant recharge of sand, the narrow beach is not backed by a dune ridge. Storms can reduce the dunes or plane them off entirely, in which case it usually takes about two years for them to rebuild.

Water Depth

Matagorda Island is the emergent top of an elongate mound of sand heaped about 40 feet thick upon compacted marine and fluvial sediments. Off its Gulf shore the firm bottom of sand and crushed shell descends through a series of bars and troughs in 5-foot-deep water in the breaker zone to a depth of 10 feet about 300 yards from shore. On the bay side the water deepens very gradually over a soft bottom of muddy sand. Although Matagorda Bay gets 12 to 14 feet deep in places, the other bays seldom go beyond 6 to 8 feet, and one can wade several hundred feet from shore with more concern about deep ooze than deep water.

The bay bottoms are laced with submerged pipelines, and many sectors have been dredged for oystershell. Most dredging scars have filled with sediment. The Army Hole, a popular fishing site, is located just off the bay shore of Matagorda Island about 1,000 yards south of the Parks and Wildlife dock. This deep spot resulted when a large quantity of bottom material was pumped onto the island in the 1940s to level the ground for the air base runways.

All of the bays have navigation channels with attendant spoil banks in various stages of emergence. The two prominent channels are the Gulf Intracoastal Waterway, a 125-foot-wide and 12-foot-deep channel that hugs the mainland until it slices across San Antonio and Matagorda bays, and the 38-foot-deep Matagorda Ship Channel, which extends from a cut through Matagorda Peninsula to Lavaca Bay. The old military Ferry Channel, main route to the north end of Matagorda Island, leaves the Gulf Intracoastal Waterway near Port O'Connor through a cut in the prominent ridge of spoil and angles 4½ miles across Espíritu Santo Bay to the Parks and Wildlife dock. The Wynne Channel exits from the Gulf Intracoastal Waterway farther south and bisects Mesquite Bay for about 5 miles to the boat dock at the Wynne lodge. This is the main access to the south end of the island.

Pass Cavallo is the durable inlet that separates the north end of Matagorda Island from the tip of Matagorda Peninsula. At the time of discovery, it was nearly 2 miles wide and had an emergent shoal— Pelican Island—capped by 20-foot dunes. The main channel was 2,000 feet across and nearly 40 feet deep. This conformation remained essentially unchanged until the 1960s. In 1961, Hurricane Carla forcefully reshaped the north end of the island, and in 1965, the Matagorda Ship Channel was cut through Matagorda Peninsula 3 miles north of the pass. This new inlet sapped much of the water flow from the natural pass, and its associated jetties interfered with the movement of sand along the coast.

The combination of the hurricane's fury and the impact of the ship channel formed a thin peninsula—the J-Hook—at the northeastern tip of Matagorda Island. This tenuous strip of sand, probably ephemeral and destined to be reshaped or erased by future storms, is the site of popular Sunday Beach. The J-Hook curves across the shallow bars to incorporate Pelican Island in its tip and encloses a deep pocket of protected water that was the main channel of Pass Cavallo. The channel has now shifted to the outside border of the sand spit. Persistent shoreline erosion and a gradual migration of Pass Cavallo westward added to this recent resculpting and have made it impossible to locate the historic structures that were once on the north end of Matagorda Island. Pass Cavallo remains a major water exchange portal that has never been known to close.

Cedar Bayou, the shallow, fickle inlet that separates the south end of Matagorda from St. Joseph Island, has opened and closed naturally in the historic past and has been dredged open several times. It ranges from 2 to 9 feet in depth and can usually be waded at its Gulf end. Its 9-mile length was most recently dredged, to a depth of 6 feet, in 1987.

Soils

The young, sandy soils of Matagorda Island derive, ultimately, from material eroded from the interior of the state and carried by rivers to the Gulf. They are low in organic matter and rapidly permeable to water, and are either *eolian* (wind-deposited) or *littoral* (wave-deposited) in origin. Two main horizons can be recognized: the main island sands and the back island sands.

The main island sands that make up the bulk of Matagorda are sands picked up by longshore currents and pushed onto the barrier shoreline by waves. The *psamment zone,* the wet sand freshly piled onto the beach, is not really soil, but a washed and sorted mix of sand grains and pulverized shell. It is the source of sand for the remainder of the island. Under slight magnification it can be seen that the rivers and the sea have already produced a highly selective blend; there is no gravel, mud, or clay and only a few bits of dark mineral matter. The uniformly small grains are washed clean and the edges of each sparkling quartz nugget are rounded from ceaseless abrasion during transport.

But, however meticulous the waves are at sorting sand, the wind is even more exacting. Once it has dried on the upper beach, the sand is subject to the onshore breeze, which picks up only the smallest particles and then re-sorts these, moving the very finest ones farther inland and piling them into dunes and the low ridges and flats across the island's interior. Once this sand is captured by vegetation, it forms the typical quick-drying, deep, sandy surface that the pedologist calls Galveston soil. In depressions and swales that hold ponds of rainwater or overwashes of salt water for variable periods, this same sand develops a higher organic content and becomes Adamsville soil.

The back island sands mainly come from sediments thrown ashore from the bays by northerly winds, waves, and tides. In this low-energy environment the sand grains are less polished and the stratum is dark with mud and clay and specked with fragments of shell; often the bacterial flora give it a sulphurous odor. Although its organic content is high, the zone is saturated with salt water and usually low in oxygen; thus, the resulting Bayucos soil supports only hardy salt-marsh vegetation.

Fresh Water

On Matagorda Island the lack of fresh water can be a serious problem for plants, animals, and humans. The Gulf Coast Aquifer underlies the Texas barriers, but at great depth; insular wells drilled nearly 2,500 feet deep have failed to tap potable water. With heavy rains, water collects in natural depressions and in artificial scrapes and ditches, where it remains for variable periods, but most of these dry up, turn brackish, or are fouled by overwash of salt water. Fortunately, there is a shallow *perched aquifer* around which the fresh-water economy of the island revolves.

A perched aquifer is a lens of fresh water trapped in the sand 8 to 10 feet below the surface of the island's interior. Rainfall, the sole source of this water, percolates rapidly down through the porous, sandy soil before it can evaporate or run off. This fresh water is slightly less dense than salt water, so it floats on the top of the salt-water table without immediate mixing. For those creatures that can reach it, this delicately suspended sand slurry of fresh water is the sustenance of life on the island, and it inhibits the rise of salt water into the root zone.

Some plants make do by catching rainfall directly; others plunge their roots to the shallow aquifer, especially in favorable spots such as swales, where the fresh water often lies within 20 to 40 inches of the surface. Many smaller animals take advantage of the heavy dew-fall for their water needs, but most of the larger ones drink from surface depressions, a few of which are deep enough to tap the aquifer and so are permanent sources of water.

Humans must have a lot of water for themselves and for their ill-adapted livestock. To get it, they drive perforated pipes into the aquifer. Tiny holes allow the water to slowly seep into the pipe while holding back most of the sand. This water is then drawn to the surface, traditionally and most economically with a windmill, and stored in cisterns or allowed to dribble into concrete troughs or "stock tanks" excavated in the sand. For drinking purposes, Matagorda Island ranchers caught rainwater from their rooftops in cisterns, but depended on windmills for water for other household uses and for livestock. Today, electric pumps and pressure tanks make the water available for routine use, but a high content of suspended solids and a strong alkaline taste force the importation of bottled water for drinking. Some people unaccustomed to island water are sickened by drinking it.

Although the shallow aquifer suffices for the natural communities on a barrier island, it is not enough for sizable groups of people. Aside from its inferior quality, the volume, always small, shrinks in direct relation to rainfall, leading to failure at the times of greatest demand. It is easily contaminated with salt water by storm overwash, and during droughts the upward diffusion of salt into the unreplenished fresh water finally renders it completely unusable. Also, sand easily passes human effluent to the water table. Once the aquifer is tainted, only heavy rainfall can purge it.

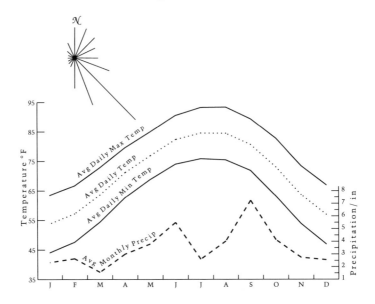

Figure 1. Temperature and rainfall averages for Port Lavaca, Texas. Wind rose shows average annual surface winds at Corpus Christi. Angle of lines indicates direction of wind origin; line length is proportional to wind frequency (data from the National Weather Service).

Climate

The climate of Matagorda Island is characterized as maritime, humid, and subtropical. The weather is both dominated and moderated by warm air masses that steam up over the Gulf of Mexico. Summers are generally sticky-hot and winters pleasantly mild.

The average annual temperature is 70° F; average daily temperature extremes are 46° and 66° F during the winter and 75° and 93° F in summer. In a typical year there are 104 days when the temperature reaches or exceeds 90° F and only 11 days when it drops to freezing or below. The frost-free period is a prolonged 300 days, from February 19 to December 16. The average annual precipitation is 38.56 inches, peaking in May–June and August–September. March and July are the driest months, and hurricane season (mostly August–September) is apt to overflow the rain gauge. Overall, the region receives 64 percent of the potentially available sunshine; the value drops to 50 percent in the winter and rises to 75 percent during the summer.

However, these weather statistics come from Port Lavaca, 18 miles inland. There are no long-term climatic data for Matagorda Island itself, and only intuition and anecdote suggest how different it may be from the mainland. And all of these averages are derived from just over a quarter-century of weather record keeping. They provide little more than a vague baseline for the climate of Matagorda Island, and they impart little significant information about extremes and the collective ecological impact of the several parameters.

Generally, the barrier would be expected to have more moderate temperatures than Port Lavaca, somewhat higher prevailing winds, and slightly higher rainfall. Because of its alignment and its length, the north end of the island receives significantly more rain than the south end. There are marked short-term differences in temperature, humidity, and so on between the bay-shore and Gulf-shore sides of Matagorda, especially during tropical storms and northers—short-lived, gusty, wintertime northwesterlies. Any visitor can verify a striking contrast in comfort at different points on the island according to the season and immediate weather pattern. No doubt the resident plants and wildlife experience a comparable sensation.

Humidity

Humidity is a measure of the amount of water vapor in the air. Because the relative humidity on Matagorda Island is persistently high, it is an important aspect of the climate. It is the wet Gulf air, slowing the rate at which the island cools off and heats up, that keeps summer and winter temperature extremes inside those on the mainland.

Gulf moisture also accounts for exceptionally heavy winter dewfalls; for the fact that northers are often preceded or accompanied by rainfall; and for the high frequency of coastal thunderstorms, tropical storms, and hurricanes. Warm air holds a lot of moisture, and when it cools, its water vapor condenses as dew, cloud, or rain. During the day, the wet air, heated by the sun-warmed land, rises. As it rises, it cools, and its moisture condenses into the endless ranks of cumulus clouds and the stupendous muttering thunderheads so characteristic of summertime near the sea.

And everyone knows that on the Gulf Coast "it's not the heat that gets you, it's the humidity." Moist air resists rapid change in temperature and retards evaporation, making a warm afternoon seem unbearably stifling and a summertime onshore breeze delightful. And it is the combination of wind and moist skin that makes a mild norther feel bone-chilling.

two, the island, which depends exclusively on rainfall for its fresh water, rapidly deteriorates into drought. Such dry intervals are apparently the climatic mode: seven severe droughts have been recorded on Matagorda Island since the 1890s, with the latest occurring in the 1950s; the early 1990s may be ushering in another withering siege.

In normal years Matagorda has just enough rain to support a good growth of grasses and forbs across the interior of the island and over the lee sides of the dunes. In the summertime, or during recurrent dry spells and outright droughts, the vegetation draws back, especially on the drier dunes and ridges, exposing previously protected sand to the wind. Then the entire landscape begins to move. The current physiography and stability of Matagorda, as well as the diversity and abundance of its wildlife, reflect the historic balance between the natural forces of rainfall and plant cover on the one hand, and wind and sand on the other. Thus, it is the geographic position of Matagorda Island along the rainfall gradient that accounts for its appearance as compared, for instance, to that of Padre Island, on the arid end of the scale, with higher, more active dunes, a more open interior, and broad barren flats bordering its bay-side lagoon.

Matagorda Island is almost always in need of a good rain. The deluge from a tropical storm may leave the depressions brimming and the swales boggy, but most of this water soon disappears into the sand. The aquifer can hold only so much, and once it is full, the excess drains away into the sea. Within days of a downpour, evaporation dries the surface enough to snap its capillary connection with the moist depths, and the wind erases the last imprints of the raindrops; then, only the spurt of green growth and the whine of mosquitoes affirm the welcome spate of moisture.

Temperature

The historical temperature extremes of 14° and 107° F recorded at Port Lavaca (both in the fitful year of 1962) have little significance for Matagorda Island, where both temperature and its rate of change are moderated by the Gulf of Mexico. The seasons are smudged between a grueling summer and a moderate winter punctuated with northers. The subtle temperature shifts of spring and fall, along with their attendant bursts of wildflowers, seem inconsequential amid the flutter and gabble of the hordes of migrating birds that dominate these periods. A nearly year-round growing season assures that there is always some greenery, shade, and shelter. The dry, hot summer is the stressful time for wildlife; many animals are driven to crepuscular or nocturnal activity patterns. Some creatures become dormant during the winter, but for most, the cool season is a time of relatively easy living.

The main impact of temperature is through indirect effects on moisture: polar fronts become wet northers, crisp mornings drip with dewfall, cool downdrafts produce frequent thunderstorms, warm tropical air swirls into hurricanes, and high humidity exacerbates the heat/cold index.

An exceptional cold snap can put skim ice on the bays, decimate fauna in exposed mud flats, and cause fish kills, but, except for frost-nipped vegetation and a temporary shortage of prey for shorebirds, island life is not adversely affected. On a summer afternoon, exposed sand gets hot enough to blister bare skin, the stagnant air in wind shadows is scarcely breathable, and the simmering shallows in the bay marshes are nearly anoxic; yet the plants are hardened to these extremes and the animals have learned to avoid them. By pacing itself, insular life persists.

Storms

Each year Matagorda Island is lashed by over forty thunderstorms and chilled by about twenty-five northers. In addition, the island lies in the most cyclone-prone section of the Texas coast. Although tropical storms and hurricanes perversely refuse to be hemmed in by statistics, over a century of records indicate that between June and October some sort of tropical tempest makes landfall in the Coastal Bend every three to four years, that the blow will be of hurricane force every four to five years, and that a severe hurricane will wrack the area every dozen years or so. In addition to these direct hits, most large tropical storms and hurricanes that enter the Gulf of Mexico have at least a glancing effect on the central Texas coast.

Despite its exposure to such repeated violence, Matagorda obviously thrives. After all, storms are an important element of the natural forces that form and mold barrier islands. Even the impact of a full-blown hurricane is not nearly so catastrophic to the natural environment of a barrier as it seems to human eyes.

Hurricanes wreak their havoc by rain, wind, and tidal surge. The island's sands passively absorb and drain away the rain, while its open, treeless landscape offers scant resistance to the wind. Only the tidal surge brings destruction in the form of massive restructuring of the beach, eroding or flattening the dune ridges, carving washover channels across the interior, smothering the vegetation with sand and blighting it with salt water, and altering the tidal inlets. The immedi-

ate aftermath of a powerful hurricane certainly is a shambles. However, although every barrier island owes some of its features to the
latest hurricane, most storms inflict no lasting ecological damage.
Waves smooth out the beach, windblown sand fills in the storm channels and rebuilds the dunes, ebb and flood tides flush the passes,
plants sprout and spread, and animals emerge and propagate. The
island heals, and within months it may actually be in better ecological
health than it was before the storm. Only shortsighted humans could
see this ageless cycle as being detrimental.

Tides, Waves, and Currents

Astronomical tides (those governed by the relative movements of the
earth, moon, and sun) are not pronounced in the Gulf of Mexico because that body of water is not particularly large. The tidal range at
Pass Cavallo is only 1.4 feet. Each tidal cycle causes the swash zone
of the beach to advance and retreat several feet on the forebeach; a
line of fresh detritus marks the latest high point. A rising tide produces strong flood currents through the passes into the bays, and a
falling tide generates even stronger ebb currents back into the Gulf.
These flows are important for scouring the inlets, flushing the bottom
sediments from the bays, maintaining bay salinities, and transporting
marine creatures to and from the estuaries. But the most noticeable
effect is on the bay side, where even a slight change in water level
over the gently sloping bottom can cause the shoreline to advance or
retreat by 20 feet or more. Here, the changing tide stimulates activity
in the marshes, mud flats, oyster reefs, and submerged grass beds by
stirring up nutrients, replenishing oxygen, and shifting temperature
and salinity gradients. Everything from fish and clams to fiddler crabs
and birds responds to the tidal cycle.

Wind tides result when air currents are strong enough to raise or
lower the water level along a shoreline. Although they may act in
concert with astronomical tides, wind tides are as erratic as the
weather that produces them. The wind has the greatest effect when
it blows across a broad fetch of shallow water, which is precisely the
situation in the bays behind Matagorda Island. In Texas bays, winds
often account for more water movement than astronomical tides. A
strong onshore wind drains the marshes on the bay side of Matagorda; a blustery norther piles muddy water 3 feet up the shore.
Strong winds at sea can generate a heavy surf that sends waves over
the berm and into the base of the dune ridge, resulting in beach
erosion.

Storm tides are simply severe wind tides associated with storms, and they culminate in the tidal surges of hurricanes. Because they are whipped into crashing waves, storm tides generally cause considerable damage.

Waves, which are as integral to the formation and maintenance of Matagorda Island as sand, are generated by the wind. Depending on the strength of the wind, depth of the water, slope of the bottom, and angle of contact with the shoreline, waves can be either constructive or destructive. Smooth oceanic swells, low breakers, and flat waves lapping ashore bring in more sand than they wash out, building up the island. Conversely, rough water with crashing waves erodes sand from the beaches and sediments from the bay shores. The elongate sandpile that we call Matagorda Island is very much a cumulative result of the constant building and wasting activity of the waves.

Three kinds of currents are important to the health of Matagorda Island. The angle at which oceanic waves strike the island creates a southward-flowing longshore current that is crucial for transporting sand onto the shoreface so that waves can push it in to replenish the beach. Tides generate the flood and ebb currents that keep the passes open and maintain the quality of the bays. Interior currents are produced by a combination of tides, winds, and discharges from the rivers. Matagorda Bay has a prevailing back-and-forth movement dominated by the flood/ebb through Pass Cavallo. There is a general southward flow of lagoon water behind the island: Espíritu Santo Bay receives saline water from Pass Cavallo. San Antonio Bay, especially its west shore around Blackjack Peninsula, carries water freshened by the discharge from the Guadalupe/San Antonio rivers. There is some flow in and out of Mesquite Bay through Cedar Bayou, but the main movement is south into Aransas Bay toward Aransas Pass. The various salinities and sedimentation patterns associated with these currents have much to do with the occurrence of shell ridges and mud flats and with the luxuriance of salt marshes on the back side of the barrier island.

The Human Factor

So far, emphasis has been placed on the natural aspects of Matagorda Island, but the barrier has a very real human dimension as well. Sometimes for better, often for worse, the island's destiny now turns on decisions people make, not only about the island itself, but also about the Texas coastal zone, the Gulf of Mexico, state and national environmental policies, and the collective stewardship of the entire biosphere. Despite their detached geographic locations, islands are not immune from—in some ways are especially susceptible to—one of the maxims of ecology: everything is connected to everything else, and the human factor runs unimpeded through every aspect of this tangled web.

After early attempts at colonization were aborted, Matagorda Island eased into the twentieth century pretty much out of sight and out of mind, visited on its periphery by local anglers, hunters, and beachcombers, but otherwise remaining inviolate as the private domain of a few ranching families. In 1942 most of it was taken over for use by the U.S. Air Force. For over thirty years it was strictly off-limits to the public, and was managed, exploited, strafed, and bombed by the military. The air base closed in 1978, and the property was turned over to the Department of the Interior in 1982. In 1988 it became the first and only Texas barrier completely under public ownership, with the added security of being designated a part of the National Wildlife Refuge System.

For those who want to see wild places protected from the ravages of real estate developers and the humiliations of banal entrepreneurs, the island's new status is gratifying. But public ownership brings its own problems. Conflicts of interest move from the small private arena to the huge public one. Contentious issues go before larger, more factious committees. Good solutions are diluted by necessary compromise. Time ticks away while red tape is unrolled. Decisions of moment are made by parties at great remove from the site under dispute. If the land belongs to everyone, then everyone has the right to enjoy it. Somewhere between the extremes of cordoning off the island entirely and providing unlimited public access exists a solution. The admonition in Garrett Hardin's "Tragedy of the Commons" must come to mind: That which is owned by everyone is treated as though it is owned by no one.

But there is good reason for optimism about Matagorda Island. It has moved into the mainstream of human activity at an opportune time. The 1970s environmental movement that raised public awareness was initially characterized by an undirected and uncompromising fervor, which has matured into a quieter, more rational, and conciliatory dedication. By 1988, both politicians and constituents were more intelligently informed about environmental issues. The National Wildlife Refuge System has a long and distinguished reputation in the custodianship of our wild heritage. Unfortunately, the state of Texas (which is involved in managing the island as well as having jurisdiction over the bays, marshes, shorelines, and the continental shelf more than 10 miles into the Gulf) is more suspect. Although the TPWD is experienced at handling people in parks, the state legislature has a sketchy reputation for protecting the general quality of the environment. Texas' independent, frontier attitude has earned it the dubious distinction of being the only one of thirty coastal states that has failed to adopt a comprehensive coastal zone management program. Instead, a hodgepodge of state and federal agencies now try to write and enforce rules for the state's congested coastline. In the resulting melee, pork barrels still surface about as frequently as barrels of hazardous waste appear on the beaches. At present, the ecological health of the mainland and marine support system around Matagorda Island is in well-meaning but erratic hands.

Despite all this, the future for Matagorda Island looks bright. Wind, sand, and sky will be let alone to interact as they always have. The far horizon, the grand cloud banks, the breathtaking sunrises will continue unobstructed. Nights will be dark, the heavens in place. The wild stretches should remain, if not wild, at least open. Our much-harassed migratory waterfowl should find winter sanctuary, which although it is not completely secure from shotguns, is better protected than most other places along the coast. The several endangered species that use the island will have their chance to hang on. It will be a place for people to quietly learn and as quietly enjoy. If we can ever admit that shooting wildlife on a wildlife refuge is not an acceptable form of recreation, it will be quieter yet. And if the current resolve holds firm, there will be no causeway, no vehicular access from the mainland; Matagorda will remain an island. That physical inconvenience will succor one of the barrier's most precious and sought-after gifts—the pleasantly eerie, increasingly rare sensation of personal isolation and the satisfying illusion, however contrived, that for awhile at least, all is well with the world.

There should be no astonishment or lament that Matagorda Island is not now and never again will be pristine. The island is undeveloped, but it is certainly not untrammeled. It helps if one can admit that primeval does not necessarily mean perfect. Indeed, the faded imprint of humanity adds an intriguing dimension.

Look into the glare of a morning sun glancing off Matagorda Bay and imagine you hear the distant blat of the *Polly Hopkins* gingerly lightering a load of blackstrap molasses and coarse brown cane sugar through Dog Island Pass, bound for the busy T-head at Saluria. Observe the breakers sweeping across the bar at Pass Cavallo. You can regard them as violent, but you cannot call them treacherous unless you can envision the *Palmetto*, its great sidewheel helplessly churning the sea to froth, being methodically battered to bits against the shoals. Visit the overgrown dogleg excavations near the lighthouse. Stand quietly until you can hear the crack of the Springfields and the ominous whine of the minié balls as Ransom's Blue closed with Bradfute's

Gray so long ago. Stare down the length of one of the great silent runways, cracking now with neglect and beelining to nowhere, and relive the tumult and thunder that it knew while the nation prepared for war. If you want to reduce the mosquitoes to a minor nuisance, do so by catching a glimpse of two glistening Karankawa ghosts poling a pirogue through the dawn mists in the bay-side marsh.

There are other, more solidly poignant reminders that you can visit to bolster your nostalgia. Stand quietly awhile facing the cluster of leaning gravestones that huddle beside the lighthouse. The information in Appendix A will help you interpret what you see, but no one alive can accurately conjure the tales or even the names of the souls whose paths finally ended here beneath the several unmarked mounds. On a breezy eminence a mile to the north, at the end of the trail leading to the J-Hook, stands the beautifully weathered marble tombstone of Judge Hugh Walker Hawes, one of the patriarchs of Matagorda Island. As will be related in Chapter 3, the good judge worked hard to entice civilization to this neglected strip of sand; he deserves your homage. Hidden amid the cotton rat runs deep in the seacoast bluestem just off the south runway of the air base are two headstones of polished granite, each bearing its own epitaph to the uncertainty and the meanness of life in the early days on the island. Here lie Cora M. Nichols, first wife of Captain William Nichols—robust wagon freighter and reliable harbor pilot—who never saw her twentieth birthday. And beside her, "Little Kate" (by the captain's second wife, Alelea), taken by God only knows which of the multitude of childhood hazards before she had fairly begun to live. Only part of the family's tribulations are commemorated here. The captain, with dying Alelea cradled in his arms, was washed into oblivion during the fierce hurricane that ravaged the island port of Saluria in September 1875. Such was the way of rough life and stark death back then; it was a tenuous existence, one that should engender in us a distant admiration and solemn contemplation.

These are sensations that nature alone cannot provide, yet the sentiments are not insignificant. They constitute a genuine part of the legacy of Matagorda Island, deserving of preservation, worthy of reflection. They remind us that we are not aliens here.

Finally, there is the matter of aesthetics. Without an admirer, Matagorda Island holds no beauty or fascination. The barrier has no cognizance of its own wonderfulness. Alone it is, if not wasted, then certainly unappreciated.

The dying onshore breeze smooths the sand with a final caress, and the tip of a pendant leaf of sea oats immediately proceeds to inscribe a cryptic rune on the fresh palette. With effortless precision, a ghost crab folds its periscope eyes into their facial grooves. Dawn is greeted with a thousand thousand yellow saucers of beach evening primroses gleaming across a terrain of soft, undulating shadows. The phalaropes return on schedule to pirouette in the shallows before resuming their unbelievable journey to faraway places. From out of the invisible chimneys of unstable air a gigantic thunderhead soars up until its windswept anvil crest surges over 5 miles above the Gulf of Mexico. This ephemeral mountain of boiling vapors is truly majestic in the late afternoon sun; with its billowing, multihued crags and bottomless purple chasms, the whole cloud mass comes ominously alive as it signifies to itself with flickering lightning and subdued rumbles.

These are phenomena that should be shared, natural occurrences that must penetrate a human conscience before they acquire value. They confirm that islands need people to admire them, to love them.

Matagorda Island State Park and Wildlife Management Area

The area is still being developed; what follows is subject to change as management plans proceed.

For general information, including how to charter a boat or take the pedestrian ferry, visit, write, or call: Matagorda Island State Park, South 16th Street & Maple Avenue, P.O. Box 117, Port O'Connor, TX, 77982-0117; (512)983-2215.

How to Get There

Most visitors embark from Port O'Connor. Suggested routes:

1. From Houston (about 164 miles): Take the South Freeway (State 288) to Angleton (36 miles); State 35 to Port Lavaca (98 miles); State 238 to FM 1289 (6 miles); FM 1289 to State 185 (16 miles); left to Port O'Connor (8 miles).

2. From San Antonio (about 167 miles): Go east on U.S. 87 to Port Lavaca (137 miles); Take State 238 to FM 1289 (6 miles); FM 1289 to State 185 (16 miles); left to Port O'Connor (8 miles).

3. From Austin (about 183 miles): Go south on IH 35 to San Marcos (27 miles); Take State 80 to Luling (21 miles); U.S. 183 to Cuero (52 miles); U.S. 87 to Port Lavaca (53 miles); State 238 to FM 1289 (6 miles); FM 1289 to State 185 (16 miles); left to Port O'Connor (8 miles).

4. From Corpus Christi (about 88 miles): Go north on U.S. 181 to State 35 (4 miles beyond Nueces Bay Causeway); east to State 185 (55 miles); 7 miles north of Tivoli turn right on State 185 to Seadrift, continue on to Port O'Connor (29 miles).

Matagorda Island

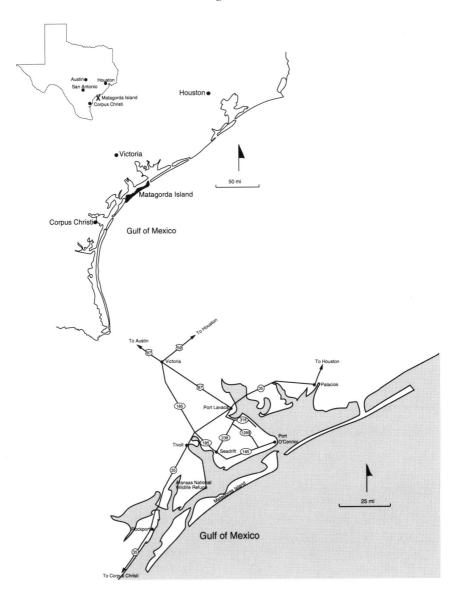

Map 3. Matagorda Island location in the Coastal Bend.

You enter Port O'Connor on Adams Avenue. On your left at the edge of town is a tall radio antenna. From that point, continue 1.7 miles to 16th Street. Turn right, go a long block to Maple Avenue. Cross Maple and enter the TPWD compound inside the chain-link fence. The headquarters building is beside the flagpole on your right. The office is open year-round from 8:00 A.M. to 5:00 P.M.

The ferry runs between the TPWD mainland dock and the island on weekends and holidays. Contact the mainland office about fees and schedule.

If you plan to get to the island in your own boat, anglers' maps are available that show the way. As you enter Port O'Connor, watch for the brown sign, "Public Boat Ramp," on the right, 0.7 mile past the tall radio antenna. Turn right one long block to the ramp on the Gulf Intracoastal Waterway. Gas, bait, ice, and information are available at many places in town, including at a shop beside the ramp. There are no launch or parking fees.

There is no access fee for the park. Once on the island, you may trek about as you wish. On weekends and holidays a shuttle vehicle transports visitors to the beach and to landmark sites on the north end, and a tour bus regularly travels to Darlington Beach and trailheads 10 miles down the island. Check at the Visitors' Center for fees and schedule.

When to Come

The park is open year-round. Although there are always some personnel on the island, the Visitors' Center is open only during duty hours: 8:00 A.M. to 5:00 P.M.

Weekday shuttle service is available by special arrangement; groups should contact the main office for reservations well in advance. There is a fee for transport on the island.

A moderate climate makes Matagorda Island a pleasant site to visit all year, but because of its exposed location, weather fronts and storms may limit access or curtail activities. Seasons are: spring (March to May); summer (June to September); fall (October to November); winter (December to February).

Depending on your proclivity, you may consider:

• November–March for whooping cranes.
• March–May for spring migrant birds.
• August–October for fall migrant birds.
• November–February for winter resident birds.
• March–May for wildflowers.

- October for cool, open weather.
- July–August for hot, sultry days on the beach.
- After wintertime northers or after springtime high surf for beachcombing.

Times to beware:

- June–November is hurricane season; keep posted.
- Strong wintertime northers make bay access dangerous.
- Strong southeasterly winds produce heavy surf and a nasty beach.
- Heavy rains are followed by clouds of mosquitoes.
- Doldrums of summer limit inland hikes to early and late in the day and demand special precautions against sun exposure on the beach.

Special Occasions

- Guided tours to otherwise inaccessible parts of Matagorda Island are conducted throughout the year for visitors who have purchased a Texas Conservation Passport. Topics include beachcombing, birding, island history, barrier island ecology, wildflowers, and marine life. Children, if accompanied by adults, are welcome. Contact the TPWD mainland office in Port O'Connor for a tour schedule, reservations, and fees.
- Hunting for deer, upland game birds, waterfowl, and wild hogs is strictly regulated. Contact TPWD personnel for arrangements.
- Fishing is permitted throughout the year from any shoreline, as long as you have a valid license. It is subject to all state regulations.

Facilities

In a word, facilities are primitive; this is by design, for protection of the island and enrichment of visitor experience. Facilities include:

- A main dock with several finger piers for small craft; the access channel is 5–6 feet deep.
- Army Hole Campground beside the dock has six shaded tables, fire rings, pit toilets, and a cold-water shower. Availability is on a first-come, first-served basis.
- Beach Campground is 1.5 miles from the dock and has four shaded tables and a pit toilet. It also is first-come, first-served.
- Visitors' Center beside the dock has information, displays, and a shuttle.

- The following are not available: electrical hookups, telephones, drinking water, trash disposal, concessions, and gasoline.

Plans for the future call for interpretive trails, guided tours, observation platforms, fishing piers, and limited access to the island's southwestern end. This is a good time to make your preferences known.

Layout

Matagorda Island State Park, a 7,300-acre tract across the island, includes a public dock, Visitors' Center, campgrounds, Army Hole, lighthouse, and a 2-mile Gulf beach. There is unlimited visitor access.

- Overnight camping is permitted only at Army Hole and Beach campgrounds.
- Daytime picnicking permitted anywhere on the open beach.
- No fires are allowed except in fire rings at designated campgrounds or on the open beach. Driftwood, but not native vegetation—live or dead—may be used for fuel.
- At present, there are no interpretive trails. Visitors are urged to remain on roads, mowed paths, bayside shoreline, and beach.
- At present, there are no fishing piers. Fishing is permitted along any shoreline.
- Bicycles are permitted; you should remain on roads or the beach.
- Swim at your own risk; there are no lifeguards. Parents should monitor children continually. Beware of high surf and offshore currents, and occasional sharks, stingrays, and man-o'-war jellyfish.
- Emergencies: Try to get to the Visitors' Center. After duty hours, try the game warden's quarters south of the dock (it has a satellite receiving dish). Personnel can only perform basic first aid and radio the mainland.

Matagorda Island Wildlife Management Area, a 36,500-acre piece on the northeastern tip of the island, includes J-Hook and 22 miles down the island's central portion. Use is limited to hiking, fishing, and regulated hunting. There is a weekend shuttle to Darlington Beach, 10 miles from the dock.

A 9-mile southwestern portion (formerly the Wynne ranch) is currently managed for wildlife by the USFWS and is not open to the public. For special group use of the Wynne lodge, contact the Texas Nature Conservancy, P.O. Box 1440, San Antonio, TX, 78295-1440; (512)224-8774.

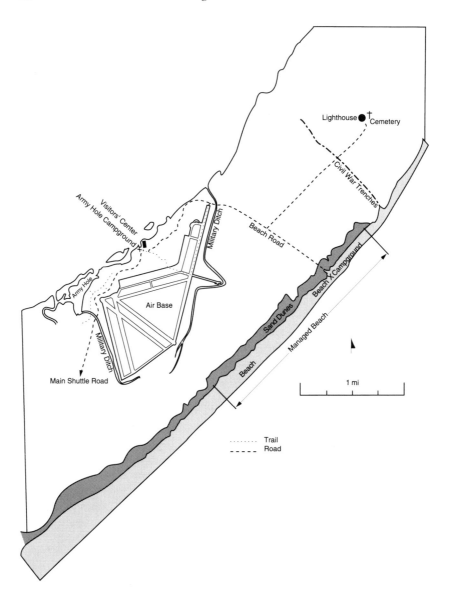

Map 4. Matagorda Island State Park landmarks.

What to Bring

For a day-use visit:

- Food.
- Drinking water. Plan for plenty, especially in the summer.
- Proper clothing:
    Long sleeves, long trousers, hat, especially in summer.
    Light walking shoes (tennis shoes) for the beach.
    Windbreaker most times, but especially in winter.
- Sunscreen lotion, all year.
- Dark glasses.
- Insect repellant, all year.
- Trash bag to haul out your waste.
- All gear in portable packs.

For an overnight visit (gear in addition to above):

- Lantern and flashlight.
- Tent or screen shelter.
- Bedding.
- Matches.
- Containerized fuel or charcoal recommended.

If you come in your own boat:

- Valid state boat license.
- Approved personal flotation devices for each person.
- Adequate fuel.
- Local navigation chart.
- If equipped with marine-band radio, you will find that Channel 16 is continually monitored by the Coast Guard; Channel 2 forecasts local weather.

What Not to Bring

- Firearms.
- Metal detector; use is illegal in all state parks.
- Alcoholic beverages.
- Any type of motorized vehicle.
- Radios permitted but discouraged.
- Pets permitted but discouraged; restricted to 6-foot leash at all times.

CHAPTER 2

Geology

Popularizations of geology focus on exaggerated topographies built of indurate rocks; things that change dramatically but so slowly as to appear ageless to man's impatient senses. A flat, apparently static barrier island is seldom thought of as a proper geological stage. Yet, a barrier island is geology in fast-forward; it is here that geological events occur often enough and rapidly enough to catch and hold our notice. Like a waterfall, the island maintains a static appearance through constant change.

A glance around verifies the geological tumult of a barrier island. Watch an incoming wave scribe its imprint on the beach. Most of the million sand grains jostled to produce that ephemeral signature are in passage on a journey that began long ago and far away. Several feet up the beach, at that just-perceptible border where the sand is dry enough to be vulnerable to the breeze, you see the beginning of an exquisite sorting. The lightest sand grains, picked up first, are whisked inland; heavier grains and bits of shell are trundled more slowly, dropped sooner. Delicate ripples and drifts of sand faithfully mirror the slightest change in the mood of the air drafts. Light wind gusts generate ghostly veils of sand that flicker across the backbeach, streak off the lee sides of the dunes, and disappear into the vegetation—restless sand on its way from one somewhere to another.

Pay heed to the static march of the plants. From the tangled mat of grasses and forbs in the interior, through the deep-rooted clumps on the dunes, to the prostrate and clutching forms on the backbeach, each green sprig obstructs the rush of the wind, and as the eddies spiral past, neat piles of sand grains sift gently down on the lee side of every branch. From such minute sandpiles mighty dunes can grow. You can find ruler-straight stretches where dense plants on one side and bright unblemished sand on the other mark silent battle lines in the endless struggle between the plants and the wind over which shall rule this kingdom of sand.

There are other signs that this island is hustling just to stay in place:

the disquieting sidewise tug felt by a swimmer that hints of powerful submarine forces; the ceaseless pound of the breakers, destroying even as they build; the line of wrack that marks exceptionally high tides; the heavy drift behind the dunes that tells of a sea gone mad; the low stature and permanent stoop of the vegetation, implying servility to a superior force; the quiet and mucky bay-side margin, so much an antipode to the surf.

Even these few geological reflections on a barrier island stimulate many questions: Where does all the sand come from? Where does it all go? Why is it clean sand and not mud or clay? How deep is the sand? How old are the dunes? How permanent are they? Can a dune move? How old is this island? How did it begin? What was here before? Is the island still growing or has it begun to dwindle? What effect does a gusting norther have? A few answers will be given here; you must search after others on your own. But this intriguing sandpile is frugal with answers to its mysteries, and that, after all, is as it should be.

Origin

Matagorda Island is one of a series of barriers that form a thin intermittent fringe on the Texas coast from the Trinity River southward and along the coast of Mexico to 150 miles beyond the Rio Grande. All of this sandy strip is one vast expression of a particular combination of conditions in the Gulf of Mexico: an ample inland source of sand, a very gradual submarine slope, vigorous longshore currents, persistent waves, and relatively low tidal range. Indeed, these islands are simply the current set in a sequence of similar barriers that have skirted the varying coastline over the past million years. As the level of the sea rose and fell, each assemblage was built up and then partly erased, most of the sand from one chain being reworked by waves and currents and redeposited in the next. Each well-traveled sand grain on Matagorda Island may have known many cycles of prehistoric exposure and inundation.

In the local Coastal Bend, loose sandy soil of the Port O'Connor peninsula and Blackjack Peninsula (the Aransas National Wildlife Refuge), and down as far as Baffin Bay south of Corpus Christi makes up the remnant of the Ingleside Barrier, an older island chain. There is a distinctive band of yellow-orange Ingleside sand in the bowels of Matagorda Island.

For hundreds of thousands of years primordial rivers trundled huge loads of silt, sand, mud, clay, and gravel from the once lofty interior of Texas down toward the sea. Heavy gravel fell aside as soon as the currents slacked across the coastal prairie, but smaller particles were carried onward. At the coastline, stream burdens were finally dropped in broad deltas that gradually built into a gently sloping continental shelf. Wave action stirred these deposits and kept the finest particles in suspension until they settled as ooze in the deeps, but the sand was just heavy enough to settle out where waves broke against the shoreline. So, as longshore currents raked the sand together and the waves rolled it in to shore, a prolonged natural sorting accumulated clean sand, the stuff of which barrier islands are made.

The fate of each set of island barriers is linked to the rise and fall of sea level, which, in turn, is dictated mainly by the degree of glaciation at the poles. Water piling up as ice in growing glaciers can so reduce the sea that even that vast reservoir shrinks; meltwater from dwindling glaciers returns to the sea, causing it to rise again. These glacial cycles induce a sequence of local events, each cycle partly obliterating evidence of previous ones; barrier islands form on a rising sea and erode when the sea retreats. The story of this particular island begins about eighteen thousand years ago with the most recent major change in sea level.

The last Pleistocene glaciers, at their maximum spread across the northern tier of the United States, had locked up enough water to reduce the sea mightily; the present site of Port O'Connor was 50 miles from the shore. Pursuing the retreating sea, rivers cut deep valleys across the ancient sediments of the exposed continental shelf. Shrunk into a deep basin with no shallow edges, the Gulf of Mexico was deprived of the vigor of its breakers, so the rivers belched their loads of sediment unopposed, building deltas directly on the coastline. And a featureless coastline it was, with no barrier islands, no estuaries, and only paltry salt marshes, nothing but a scant beach flanked by a low line of dunes. With so few different habitats, there were few different kinds of creatures in this primordial landscape. But things were about to change, for this was the end of an era.

A shift in climate marked what today we recognize as the close of the Pleistocene and the beginning of the Holocene; glaciers began to retreat and the sea to rise. The progress, though slow and vacillating, was inexorable. The bland primordial shore and the river-cut continental shelf were gradually submerged as the Gulf of Mexico reclaimed its domain.

Head-on encounter with the advancing sea caused the sluggish streams to double back upon themselves, to cut into their own banks, and to drop their sediments in the lower reaches of their valleys, clogging the channels with mud and sand. But before the valleys were silted full, the sea poured into them, and the shortened rivers began to build fresh deltas near where we find them today. The old stream valleys, deep indentations in the shoreline now flooded by the sea, were the antecedents of our modern bays and lagoons. All of this culminated about five thousand years ago when the climate stabilized, the glaciers ceased to retreat and the sea to rise, and the Gulf reached stillstand[1] at just about its modern level.

Picture a newly minted local coastline, nearly modern except that it lacked its chain of barrier islands. In Egypt, the Great Pyramids were new; Sumer was 500 years old; Rome's day of birth still 1,800 years away. But humans had been roaming the New World for at least 15,000 years and aborigines—Indians, if you will—already inhabited the developing Coastal Bend.

With the river mouths stabilized and the sea paused at stillstand, the longshore currents and incoming waves resumed their concert of sorting, piling, and pushing sand shoreward. Several miles from land, this long roll of sand reached a point on the gently inclined shelf where the water was shallow enough for its soft backbone to break the surface as a series of shoals. The emergence of these low bars had far-reaching effects. They hampered the action of the currents and waves, so that more sand accumulated directly on the bars, and they cordoned off a lagoon, a broad expanse of quiet water between the open Gulf and the shoreline. Here we see the birth of our modern bays and the barest beginnings of our barrier islands.

In these lagoons, the capture of fine sediments that had previously escaped into the Gulf now made fertile estuaries where quiet, brackish waters spawned thick submarine grass flats and fringing salt marshes. A growing accumulation of detritus and muck derived from these productive areas compacted into a thick layer of gray-green mud, the firm pavement upon which the barrier islands would come to rest.

Continuing to roll across the estuarine mud, the sand shoals finally lodged about 5 miles offshore, the old sunken stream valleys becoming channels between emergent ridges. Flood and storm tides still easily breached these low bars and kept the intervening channels clear, but the main sand mass remained piled as far into the shallows as the sea could push it. Where these old sand ridges came to a halt dictated the landward margins of sand on the current barrier islands. For Matagorda, this is approximately the route of the shuttle road.

As more sand came in, it was piled up on the shoals and diverted around their ends until it closed many of the channels, coalescing the

---

1. A stillstand is a stationary interval during normal, nontidal oscillations in sea level.

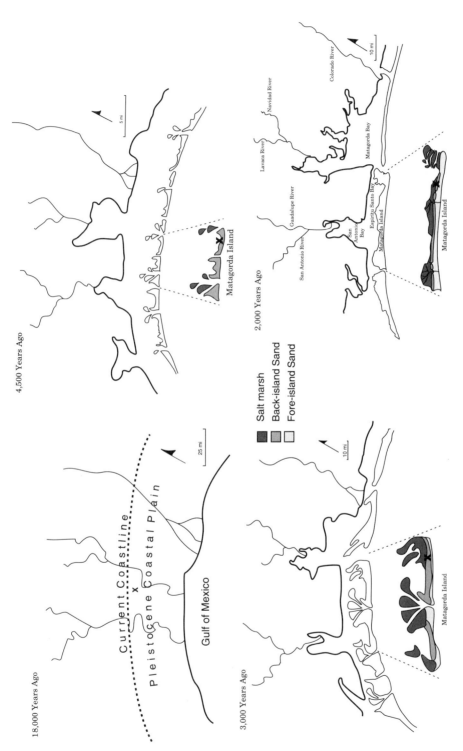

18,000 Years Ago

Current Coastline
x
Pleistocene Coastal Plain

Gulf of Mexico

25 mi

4,500 Years Ago

5 mi

Matagorda Island

3,000 Years Ago

10 mi

Matagorda Island

Salt marsh
Back-island Sand
Fore-island Sand

2,000 Years Ago

Lavaca River
Navidad River
Guadalupe River
San Antonio River
San Antonio Bay
Espíritu Santo Bay
Matagorda Island
Matagorda Bay
Colorado River

10 mi

Matagorda Island

Map 5. The origins of Matagorda Island: 18,000, 4,500, 3,000, and 2,000 years ago. (The present location of the air base is marked by the X.)

bars into elongate islands. Storm tides still broke over these low barriers and occasionally reopened a channel, sending a great belch of sand into the lagoon. These events, repeated many times at the same site, distorted the smooth contour of the back side, producing intricately dissected, fan-shaped lobes of sand that protruded into the lagoon. Today, these old storm-tide deltas support the maze of interconnected ponds and salt marshes on the bay sides of the islands. The prominent bayward bulge on the south end of Matagorda Island called Ayers Point and the long irregular extrusion into Espíritu Santo Bay between Panther Point and Pringle Lake represent the mouths of old storm passes. The jagged enlargement of the northeastern end of the island, including Bayucos Island and the many small exposures in the vicinity, is an active tidal delta where sand, funneled through Pass Cavallo, is spun to the west and packed in place by strong northers.

Eventually, only the major channels near river mouths remained open. Some of these, such as Pass Cavallo, have persisted as the passes we know today. Until about five hundred years ago, the south end of Matagorda Island was marked by a large pass; all that shows of it now is the large bay-side tidal delta on the north end of St. Joseph Island. When this major pass closed, the much smaller Cedar Bayou took on historical significance as the tenuous boundary between the two islands.

Once the islands and principal passes were in place, a period of rapid growth began. The substantial shoals now withstood the assault of the routine breakers and diverted the longshore current so that sand was piled in ever increasing amounts against their seaward edges. At this time "old" sand was still being rolled in from the adjacent submarine shelf and "new" sand was being dragged down the shore from the huge deltas of the Brazos and Colorado rivers to the north. Though much of this river sand was deposited in the growing spit called Matagorda Peninsula, budding Matagorda Island had no dearth of building material.

As sand accumulated against the Gulf side of the island, the beach broadened. When the sand dried enough to be picked up and mounded by the wind, the first tier of low dunes was formed. By the time this dune line, pushed inland by the wind, could be smoothed and captured by encroaching vegetation, the beach had grown seaward more, and a fresh row of dunes had developed. This next line of dunes stabilized a short distance seaward of the first, leaving a swag between the two. This process, called *progradation,* continued apace, and the island grew uniformly along its gulfward edge in a corrugated, low, ridge-and-swale topography. The growth, rapid at

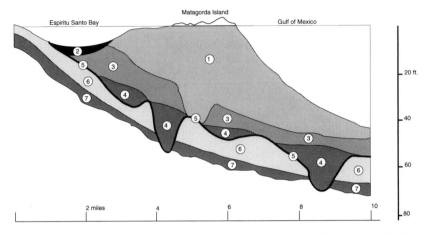

Figure 2. Cross section of the geological strata beneath Matagorda Island: (1) barrier island sand, 4,500 yrs.–present; (2) lagoon mud, recent; (3) lagoon mud, 10,000–4,500 yrs.; (4) river deposits in old stream channels, 18,000–10,000 yrs.; (5) Pleistocene-Holocene boundary, 18,000 yrs.; (6) Ingleside sand, 135,000 yrs.; (7) Pleistocene coastal plain, 200,000 yrs. (modified from Wilkinson, 1975).

first, slowed in time as the supply of sand petered out and as the island edge pushed into water too deep for the waves to pick up sand from the bottom.

While the island was prograding gulfward, it was also growing on the bay side. Here, the irregular and erratic expansion resulted mostly from the accumulation of sand washed continually through the active passes or pushed across the island by storm surges. These lobes of virgin sand, rapidly veneered with organic bay sediments, were soon invaded by estuarine vegetation. The plants served as an additional trap for the accumulation of more sediment whipped up and pushed in by northers, and so bay-side growth accelerated. Along stretches of shore with an eastern exposure fronting a broad expanse of bay, northers piled up narrow but solid and stable ridges of oystershell, like the one called Vanderveer Island on the back side of Matagorda Island.

By about two thousand years ago, Matagorda Island had matured to very nearly its present size and shape. Progradation, at a rate of about 250 feet per century, had progressed a mile into the Gulf before equilibrium between the forces of construction and demolition was reached. Irregular bay-side growth shaped the island to between 1 and 4 miles across. Sand had accumulated in the interior to a depth of 35 to 40 feet, enough to resist overwash by anything short of the surge from a major hurricane. Except for activity at the passes, Matagorda Island has been delicately poised in a dynamic steady state for the last two millennia.

Physiographic Zones

Barrier islands have a rigid stratification reflecting the forces that forged them. Vegetation may affect the shifting patterns of sand, but the intrinsic alignment of the island is dictated by the inorganic forces of wind and water. The Gulf of Mexico being the dominating influence on Texas barriers, the surface layering runs up and down the islands parallel with the surf line.

If you think of the basin of the Gulf of Mexico as a huge saucer, the gently concave rim is the shoreface. Oceanic swells come rolling up this slope until they stumble in the shallows and their crests sprawl forward, creating breakers, while their bases gouge out a series of bars and troughs. The dying waves expend themselves at the shoreline, dropping their load of suspended sand, reshaping and packing sand left by preceding waves, and dragging sand away in their backwash. This is the cutting edge, the continually replenishing source, the beginning point for every other geological feature on the island. Although storms may drastically modify this exchange, Matagorda Island, its surfline poised between the forces of construction and demolition, has enjoyed a stable relationship with the Gulf of Mexico for two millennia. The island is as large today as it has ever been.

Between the waterline and the dunes lies the beach. The width of a barrier beach depends upon several factors; a conjunction of very fine sand and a moderately steep shoreface meeting strong breakers nearly head-on has endowed Matagorda Island with a broad beach, typically about 300 feet, as at the northern beach access trailhead. From the surfline to the dunes, there is a distinct zonation of the beach, and as there is no big difference in these zones from one end of Matagorda Island to the other, they can all be observed, to a greater or lesser extent, anywhere along its length.

The *swash zone* is the interface between island and sea. Repeatedly covered and exposed by the pulse of the waves, its inland border advancing and retreating with the tides, it is seldom more than 20 feet wide. Here the constantly wet sand, smoothed into a seaward slope, bears the fleeting imprint of the last foam-flecked wave front; and here the most recent wrack from the Gulf makes landfall.

From the swash zone the forebeach slopes up to a low crest about 150 feet inland. Though occasionally remodeled and refurnished by flood and storm tides, this stretch of sand, kept moist by spray from the surf, is usually smooth and free of debris. Smears of tar may mar its surface, but the forebeach is the place for sunbathers.

The low crest at the interior margin of the forebeach is the *berm*, the high point of the beach. This is the level to which the strongest waves at the highest ordinary tides can push the sand and where they drop their load of natural wrack and human offal. Because of its windrow of debris, the berm is often called the strandline; it is usually the best place to beachcomb. Wind and those storm waves that breach the berm scatter this detritus toward the interior. On the berm, sand, at last surrendering the moisture of the sea, is claimed by the wind. From here its odyssey will continue to the beat of a more fickle drummer.

The backbeach, the slight inward slope from the berm to the first line of dunes, is a temporary repository of sand blown from the berm, and a more permanent resting place for the shells, driftwood, and assorted debris thrown over the berm by storms. At the least obstruction, driftwood, even a seashell, the onshore breeze snags and slows, dropping sand grains, which collect in wind shadows (the downwind side of an object where air currents decrease and drop their load of suspended material). On the inner side of the backbeach there is just enough protection from wind and salt spray to allow the first prostrate beach plants to take advantage of these sand accumulations. A plant takes root and grows, holding a tiny sandpile and increasing its wind resistance, which causes more sand to gather on which more plants can grow; eventually a *coppice dune* may develop. Dozens of these knee-high hillocks will be scattered in irregular tiers across the inner quarter of the backbeach. Most coppice dunes are short-lived. They and the plants that fostered them succumb to the harsh extremes of the backbeach; the plants deteriorate and the sand moves on; more sand and new plants form fresh coppice dunes.

The position, height, and durability of the vital primary dune ridge grow out of the most delicate balance of natural forces on the island—the active urge of the onshore wind to move the sand and the passive coaxing of the vegetation to hold it in place. As the wind passes inland it loses strength and begins to drop sand; as the vegetation moves seaward it meets conditions too harsh to tolerate. The strike of the primary dune ridge is where the opposing elements have met in a standoff. At this point the plants are able to close ranks tightly enough to trap the bulk of the sand, and the dune grows. Once begun, the process is self-nourishing, coalescing adjacent dunes to form the ridge. On Matagorda, this is a relatively continuous line of dunes that rears from 6 to over 20 feet in height behind the backbeach.

As with the island of which it is an integral part, a sand dune exists in a state of tenuous equilibrium. The onshore wind can push sand grains just up to the peak of the smooth, windward side of the dune, where they tumble down the abrupt leeward slipface. If the wind increases, sand is whisked off the dune crest into the interior. Normally, the vegetation grows fast enough to stay exposed and to restrain most of the sand; a stabilized dune increases slowly in height and breadth, but remains in place. But if conditions shift, and so much sand is blown over the crest that it smothers the plants, the entire dune may begin to migrate inland.

Storms, droughts, strong dry northers, and human interference can all upset the balance and tip the advantage to the wind. The results are washover channels, "blowouts" (enlarging, saucer-shaped excavations), and rapidly migrating dunes. Rampant migration of loose sand destroys the stability of the island's interior and spills into the lagoon; so the damage to the ridge can lead to disintegration of an entire section of a barrier island and rapid filling of the lagoon.

Such wounds heal slowly. In 1961 Hurricane Carla caused wholesale devastation, gouging a washover channel 6 miles wide that cut completely across the central part of Matagorda Island; the effect is still evident. There are several natural blowouts, but in normal years there is enough rain to maintain a dense plant cover; thus, Matagorda Island does not suffer from the desolate sandy wastes and rampant dune fields seen on drier Mustang and Padre islands. The shuttle road to the beach has created a dangerous wind gap, and old cattle trails and paths used by wildlife and people are incipient blowouts.

The irregular clumps of high mounds about a quarter mile inland of the primary dune ridge are secondary dunes. These are dunes that broke from the primary ridge and traveled across the interior until they were finally stabilized by the vegetation. Aerial photos show that the period of migration occurred from the late 1920s to the mid-1930s. Hurricanes may have instigated the activity, but these were the "Dust Bowl" years, when poor land management caused massive erosion. Clogged rivers delivered heavy burdens to the sea and excess sand began to pile up on the barrier beaches, becoming extra fodder for the wind.

The strip of island interior about a mile wide, from the primary dune ridge nearly to the bay shore, is what was laid down by gulfward progradation after the sea came to stillstand about forty-five hundred years ago. The topography of this fore-island area reveals its origin—a series of long, low ridges separated by shallow troughs, each closely paralleling the current surfline. These old primary dune ridges did not migrate to their present positions but were left in succeeding rows as the island grew gulfward. The low height of these old dune crests is only slightly due to weathering. During the very active phase, the leading edge of the island grew so rapidly that before a developing ridge could get very high, it was deprived of more sand by the growth of a new ridge between it and the beach. If small dunes reflect rapid growth, then larger dunes indicate slower growth. Today, Matagorda Island is not growing at all; its primary dune ridge is probably the highest in its history.

Where the secondary dunes migrated across, they obliterated the old topography, planing down the ridges and filling in the swales. Portions of the corrugated pattern have been smothered by hurricane washovers and extensive stretches have been erased by the construction of the air base and bombing range. Some features on the island's southern end were altered by land management practices. But down the length of Matagorda, vestiges of the fore-island area are still evident here and there seaward of the main shuttle road. It shows up clearly on aerial photographs, where uninterrupted ridges can be traced for 10 miles. This region can best be appreciated on foot on either side of the beach access road between the trailhead to the lighthouse and the primary dune ridge. Sight along the long axis of the island; the taller, darker vegetation of the moister swales stands out in the dense, matted cover.

The oldest part of Matagorda Island, the back-island area, is a half-mile-wide strip between the inner edge of the fore-island area and the modern salt marshes that have built up in the bay. Although not evident on the surface, the sharp geological boundary between the fore- and back-island areas shows clearly in the sand distribution pattern. In the back-island area the grain of deposition is flattened and oriented northwest-by-southeast, reflecting the island's birth as a shoal frequently washed over by flood tides and storms approaching from the southeast. Much of the original sand that washed up forty-five hundred years ago still lies at the heart of this sector.

This narrow strip of archaic island sand disappears beneath the more recent flood tidal delta that splays out into Mesquite Bay, and both it and the fore-island area have been erased by the migration of Cedar Bayou across Matagorda's southern tip. From the level of Pringle Lake northward, shoreline erosion has stripped away the back-island area. It does not have a distinctive surface characteristic and it grades imperceptibly into the bay-side marshes, but the back-island area is best observed on the bay side of the main shuttle road.

Passes

By their very nature, passes between barrier islands are sites of unusual activity. Even more than the islands themselves, passes persist in a constant state of flux. The inlets are kept open only if the flush and scour of tides, river floods, and storms successfully counter clo-

sure by sand brought in by longshore currents, waves, and hurricanes. On the Texas coast, the most stable passes are those oriented
north-northeast by south-southwest. These benefit from strong purg-
ing currents produced by the prevailing sea breeze and by gusting
northers.

Pass Cavallo is one of the most enduring natural inlets on the Texas
coast, and at up to 30 feet, one of the deepest. Yet, it is notorious for
its unstable channel and shifting shoals. Old maps show the edge of
Matagorda Island bordering the entrance to the pass as being smooth
in profile; today the J-Hook and Sunday Beach have emerged and
prograded up the inlet. A century ago Pelican Island, east of the main
channel off Decros Point,[2] supported mesquite trees and grass-cov-
ered dunes 20 feet high. Today, the channel has shifted eastward, and
the remnants of Pelican Island are fused into the low wastes at the tip
of the J-Hook. Sandy bluffs shown on old surveys of Decros Point and
along the northern edge of Matagorda Island no longer exist.

Less obvious is the insidious movement of the whole pass to the
southwest as prevailing currents deposit sand on the tip of Matagorda
Peninsula and cut it away from the northeastern edge of Matagorda
Island. It is this relatively rapid lateral migration, faster during storms
but averaging nearly 10 feet a year, that has destroyed historical sites
along the north end of the island over the past 150 years. It is reasonable to guess that Pass Cavallo originated near the mouth of the Colorado River, and for much of its existence has been migrating southwestward, continually shifting the geographic terminus of Matagorda
Island.

Cedar Bayou, at the south end of Matagorda Island, has a more
checkered history. This inlet began as nothing more than one of the
narrow washover channels on the west side of the huge storm-tide
delta of Ayers Point. Four miles south of this delta, a large pass once
separated Matagorda from St. Joseph Island but, about 450 years ago,
this pass closed, leaving Cedar Bayou as the nearest valve to relieve
the local energy of the Gulf. Rather than enlarging the small inlet,
the fickle forces of water and wind caused Cedar Bayou to migrate
across the toe of the island to the approximate geographic position
and northwest alignment of the original pass. The area between
the Wynne lodge and the toe of the island, called South Pasture, has
a distinctive topography of relatively active, crescent-shaped dune
fields that reflect the recent fill behind the moving channel.

---

2. The tip of Matagorda Peninsula called Decros Point was originally named
Decrow's Point, in reference to the Thomas Decrow family, who settled on
the site in the 1840s. Older maps will refer to it by the latter name.

Neither Mother Nature nor humanity is done with Cedar Bayou. Although occasionally enlarged by hurricanes, it is as often closed by them, and it is still slowly moving southwestward at the expense of St. Joseph Island. Cedar Bayou has been dredged open several times over the past decades, and was purposely closed in 1979 to protect the bays from possible oil contamination from the IXTOC oil spill. Most recently dredged in 1987 to allow water exchange in the bays, it has remained open to date.

Wind

Barrier islands are formed and maintained by the action of wind and water on sand. Wind, the prime mover of water, is the more fundamental force. Can you back up another step? What moves the air and so causes the wind?

Routine geological maintenance of Matagorda Island is handled by the onshore southeasterly breeze, by longshore current, and by lapping waves. Northers have less influence on overall island form. They occur when the water table is apt to be high and they often bring rain, so there is less dry sand to be blown about. A stiff, dry norther can reverse normal sand movement, driving it into the Gulf, from where it is eventually returned by normal wave action. Northers have more lasting effects on the island's bay side. Strong winds howling across the broad fetches of Espíritu Santo and Matagorda bays pile up the water and beat the shoreline with resounding force. Marshes serve as buffers, but in exposed stretches significant erosion or accretion of mud and shell often results. In addition to shaping the bay side, northers drive strong currents through the inlets, flushing the passes.

Over the long haul, prevailing southeasterly and periodic northerly winds with their attendant waves and water currents mostly account for the origin, appearance, and persistence of a barrier island. Storms are episodic exaggerations of these everyday forces. With increased winds and high, turbulent water, tempests from the sea may shift more sand in hours than conventional forces will move in years. Because of their position, barrier islands catch the brunt of the violence; each one owes much of its shape and surface conformation to the cumulative effect of storms and all bear old storm wounds in various stages of convalescence. Although any intensification of wind and wave will leave some mark on a barrier island for awhile, it is the culmination of these forces—the full-blown hurricane—that leaves the most lasting aftermath, not only in the minds of the people who witness it, but also in the geology of the island.

A hurricane's greatest geological impact on a barrier island comes from the storm surge, the sudden rise and inland rush of a rough sea. In the Gulf of Mexico a major hurricane generates a surge of 10 feet along the barriers and more than that in the bays; a powerful, slow-moving hurricane has time to push even more water to its fore. Gale-force wind, low barometric pressure, and a sloping shoreface combine to pile the rising water against the shoreline; the right-hand side of an advancing cyclone is especially vicious because the counter-clockwise wind direction is supplemented by the forward movement of the storm front. Aside from flooding, the surge generates colossal waves that repeatedly pound the shore with explosive force. Each breaker pushed by a 150-MPH wind swells forward at nearly 50 MPH and slams uncounted tons of water against the shoreline. Clearly, nothing short of catastrophe can result. And once the storm passes, a subsequent swift and massive backwash of all that water creates its own havoc.

During a hurricane, a barrier island lives up to its name, standing completely exposed to the full fury of the onslaught. Because it passively rolls with each punch rather than offering resistance, the island comes out intact, although never unscathed. Immediately after a hurricane, a barrier island looks a shambles. All of the intricate subdivisions of the beach are gone, replaced with a single broad expanse of fresh and reworked sand littered with the remains of sea creatures and bottom debris from offshore. The primary dune ridge, battered and cut by washover channels, may be carved into cliff-like sections prone to blowouts, pushed inland 100 feet or planed off entirely. But the damage is not so consequential or as lasting as it appears. Despite the razing, the ordinary beach zones begin to reappear within days, and coppice dunes soon crop up as forerunners of a new dune ridge, which may be in place within a year of the storm. Most of the details of today's primary dune ridge on Matagorda Island have been built up since Hurricane Carla in 1961.

Washover channels, where the storm surge cuts through the seaward side of the island and heaves a great gout of sand, shell, and debris across the interior and into the lagoon, have a more lasting effect. Although the edges of a channel are subject to wind erosion, most cuts are rapidly plugged with sand pushed in from the Gulf. However, the washover fans are recognizable at the surface for centuries, and may become permanent geological strata in the bowels of the island. Where a hurricane cuts through is determined by interaction of the forces that generate the storms with the configuration of the island. There are inherent "weak spots" where the accumulated washovers of successive storms create large deltas on the bay side of the island. Across the interior, the wind gradually blows most of the sand onward, leaving ancient chunks of driftwood improbably stranded behind the dunes and all across the island.

The passes that mark the island's ends are also variously affected by hurricanes. They may be broadened, narrowed, straightened, closed, deepened, or pushed aside, and all may be undone as soon as conditions return to normal.

On September 7, 1961, Hurricane Carla charged out of the Atlantic through the Yucatan Channel and entered the Gulf of Mexico. On September 11, the eye of this powerful and slow-moving cyclone crossed the north end of Matagorda Island and made landfall at Port O'Connor. Winds of over 175 MPH raised the most extensive storm surge in the history of the Texas coast, pushing salt water in over nearly 500 square miles of the Coastal Bend and sucking it back out with comparable force. Carla completely inundated 95 percent of Matagorda Island; the water was 2 feet deep at the Visitors' Center, 10 feet deep at Port O'Connor and an incredible 12 feet deep at Port Lavaca. Half of the Port O'Connor peninsula went under water.

When Carla had passed on, Matagorda Island was a mess. Over a hundred million tons of sand had been scooped up and shoved about along Pass Cavallo, where 800 feet of shoreline was carved away and the J-Hook appeared. The typical wide "hurricane beach" was formed, the primary dune ridge shattered, and a miles-wide wash-over channel gouged across the central part of the island, smothering the interior beneath a coat of muddy sand. Yet, Matagorda Island persisted and today only a geologist can detect the scars. Such is the remarkable resilience of a barrier island to natural disasters.

Prehistoric Life

If Matagorda Island is no more than forty-five hundred years old, then the last of the mammoths, camels, saber-toothed cats, bison with great sweeping horns, and other members of the late Pleistocene fauna were long extinct before the island came into existence. Storms occasionally throw worn bits of fossilized bone, palm wood, or the teeth of ancient horses onto the barrier beaches, but these have been either trundled down by rivers or they derive from the glacial periods when animals foraged out across the exposed continental shelf.

CHAPTER 3

History

Rarely do we encounter a major landform having a shorter lineage than its human inhabitants, yet such is the case with Matagorda Island. The land is only about forty-five hundred years old, while definite evidence places humans in Texas thirteen thousand years ago, and good reason suggests they were here considerably earlier than that. It is not only possible but probable that when the rising Holocene sea first rolled up the sand ridges that would grow into the barrier islands, sharp-eyed aborigines, perpetually on the lookout for a windfall, immediately visited these newly emerged bars. From their very beginning, the shifting sands of Matagorda Island have registered and erased questing human footprints.

Who were these first peoples? They were, of course, American Indians, descendants of Paleohunters from Asia who spread across the New World ferreting out every habitable niche. Their habits, their lore, and their legends were expressions of the environmental intimacy forced upon them by brute survival. These particular people struck upon the vacant littoral margin of the Texas Coastal Bend, and over the generations all of their cultural adaptations and accumulated wisdom came to reflect that happenstance. Even as they became identified with their land, so the land came to be identified by them. Without intent, they became Karankawas, and their land would be forever known as Karankawa Country.

Karankawas

They had little social organization; there was never a unified Karankawa tribe. Rather, there were half a dozen groups of related peoples sharing a common language and life-style and maintaining relatively amicable relations among themselves. There may never have been more than a few thousand of them alive at one time, thinly scattered from Galveston Bay to Corpus Christi Bay. Each subgroup had its designated strip of coastal territory. Locally, the Cujanes occupied the delta of the Colorado River. The heartland, Matagorda Bay and Matagorda Island, was claimed by a group that used the generic name Karankawa. The Coapite lived on St. Joseph Island and on the mainland between San Antonio and Copano bays. Inland, on the lower reaches of the Guadalupe and San Antonio rivers and on through the dry brushland of South Texas, the linguistically related Coahuiltecans roamed.

The Karankawan life-style was classic hunting and gathering. Each nomadic band, an extended family group of several dozen individuals, working on tradition and intuition and moving with the seasons, the tides, and the weather, roamed over familiar ground in an incessant search for subsistence. They killed what animals they could; appropriated any carrion they found; plucked and grubbed all edible fruits, roots, and greenery; patrolled the shoreline, marshes, lagoons, and barrier islands with dedicated regularity for any favor from the sea; harvested what they could from the periodic clouds of passing migratory water birds; and generally managed to scrounge an enduring existence from their bountiful but occasionally treacherous coastal environment.

According to early explorers, the Karankawas kept a type of barkless dog, deprecated by the haughty Spaniards as cur-like, that probably lived on camp scraps and doubtless participated to some extent in the hunt. According to one interpretation, "karankawa"—an appellation the Indians themselves used—translates as "dog lover."

They lived in portable lean-tos, animal skins thrown over a cluster of canes or saplings. Their original weapon was doubtless a spear launched with an *atlatl,* a notched stick used to supplement the length of the spear thrower's arm and so gain added distance and penetration power. Long before Europeans came, however, they acquired the bow and arrow and learned to live by it. Their stout long bows, fashioned from red cedar and strung with twisted deer sinew, could propel a fletched, flint-tipped cane arrow through a person or a beast, and they were used with great facility from the prow of a heavy pirogue to skewer fish and other creatures in the bays.

Although they apparently never fished with hook and line, these Indians did fashion weirs of cane to trap fish, turtles, and crustaceans in streams and tidal inlets, and they made baskets and pouches from split cane, the fibers of Spanish dagger, and the wiry leaves of Gulf Coast cordgrass. They made glue and caulk from a mixture of coagulated animal blood, mesquite resin, and natural asphaltum from the beach. In their later history they learned of ceramics and fired gray clay pots and bowls for containers and cooking vessels.

If the Karankawas had a specialty, it was in utilizing products of the sea. They used the shells of clams and large snails for dishes and containers. They pierced and strung small shells for ornaments. Shell fragments were fashioned by abrasion with sandstone or pumice to form scrapers, awls, and other hand tools, and the central columns of whelk shells were employed for hammerstones and gouges. Sometimes they floored their lean-tos with oystershell, perhaps to hold down the blowing sand. Although these coastal Indians must have occasionally journeyed inland to gravel bars on the lower rivers for flintstone and even farther for a supply of cedar, they probably also bartered seashells and other marine materials for these and other commodities.

As usual, there is little mention of the women's appearance, beyond the description of short, dumpy, and tattooed, and even less of their activities. By all accounts, the Karankawa men fitted the stereotype of the quintessential savage: impressively tall, powerfully built, well-proportioned, and in perfect health; their skin was a mahogany-brown, their coarse, black hair flowing or loosely braided. They proudly strode the coastline stark naked and barefoot in fair weather and foul, their only raiment a liberal daubing of fish oil to ward off the ever-present mosquitoes. Personal ornaments were few—a rattlesnake rattle in the braids, a bracelet or anklet of small shells. They routinely painted themselves and tattooed their faces with blue-black lines and circles, using thorns to introduce charcoal dust beneath the skin. And as a rite of passage to manhood they pierced nipples and lower lip with cane splints. Little wonder that these wild, strapping aborigines inspired awe and trepidation in the Europeans who met them and continue to evoke admiration and intrigue in those of us who can but contemplate them.

It was the Karankawas' double misfortune to live precisely in the cradle of Texas history and to dare to resent it. As a consequence, they went quickly to their destiny. Their final, recalcitrant three centuries were punctuated by repeated conflict and disaster, and their reputation was stigmatized with savagery, cannibalism, thievery, fecklessness, and deceit.

The local Indians first contacted Europeans on the surf-side of Matagorda Island in the winter of 1528, when they met two boatloads of half-dead Spaniards from the ill-starred Narváez expedition. The next spring more survivors straggled in, including Cabeza de Vaca, who was to give the world the first eyewitness account of the Karankawas. The few Spaniards who survived the rigors of exposure and unaccustomed privation lived with the Indians for five years before trekking to the nearest outpost of civilization in Mexico.

The Karankawas had their coastline to themselves for the next 150 years until, in 1685, they met the French when René-Robert Cavelier,

Sieur de La Salle, established a camp on the northern tip of Matagorda Island while his ships were navigating Pass Cavallo. This was
to be a prophetic encounter. The colonists were soon in open conflict
with the Indians and news of the French presence stimulated the
Spanish to reaffirm their claim to the land.

For the Karankawas it was the beginning of the end. In 1689, after
repeated quarrels and skirmishes, they massacred all but a handful of
the French. When the Spanish moved in they found the Indians had
turned surly, suspicious, and downright dangerous.

During the eighteenth century Spain tried, with singularly poor
success, to missionize the Karankawas. The Indians accepted the
handouts, mumbled the (to them) meaningless catechisms, and then
perversely hied off into the salt marsh from where they emerged sporadically to rustle cattle, ambush travelers, snipe at unwary settlers,
plunder ships in distress, pilfer anything loose, and generally make
life miserable and risky for all interlopers. In frustration, the Spanish
finally moved their missions further inland. As relations deteriorated,
an exasperated Flemish trader was driven to suggest a dastardly
scheme. His idea was to gain the Indians' trust with lavish overtures
and gifts; then, when the savages were at the height of celebration in
one of their wild mitotes,[1] to lace their frothy yaupon brew with poison, and so be done with the lot of them. Fortunately the Spanish
viceroy had enough humanity to veto this plot.

By the dawn of the nineteenth century the tide was flowing strong
against the badly outnumbered Karankawas. Spanish colonizers,
moving up from Mexico, pushed in displaced and disgruntled Indians from other regions. In 1821 the area came under Mexican rule and
the new empresario system of land management invited colonization
by both Mexican and Anglo settlers. With one colony on the Karankawas' doorstep at the mouth of the Colorado River, another on the
lower Guadalupe, and yet more settlers on the coast south of the San
Antonio River, the Indians were hemmed in.

With the appearance of the aspiring and intolerant Anglos the war
of attrition against the Indians went into high gear. Long bows were
no match for long rifles, and every skirmish between Indian and European was now followed by all-out pursuit, invariably ending in resounding defeat for the Indians and fearful loss in their rapidly
dwindling stock of warriors. The reckoning was always the same:
1823—two whites and nineteen Karankawas killed; 1824—three
whites and fifteen Karankawas slain; 1826—five whites killed and an

---

1. A term used by early Spaniards for pagan dances and demonstrative cele-
brations in general.

entire band of Karankawas wiped out. When the Indians were reduced to a negligible threat, the original self-protective motive lapsed
into hunting "Kronks" for sport.

Eventually the Indians could take no more. What had begun three
centuries before as a fair match of wits and arms now came to a pitiful
and inglorious finish in disease, genetic dilution, habitat destruction,
incessant harassment, social disintegration, and—ultimately even to
the stalwart—utter despair. By 1852 the Karankawas were gone.

Gone forever the curious sighing, almost breathless speech. Irrevo-
cably lost, the virgin, haughty demeanor and the menacing dark-eyed
gaze. Finally erased from the restless coastal sands, the huge, splayed
footprints. Vanished unplumbed, the alien source of inspiration behind the mysterious sunrise trance. They are all gone, but because
the Karankawas once strode this lonely stretch of sand, the island is
endowed with extra charm. It could hardly have ended otherwise,
but the inevitability of the outcome does not render it the less tragic.
However, time not only heals all, it erases much; today the special
vacuum left by the passing of the Karankawas is so faint and unreal
that it takes a long, solitary stroll along an empty barrier island to
unleash the imagination and conjure a mood wistful enough to believe that these remarkable aborigines ever existed here at all.

The Karankawas routinely poled their heavy dugouts between the
mainland and Matagorda Island, and they probably lived offshore for
extended periods when weather, mosquitoes, and food resources
permitted. However, because they had few durable goods and the
climate is exceptionally erosive, material evidence of their occupation
is scanty.

In a preliminary 1971 archaeological survey of the Matagorda Bay
region, including the northern rim of the island, only three aboriginal
sites were recorded. Fully 80 percent of the island remains unex-
plored by professional archaeologists; surely, many other sites exist.

The typical coastal Indian site is a shell midden, an accumulation
of shells, bones, flints, plugs of asphaltum, and occasional potsherds
that hardly differs in appearance from the frequent low ridges of oystershell and sand thrown up by storm waves. At favored sites successive generations of Karankawas occasionally paused, camped, ate,
busied themselves, idled, and then moved on, leaving their refuse.

Archaeologists speak of a Rockport Focus, generally identified as
Karankawan by the presence of the distinctive, but uninspired gray
pottery ware and characteristic flint bird points. One well-studied
midden on the adjacent mainland yielded evidence of the Indians'
catholic diet: the shells of one land snail and three kinds of marine
snails; shells of four kinds of marine clams, including the most com-

mon item at any local site—oystershell; bones of two kinds of marine fish, two kinds of marine turtles, and two kinds of freshwater turtles; and the bones of gophers, raccoons, coyotes, javelinas, deer, and bison. At this site, as in some others, items indicating European contact appeared in the superficial layer: metal knife blades, gunflints, clay pipes, trade beads, and arrow points skillfully chipped from bits of green bottle glass.

So, there is a passing chance that when you pluck a mud-stained oyster half shell from a bay-side spit on Matagorda Island, you might be handling something once handled by a 6-foot Karankawan who would have heaved it into the fire until it popped apart, then dragged it out and downed the steaming viscid mass, entrails, ashes, sand, and all, and unceremoniously cast the shell aside. There it lay, alternately covered and uncovered by sea, silt, and sand, until you happened along to feel its faint vibrations still capable of forging if not a direct filial tie, then at least an emotional bond across the ages. The incident would mean nothing to the Karankawa who was of this island; it is much to you who would savor a vital part of that vanished heritage.

Explorers and Pirates

Matagorda Bay, though not Matagorda Island, eases unobtrusively into the historical record in Alonso Alvarez de Pineda's ink sketch of 1519, a nondescript indentation in the thin, misshapen arc that represents the Gulf of Mexico. There is no notation at the site; it is recognizable only on faith because it is in about the right place between the crude bulges that must be Florida and Yucatan.

Until rather recently, Matagorda Island has existed only by implication as the west bank of all-important Pass Cavallo. Except as a vantage point from which to protect the pass, the island had no value to the early explorers, some not even appreciating that it was an island. The early settlers regarded it as a good spot for a pilot house and customshouse, a great place to hunt, fish, and beachcomb, and later as a conveniently confined cattle range, but the exposed strip of sand never knew the vigor of civilization that agitated the adjacent mainland.

The island quietly persisted, for the longest time so lacking in recognition that it did not even have an accepted name. It was always there, passively absorbing the force of the Gulf's incessant swells, keeping all but the most powerful cyclones from overwashing the interior busywork of humans, and funneling the tides through the pass. Because of its location fronting a deep-water bay, but exposed to the elements, this barrier island was continually brushed by history, yet always removed from the main flow.

For over 450 years, Matagorda Island has touched the lives of a few of the famous and notorious and of many ordinary folks. It has seen human aspirations soar and collapse, witnessed a few births and many more deaths, watched occasional high drama, and patiently marked interminable intervals when absolutely nothing of note occurred. Always, the blowing sand has yielded, bided its time, and then covered over. In the end, it is as though nothing of significance ever has happened. But that is not so.

The local coast was indifferent, even unfriendly to early passersby, but it was not until some of them tried to settle in the area that it mounted trials which seemed specially designed to crush human ambitions. The cumulative tragedies of three star-crossed expeditions bring Matagorda Island into the stream of what we call history.

In November of 1528, a pitiful remnant of the shattered Narváez voyage to Florida washed up on the desolate Texas coast. The crusty leader himself was swept out to sea off Pass Cavallo. The few survivors, including Cabeza de Vaca, who was to chronicle his observations and miseries, suffered a precarious existence among the inhospitable Karankawas on and near Matagorda Island for over five years before making their remarkable journey to Mexico.

In the summer of 1543, several dilapidated barges, the sad remains of the once proud Hernando de Soto expedition, put in at Matagorda Bay. Now led by Luis de Moscoso, they were in dire need of fresh water, food, and a rest to bolster their spent bodies and worn spirits for the final push to Tampico. They very likely walked the beach of Matagorda Island, for they found bitumen to caulk their failing craft before pushing on.

In February of 1685, La Salle was already seven months along a collision course with disaster when he tried to steer his three shiploads of French colonists over the bar at Pass Cavallo. *L'Aimable*, loaded with precious supplies and ammunition, shoaled and then split open in the passage, becoming the first of many vessels to succumb to the veiled treachery of the inlet. This was but one more in a series of misfortunes for La Salle. He had already lost one ship to Spanish corsairs. This clearly was not the delta of the Mississippi River, his intended destination. His men quickly alienated the Karankawas. Long-standing dissension among the crew soon culminated in a boatload of the French sailing back home, leaving La Salle and about 180 distraught settlers stranded on an alien shore with one frigate for security. The demolition of that vessel on a reef inside the bay was the final unlucky cast of the die.

The French managed to install themselves at the head of Venado Creek, between the mouths of the Lavaca River and Garcitas Creek at the far end of Lavaca Bay, bravely christening their rubble of ship's timbers and logs Fort Saint Louis. Here they were safe from detection by passing Spanish vessels, but not secure from their destiny. In 1687, La Salle, trekking northeast in hope of contacting a French outpost, was murdered by one of his own men. The withering climate and a final vicious assault by the Karankawas in 1689 terminated the utter despair that had settled over Fort Saint Louis. The first European settlement on the Texas coast had lasted a scant five years.

The significance of the French was not that they were the first civilized men to know Matagorda Island in over 150 years, but that news of their presence prompted the Spanish to take sudden interest in the neglected dominion of Nueva España, and to frantically seek out the intruders. Before he was done, the viceroy in Mexico City had ordered five search sorties by sea and six by land. What was left of Fort Saint Louis was finally discovered and burned to the ground. Meanwhile, the strategic location of Lago de San Bernardo (Matagorda/Lavaca bays) and its potential as a deep-water port was not lost on the sharp-eyed Spanish sea captains. In 1690, a ship's cartographer, Manuel José de Cardenas produced the first creditable map of the local area. The north end of Matagorda Island appears on this map, though it is not named and is incorrectly shown as a continuation of the mainland.

In 1719 a French vessel bound for New Orleans overshot its port and ended up marooning a landing party on Matagorda Island. The lone survivor of this group, Simars de Bellisle, eventually made it back to Louisiana overland. There he drew a map—finally showing unnamed Matagorda Island as an island—and convinced the governor of the potential of the area as a beachhead. In 1721 a French vessel under Bernard de la Harpe, with Bellisle on board as guide, sailed into Matagorda Bay. However, after observing the low-lying, mosquito-infested coastal country and meeting the Karankawas, he aborted the colonization effort; with that decision, the French gave up on the Texas coast.

Spain was in no mood to rely upon the French indifference. In 1720 the impressive *entrada* (expedition of discovery) of the Marquis de Aguayo set out from Monclova, Mexico, with orders to re-establish the Spanish presence by activating the abandoned missions in East Texas and by securing La Bahía del Espíritu Santo, the name now favored for Matagorda and Lavaca bays. In 1722 the marquis formally dedicated El Presidio de Nuestra Señora de Loreto and the mission Nuestra Señora del Espíritu Santo de Zuñiga on the banks of Garcitas

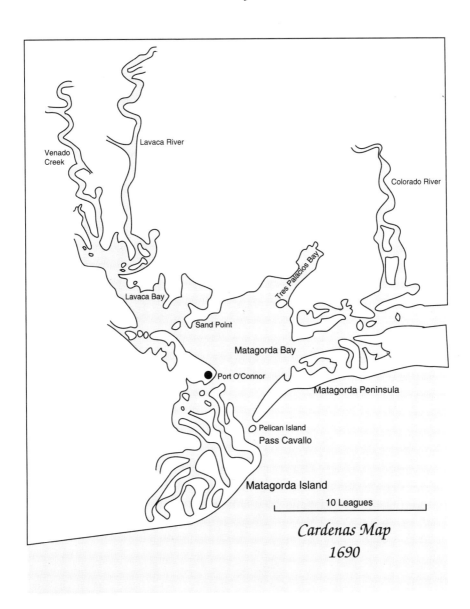

Map 6. The Cardenas map, 1690: earliest detailed map of Matagorda Bay and vicinity. Ten leagues are equivalent to 26 miles (modified from a photocopy, National Archives).

Creek, about 5 miles upstream from its mouth, just over 4 miles west of the site of Fort Saint Louis. This enclave, referred to simply as La Bahía, the first Spanish settlement on Matagorda Bay, fared little better than La Salle's endeavor. Within a year the Karankawas had killed the commander of the presidio. In 1726, La Bahía was moved to a site up the Guadalupe River.

Although the settlers of La Bahía failed to pacify the Karankawas and never confronted the French, they did stimulate a minute exploration of the local coastline and the naming of prominent landmarks. In Aguayo's day Matagorda and St. Joseph islands were regarded as one, called La Isla de San José. Cedar Bayou was referred to as Passo del Espíritu Santo. Passo Caballo (Pass Cavallo), which had long been applied to the important inlet at the north end of the island, stemmed from an early fancy that the entranceway resembled the outline of a horse. The edge of Matagorda Island bordering the pass was called Nuestra Señora del Buen Suceso, and the end of Matagorda Peninsula on the opposite bank was La Punta de Culebra. Probably because one or more of the ephemeral cuts across that narrow neck was open at that time, the Spanish consistently considered Matagorda Peninsula an island—La Isla de Culebra, (Snake Island). La Bahía del Espíritu Santo encompassed both Matagorda and Lavaca bays. San Antonio Bay was sometimes called Lago de San José, but both it and modern Espírito Santo Bay were regarded as the expanded mouth of the Guadalupe River, with Saluria and Bayucos islands on the river delta. The other major tributaries into the bay were Garcitas Creek (Río de San Miguel de Aguayo), the combined Lavaca-Navidad rivers (ríos de Venado y Santa Rosa) and the broad Colorado (Río San Marcos). So by the early eighteenth century, the local coast was no longer terra incognita.

In 1746 José de Escandón, commissioned to begin colonizing Texas south of the San Antonio River, sent several boatloads of explorers and surveyors through Pass Cavallo. The voyagers wended their way west through Espírito Santo and San Antonio bays to the mouth of the Guadalupe River and on up that stream. On the west bank of the Guadalupe, just below its junction with the San Antonio River, they established a landing that they called Los Mosquitos, a docking site to be used for years thereafter and later called Mesquite Landing. These earliest parties felt out routes through the oyster reefs, mud flats, and islets between Matagorda Bay and the Guadalupe River that steamships would one day ply.

In 1793, as part of the opening up of the local coastline, the Zacatecan mission Nuestra Señora del Refugio was established near Green Lake for the Coapites. But as with La Bahía, neither the climate nor the Indians were conducive to success. The mission was soon moved to a site near Mesquite Landing, and then, in 1795, to Copano Bay at present-day Refugio (reh-FURY-oh).

The earliest recorded, deliberate Spanish exploration of Matagorda Island occurred in 1793, when Captain Juan Cortés and four men left La Bahía (by then at its final location at Goliad) and rode down the east side of San Antonio Bay to the coast at Welder Flats. There they took advantage of a low tide to push their mounts, on hooves lacerated by oystershell, across the First Chain of Islands and onto Matagorda Island in the vicinity of Contee Lake. Their stay was not a pleasant one; both men and horses were plagued by horseflies and mosquitoes. They did journey to the north end of the island and back down to their entry point. En route Captain Cortés commented on the live oak mottes, which he thought should be removed so the island could be more easily defended. It took the party two strenuous hours to regain the mainland on a rising tide. In a rare show of wry amusement, the captain suggested in his report that the island be named Purgatorio.

By the turn of the nineteenth century, the area around Matagorda Bay, while not yet confidently settled, was at least better known. But changes were stirring. The Karankawas were on the wane, but Lipan Apache raiding parties were already a serious local menace and the dreaded Pinateka Comanche had begun to make travel hazardous as far south as El Camino Real. In 1803, the United States purchased Louisiana, and visionary Anglos immediately began to pour across the Mississippi and on toward the Sabine. Unrest was fomenting in Mexico and in 1810 Father Hidalgo ignited the Mexican Revolution. As part of the general turmoil, everything from smugglers and pirates to filibusters (Spanish buccaneers) began to appear off Pass Cavallo.

In an effort to control trade, Spain had decreed that all missions and colonies in Texas be provisioned overland from Mexico. In no time at all, freebooters appeared to participate in and prey upon a lucrative commerce in contraband. Most of the agile sloops sailed out of New Orleans to hastily unload along the shores of Lavaca Bay, a stretch loosely designated as the Port of San Bernardo. Soon the Mexican revolutionaries were commissioning privateers to prey on Spanish ships while Spain was propositioning others, or the same ones, in its own behalf. Plots and counterplots fostered three turbulent decades of piracy in the Gulf and back bays; this was the swashbuckling time of Jean Lafitte and Louis-Michel d'Aury.

How often these two buccaneers sailed through Pass Cavallo—or if indeed they ever did—and what escapades they were involved in cannot be known. Both were definitely in the area from 1817 to 1821, and because of the clandestine nature of their business, they surely knew all the inlets and navigable bays. One good tale linking pirates with Matagorda Island contains just enough marginally reliable hearsay and fascinating speculation to make it a lasting part of lore and legend.

In the summer of 1817, d'Aury, usurped from his stronghold on Galveston Island by Lafitte, established himself on Matagorda Bay. His encampment was on the mainland at the mouth of the Colorado River, with lookout posts across the bay on Matagorda Peninsula and probably on Matagorda Island as well. Here the pirates, feeling secure, rested and recuperated from their hectic life in the open Gulf. They lived in their accustomed paramilitary fashion, even firing their cannon at reveille and retreat.

Eventually, inevitably, some of the men tangled with the Karankawas, and rumor of their presence was transmitted by Indian grapevine to Captain Juan de Castañeda, the Spanish commandant at La Bahía. He set up an ineffectual observation post at Los Mosquitos, too far from the objective to do any good, but convenient to the presidio. When more Indians arrived with accounts of a wholesale disaster on Matagorda Bay, an immediate sortie to the mouth of the Colorado confirmed the news. If several written reports and related correspondence can be trusted, the bay was indeed a scene of carnage. The plundered wrecks of thirteen of d'Aury's ships were silently listing in the shallows or grounded on reefs. The wooden barracks were a shambles. There were corpses on the shore, in the ships, and on the peninsula, over a hundred in all. Obviously, this was the brutally efficient work of professionals—mutineers, perhaps.

Perhaps. There was no love lost between d'Aury and Lafitte. Jean Lafitte loved a good fight for its own sake, and he had been promised a reward for forcing d'Aury out of the Gulf and away from the Spanish shipping lanes. Did he have spies planted at Matagorda Bay? Did he carefully plan and execute a lightning raid on the sheltered bailiwick there? Did he send his light corsairs through Pass Cavallo, up from Cedar Bayou, and down from Brown Cedar Cut? Did he personally direct his seasoned cutthroats in a battle royal for both fun and profit? Certainly he was capable of it. But much of the intrigue in such a story is that no one really knows. The corpse of d'Aury was not among those scattered around Matagorda Bay; he is known to have died in the West Indies four years later.

We cannot speak of pirates without mentioning buried treasure. Every barrier island on the Texas coast, including Matagorda, has its legends of hidden troves, usually associated with Jean Lafitte. This most colorful of the Gulf freebooters is reputed to have routinely slipped through Cedar Bayou and to have established a stronghold on the southern tip of the island. Did he bury booty there? Maybe so, but it is well-documented that in his later years Lafitte was hard-up. The prosaic consensus is that if he did stash valuables against a rainy day, he would surely have recovered them in his own bad weather. Of course, if you should spy a moldering trunk half exposed among the dunes . . .

Mexico

From 1820 through 1835, the fading Spanish viceroys and then a rapid succession of contradictory Mexican regimes clearly recognized that they must quickly contrive to populate Texas or lose the province entirely. Ironically, their liberal colonization laws achieved both results. Under the empresario land-grant system, hundreds of thousands of acres of Texas real estate moved from public to private hands, and most of the recipients were shrewd and aspiring Anglos.

Fertile river valleys adjacent to the potential port sites on Matagorda Bay convinced Stephen F. Austin, the first and most prolific of the empresarios, to locate his colony between the lower reaches of the San Jacinto and Lavaca rivers, with a principal port at the mouth of the Colorado and outlet to the sea via Pass Cavallo.

Because of Austin's success and his influence with the Mexican authorities, other aspirants quickly followed his lead and the local area became a focus of early Anglo colonization. Austin's colonists began arriving in 1821. In 1824, Martín de Leon obtained a grant of land between the Lavaca and Guadalupe rivers. A year later Green DeWitt started his colony upriver of de Leon. In 1828, the pair of Irish empresarios, James Power and James Hewetson, received their grant to introduce colonists between the Guadalupe and the Nueces rivers.

By 1830, several thousand multinational immigrants and westward-moving Americans were in the area. For the most part this was a new breed: self-reliant, hard-working, conniving, ambitious, and possessed of reckless courage, grim determination, boundless energy, irrepressible ingenuity, and the tools and weapons not just to hold the land, but to render it livable and productive. They were hard on the land, harder on its prior inhabitants, and hard for local officialdom to comprehend. Despite governmental attempts to restrain them, their tide would not be turned. The Matagorda Bay area was finally getting permanently settled.

By 1835 barks, sloops, and ocean schooners were trafficking people and supplies through Pass Cavallo, bound for docks at the old Mesquite Landing and at the new ports of Linnville on Lavaca Bay, Dimitt's Landing at the mouth of the Lavaca River, and Matagorda at the mouth of the Colorado. The old establishment of Bahía (modern Goliad) was joined by the budding settlements of Gonzales, Guadalupe Victoria, and Refugio. Cattle and horses, corn and cotton, wooden wharves and tabby foundations, crude trails and rutted traces, wood smoke and human sweat, conflicts and cholera all began to appear.

As always, Matagorda Island was a witness to history without actually participating in the making of it; the early action was all on the mainland. Nevertheless, on paper at least, the island was being drawn into the flow. In 1824 it became a part of the newly formed Mexican state of Coahuila y Texas. In 1830, Power and Hewetson asked to have St. Joseph and Matagorda islands included in their premium for introducing colonists.[2] The Mexican commandant, in refusing their petition, commented that "these little islands are not suitable for agriculture but are ideal for pirates and as bases for contraband trade." But the astute empresarios could see the additional value of the islands as port sites for the growing maritime trade, so they persisted. After considerable wheedling, they got what they wanted. Hewetson later sold out to his partner, and in 1835 Colonel James Power became the first owner of record of Matagorda Island, but his was a cloudy title and it was consummated on the eve of tumult.

When the friction between Anglo and Mexican cultures finally flared into the Texas Revolution, Matagorda Island played its usual spectator role. It lay just out of earshot of Gonzales and San Jacinto, and General Urrea's fierce advance up the mainland ignored the uninhabited barrier islands. The local ports swelled first with inbound vessels provisioning the conflict and then with outbound craft crammed with frightened refugees. When the war was over, the people quickly returned to a land that was finally "rightfully theirs," with the single resolve to enjoy their reward in a new country, the Republic of Texas.

Republic of Texas

Enjoyment took the immediate form of rampant growth—in numbers of people, in facilities, in material goods, and in grandiose plans. Local activity centered around the booming shipping industry. In the 1840s wharves were built at Lavaca,[3] Cox's Point, Indian Point and

---

2. A premium was a special dispensation of land awarded to an empresario for timely completion of the terms of that person's land grant.
3. Lavaca was the original name for Port Lavaca.

Decrow's Point on Matagorda Bay, and up the Navidad River at the inland port of Texana. The Morgan shipping line began using docks on Powderhorn Bayou and the busy port of Indianola grew there. In 1844 the *Adelsverein* debarked the first of thousands of German immigrants at Indian Point. The deplorable conditions of the times are revealed by the litany of diseases that struck down these hopefuls by the dozen: cholera, black vomit, typhus, typhoid fever, consumption, yellow fever, scurvy, the pox, meningitis, malaria. But nothing could suppress the tempo of growth.

Barks, ketches, brigs, clippers, schooners, and the first steamers inbound from Galveston, New Orleans, Mobile, Boston, New York, and from across the bounding main, came with full charges of expectant passengers and ladings of furnishings for a civilized existence covering the gamut from Florida cypress and Louisiana pine to Boston ice, from wrought iron tools to lamp wicks. Outbound ships hauled the bounty of the raw land: animal pelts, alligator hides, honey, beeswax, pecans, wild grapes, Spanish moss, beef tallow, barrels of iced oysters and salted ducks, drums of blackstrap molasses, bags of crude brown sugar, a few early bales of cotton, and the first longhorns on the hoof.

The shifting shoals inside Pass Cavallo and the numerous oyster reefs and uncharted shallows in the bays made local pilots a necessity and fostered the industry of lightering—off-loading cargoes from deep-water craft onto skiffs and barges for transport to the docks. All of this commerce was not ignored by the republic: A customshouse was established at the port of Matagorda for administering such a burden of tariffs that a lucrative smuggling trade took over by night.

The local coast began to lose its raw edge. In 1840 Comanches sacked Linnville, but by the end of the decade the Indian frontier had moved on west. The remarkable canebrake along the lower Colorado River was going up in flames, to be replaced with sugarcane and corn. The riparian forests were falling and rich topsoil was muddying the rivers. The buffalo no longer appeared in the wintertime, and migrating swans were getting scarce, although wintering ducks and geese were still too numerous to be shot out. Black bears were receding to the east and passenger pigeons toward oblivion. Even the alligators had learned not to bask on the riverbanks in broad daylight.

Through it all Matagorda Island maintained its isolation. It had officially become part of Refugio County in 1838, and in 1846 was transferred into newly organized Calhoun County, but it still had no permanent population. Some vintage maps designated it St. Joseph Island. The Spanish name of Matagorda, meaning "thick brush," probably for the canebrakes, was primarily used for the port and settlement at the mouth of the Colorado River, and by extension, for the main bay, and the island and peninsula guarding Pass Cavallo.

In 1839 the congress of the republic decided to establish a port of entry, customshouse, and a fort on the outer, northeastern edge of Matagorda Island at the entrance to the pass. Unfortunately, this spot was apparently chosen on a map rather than by preliminary survey. Nonetheless, a 640-acre townsite was platted and 173 lots were put up for public sale in 1841. But the lack of a natural harbor, the inaccessibility to overland transport, and the existence of numerous competing ports, in addition to the government's preoccupation with other matters, caused the proposed Port of Calhoun to die aborning. Fort Washington, conceived while there was still fear of reprisal from Mexico, was no more than a sandy embankment reinforced with driftwood; it was never consistently manned. The paltry sites of both town and fort have long since been consumed by shore erosion along the west bank of the pass.

But this impotent venture on Matagorda Island had one important consequence—it riled Colonel James Power, who considered it an infringement upon his private property rights. By the time the Republic of Texas became the state of Texas, he moved to firm his contested claim by drawing up a townsite of his own, just north of aborted Port Calhoun. He called his vision Saluria, and it was destined to bring civilization at last to Matagorda Island.

Most of the townsite, on the northwestern tip of Matagorda Island at the mouth of Saluria Bayou (then called McHenry Bayou), is now under the sediments and shallow water of Matagorda Bay. There are no visible foundations, no monument or marker, not even a cemetery. Generations of bottle hunters rummaging along the current shoreline have left little more than occasional chunks of brick and crumbles of tabby. A canal, the "Oilfield Cut," bisects the area. The location is rendered more stark by the looming concrete skeleton of the U.S. Coast Guard station, appropriately named Saluria Station, erected there in 1932 and gutted by Hurricane Carla in 1961. Brown pelicans crouch on old boat-shed pilings and porpoises crowd schools of mullet over the once busy intersection of Resaca and Buena Vista streets at the commercial heart of Saluria.

In 1847, Colonel Power and a consortium of investors founded Saluria. Power quitclaimed 640 acres of land to Alexander Somervell, his land agent and trustee, who promoted the plat of over 300 lots as a port, pilot station, resort, and a pleasant and profitable place to settle. The enterprise achieved respectability when the legislature validated Power's title to the land.

As it turned out, Judge Hugh W. Hawes, a transplanted Virginian,

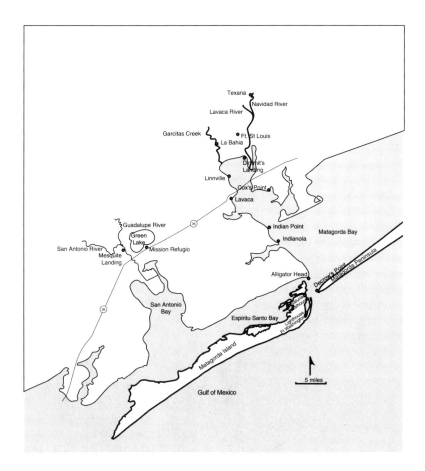

Map 7. Historical sites of the latter half of the nineteenth century on and near Matagorda Island. Offshore sites are now submerged.

bought many of the lots and became the commercial and developmental driving force of the community. The Hawes warehouse and wharf were the center of maritime commerce. Although incoming vessels had to bank sharply across the strong current through the pass, good docks over 11 feet of water enticed full-rigged transoceanic vessels to heave to at Saluria, and freighters from the Atlantic seaboard lightered there. River steamers like Captain Wheeler's *Kate Ward* made routine round trips between Saluria and inland river ports.

In 1852 Judge Hawes promoted the growing commercial bustle at Saluria by financing the opening of the Indianola Road. From Alligator Head (modern Port O'Connor), to Bayucos Island, with a ferry over

McHenry Bayou to Saluria, it gave Hawes' adopted home port access to land transport into the interior. In 1857 he financed Saluria's first school. In addition to being the town's major benefactor, H.W. Hawes was one of the island's largest landholders, eventually passing his estate to a widening succession of descendants so that the Hawes name is inseparable from the later history of Matagorda Island. The good judge saw Saluria born, rise, and succumb. He died there in 1883, at the age of eighty, and rests today in a solitary grave on a breezy hillock of sand on what was once Hawes land on the north end of the island.

Throughout the decade of the 1850s, Saluria lived up to its potential, overshadowing Port Cavallo, which had been established about the same time across the pass on the tip of Matagorda Peninsula. In addition to the lure of its docks and warehouses, Saluria became the main pilot station on Pass Cavallo. At busy times, several vessels would be anchored outside the pass with pilot flags flying, awaiting an experienced hand to guide them across the bar. Captains who got impatient and tried navigating on their own often ran aground. Harris and Morgan mail-packet steamers arrived weekly, and eventually a post office was established in town. Directly across McHenry Bayou the federal government erected a 55-foot wooden tower capped by a whale-oil lamp. Although its range was restricted, this Saluria Light guided ships at sea to safe anchor before they shoaled in the pass. The similar Swash Light was erected off Alligator Head and the Halfmoon Reef Light was perched atop that great oyster reef off Palacios Point on the east side of Matagorda Bay.

As both ship traffic and shipping disasters increased in Pass Cavallo, the need for a full-scale lighthouse became critical. In 1847 the federal government appropriated $15,000 and a year later acquired several acres of land. This original site, on the edge of Matagorda Island bordering the entrance to the pass, was about 2 miles east of the present location of the lighthouse and half a mile north of Fort Washington.

The heavy metal columns and trusses and the huge cast-iron sheathing plates of the lighthouse were prefabricated in Baltimore and bolted together on the site by a special crew who traveled down with the parts. They began assembly in March 1852. The 79-foot metal tower, gaudily painted with horizontal bands of red, white, and black to serve as a daymark, contained a giddy 100-step spiral staircase up to the lantern—the glass-walled cylindrical room that housed the actual light, 96 feet above sea level.

In the lantern was a third-order Fresnel lens imported from France. This huge lens, 7 feet tall and 4 feet across, had an elaborate array of

Lighthouse

prisms above and below that refracted the light into a thin sheet, which was then concentrated into an intense beam as it emerged through one of six "bull's-eye" lenses equally spaced around the middle of the apparatus. The whole affair, with its tiers of gleaming crystalline prisms supported on polished brass fixtures, resembled an enormous hornets' nest by Fabergé.

The light itself was a concentric series of smokeless, hollow wicks fueled by colza oil (extracted from rapeseeds) mounted in a special lamp positioned on a stationary table inside the lens. The Fresnel lens was fixed to a rotating platform that was driven by a precision clockwork powered by the descent of a heavy counterweight, which the keeper periodically cranked back up the tower, as though winding a gigantic grandfather clock. The lens made a complete revolution in 9 minutes, so one of the six bull's-eye lenses passed a given point every minute and a half. Within the 16-mile range of the light, a ship's captain in the Gulf would see a 2-second flash of light every 90 seconds.

The light was fired up each evening 15 minutes before sundown and extinguished 15 minutes after sunrise. In between the prisms were scrupulously polished, the brass mountings shined, and the whole affair draped in fine linen curtains by a succession of keepers-of-the-light. These were men imbued with near monastic concern for their charge and as reliable and as dauntless as the faultless machine itself. Captain James Cummings, the first head keeper, ignited the

Matagorda Light for the first time on December 21, 1852. (More information on Matagorda Lighthouse can be found in Appendix A.)

As Saluria's star continued its rise, so did the outlying population on Matagorda Island. Soon the interior grassy flats down the length of the island were cross-fenced into cattle and sheep ranches. The most prominent landholders were the Hawes and the Littles, but there were others: Byrne, Boone, Brundrett, Dubois, Hill, Holzheuser, Madden, Storrs, Vandeveer. The census of 1850 recorded 120 "free people" and 44 slaves on Matagorda Island; by 1860 the population had climbed to an all-time high of 258.

By this time there was enough activity on the island for brothers Pete and Theo "Charlie" Johnson to launch another public transportation system linking island and mainland. They deftly threaded two three-masted schooners through the oyster reefs and mud flats in the back bays, hauling passengers, mail, and goods to all ports between Corpus Christi on the west and Saluria, Indianola, and Port Lavaca on the east. At the same time, they operated a 60-mile stage line connecting Saluria via a ferry on Cedar Bayou with the village of St. Joseph's on the southern tip of St. Joseph Island. Matagorda Island must have been at its vintage best when the morning stagecoach pulled out of Saluria and came high-balling down the firm forebeach with colorful Charlie Johnson letting the fresh team have its head.

The Civil War

Through 1860, everything on Matagorda Bay was looking up. Lying at one end of an endless stream of oxcarts and muletrains plying the Chihuahua Trail, the area had access to the ports and markets of the world. It was a mecca for immigrants and the gateway for provisions for military forts in the west. Work was proceeding on a railroad; there was an endless demand for cotton; the ranching enterprise was starting to pay off. No one foresaw the coming misfortunes that would totally wipe out much that had been done and leave the remainder in chaos and depression.

The first blow was the Civil War. The immediate issue was clear-cut: the Union under Major General Nathaniel P. Banks wanted to close the ports to halt the cotton trade and cut military supply lines; the Confederates under Major General John Bankhead Magruder were determined to keep the ports open. So most military action in Texas was concentrated along the coast, and Matagorda Bay was occasionally in the thick of it. What occurred in Texas during 1861–1865 was not paramount to the overall conflict, but vast destruction of facilities and complete disruption of society had a devastating impact, causing widespread misery and hardship, and an aftermath of resentment and despair.

Even before conflict began, U.S. soldiers at military posts across Texas started to evacuate the state, many ordered to Matagorda Bay to await transport. When the opening shots were fired at Fort Sumter and Confederate President Jefferson Davis gave orders to detain all Federal soldiers, Confederate Colonel Earl van Dorn and 125 scrappy volunteers steamed out of Galveston bound for Saluria, where 500 Union soldiers had not yet debarked. Less than a week after the war began, it was already on its way to Matagorda Island.

On April 17, 1861, van Dorn encountered the transport steamer, *Star of the West*, anchored outside Pass Cavallo awaiting a shuttle of troops. Waiting for darkness to conceal their identity and inferior strength, the Confederates pulled alongside the Union ship and pretended to be the expected lighter. The captain of the *Star* took the bait and van Dorn's men turned their ruse into a quick and bloodless capture. All of this occurred practically under the guns of the guardian ship *Mohawk*, which quietly rode the night out before discovering that the *Star* had been seized and taken up the coast.

A few days later the plucky van Dorn docked at Saluria, backed by three Confederate ships and a carefully choreographed show of force. There, in the parlor of Judge Hawes' home, the Confederate colonel, in full dress uniform, brusquely informed Major Caleb C. Sibley that he and his troops had just become prisoners of war, a circumstance which the major thought it prudent to accept. In just over a week, the Confederates had scored two easy coups on Matagorda Bay, and their morale and confidence were sky-high; but the war was hardly begun.

By the summer of 1861, five Union gunboats of the West Gulf Squadron were effectively enforcing the blockade of the major Texas ports, and even wily Confederate blockade runners were frequently outsmarted and waylaid in the back bays by shallow-draft Union cutters. Grim reality was beginning to replace earlier cocksureness.

On October 25, 1862, the ominous sounds of war reverberated on Matagorda Bay. When three heavily armed Union warships appeared off Pass Cavallo, the company of Indianola Artillery Guards occupying Fort Esperanza, overlooking the pass, were delighted to finally have a target to break their tedium, and they readily opened up with their 24-pounders. This salvo was immediately returned by such a withering fire from the ships that Guards Captain Joseph M. Reuss' order to retreat to the mainland before they were either blown apart or cut off was obeyed with alacrity.

So the gunboats continued undeterred through the pass and anchored off Indianola. The next day Union Captain William B. Renshaw met a citizens' delegation to demand that the town capitulate; he was summarily refused. After a 90-minute truce to allow evacuation of women and children, a sustained bombardment began. By noon the next day Indianola ran up the white flag. Union soldiers entered the town and pillaged some stores before returning to their vessels, and the fleet continued up the bay until it was stopped by the shallows over Gallinipper Reef. On October 31 they shelled Port Lavaca, and then they steamed away as abruptly as they had arrived. Their objective, apparently, had been to feel out the defenses and to decisively show the Confederates where the power lay.

Confederate General Magruder got the point. He ordered civilian evacuation of the barrier islands and establishment of forts at critical locations. Then he designed a scorched-earth program that wreaked more damage than anything the Union commanders even contemplated. It also elicited furious local resistance. The orders were detailed and explicit: tear up the wharves, destroy the bridges, burn the warehouses, pull up all channel markers and sink private vessels in the shipping lanes, rip up the railroad and burn or splinter the ties, drive the cattle over the reefs to the mainland, fire all the houses on the islands; burn Saluria to the ground, topple the Saluria Light, wreck the lights on Halfmoon Reef and off Alligator Head, and blow up the U.S. lighthouse at the pass. Local responsibility for this destruction devolved to Major Daniel Shea, who allocated the dismal work to Captain John T. Brackenridge's cavalry detachment at Indianola.

Apparently Brackenridge's men performed their grim mission with solemn efficiency, except for the lighthouse. They removed the valuable lens and buried it in the sand, but the single keg of powder they had been issued for the demolition work did no more than put a few splits in the casing of the sturdy iron structure. So, the tower remained, staring hollow-eyed over the scene of general destruction.

In November 1863 Union General Banks initiated a major offensive up the Texas coast. After landing at Brazos Santiago and capturing Brownsville, several thousand disciplined Union troops under generals C. C. Washburn and N. J. T. Dana moved rapidly up the nearly deserted lower coast, taking Corpus Christi on November 16. They marched unopposed up Mustang Island, crossing Aransas Pass onto St. Joseph Island on the 18th. They met barely token resistance, but their advance slowed to allow Union gunboats to precede them to Pass Cavallo, where they knew the Confederates were dug in. When the Federal soldiers crossed Cedar Bayou and for the first time set foot on Matagorda Island on November 25, they were back in stride

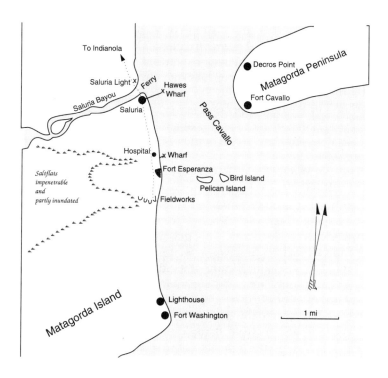

Map 8. The Bluecher map, 1863; drawn by Major Felix A. Bluecher, CSA, showing Civil War–era sites on Matagorda Island. Note the presence of islands, original location of lighthouse, and absence of J-Hook (modified from a photocopy, National Archives).

and doubtless could hear the occasional muffled boom of their ships' heavy guns over the pounding of the surf.

The Confederates, determined to make a stand at Matagorda Bay, had raised crude breastworks at strategic locations. At least several of these "forts" had artillery emplacements with whatever cannon or scavenged ship's guns were at hand. Pass Cavallo was guarded by Fort Esperanza (Hope) on the north end of Matagorda Island and by Fort Cavallo on Decrow's Point at the tip of Matagorda Peninsula.

The site for Fort Esperanza was selected, in December 1861, by Major Daniel Shea. His artillery company had been stationed in the remnants of old Fort Washington, a location he rightly considered too exposed to long-range ships' guns. He had his men dig in at a more protected location 2½ miles up the pass, opposite Pelican Island, and about 200 yards inland from the pass. On some maps this place is referred to as Fort Debray, but Esperanza was the accepted name. In February 1862 Major Caleb C. Forshey, in charge of engineering Confederate defenses along the Texas coast, visited and approved this location and hastened its completion. Thirty slaves were brought in to help the fifty or so soldiers toiling on the garrison. A wharf was built, and a short, mule-powered rail line was laid up the shore to the stronghold.

Details of the layout of Fort Esperanza are sketchy. There was one main wall parallel to the pass, a jagged heap of sand 200 yards long and 20 feet thick. Logs extracted from the great jam at the mouth of the Colorado River were floated across the bay and fixed into the earthworks with shellcrete. This massive rampart, with its seven cannon pads all facing the pass, was doubtless the principal structure, but there was also a barricade of sand and timbers inside the frontal wall. The cannon were to be enclosed, probably with logs, and some sort of "bombproof cover" was planned for the men, but how much of this work was actually done is not known.

To protect the fort from flank and rear assault by land a series of "fieldworks," a quarter-mile line of rifle pits and crude redoubts, was dug from the pass to the nearby bay-side marshes. All traces of Fort Esperanza and its associated fieldworks have long since been obliterated by shore erosion; the site now lies offshore between the tip of the J-Hook and Mule Slough. The overgrown zigzag line of knee-deep ditches extending from the Gulf beach across the uplands and to the bay-side marshes at Lighthouse Cove, although popularly referred to as "Confederate trenches," is displaced nearly 2 miles from the fieldworks shown on maps of the time. This may be an outer perimeter hastily scooped out when the Confederates realized that the Union troops were indeed advancing up the coast, or the trenches may have been dug by the Federals themselves.

While Washburn's troops were starting up Matagorda Island, two Union gunboats off Pass Cavallo opened fire on Fort Esperanza with 9-inch Dahlgrens. This harsh greeting elicited a crackle of harmless rifle fire and a series of retorts from the one 12-pound and several 24-pound cannon mounted on the wall. The garrison was manned by about 500 men, most belonging to infantry units of Major A. F. Hobby's regiment and the rest composing Major Shea's seasoned artillery battalion, all under the command of Colonel W. T. Bradfute. Fort Cavallo across the pass was at this time unmanned.

For three days Fort Esperanza and the warships kept each other alert and in place with occasional salvos from their big guns. Then, on November 29, Washburn's men arrived and the fighting got serious. The gunboats stepped up their pounding while the infantry advanced on the trenches. A heavy exchange of small-arms fire generated a pall of black powder smoke but few casualties on either side. By nightfall, the Union soldiers had taken the outer perimeter trenches, but the embattled Confederates were still in command of their shell-pocked position. Colonel Bradfute, though he could see the futility of continuing, would not consider the ignominy of surrender. So he ordered the cannons spiked and the remaining ammunition blown, and about midnight he and his weary command slipped away and threaded the cold back bays to the mainland. The next morning the stars and stripes were quietly run up over Fort Esperanza.

Union troops went on to take and occupy Port Lavaca and Indianola. In addition, there were skirmishes on Matagorda Peninsula, while gunboats lobbed shells over into Fort Caney at the mouth of the Colorado River, but the Union offensive stalled and never reached Galveston. In March 1864 the invading troops finally steamed out of Pass Cavallo for New Orleans, and with them went the last local direct confrontation of the dreary war.

In the summer of 1865 the stifling blockade was finally lifted. Occupation troops were pulled out in 1869, and by 1870 a glimmer of life and hope was revitalizing the upper Texas coast. Local ports, especially Indianola, rebuilt to handle the reviving maritime trade. Longhorns, cotton fields, and a functioning railroad stirred the local economy. Even a severe outbreak of yellow fever could not quash the determination to pick up the pieces and get on with the good life.

Things on Matagorda Island were not so bright. Returning ranchers had to rebuild from scratch. Saluria was a shambles, its commercial center burned out by the Confederates, what lumber remained scavenged by the Union troops. There was precious little capital, and even the resourceful Judge Hawes could not confer a competitive edge over booming Indianola. Yet, the 1870 census showed that 166 people were trying to make a go of it on the island.

At this time the lighthouse was listing badly seaward from a combination of the attempted destruction, subsequent neglect, and an undercutting shoreline. In 1867 a temporary scaffold with a smaller, fifth-order lens was put into operation nearby while the tower was dismantled and the salvageable pieces stacked on the sand. In 1872, when Congress appropriated funds for rebuilding, the ponderous structural pieces, the intricate gear mechanism, and the spiral staircase were all carefully loaded onto flatcars on a specially laid narrow-gauge track. With a combination of ox power and human determination, everything was moved 2 miles inland to the present location, where it was reassembled on a new foundation.

There were a few modifications. The tower, with its several damaged plates replaced, was painted solid black. A new third-order Fresnel lens was installed. "Mineral oil" (kerosene) replaced colza oil as fuel for the lamp. The new installation included a comfortable house for the keeper (whose name has apparently been lost to history) and another for his assistant, a cement rainwater cistern, and sundry outbuildings. The new light blinked on in September 1873. Soon thereafter, the illumination was again updated to an incandescent oil-vapor light. This device, its glowing mantle primed with kerosene vapors at a pressure of 80 psi, looked very much like a large version of a modern Coleman lantern and produced a brighter, whiter beam.

Reconstruction on Matagorda Bay was rudely interrupted in the fall of 1875. Hurricanes and severe tropical storms had visited the local coast, notably in 1851 and 1854, and as recently as 1871, so people certainly knew that their coastline was occasionally raked by violent "West India cyclones." But then as now, their aspirations and sanguine expectations drove them to build and settle in exposed sites where they were clearly asking for trouble.

No European had ever witnessed the sort of trouble that began on September 14, 1875, with scudding clouds and rain showers pushed by a steady northeasterly wind. Next day the sky was dark, the wind had reached gale force, the barometer was plummeting, and the ugly water of the bay was rising at an alarming rate. By now people were genuinely alarmed, but it was too late to evacuate or even to properly secure anything, so they simply hunkered down to ride the cyclone out. Through the day and night of the 16th, the full fury of the hurricane lashed the area with winds estimated at nearly 150 MPH and a vicious tidal surge cresting at 15 feet that totally engulfed Matagorda Island and spread far across the low coastal prairie and then dragged everything into the bay with its backwash. This was definitely not the sort of cyclone to be ridden out.

When it was over, little of human devising was left intact on Matagorda Bay and every nuance of the shores of the mainland and barrier island was changed in some detail. All of the ports with their attendant commercial and residential districts were gone—Indianola, Port Lavaca, Alligator Head, Decrow's Point, Saluria. The recently resurrected lighthouse on Matagorda Island weathered the storm, but both the Halfmoon Reef lighthouse and the Swash lighthouse, along with the families who served them, were erased from their reef pilings. Several hundred people died, mostly drowned or crushed in the horror of wildly heaving debris. Ninety percent of the residents of Saluria were killed, but plucky old Judge Hawes survived by chopping holes in the floor to dissipate the energy of the waves threatening to lift his house off its foundation. The dunes on Matagorda Island were flattened; Matagorda Peninsula was shorter by 300 yards; Pelican Island was sliced off at the waterline.

"Hope springs eternal in the human breast: Man never is, but always to be, blest:"[4] At least some of those who were left could look upon the scene of splintered timbers, bloated cattle, and human grief and summon up the resolve to rebuild. But not at Saluria; that port was finished, and with its demise went all prospects for commercial development on Matagorda Island. Only the most determined ranchers came straggling back.

In 1877 high tides from a passing hurricane sapped Fort Esperanza into Pass Cavallo. In 1878 the U.S. Life-Saving Service established the Lifeboat Station on a sandy eminence inland of the original lighthouse location. Concern about rapid erosion and shoaling in the pass prompted the idea of a jetty to protect the entrance. Work was begun in 1881, using mattresses of brush stabilized with rocks and concrete. Miraculously, by 1884 the precarious structure extended from the island side of the pass nearly a mile into the heavy Gulf swells. But all of this was merely an interlude before the final disaster.

On the sultry afternoon of August 18, 1886, people on Matagorda Bay were glad to see the sky cloud over with a promise of rain; but when a sustained northeasterly wind sprang up, old fears were quickly aroused. They proved well-founded. On August 20, a hurricane more fierce than the cyclone of 1875 roared through the area. There was less damage and loss of life, mainly because civilization had not rebuilt to its former level. Nevertheless, what had been done was completely undone. Again the ports were demolished, new homes and stores destroyed, the primitive island jetty obliterated, Pass Cavallo reshaped, and Matagorda Island swept clean. On the island the lighthouse again weathered the storm, and this time Judge Hawes rode it out unperturbed in his final slumber.

The 1886 hurricane was the final blow for many of the ill-starred early settlements on Matagorda Bay. It not only took the goods and the lives of many of the residents, it finally made believers out of the rest. They abandoned the exposed locations, many of them moving inland to Victoria, Cuero, and elsewhere on the coastal prairie. For awhile Matagorda Island returned to its ages-old somnolence of sea breeze, sand, and surf.

---

4. Alexander Pope. *An Essay on Man,* Epistle I.

Ranching

Properly managed, stock raising is not far removed from nature: grass grows; cattle reproduce. An astute rancher can make a living off that viable balance. On a barrier island, the manifestly finite resources dictate that livestock can never be a big-time operation; any tendency to overstock quickly turns the grassland into stretches of wind-blown sand. From the earliest days of ranching on Matagorda Island, there was neither opportunity for, nor expectation of, much more than a subsistence living; the open life-style had to be reward enough. A ranch house, rainwater cistern, barn, corral, cross-fences, and windmills were about all the constructions necessary. Large families and hard work were part of the deal. When a cyclone came, there was little to wreck. The families temporarily evacuated to the mainland. Stock sought the high ground and, if necessary, could be replenished from herds on the coastal prairie. Frame houses were quickly rebuilt and fences mended. Life went on. Ranching was thus a sustainable, relatively low-risk means of ekeing out a living on a storm-prone barrier island.

So, by the 1890s the Hawes, the Hills, the Littles, and others like them had begun to filter back onto their insular spreads. There on isolated Matagorda Island, while the mainland marched into the twentieth century, they settled into a fiercely independent, clannish, pioneer/cowboy life-style, rough but enviable, destined to remain unchanged until 1940.

Ranch houses were thinly sprinkled on sandy uplands. There was no electricity: light came from kerosene lamps; radios crackled off batteries; brine kept meat from spoiling. Because of the scarcity of wood, kerosene also fueled the cooking and heating stoves. A diet of fresh fish, crabs, oysters, waterfowl, beef, poultry, pork, and home-canned vegetables was supplemented on occasional boat trips to the mainland by store-bought goods. Families living on the north end of the island routinely docked at the "lighthouse wharf" where the current TPWD Visitors' Center is located.

In the heavy, salty air everything made of metal corroded, machined parts jammed, textiles molded, wood swelled, smoked meat decayed, saltshakers clogged, and human sweat dripped off without cooling the body. There were no window screens until later on; smoke pots guarded the doors and everyone slept under mosquito bars draped over the beds; women set up bars at their sewing chairs. The seasons and the sea breeze often helped; other times, everyone simply tolerated the voracious pests. Despite the nuisance, there was hardly any mosquito-borne disease on the island; the insects did not have the sources of infection accessible to those on the crowded mainland.

An island ranch was a great place for a kid to grow up, at least for a boy. When he wasn't put to work, he had the vast rattler-infested interior to explore afoot or on horseback, the bountiful bay-side marshes to fish and hunt, uninterrupted miles of native beach to enjoy, and peer-aged relatives to consort with. The family was together all summer, but during the school year the women and school-age children moved to the mainland and returned to the island on weekends. Every boy's ambition was to finish or quit school and become a part of the extended family enterprise on the island.

The central business was cattle, and as one old-time rancher remarked, "You don't have to spend much time around cattle to learn that they don't just raise theirselves." If they are to yield a living, they must be worked constantly—looked after, branded, watered, rotated, winter-fed, smeared for screw worms, sprayed for blackflies, dipped for ticks, pulled out of boggy ground, selectively bred, culled, rounded up, sold. In the earliest days, market stock was hazed down to the south end of the island and forced to swim to Ayers Reef and then hobble across the oyster islets to the Black Jacks (the Aransas National Wildlife Refuge). It must have been a wild scramble—the riders on mounts with tow sacks tied around their hoofs for protection from the sharp shell, and bawling half-wild cattle reluctant to move from one reef to the next. As one participant described it: "Well, it was a good mix of excitement and damned hard work, and of course, your livelihood depended on things going right." In later days the cattle were pushed to Saluria ("You had to get them started on the run so they'd swim the Fish Pond, or they'd cut back on you."), where they were loaded on a barge for transport to pens in Port O'Connor.

As the decades passed, the good life on Matagorda Island held its course. The people lived, worked, and died, and the land passed on to the next of kin. Theodore Olsen and William Heinroth kept the lighthouse in trim. Memorable hurricanes made local landfall in 1914 and 1919. In 1929 the Lifeboat Station overlooking the entrance to Pass Cavallo was closed, and a new facility was opened in 1932, at the old townsite on the mouth of Saluria Bayou. In 1930 the first causeway was built across Lavaca Bay. The first oil and natural gas leases were being bought up on the mainland in the 1930s. The availability of outboard motors and metal boats brought an increase in seasonal waterfowl hunters and anglers and occasional beachcombers to the margin of the island. Heavy barge traffic commenced when the Gulf Intracoastal Waterway was dredged across Matagorda Bay in 1939.

1930s to the Present

None of this really altered the way of life on the island; but as it must to all places, change did finally come its way. In the 1930s, two unrelated events of hugely unequal global significance combined to push Matagorda Island into the real world of the twentieth century: in 1933 a Dallas oil tycoon decided that a barrier island would be an ideal place to set up a fiefdom; in 1939 Hitler invaded Poland.

Clint Murchison, Sr., was one of those legendary, independent wheeler-dealers who made a fortune negotiating leases, drilling wells, and running hot oil (oil illegally pumped beyond the daily allowance) in the wide open oil and gas fields of Texas during the colorful boom days after World War I. True to his nature, Murchison (Mur-ka-son) spent the rest of his life expanding and diversifying his empire. The Murchison name may be more familiar from Clint, Jr., who carried on the family tradition and founded the Dallas Cowboys football team.

In 1933, Clint tried to buy Matagorda Island outright, but was astounded to find that even during the Depression years, ready cash would not turn the heads of most of the longtime ranching families. So he began to nibble at their stubborn resistance. By 1941 he had acquired the southern 9 miles of the island, 11,500 acres. The title to the property actually belonged to the American Liberty Oil Company, of which Clint Murchison and Dudley Golding each owned 45 percent of the stock, with the remaining 10 percent owned by Toddie Lee Wynne, Sr. But Clint founded and actually ran American Liberty, and the island purchase was his idea. It was he who, after sinking several dry holes, decided to convert the tract into a working cattle ranch and a recreational retreat for family, friends, and dignitaries.

Once he had installed some of the amenities to which he was accustomed, Clint Murchison truly enjoyed Matagorda Island. An early priority was the construction of a richly furnished bungalow. It was begun in 1934, and over the years it was expanded into the house now called the Wynne lodge, a rambling, one-story clubhouse with breezy, full-length verandas facing both east and west and multiple accommodations for family and guests. He quickly added a bunkhouse for the ranchhands, sundry outbuildings and corrals, a large electric generator, a water well, a maze of shell roads, a hangar, and an airstrip of packed shell.

This compound is situated about 4 miles up the island from the entrance to Cedar Bayou, on a sandy eminence between Bray Cove and the Gulf. Here, on an acre of landscaped grounds surrounded by a neat white fence with net wire around the bottom to keep the rattlesnakes out, Clint Murchison came down from Dallas to relax, hunt, fish, entertain, hatch business deals, and watch the young people enjoy themselves. In 1940 he even managed to lure President Franklin D. Roosevelt to his island paradise for a grand tour in a stripped-down Ford, followed by a scrumptious luncheon in the clubhouse breezeway. For better or worse, with Clint Murchison running things, the southern quarter of Matagorda Island was no longer a somnolent strip of sand.

In 1940 the grim news from Europe put the nation in a somber mood, and in November of that year the growing anxiety came home to the Texas Coastal Bend in the form of federal marshals with condemnation papers in their hands. The secretary of war, by right of eminent domain, intended to acquire 55 miles of Texas coastline—all of Matagorda Peninsula and Matagorda Island—on which to train military pilots. The locale lent itself admirably. It was sparsely populated, undeveloped, open, remote from a population center, and easily cordoned off from civilian trespass, and the surrounding water would serve as a convenient buffer for ordnance gone astray.

By 1942 the nation was at war and the condemnation proceedings in Texas were hastened to completion. All of Matagorda Peninsula was put under lease to the federal government. The northern 28 miles of Matagorda Island were purchased outright for a generous $7.00 per acre, and the adjoining state-owned tidelands and beaches were put under lease. Clint Murchison retained title to his insular domain but readily leased it to the government for a token $1.00 per year. Understandably, there was grumbling among longtime ranchers who were forced to sell while an upstart fat cat across the fence was allowed to keep his title. In retrospect, many wondered what the wily wildcatter had discussed with FDR over that leisurely lunch in the clubhouse just before the war. For the moment it didn't matter. The war machine was a'building and Matagorda Island was to be an important part of the frenzied effort.

Initial construction was wiped out by a powerful hurricane in August 1942, but work was begun afresh in the fall of that year on two large airfields. One of these was located on the north end of Matagorda Island beside the old lighthouse wharf; its twin was built on Matagorda Peninsula, just north of the current Matagorda Ship Channel. Round-the-clock work by the Army Corps of Engineers brought the Matagorda Bombing and Gunnery Range into reality in July 1943, and it was immediately taken over by the Air Training Command of the U.S. Army Air Corps for the duration of the war. The base was deactivated in 1945, but returned to duty in February 1949 as a pre-amble to the Korean conflict. Transferred to the Strategic Air Command (SAC) and maintained by the 4004th Air Base Squadron with a resident crew of 125, the base was used for training by various branches of the air force and army through the 1950s.

The 8,000-foot primary runway, secondary runways, and broad cement apron and forty-four buildings of the island base sprawled over 1,100 acres. The current TPWD buildings were renovated from this military complex; the Visitors' Center was originally a dockside warehouse. The nearby popular fishing site called the Army Hole is the deep basin from which fill material was dredged to level the landing strip. The TPWD mainland information center for Matagorda Island State Park in Port O'Connor is located on 6 acres of land where the air force ferry docked daily to shuttle personnel to and from the island.

The main focus of the military enterprise was the 20-mile long bombing and gunnery range established on the central part of the island. With its cement bunkers, signal beacons, and six spotting towers, this is where the action was. Throughout World War II and on through Korea and Vietnam, military pilots and bombardiers honed their deadly skills by dropping tons of live and dummy explosives on targets along the edges of Matagorda's midsection. SAC B-52s and FB-111s came hurtling in across the Gulf on ultralow trajectories from Lake Charles and Grand Isle, Louisiana. TAC F4s, A7s, and T33s streaked down at supersonic speed from Bergstrom Air Force Base in Austin. Squadrons of Huey Cobra helicopters routinely batted over from Corpus Christi to test-fire their 7.62-mm guns and 40-mm cannons. Night bombing, horizontal bombing, dive-bombing, radar bombing, laser bombing, strafing, and incidental sonic booming—Matagorda Island definitely earned its stripes as it continually quaked and reverberated to the real roar of mock war.

By 1960 most training programs on Matagorda Island had wound down. Throughout its wartime tenure, the island had been freely used for recreation by resident personnel, pilot trainees, and especially by visiting brass. Now, with a skeleton staff, the installation had little local economic impact, and rumor had it that Matagorda was serving the air force mainly as an exclusive hunting and fishing reserve, an "officer's country club." County and state officials began to agitate for public access. The USFWS was interested in the area because whooping cranes used the bay-side tidal flats. Prior landowners petitioned to buy back their holdings. The once-isolated barrier was no longer on the fringe of local controversy; it was at the center of it.

In November 1971 the Matagorda Island Unit of the Aransas National Wildlife Refuge was established when the air force agreed to let the USFSW manage, for the benefit of the whooping cranes and other wildlife, the part of the island that the federal government owned. In 1975, the air base was deactivated; by 1977 all military personnel and equipment were off the island, and the installation was officially closed on June 30, 1978. Immediately, there began a tug-of-war over final disposition of the land.

The 19,000 acres of federally owned land, the backbone of the northern three-quarters of the island, were transferred to the USFWS for permanent inclusion in the National Refuge System, specifically for the conservation of migratory birds. Control of the 26,000 acres of beaches and tidal flats leased from the state of Texas was returned, and in 1979 these were designated the Matagorda Island State Park and Wildlife Management Area under the supervision of the TPWD. The southern 11,500 acres of Matagorda Island reverted to private use, which, by this time, no longer meant Clint Murchison.

When Dudley Golding died, Murchison and his longtime associate, Toddie Lee Wynne, negotiated a 50:50 ownership of American Liberty Oil. Like Murchison, Wynne had matured in the rough and tumble east Texas oil fields. But rather than entering the risky drilling business directly, he was a lawyer who shrewdly shuffled lease papers worth millions, nearly always managing to negotiate a percentage of the deal for himself. He was already a wealthy man when he teamed up with Murchison in Dallas. They made a well-matched pair; together, the two men routinely manipulated hundreds of millions of dollars in far-flung enterprises. It was only when he thought his lawyer was dealing behind his back that Clint Murchison bitterly demanded that the two split their assets. An irreconcilable rift developed, and when they dissolved their partnership in 1946, Wynne got the Matagorda property.

Toddie Lee took to Matagorda much as Clint had done. He showed a keen interest in operating the Star Brand Ranch, upgrading the herd with high-bred bulls. He kept about a dozen cowhands to work the cattle from horses and an assortment of stripped-down motor vehicles, and he frequently rode out with them. Once a year surplus animals were driven onto a wooden barge and ferried across the bay to waiting trucks at Rockport. Wynne installed additional windmills and cross-fences, sprigged coastal Bermuda grass in the barrier flat, and brought in draglines and bulldozers to construct a series of dikes around the bay-side perimeter of the island to prevent tidal overwash across potential rangeland. In 1979 these dikes were ruled to be in violation of state tideland sovereignty, and Wynne was forced to install culverts that allowed for normal tidal fluctuation into the flats. This series of dikes and levees and their contained brackish pools—extending completely across Ayers Point, from Bray Cove to Shell Reef Bayou—now provides some of the best shorebird habitat on the island.

It was under Toddie Lee Wynne's hand that the south end of Matagorda took on its present aspect. He paved the runway and built the huge hangar to house the customized DC-3 he shuttled down from Dallas. He had a ring of stately palm trees planted around the yard to lend an oasis-like ambiance (most of these have since succumbed to hard winters), and he added a grandiose living room to the clubhouse. The tight-knit Wynne clan was (and still is) a big and a fun-loving group, and the charismatic Toddie Lee had as many friends as Clint Murchison; there was always something going on in and around the clubhouse. However, nothing quite matched the grand bash that Toddie Lee planned for September 1982.

Space Services Inc. of America (SSIA) was a Houston-based consortium of well-heeled investors determined to prove that private enterprise had the wherewithal to do business in outer space. Toddie Lee Wynne was not only SSIA's first and most enthusiastic backer, he offered his island as a launch site for the maiden blast-off. On August 5, 1981, the well-publicized event ended in disaster when the 55-foot Percheron exploded on the pad. The massive iron gantry stills looms beside the road 4 miles up the island from the Wynne lodge. More determined than ever, SSIA's technicians went back to the drawing board and its playboy investors willingly passed the hat again.

In less than a year, on September 8, 1982, they had sleek, white Conestoga I standing erect and ready on a new pad on the southern tip of Matagorda Island a mile from the mouth of Cedar Bayou. No one was more proud, excited, or confident of success than Toddie Lee Wynne. He had primped his end of the island, set up colorful pavilions to fete the guests, and arranged for his private jet to fly reporters and dignitaries over from Rockport. But he could not control the weather, and the low clouds forced a postponement until the following day.

September 9 dawned murky, but the 10:00 A.M. countdown proceeded. Finally, at 10:18 A.M., Conestoga lifted off flawlessly and did what it was designed to do: climb to 195 miles carrying a 1,079-pound mock payload before arcing down to splash into the Gulf of Mexico 10½ minutes later and 260 miles offshore. SSIA had taken the first giant step for private enterprise and in so doing it had introduced Matagorda Island to the space age. Despite the unqualified success, gloom hung over the crowd because the man who had done so much to bring the big moment off was not there to enjoy it with them. Toddie Lee Wynne had suffered a massive heart attack early that morning and died aboard his jet en route to a Dallas hospital.

On December 8, 1982, the state of Texas and the U.S. Department of Interior entered into an agreement that was to become the basis for the modern supervision of Matagorda Island. The intent was to bring the publicly owned northern 28 miles of the island and its adjacent tidelands under a unified plan that would manage the barrier as an ecosystem. No property titles would be transferred: The state would retain ownership of its 25,000 acres of tidelands and Gulf beaches. The federal government would keep title to its 19,000 acres of barrier flat and dunes. What would be swapped were conservation easements—carefully worded stipulations on how the respective tracts would be administered. The state agreed to place its holdings into the National Refuge System, thus giving USFWS authority to manage these important fringing wetlands and beaches, along with the rest of the island, as habitat for wildlife. In return, the Department of Interior agreed to let the TPWD include all federal land in its Matagorda Island State Park and Wildlife Management Area.

In effect, the plan made USFWS the primary authority for habitat management on the entire 44,000-acre tract, while it gave TPWD the primary authority for supervising public access and use of the area. In addition, both authorities agreed that, for the duration of their 100-year agreement, there would be no public access to the island by motorized vehicle or by aircraft—in effect, that Matagorda Island would remain an island. This unprecedented arrangement was ratified by the U.S. Congress on August 4, 1983.

On December 29, 1986, the privately financed Texas Nature Conservancy (TNC) purchased the Wynne property for $13 million. Matagorda Island became the only Texas barrier entirely under public ownership when the Department of Interior acquired title to the TNC land on November 8, 1988. In December 1990 the original agreement between state and federal governments was modified to include this final land acquisition, and a lease was negotiated to allow TNC personnel the use of the Wynne lodge for environmental education. The proposed name for the all-inclusive entity was Matagorda Island National Wildlife Refuge and State Natural Area. As of February 1992, ratification by the U.S. Congress and subsequent signing of the agreement by the governor of Texas and the secretary of the Department of Interior are still pending.

So, after 450 mostly quiet years of recorded history under six aspiring sovereigns and a diverse assortment of private landholders, the
destiny of Matagorda Island finally rests with the public. As might be
expected in this polyglot nation, its current status has been met with
a mixture of rejoicing, suspicion, disgust, and indifference. Regardless of what is planned for it, so long as the Gulf breakers continue to
roll in and the sea breeze blows and the fine sand sifts across the
interior, there is always hope that Matagorda Island will continue to
be itself, which is enough.

CHAPTER 4

Ecology

Matagorda Island, with its neatly packaged, mostly self-sustaining dynamic mix of wind, water, sand, sunshine, and living creatures, is an ecosystem. Although not so disjunct from the rest of the world as its geographic remove suggests, the island does possess a recognizable ecological identity with exquisite anatomy, intricate metabolism, determined resilience, and, when it chooses to reveal it, a palpable sort of insular sentience. Those who know the island well insist that Matagorda's ecological personality distinguishes it even from other Texas barriers. But we must not push the analogy with a superorganism too far. An ecosystem is the weighted sum of lesser units, and it is within those lower levels that we find the roots of the fascination with the whole.

An ecosystem is made up of living and nonliving components. And in such an exposed location as Matagorda, the nonliving elements—sand, wind, waves, climate, sunshine—are the powerful setters of the ecological stage upon which the living inhabitants play out their roles. But the activities of living things do have some influence on the nature of the landscape. On barriers a critical relationship is the constant struggle between the push of the onshore wind, urging the sand to move, and the embrace of the vegetation, holding it in place. Without its plants, Matagorda Island would be nothing more than a barren bar of sand overwashed by the sea.

The most potent molding forces on a barrier island come from the sea—the energy of wind and wave expressed in the principal medium of sand. The Gulf shore is the high-energy side of the island. Even on a quiet day, the sand, constantly moved back and forth by the waves and whipped inland by the wind, knows no rest. During storms the Gulf side gets positively violent. By contrast, the bay shore is a low-energy environment where fine sediments, with little more disturbance than the gentle pulse of a feeble tide, quietly settle among the roots of smooth cordgrass. The gradation between these extremes impresses a zonality on the architecture of the entire island. Wind velocity, average size of sand grains, surface topography, prevailing temperature—everything is ordered into a sequence of parallel bands running up and down the barrier. Consequently, there is always a more striking environmental difference between two points on opposite sides of the island than between two points on the same side, even at opposite ends of the island.

Even casual visitors to Matagorda will notice that the living things they see are not scattered randomly across the island: Meadowlarks do not alight on bare shell ridges nor do oystercatchers stalk through the interior grassland. Dewberries can't be found on the beach or sea oats edging the bay-side tidal flat. Each kind of organism occurs in a restricted habitat, a kind of place in which it finds life most secure. Each species of plant and animal settles where its own set of biological needs and tolerances is most satisfied and least stressed. Suitable habitats are defined not only by the lay of the land but by the other creatures that live in them. The presence of grasshoppers and Gulf Coast ticks are as much a part of meadowlark habitat as sunshine and an open vista.

Habitats are framed within the dominating longitudinal pattern. Because rooted plants are more dependent than animals on substrate and local climatic gradients, vegetation zones are the most obvious indicators of changes in living conditions. You do not need to know the names of the plants to perceive a definite shift in their ranks as you go from the bay-side dock on the north end of Matagorda across the interior to the beach. In a little more than a mile you will cross several recognizably different bands of plants, and when you reach the surf you will have outstripped the tolerances of even the toughest of rooted species; the forebeach is bare of greenery. On the other hand, you can ride the shuttle for miles down the center of the island and remain among the same association of grasses and forbs.

The plant zones are convenient indicators of the limits of biotic communities, but each vegetation zone is more than a distinctive band of plants; it is a swath of greenery populated with associated animals. Among the island communities, only the forebeach, rendered distinctive by its barrenness, lacks a marker of rooted plants.

In addition to its physical qualities, an area is attractive to animals because of the vegetation it supports. Most animals, because they can move about and avoid extremes by seeking shelter, are less narrowly restricted to a particular life zone than plants are. Yet even a highly mobile creature like a seaside sparrow seldom strays far from its preferred tidal flat habitat, and more sedentary organisms like fiddler crabs and ground skinks are almost as loyal to a site as the plants themselves.

All of these components mesh with each other: the living things respond to the nonliving elements and interact in complex ways

Tiger beetle

among themselves. Inevitably, dependencies are established; discrete assemblages of creatures come to characterize a given kind of terrain. These natural associations of living things sharing the same habitat and coexisting with interwoven life-styles are recognized as biotic communities—the fundamental working units of ecosystems and the delights of anyone interested in the wonders of nature. If you would comprehend the ecology of Matagorda Island, it must be through an appreciation of its biotic communities.

The glue that holds a biotic community together is the constant, diversified intercourse among its component species. Each kind of creature, while satisfying its own needs, necessarily intermeshes its activities with those of neighboring organisms, and so the fabric of the community is woven. Quite unwittingly, every species takes a part in the construction and maintenance of this natural tapestry. The threads and twists contributed by each kind of organism constitute its particular niche, and the collective niches of all member species make up the mesh that binds the assemblage into a biotic community. In this natural scheme, think of a species' habitat as its address and of its niche as its occupation.

Much of our appreciation for nature comes from thoughtful observation of the subtleties of niches. Take tiger beetles, for example. What is their niche? Visitors on the sunny beach notice the movements of crowds of speckled tiger beetles that flit and dart along the waveline. Watched more closely, these alert and socially active insects are seen to spend considerable time in gesturing to each other. They are aggressive predators on shore flies and on the tiny worms and crustaceans stranded by each receding wave, and they nibble on dead stuff left by the waves. In their turn, the beetles are dive-bombed by robber flies or pecked up by passing willets. Female beetles are often seen running along with males clinging tightly on their backs. Each solitary egg, scattered in hard-packed sand in sites carefully chosen to avoid inundation by the normal high tide, hatches into a grub-like larva that digs a vertical burrow where it stays, most of the time waiting at the mouth to snatch any hapless amphipod, ant, or sand roach that happens by. Keen-eyed plovers occasionally snap up an unwary

tiger beetle larva before it can drop to safety in the depths of its burrow. But this response is no defense against the several species of
small flies and wasps that enter the tunnel to lay an egg on the grub.
The egg hatches into a parasitic worm that feeds on the tissues of its
host, eventually reducing it to a wisp of dried skin.

Just what is the tiger beetle's niche in the beach community? It is
all of the multifarious things that tiger beetles do and the many ways
that tiger beetle activity figures in what associated creatures do.
Niches encompass every vital function: food, shelter, reproduction,
social interactions, and so on. The common theme is survival, and
the most fundamental and ongoing relationship is that of food—what
to eat and how to avoid being eaten. An outline of food pathways is
as revealing of a biotic community as an outline of agriculture and
marketing systems is of a modern human society. So, the ecological
niches in a given community are usually described in terms of food
pathways.

Things always begin with sunshine and green plants. In any community the plants, performing the original magic of converting the
energy from the sun into protoplasm, constitute the vital producer
caste. Most plants are eaten to some extent by some animals—
herbivores or first-order consumers. These animals commonly fall
prey to other animals—predators or second-order consumers. Predatory animals may themselves be eaten by higher predators—third-
order consumers, and so on. Such a sequence of eat-and-be-eaten is
called a food chain. Ordering creatures into feeding echelons of producers, consumers, and decomposers is artificial, but it can help human observers comprehend and describe communities.

Food chains can be diagrammed with arrows pointing in the direction of energy transfer. A straightforward example from the grassy
interior of Matagorda Island might be:

sunshine→Texas brome→jackrabbit→coyote

But the Texas brome grass might as easily have nourished a harvest
mouse in the same community, and from there the chain could be
forged of other links:

sunshine→Texas brome→harvest mouse→speckled
kingsnake→white-tailed hawk

Or the coyote could have eaten the mouse instead of the jackrabbit,
producing another variant series of arrows.

Inevitably, fleas, lice, etc., would slip into the sequence. Scavengers, such as ghost crabs, consume dead plants and animals. Detriti-

vores,[1] like fiddler crabs, sift through water or muck for microscopic bits of decayed matter, and much of their energy is derived from the bacteria clinging to the particles. And of course, there are always the decomposers, the bacteria and fungi that degrade protoplasm and so make its chemical components available for yet another cycle through the roots of other plants and the bowels of other animals.

Food chains are usually short and direct, but they may take a more involved route. This one starts out simply enough:

sunshine→brownseed paspalum grass→cotton rat→barn owl

Like most birds of prey, an owl swallows its meal whole, and the indigestible hair and bones are compacted into a wad and regurgitated as a thumb-sized pellet. Complications enter with the carpet moth, a small moth closely related to the sort that damages unprotected woolens and furs in the home closet. On the natural felt of rat hair in the discarded barn owl pellet these moths lay eggs that hatch into larvae with a battery of rugged digestive enzymes that allows them to extract nourishment from hair and bits of sinew. Each larva constructs a silken case and camouflages it with a mat of hair. After a week or so, when they have reduced the pellet to a scatter of tiny bones, the little grubs disperse to pupate, laboriously dragging their hair tubes along with them. Bacteria finish cleaning the bones, leaving them odorless and shining white. Now, perhaps another cotton rat happens by and gnaws on the bones for their mineral content, and maybe the fantastic ear of a barn owl catches the whispered grinding and a loop is cast in the chain.

Just for fun, try this simple food chain.

frog→dragonfly

There is no mistake in the direction of the arrow—it says dragonfly eats frog, not, at least in this case, the other way around. How can that be? Substitute "tadpole" for frog and "naiad" (dragonfly larva) for dragonfly and the relationship becomes a credible one in any pond in the grassy interior of Matagorda Island.

It is a revealing and humbling exercise in ecology to work out the food relations of the creatures you observe in nature. Can you trace a long-billed curlew with a mud fiddler in its beak back to sunshine? What about a ribbonsnake in hot pursuit of a meadowfrog, or a flower spider clutching a fluttering hairstreak butterfly on a bull thistle blossom? Observing and pondering such relationships are fundamental

---

1. Creatures that feed on organic refuse of plant and animal origin.

88

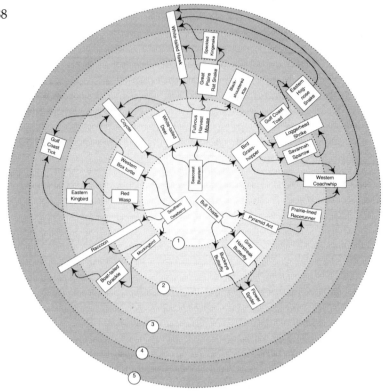

Figure 3. Hypothetical food web in the barrier flat community. Numbers indicate trophic levels. 1: producers, the plants; 2: primary consumers, the herbivores; 3: secondary consumers, carnivores; 4 and 5: higher-level carnivores. Arrows are links in food chains and point in direction of consumption. Biomass and numbers of individuals decrease as trophic level increases. The actual food web would have many more food chains.

to understanding the ecosystem that is Matagorda Island, and they add a significant dimension to nature watching.

Food webs, made up of the tangle of food chains spreading through each biotic community, are the most important binding forces in communities. Food webs also provide a starting point for understanding the varying abundance of different kinds of organisms in a community. If you were to extract all the rooted plants from a sand dune, and dry and weigh them, you would learn the biomass of the plants in that particular sample of the sand dune community. If you did the same thing with the resident herbivores and again with each of the various levels of carnivores, you would find the largest biomass at the producer level. From there the values would dwindle rapidly up the sequence. Why is this? Consider that the lower levels have to support the upper levels. Biological processes are inefficient; the marvel of photosynthesis converts only about 3 percent of the energy in sunshine into protoplasm, and each time a precious dab is handed up a step in a food chain incidental waste and metabolic digression allow only some 10 percent of the available calories to move from one consumer level to the next. The attrition in biomass is equally rapid:

100 lbs brome grass→10 lbs harvest mouse→1 lb speckled king-
snake→1/10 lb white-tailed hawk

Is there any wonder that there are more pounds of mouse meat than of hawk meat on Matagorda?

Correlating numbers of individuals with available energy in biomass relations, you can easily construe a community food web into a food pyramid. The broad base of the pyramid represents the abundant producers, with the sides of the figure sloping sharply to the relatively rare top-level carnivores. When you think about it, nothing else makes good ecological sense. You can also see why in any given food stratum there are more small creatures than large ones: more grasshoppers than deer per acre of grassland; more beach fleas than ghost crabs per linear foot of Gulf shoreline. It takes more of the "tinies" to build up a given biomass. Go one step further. The first-order consumers—the herbivores—are positioned directly above the broad base of the pyramid, closest to the original protoplasmic bank laid down by the plants. Doesn't it seem reasonable that most communities would have more herbivores than carnivores simply because the plant eaters are closer to the largest stock of goodies? The exceptions are in the tidal flat and beach communities, the sinks for all that energy lost in transfers from one level to the next. Here detritus accumulates so rapidly that detritivores outnumber herbivores.

Food relationships help in understanding the carrying capacity, the population level of a species that a biotic community can support without causing undue stress among the individual creatures or deterioration of the habitat.

Every member of the community has critical needs: food certainly, but also water, air, shelter, etc. And there are more nebulous but still vital things: elbow room, interactions with fellows, and something equivalent to what we call "peace of mind." These requirements are met by tapping resources in the community. Some resources are renewable, but all are finite; at any given time the habitat can support only so many individuals of a given species—for instance, more of shore flies that make small demands, fewer of badgers that make large demands.

As population numbers build, the effects of crowding set in; competition escalates for dwindling resources; the struggle for existence gets tougher. Some individuals move out. Among those that stay, the death rate climbs. Stress reduces the birthrate. So, for one reason or another, population numbers decline. For each member species, a biotic community will have a carrying capacity. Below capacity, life is relatively easy and numbers rise; above that critical level, life gets increasingly chancy. Here we are close to that fabled "balance of nature" that keeps biotic communities in trim.

The carrying capacities of a habitat vary; there are good times and bad times. So population numbers oscillate around some average; the difference between high and low depends on the reproductive ability of the creatures concerned. After a big early-summer rain, for instance, the flooded swales in the grassy interior of Matagorda are suddenly capable of supporting a whining horde of millions of salt-marsh mosquitoes. However, that same rain might wipe out most of the nesting effort of meadowlarks. The rain raised the carrying capacity for mosquitoes but lowered it for hatchling meadowlarks. (What might it do for hatchling barn swallows?) A hurricane can cause wholesale physical damage to the island topography, drown many animals, and uproot vegetation and expose it to salt water. Obviously, the carrying capacity of the wrecked habitats will be lowered for everything except the scavengers and detritivores. But as the environment recovers, carrying capacities will climb back to normal and populations of inhabitants will increase rapidly until biotic equilibrium is again established, leaving us to marvel over the natural feedback that keeps the ecosystem functioning.

Each kind of organism can be thought of as a delicate survival machine. To keep this contrivance in continual operation, it must be nourished on a constant source of energy (food for animals; sunshine for plants). Within a given community, if two different species use the same tactic to glean the same energy source, they will come into direct competition. Each would be better-off if one or both shifted its demands so that they occupied at least partly separate niches. The evolutionary consequence of this involvement is just what you might expect—an amazing diversity of kinds of creatures, each equipped with adaptations in body and behavior for a particular means of making a living—each survival machine plugged into the power supply of the ecosystem in a slightly different way.

This diversification on a theme by a group of similar species is called *adaptive radiation,* and you can't find a better example than the fall and winter birds feeding on a tidal flat on the bay side of the island. Each kind has a different way of acquiring the bounty of the flat: dowitchers probe, plovers peck, egrets spear, avocets scoop, terns dive-bomb, skimmers skim, gulls scrounge. Some species may seem to be doing the same thing, but a closer look will surely discover subtle differences in approach. For instance, marbled godwits, long-billed dowitchers, and western sandpipers all probe for marine worms, clams, and crustaceans burrowing in the muddy bottom. But the tall godwits use their long, upswept bills to extract sizable prey in relatively deep water, while the smaller dowitchers use their straight beaks on smaller prey in shallower water, and the little sandpipers get tiny prey at the water's edge. A willet can't peck up the tiny shore flies that a black-necked stilt can easily get with its stiletto bill. Wood storks and clapper rails aren't even interested in the same kind of food items. You can start all over again with birds on the beach or with the birds of prey.

Birds, highly visible and easy for us to relate to, provide good examples of adaptive radiation, but you can observe the same principle among crabs, beetles, spiders, or sand wasps. With keen eye and open mind, you can perceive this diversifying rule at work in the passive world of plants, where the less-evident responses include tolerance of salt, submission to wind, rate of seed germination, capacity to store water, a cryptic ingenuity among roots, and an ability to keep greenery from being smothered beneath the sand. The upshot is the same as with animals—each community has its characteristic varieties of daisies, legumes, and rushes; each species exploits a slightly different niche. Once you know what to look for, you will have an understanding of what turns lovers of nature into avid naturalists who know that Matagorda Island has no season too dull, no weather too inclement, no day quite like another, no end of fascination.

Despite their variety of resident and migrant species, barrier islands generally support a less-diverse array of living creatures than comparable strips of adjacent mainland, and Matagorda Island is no exception. As Table 1 indicates, compared to the nearby Aransas National Wildlife Refuge on Blackjack Peninsula, the natural biota of Matagorda is indeed meager. Ecological reasons are not hard to find.

Twelve major biotic communities are recognized on the Aransas Refuge, only six on Matagorda. The monotonous physiography and topography of a barrier provide few kinds of habitats. This lack of habitats means a comparable lack of potential niches; with fewer ways to make a living, there will be fewer species. Consider the general lack of shrubs and trees on Matagorda; without this stratum there is

Table 1. *Comparison of native biota on Matagorda Island and the adjacent Aransas National Wildlife Refuge*

	Number of Species	
	ANWR	Matagorda
Mammals	35	9
Birds	389	317
Reptiles	48	21
Amphibians	17	5
Flowering plants	845	301
Trees	20	8
Grasses	119	49

scant opportunity for arboreal insects and their larvae, small perching birds, orb-weaving spiders, wood-boring beetles, high-climbing vines, shade-loving herbs, and tiny creatures that live in leaf litter and humus, all common on the mainland. The insular soils, with little organic matter in them, limit the variety of plants that can take root and the kinds of animals that can keep burrows open. The loose, dry sand inhibits invasion by all but a few kinds of ground-living ants and beetles, important elements of most terrestrial communities.

But fewer kinds does not necessarily mean fewer individuals on a barrier. Lack of diversity is frequently balanced by marked abundance of the species that have successfully carved niches there. In most instances, high populations tap the prodigal resources of the sea (fiddler crabs, ghost shrimp, beach fleas), and in some cases their numbers are markedly seasonal (migrating dunlin, semipalmated plovers, least sandpipers). In other cases, populations soar when conditions in certain insular habitats become especially favorable (fresh greenery and grasshoppers, standing water and mosquitoes, summer rains and Indian blankets.)

Another factor limiting island biota is the open and generally harsh nature of the environment, with its tendency to swing through seasonal extremes and its periodic wholesale devastation by storms. The plants are all exposed to intense sunshine, continual wind, withering temperatures, scarce fresh water, and the potential of salt-water overwash. The sandy soil is low in nutrients and gives plants an abrasive, insecure substrate that may at any time be blown away from their roots or piled atop their leaves. Matagorda is no place for delicate greenery such as ferns and tender herbs.

Resident animals must survive in the same austere world. Amphibians, with their moist skins and freshwater larvae, are at a particular disadvantage. Land snails are equally constrained. The constant wind renders the island inhospitable to large-winged butterflies, and it shreds the webs of orb-weaving spiders. With only three native rodents and one sort of hare to exploit, there can hardly be a rich order of predaceous birds and mammals and relatively few snakes. An impoverished soil fauna means no niches for moles or ground snakes. Although Matagorda is a mecca for shorebirds and large waders, very few of these birds nest on the island because most potential sites are open to predation by raccoons and coyotes. Beyond these considerations, each kind of animal has to have the ability to avoid dehydration, traverse the sand, dig in during storms, and make it through the long, hot summer. As with the plants, there is no place for those without special adaptations to cope with the generally hostile environment.

And there is always the initial problem: colonization. Each species must somehow contrive to get to the island. Matagorda is no more than five thousand years old, so all immigration must have been relatively recent and is probably not finished yet. As it seems likely there was never a connection to the mainland, the obstacle of salt water, though not extensive, has always been there to be reckoned with. Five miles of brackish water presents a formidable barrier to some potential colonists, whereas it causes no pause for others. For this reason, the intervening bays act as a biotic sieve, allowing some immigrants easy access while barring others entirely; the native residents we see on the island today are the ones that have managed to trickle through this natural filter.

Colonization of Matagorda Island has come from the land, sea, and air. Creatures from the sea have no problem getting to the island, but as they have difficulty breathing and maintaining water balance on land, most of them must remain near the shoreline, where they can return to their native element to regain their vigor and procreate their kind. Of all the many and varied creatures of the bays and shallow Gulf, only a few crustaceans have made even a partial transition to life on the island. Although only a few species are represented, these often occur in such huge populations that they are significant elements in the food webs of the perimeter communities. Ghost and fiddler crabs, beach amphipods, and a few terrestrial pillbug-like isopods represent this terrestrial marine element.

For airborne creatures, Matagorda Island is simply one more site to make landfall. Birds, bats, and strong flying insects like dragonflies and bird grasshoppers have easy access, though prevailing winds and the considerable expanse of open water may inhibit many small flying insects. But wings are only the most obvious means of air transport. The lightly floating parachute of a bull thistle seed, the ultralight spores of fungi, and the fleecy dispersal webs of tiny spiders are just as effective. Offshore winds can loft millions of seeds, spores, large and small insects, and arachnids for miles. Along with the fliers and the drifters there will be a load of hitchhikers: ticks among the feathers, parasitic worms in the bowels, and seeds, snails, and protozoans in mud on the feet of waterbirds; pseudoscorpions clinging to flying beetles; fly larvae stuck to dragonflies; and flower mites riding comfortably in the nostrils of hummingbirds.

Species that cannot get airborne can still cross the bays in a variety of ways. Most directly, some can swim or wade. The red-eared turtle tolerates brackish water and can easily cruise the bay and invade the island's fresh-water depressions. Certainly, if the early ranchers could move their stock from island to mainland at low tide, animals like coyotes, raccoons, and white-tailed deer can make it in the other direction. Of course, cattle and horses were prodded into making the trip. Why would a coyote set off to sea? Probably the answer is emigration rather than immigration. Population pressure on the mainland—juveniles seeking home ranges; young males seeking mates—impelled animals, sometimes with amazing determination, into leaving the congestion behind. If a series of oyster reefs provides an avenue, it is exploited to get away from the mainland rather than with a vision of reaching a virgin island paradise.

Most kinds of terrestrial creatures can swim if pressed to it, but many lack the endurance and perseverance to cross the bays. However, some of them can float for prolonged periods, and with the aid of offshore winds or discharge currents from the Guadalupe/San Antonio rivers, they could easily make it to Matagorda. Coiled rattlesnakes, bobbing lightly with inflated air, have been found far from the mainland shore. A variety of insects can ride the surface film, including entire colonies of imported fire ants balled up for the protection of their brood stock. Because they can often resist infiltration by salt water for days or weeks, flotation is the routine means of dispersal for the seeds of many plants. An important variation on floating is rafting. All sorts of creatures, marooned on flotillas of logs and buoyant patches of vegetation, wash into the bays during floods. They cling to these natural floats until death or landfall. This is the probable avenue onto Matagorda Island for many insects, for scorpions, spiders, rodents, and even an occasional armadillo.

"Sweepstakes dispersal" by floating and rafting is chancy, and happenstance may explain some peculiar omissions. Although kangaroo rats, ground squirrels, and earless lizards inhabit some of the other

Texas barriers, there are none on Matagorda; perhaps the numbers for these animals just have not come up yet.

And many residents on Matagorda have gained access through human intervention. Sometimes, as with the sprigging of coastal Bermuda grass, planting of Macartney rose, and the release of wild turkeys, the introduction was deliberate. More often it was inadvertent; weed seeds and insects and their eggs easily stow away in all sorts of goods hauled to the island; once there, they take advantage of human disturbance to gain a foothold. The feral hogs, though they owe their origin to escape from domestication, may well have gotten to the island on their own.

Gaining access to Matagorda Island is a necessary but only preliminary step to successful colonization. For immigrants to become residents, they must establish a proliferating population, and this can be a difficult ecological feat. The new arrivals not only must contrive to withstand the physical rigors of their new environment, they must also work their way into already established close-knit food webs. Competition with well-adapted residents for space and food, and vulnerability to new predators and parasites, can quickly wipe out small beachheads of potential colonists. Sometimes a species manages to establish an island population but is wiped out by catastrophe, as happened to the pocket gophers on the south end of the island—all were drowned in Hurricane Celia in 1970. Of course, recolonization is always a possibility. Nonetheless, the struggle is an extension of the filter that started at the shore of the mainland. Only a few of the most durable species become part of the island's resident biota.

Occasionally, scientists have been able to study the recolonization of islands sterilized by volcanic eruptions or of islets purposely depopulated by fumigation. But in the normal course of events, the arrival and subsequent establishment of a new species is so rare and unpredictable as to preclude actual observation. The successful invasion of the cattle egret into the grasshopper-eating food niche in the 1950s is the only documented instance of natural colonization on Matagorda. So, it should be readily evident that any discussion of the natural colonization of a barrier island is based on little more than speculation.

Biogeographers (the people who study the geographic distributions of plants and animals) mostly do what any amateur naturalist can do: study the abilities and tolerances of creatures, figure in the vagaries of the climate and terrain, note the distances involved, consider prehistoric conditions, judge possibilities and weigh probabilities, dream up scenarios, and finally, throw it all up for grabs. What they strive for is credibility—a believable story. You can do the same.

How might badgers, black widow spiders, passion flowers, and Spanish daggers have gotten onto Matagorda? Why are diamondback rattlesnakes common and cottonmouth moccasins rare? If a raccoon can make it on Matagorda Island, why not an opossum? If a mesquite, why not a scrubby live oak? Why don't the several kinds of exotic seabeans on the beach sprout into tangles of tropical vegetation? What about migration routes from adjacent Matagorda Peninsula or St. Joseph Island, rather than directly from the mainland? Conjecture over these and other biogeographic enigmas is not only fun, it is necessary for a full grasp of the island ecosystem.

Biotic Communities

On the broadest scale, Matagorda Island has three physiographic regions readily evident to any visitor:

- Beach and primary dunes—the smooth gulf-side strip of beach backed by a ridge of dunes. Dominated by the Gulf, this region is characterized by high energy, exposed substrate, and active geological processes. It borders the whole 38 miles from Pass Cavallo to Cedar Bayou and covers about 5,000 acres, 9 percent of the island's area.
- Bay side—the serpentine, marshy side of the island. Dominated by adjacent bays, this low-energy, depositing shoreline of muddy sand and shell is captured by squat, hardy plants that can survive tidal flooding. Much dissected by lakes, ponds, and inlets, it stretches over 80 miles of shoreline, covering 39 percent of the area, some 22,000 acres, much of it tidally influenced open water.
- Interior—this central core of the island covers 30,000 acres, 52 percent of the area. Protected from the Gulf, the sandy but stable soil is mostly well-vegetated. There are scattered clumps of grassy interior dunes and freshwater depressions.

Within these regions are six major biotic communities, most of which include recognizable minor subdivisions called *associations*. With the exception of one restricted association, the determined visitor can see examples of all of these areas. In fact, most of the diversity that Matagorda has to offer can be sampled between bay side and surf side anywhere in the strip between the Army Hole and the lighthouse. The locations of the major communities are shown on Map 9.

The following brief descriptions of communities and associations are meant to give an overall view; the plants and animals mentioned are detailed in other chapters in this guidebook, and most of them are described and illustrated in field guides listed in the bibliography.

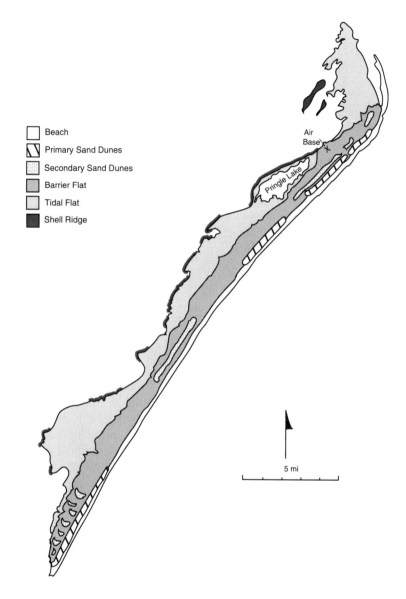

Beach
Primary Sand Dunes
Secondary Sand Dunes
Barrier Flat
Tidal Flat
Shell Ridge

Air
Base

Pringle Lake

5 mi

Map 9. Major biotic communities on Matagorda Island. (Minor dune fields and fresh-water sites are not shown.)

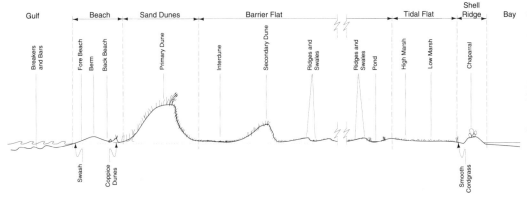

Figure 4. A typical surface profile across Matagorda Island.

Biotic communities and associations are identified by their dominant species or by some prominent physical attribute. Because of the strong alignment of the surface of Matagorda Island, the superimposed biological habitats are named for underlying physiographic features, using terms that are formally defined in Chapter 2.

Beach Community

No one really needs directions to the beach or help in recognizing it. Listen for the muffled boom of the surf. Move upwind into the on-shore breeze. Squint at the bright sand, marvel at the breakers, and rush to get your feet wet when you get there.

It varies some in width, but the beach community is essentially uniform along the length of the island. Beginning on the surfside there are four associations: (1) the narrow swash zone, washed by the waves and varying in position according to the tides; (2) the fore-beach, sloping gently up from the swash to (3) the berm or strandline, which marks the limit of normal high tide; and (4) the backbeach, which extends to the base of the sand dunes.

There may be birds in the distance and low plants on the back-beach, but your first impression of this community will be of an un-inhabitable waste of sand fit only for beachcombing and bathing. Actually, that's not far off the mark; the beach habitat is indeed a harsh place to live. Even on a pretty day, this is a violent, thunderous world of slamming waves, ceaselessly shifting sand, and pitiless exposure to drying wind, salt spray, and the full glare of the sun. (If you are prudent, you will temper your own visit with long sleeves, a liberal slather of sunscreen, dark glasses, plenty of fluids, and a shower when you're done.) Here, all existence depends upon the mood of the sea; when the sea turns ugly with storm, the beach bears the brunt of its anger. Little wonder, then, that the animals of the beach are all burrowers and that the rooted plants crouch well back from the edge of the water. But the beach community is not as barren as it seems. Though most of the relatively few kinds of residents are small, and all are hidden, at least some of them occur in great abundance. You just have to know how to look for them.

Strictly speaking, the swash zone belongs to the sea, and all the creatures that inhabit it are marine in origin. The only producers are microscopic algae, which eke out an existence in the film of water between sand grains. These do not completely support the association; detritus shares that burden. The fine particles of plant and animal matter brought in by the waves from the offshore shallows emphasize that the ecosystem of Matagorda Island does not end at the waterline. The sea nourishes them, and all of the small creatures of the swash are provided with mechanisms for filtering the bounty of the waves or with strategies for preying on each other. And every species is geared to burrowing and to frantically reburying itself when exposed at the surface of the sand.

This is the realm of small detritivores: mole crabs, surf crabs, coquina clams, ghost shrimp, sand digger amphipods, and miniscule palp worms—a huge biomass that easily supports hunters. Predatory snails—Atlantic moons, lettered olives, and Salle's augers—cruise through and over the sand; blue and speckled crabs lie in ambush; sharp-eyed shorebirds probe telltale movements in the wake of each receding wave. After dark, ghost crabs emerge from their burrows up the beach and move down to glean in the swash. Getting down on your hands and knees with a sieve and trowel is the way to delve into this hidden world at the cutting edge of Matagorda.

The forebeach, lacking the cushion of water between the sand grains, is even more hostile to life than the swash. Burrowing and breathing with gills are difficult in the dry sand. And food is limited to fine particles of dehydrated organic matter blown in from the shoreline. Even the juvenile ghost crabs that dig their tiny burrows here find most of their food elsewhere. The few other creatures of the forebeach, most evidently the tiger beetles, are transient feeders. Dragonflies and robber flies hawk small insects here but spend most of their time further inland. Gulls, terns, and brown pelicans frequently loaf through the doldrums of midday on isolated stretches of forebeach.

High tide leaves wrack along the strandline, and this windrow of dismembered crabs, dehydrating jellyfish, bleaching mollusc shells, and moldering mounds of gulfweed means food, moisture, and shelter for the scavengers of the beach. Legions of beach fleas live within this mass, and swarms of shore flies, seaweed flies, carrion flies, and flesh flies feed and lay their eggs on the rotting material. Most shorebirds, especially willets, plovers, turnstones, and gulls, pick over the refuse. At night the strand is prime foraging area for ghost crabs and coyotes.

The strand is also where beachcombing is most profitable. Although Matagorda Island is not so favorably positioned as Mustang and Padre islands for receiving exotic drift from the longshore currents, it collects enough shells, seabeans, and assorted natural flotsam to keep any beachgoer strolling for miles. Unfortunately, there is also a staggering accumulation of human litter from offshore drilling platforms, oceangoing ships, small pleasure craft, flooding streams, and careless beachgoers. To indicate the magnitude of the problem, during a recent beach cleanup campaign, in a single day on Matagorda Island volunteers picked up over 45 tons of artificial debris from the 3-mile stretch between Pass Cavallo and the main access road. As you might expect, the bulk was composed of lightweight plastic items, so the volume was staggering; it filled over twelve hundred large garbage bags. Legislation passed in 1986 was aimed at limiting dumping of plastic waste at sea, but the only lasting solutions can come from a less disposable-oriented economy, personal discipline, and relentless education.

Still, without in the least condoning this reckless discarding of waste, it is a fact that this continually replenished depository of domestic and foreign trash provides an unparalleled bonanza for the casual beachcomber. Where else can you find a can from Singapore that contained soya bean drink, an oddly proportioned, translucent, blue plastic bottle molded with unintelligible but artistic Arabic script, a graceful amber wine bottle with 4-inch cork, and a monstrous light bulb enclosing a filigreed filament worthy of a jeweler's craft, all within 50 yards of linear strand? We may be heedless, negligent, and even callous toward our environment, but the fact that one person's offal becomes another's treasure proves what we all know—we are endlessly fascinated with our own estate. We have rendered the beach a window on the world and a reflection of ourselves, and, for better or worse, a most interesting avenue down which to amble and reflect.

The backbeach, the broad, rear-sloping inner perimeter of the beach community, is where the first daring outliers of rooted plants are encountered. These plants must withstand not only desert-like conditions but occasional ponding from heavy rains and saltwater overwash during storms. Here, the tips of long runners of goat-foot morning glory snake among knots of sea rocket, sea purslane, wooly

honeysweet, beach ground-cherry, and occasional wiry tufts of fimbry and marshhay cordgrass. Behind these pioneers, small piles of
wind-blown sand accumulated by more robust clumps of marshhay
cordgrass form low coppice dunes that provide meager but important
protection for an array of hardy beach plants. Despite the rigors, the
first wildflowers appear here: Corpus Christi fleabane, frogfruit, sand
pinks, the white curls of seaside heliotrope and the beautiful yellow
saucers of beach evening primrose. Depressions usually support a
shoetop forest of dark green umbrellas of coast pennywort. The
weedy beach amaranth and occasional Gulf croton catch their own
piles of sand, and widespread clumps of gulfdune paspalum and sea
oats, two important sand-binding grasses, make their appearance.

Even with this scattered vegetation and thin patches of shade, the
backbeach is too harsh and fickle to maintain a permanent food web.
The most common animal here is the ghost crab. Adult crabs—as
evidenced by their large burrow openings—dig in here, but travel to
the strand and swash to feed at night. Bees and wasps are attracted
in season to the flowers, but grasshoppers and other herbivorous insects keep mostly to denser vegetation further inland. With scarce
insects and scanty fruits and seeds, few birds visit the backbeach and
none nest here. However, three mammals find it profitable to spend
time among the coppice dunes after dark. Jackrabbits come to crop
the sparse greenery in the sort of open terrain where all-around visual
field and great speed give an advantage over a coyote. Coyotes trot
down the strand, scrounging what they can and occasionally detouring across the backbeach to ambush a jackrabbit or waylay a tardy
ghost crab. The methodical badger treks in to dig ghost crabs from
their burrows. With a little experience, you can easily read the stories
of these nocturnal animals in their tracks; wherever they have tried
to unearth ghost crabs, you should be able to distinguish the narrow,
typically dog-like dig of a coyote from the broader excavation of a
badger.

Sand Dunes Community

Of the three associations in this community, the most easily recognized and most appealing to visitors is the primary dunes, the
sparsely vegetated sandy ridge directly behind the backbeach. Further inland, isolated clusters and short rows of secondary dunes rise
out of the flat grassland, and between these two masses is the low-
lying interdune association.

The primary dunes association parallels the beach community, but
the dunes are not as continuous as the beach. The largest dunes are

at the south end, but several near the main beach-access road are only slightly less impressive and display all of the typical features. Northward from the beach-access road the primary dunes rapidly fade away, and in most of the central part of the island they are low or absent, with the backbeach grading through low coppice dunes directly into the interior grasslands.

Like the beach, the beguiling primary dunes association is not an easy place to make a living. Plants have difficulty establishing and maintaining themselves where rainwater rapidly percolates through, taking the sparse nutrients with it and leaving the deep sand chronically dry and deficient. The onshore wind constantly moves the loose sand, uncovering roots and sandblasting or covering up green shoots. Animals on foot have trouble traversing the sliding substrate and burrowers cannot easily keep tunnels open. These trials are harsh on the sloping, windward side, but the protection of the dune itself makes its abrupt leeward side more amenable for both plants and animals.

The vegetation of a primary dune is characterized more by subtle changes in densities than by unique species. On the windward side, the most important grasses are marshhay cordgrass and gulfdune paspalum, assisted in sand binding by the mounds of Gulf croton, patches of beach evening primrose, and the trailing stems of goat-foot and fiddleleaf morning glories. The crests of many taller dunes are capped by swaying, picturesque tussocks of sea oats. The lee side of a dune is densely clothed in marshhay cordgrass and gulfdune paspalum mixed through with camphorweed, beach ground-cherry, partridge pea, western ragweed, and broom groundsel. Beach croton and beach evening primrose descend the lee face wherever the thick grass cover is broken.

Despite an abundant producer level of rooted plants, the harsh physical conditions on a primary dune shut out most resident animals; several species of dunes grasshoppers and katydids, two kinds of cicadas and two of ants, several sorts of butterfly and moth caterpillars, sundry kinds of sap-sucking planthoppers, and a few species of ground beetles constitute the permanent herbivore assemblage. But when conditions are favorable, many others visit the dunes to feed. Flowers are attended by swarms of flies and wasps, buzzing bumblebees, whining hover flies, and fluttering hairstreak, dog-faced sulphur, and checkerspot butterflies. Throughout the dunes, ghost crabs dig deep burrows around the bases of plants, and although they feed mostly on the beach, they do nibble on some of the plants and consume the seeds of sea oats. Early and late in the day, bobwhite quail filter into the dunes to pick up seeds and bathe in the sand. At night, cotton rats from the interior grassland move onto the leeward dune faces. Tracks, fecal pellets, and yellowed urination sites indicate that jackrabbits routinely feed on greenery and grains of sea oats. But, the kangaroo rat, that distinctive rodent of the sand dunes so abundant on Mustang and Padre islands, does not occur on Matagorda.

Predators of many sorts patrol the sand dunes by day and by night. Sand wasps, cicada killers, dunes spiders, assassin bugs, robber flies, and dragonflies prey on the insects; prairie-lined racerunners (a kind of lizard) pursue the grasshoppers. Kestrels, marsh hawks, and short-eared owls occasionally glide over the leeward dunes in the wintertime, but spend most of their time further inland; a barn owl may make nocturnal forays into the dunes, but it also prefers the more vegetated interior. Tracks indicate that coyotes regularly pass through the dunes at night, pouncing on whatever comes their way. Badgers sometimes den at the base of a dune, but they seldom forage there.

Secondary dunes are mounds of sand from the primary dune ridge, driven by the wind across the interior of the island until the pull of the vegetation overcame the push of the wind and they slowed and were finally captured. These inland dunes occur sporadically down the length of the island, especially in the old washover area opposite Panther Point. Good examples of secondary dune association can be seen on each side of the main beach-access road not far behind the primary dune ridge.

The thick vegetation on a secondary dune, resembling that on the leeward side of a primary dune, is dominated by marshhay cordgrass and gulfdune paspalum, but is interlaced with vines of American snoutbean and hoary milkpea. Some secondary dunes support a cap of sea oats not yet crowded out by the dominants. Here and there, clumps of coast prickly pear and patches of partridge pea and California loosestrife manage to overtop the thick cover, and occasional sandy openings support tall stands of the handsome silverleaf sunflower.

The animal assemblage on secondary dunes is not different from that of the surrounding grassland. Eastern meadowlarks use the vantage of tall sunflower stalks to announce their territories with the melodious, flutelike calls so characteristic of the island interior. Wintering sparrows prefer the dense cover on these dunes to the more open ground in the primary dunes and to the thicker vegetation of the surrounding lower ground. In a flat land even a slight eminence provides visual advantage, so it is not surprising that the tops of secondary dunes are commonly spattered with guano from turkey vultures that settle there to rest and white-tailed hawks that stop to scan the surrounding grass for prey.

The interdune association develops in the moist pockets between the primary and secondary dunes. In dry years this area dehydrates and loses some of its distinction. After severe storms it is laid waste by the incursion of salt water. But in good years, with ample rain, it is choked with moistland plants and pocked with knee-deep pools of fresh water.

Marshhay cordgrass covers most of the interdune association, over-topped in wet sites by stands of American bulrush and cattail. Early in the day, wet places may be graced by the large purple blossoms of salt-marsh morning glory, and the mucky ground supports many other moisture-loving species: water hyssop, frogfruit, spikesedge, flatsedge, white-topped umbrella grass, and several species of rushes. Better drained spots harbor many wildflowers in sea-son—sand pinks, bluebells, purple pleatleaf, prairie bluets, fleabane, lazy daisy, skullcap, pink-net evening primroses, Indian blanket, and ladies' tresses, the island's only orchid.

This association is not large enough, different enough, or stable enough to have a distinctive animal assemblage. According to its state of hydration, creatures come and go from the grassland, from the dunes, or from fresh-water pond communities. In a typical year, when the area is wet, both yellow and black rails occur here, and there is a reasonable chance that a birder slogging across it will spook one of these secretive little birds. Mottled ducks, American coots, and blue-winged teal feed in the ponds. If the water lasts, red-winged blackbirds nest in the cattails, rice rats replace cotton rats among the rushes, and yellow mud turtles dig out of their entombment in the mud to feed in the ponds. Leopard frogs, attracted by the insects, are followed by their own predators—raccoons, ribbonsnakes, speckled kingsnakes, and an occasional massasauga rattler. Unfortunately for human visitors, even the numerous hawking dragonflies and swoop-ing barn swallows make only scant inroads on the horde of mosqui-toes emerging from the water.

Within the interdune association one specialized habitat bears men-tion. A hurricane surge that breaches the primary dune ridge deposits debris in the interdune zone. Most of this soon rots away or is cov-ered by sand, but big pieces—logs, boards, sections of marine ply-wood that last for years—provide a microhabitat for secretive species that live or retreat in such places. These, along with fallen trunks of large Spanish daggers, are the only places for such animals. Here are found several species of field crickets and cockroaches, bombardier beetles, staphylinid beetles, termites, ants, harvestmen, the few spe-cies of land snails, and the numerous pillbug-like terrestrial crusta-ceans. These creatures are preyed upon by earwigs, carabid beetles, centipedes, black widow spiders, wolf spiders, scorpions, pseudo-scorpions, and ground skinks. This is the commonest habitat for a Mexican milksnake; does it come for food, shelter, or both? Diamond-back rattlers sometimes linger here after searching out cotton rat and harvest mouse nests among the recesses. And all of these creatures are eaten by feral hogs, badgers, and coyotes, if they can raise or dig under the cover.

Barrier Flat Community

This is the broad grassland that fills the interior of Matagorda Island between the sand dunes and the bay-side communities. In the central part of the island, where the primary dunes are absent, it borders the backbeach, and in many areas it completely surrounds outlying clusters of secondary dunes. Under thick vegetation, the apparently flat terrain is corrugated, the low wrinkles parallel with the length of the island. Even this slight variation in elevation produces distinctive bands of vegetation: the ridge association and the swale association. Three other minor, specialized habitats are scattered through this community.

The ridge association is dominated by that ubiquitous pair, gulf-dune paspalum and marshhay cordgrass, with a little more of the paspalum. These grasses, bound together by the viny stems of American snoutbean, hoary milkpea, southern dewberry, and wild bean, make a thigh-high tangle that is difficult to walk through. The onshore wind bends the grasses to the northwest, forming a nearly unbroken canopy over a dark, moist jungle.

Where a ridge is somewhat higher and drier, shorter grasses allow herbaceous and succulent plants a chance at the sun. Silverleaf sunflowers, bull thistle, beach ground cherry, partridge pea, clumps of yankeeweed, and expanses of wooly goatweed, ragweed, and broomweed capture the hillocks. Both Texas prickly pear and plains prickly pear are common on more open ridges. In the southcentral part of the island there is enough elevation to support a fine sward of seacoast bluestem grass and occasional patches of Gulf muhly and crinkleawn grass. Between Shell Reef Bayou and the Wynne lodge an open mesquite/bluestem savannah covers the higher ground.

The dark vegetation of the swales is essentially like that of the interdune association. Marshhay cordgrass forms most of the cover, and in any slightly saline spot, dark clumps of Gulf Coast cordgrass appear. Certainly the most easily recognized plant is the dense, spear-like border of American bulrush.

A variety of grasshoppers, katydids, and leafhoppers lives in the sunlit canopy of the grassland, and these are exploited by funnelweb spiders, which lay traps there, and by jumping spiders, which leap from ambush. Flowers are attended by the usual retinue of wasps, bees, flies, and butterflies, and many blossoms conceal crab spiders, assassin bugs, and an occasional praying mantis lying in wait for the pollinators. The dark understory beneath the grass is honeycombed with the trails of cotton rats, and here also live harvest mice, rice rats, crickets, ground beetles and their grub-like larvae, earwigs, crane flies, roaches, and pillbug-like isopods. Predators pursue these creatures, as well as each other, through the dank jungle of stems: carabid beetles, wolf spiders, narrow-mouthed toads, slender glass lizards, speckled kingsnakes, and massasauga rattlesnakes. Where the grass thins somewhat, western diamondback rattlesnakes commonly search for cotton rats and young jackrabbits, and coachwhip snakes streak after prairie-lined racerunners.

Where the grass cover is deep and continuous, birds seldom perch, but over this terrain the raptors soar and repeatedly drop on rodent and insect prey, and several species of swallows skim tirelessly for mosquitoes and midges. Sedge wrens set up their winter territories along the ribbons of bulrush. In thinner vegetation eastern meadowlarks and northern bobwhite quail feed and nest, visiting sparrows spend the winter, and long-billed curlews and sandhill cranes forage. The diversity of small birds, like mockingbirds, loggerhead shrikes, scissor-tailed flycatchers, and a host of migrant species, increases where mesquite and other plants afford perching sites and protection.

Rodents like it, but larger mammals have difficulty maneuvering through the thickest ground cover in the barrier flat community. Jackrabbits only dive into the deep grass to escape a close pursuit. The long-legged white-tailed deer and the heavy feral hogs can traverse the tangle, and they form paths that are used by coyotes, badgers, and raccoons. But most hunting and grazing is done on the more open uplands or along the island's perimeter. In this flat, nearly treeless landscape, the dark recess under the grass canopy does serve as a daytime shelter for the larger mammals. Here raccoons, coyotes, and feral hogs can lie up in temporary lairs, out of sight and ready to slink off at the slightest disturbance. They also bear their young in such hideouts. In bad weather even deer bed down in the thick vegetation.

The three minor habitats scattered through the barrier flats community all result from human activity.

The Macartney rose habitat is made up of the isolated, head-high, rounded mounds of this dense, thorny briar, which dot the grassland in the northern third of the island. This plant, sprigged around the air base to form shelters for bobwhite quail, has since moved southward to the level of Pringle Lake. Quail, as well as raccoons and feral hogs, do indeed utilize the rose clumps for shady daytime retreats. Insects visit the large white blossoms in early summer, and flocks of migrating perching birds descend into the clumps to feed and roost.

The saltcedar habitat is also clumped through the grassland around the air base, and, like the rose, was purposely planted for protection of quail. The supple growth of these fine-leaved evergreen trees is well adapted to moist saline ground, and they produce bountiful crops of tiny seeds that disperse widely. Consequently, saltcedar mottes—either from the artificial plantings or invasion from the adjacent mainland—dot the interior of Matagorda throughout its length and are also in the tidal flat community.

The trees colonize moist depressions; so with the dense shade, the ground within a saltcedar clump is bare and cool, ideal for the daytime retreat of feral hogs and for hordes of salt-marsh mosquitoes. Black-crowned night-herons and an occasional horned owl roost and nest in the cedars, many wading birds use them for incidental nighttime roosts, and migrating perching birds flock into these trees, too. During northers, white-tailed deer commonly bed down on the lee sides of saltcedars.

In this monotonous climax grassland, any maintained opening offers a distinctly different microhabitat, altering the distributions of some plants and animals. The roads and runways habitat includes all of the roadways that dissect the grasslands—simple jeep trails, shell-topped drives, and the partly paved main island road, as well as the surfaces and borders of the large airstrip at the air base and the smaller one beside the Wynne lodge. These structures influence the biota in several ways.

Hard road surfaces absorb and hold heat, attracting slender glass lizards, Texas horned lizards, and various snakes that come to bask on the runways and topped roads early and late in the day. Cracks and irregularities in the surface of the northern airstrip are routinely used as nesting sites by least terns and common nighthawks. Asphalt-surfaced and built-up shell roads direct rainwater to their borders, where the vegetation benefits with luxuriant, usually weedy growth. Crushed-shell and raised and compacted roadbeds also provide favorable habitat in extensive strips for plants like annual sunflowers, silver-leaf nightshade, broomweed, bitterweed, doveweed, and western ragweed, and for several woody species such as mesquite, huisache, and wild lime that would naturally occur only in isolated patches in the grassland.

Runways and roads provide avenues for various animals through what would otherwise be a continuous expanse of impenetrable vegetation. Jackrabbits are especially attracted to the roadsides, where they can use their speed and vision to maximum advantage. Bobwhites, horned larks, mourning doves, and the several species of wintering sparrows use the weedy roadside growth for both protection and its abundance of seeds. The Texas horned lizard is nearly restricted to this habitat on the island. A variety of insects, including crackle-wing grasshoppers, ants, and tiger beetles are also attracted to the open ground, and their presence entices prairie-lined racerunners, which, in turn, are followed by western coachwhip snakes. American kestrels, black-shouldered kites, and other raptors patrol the roads where prey is apt to show itself.

The runways and roads are clearly artificially disturbed areas, but a diversification of niches in the otherwise unrelieved grassland has certainly worked to the benefit of at least some of the island's native and introduced species.

Tidal Flat Community

The meandering 5-foot elevation line marks the limit of normal high tides and wind tides on the inland side of Matagorda Island and neatly sketches the border between the central grassland and this extensive, tidally influenced, bay-side habitat.

The tidal flat community is often called "salt marsh," but this term is more applicable to the extensive growth of emergent grasses, reeds, and rushes that characterizes the Eastern seaboard, where the tidal range is higher, and to the northwestern rim of the Gulf of Mexico (from the Colorado River eastward) where, because of more rainfall, there is a higher volume of fresh-water discharge to the coast. The Coastal Bend lies in a transition zone where decreasing precipitation and attendant scanty and sporadic runoff do not encourage broad salt marshes. (Two salt-marsh index species—the black rush and the winter-resident sharp-tailed sparrow—both become scarce halfway between Galveston and Matagorda islands.) The slight tidal flushing of our local bays leaves a mucky substrate, low in oxygen and high in hydrogen sulfide. Hot sun evaporates the shallow water, resulting in saltiness sometimes triple that of normal seawater. Because of all this, except for a thin, chest-high fringe, most of the vegetation of the local tidal flat association is low-growing and scrubby. Nevertheless, despite the grueling conditions, this is by far the most productive portion of the barrier.

Few herbivores feed directly on the rank tidal flat plants; the foundation for the stupendous biomass of this community lies in its dark, vile-smelling sediment. Here thrives an immense population of marine bacteria feeding on the inwash of organic material from the surrounding bays and estuaries, the fallen stalks and leaves of plants, and the feces and dismembered bodies of animals. This natural microbial culture is a continual source of recycled nutrients and bits of detritus softened by decomposition and enriched by protein-packed layers of attached microorganisms. An energy-rich soup, sucked and sifted first through the many detritivores and then variously gobbled up by the higher consumers, it powers the complex food web of the tidal flat.

The outer margin of the tidal flat community is a band of smooth cordgrass, the only species that can withstand continual flooding—even complete submergence—by brackish water. An extensive network of underground rhizomes allows smooth cordgrass to hold in the soft mud even when wind-driven waves pound the shore. It strikes a dynamic balance with the open bay; during quiet intervals, the grass accumulates sediment and extends its root system bayward; before rough seas the cordgrass zone is trimmed back to its normal width of only 10–20 yards. Smooth cordgrass prefers the better water exchange provided by Pass Cavallo, so the most extensive growths occur in the sheltered coves behind the northern tip of the island.

Depending on the tide, the actual shoreline starts at or just behind the strip of smooth cordgrass. This imperceptibly rising ground is a mucky region of saturated, saline, muddy sand, routinely baked by the sun but pocked with salty pools, lakes, and channels and still prone to flooding by spring and wind tides. This low marsh association may be from a few yards to a mile or more wide. It is widest in the old flood deltas at Ayers Point and between Panther Point and Pringle Lake, where it is protected from the open bay; wind tides and currents have virtually eliminated the zone between Lighthouse Cove and the Army Hole. This rigorous subdivision supports a dense shin-high cover of exceptionally hardy, salt-tolerant succulent plants. The hallmark of the low marsh is the bright yellow-green cover of maritime saltwort intermixed with darker green patches of perennial glasswort and annual seepweed. Although these are all rooted, flowering plants, the only sign of their seasonal reproduction is a dust of yellow pollen at the bases of the succulent leaves.

A windrow of dead widgeon grass and shoalgrass washed in from the bay marks the extent of normal high tides and a shift from the low to the high marsh association. This slightly higher region, though still occasionally washed by wind tides, provides better drainage and supports a noticeable shift in plant species. Dark patches of saltgrass appear, along with occasional stretches of seashore dropseed. The distinctive plant is the bushy sea oxeye, which displays a few of its yellow daisy blossoms and prickly fruit heads at almost any time of the year. Varying with the slope of the land, the sea oxeye zone may be from a few yards to half a mile in width. The inner margin is invaded by the large leaves and pretty flowering stalks of sea lavender, the bright yellow blossoms of camphor daisy, and dark green carpets of shore grass. Beyond this, secure from all but exceptional storm overwash, is a strip dominated by large mounds of Gulf Coast cordgrass. From there the ground continues to rise through a thin line of sumpweeds and groundsels, into scrubby mesquites and low clumps of Texas prickly pears, and grades into the grasses of the interior.

If you stood on its inner margin, you might be able to pitch an oystershell across the entire tidal flat community into the adjacent bay, or you might need binoculars to see open water; it all depends on the grade of the shoreline.

Just as the beach community is nourished by the Gulf, so the tidal flat community is nourished by the bays. In both, the detritivore base of the food web is filled by marine animals, but the cast of characters on the tidal flat is totally different. Hidden in burrows and tubes in the mud around the smooth cordgrass lies a huge biomass of creatures, all busy filtering the detritus-laden water or stalking those that are. Most of this mass is made up of a variety of marine worms, half a dozen species of clams, ghost shrimp (a different species from the one in the surf), and sundry kinds of tiny crustaceans. In addition to burrowers, the shallows are usually teeming with swimming and skittering life: grass shrimp, juvenile brown shrimp, pistol shrimp, blue crabs, marsh crabs, mud crabs, stone crabs, striped hermit crabs, several kinds of scavenging and predatory marine snails, and active schools of striped mullet and killifishes. Swarms of shore flies, dance flies, long-legged flies, and clusters of shorebugs animate the waterline, and hordes of beach fleas live in the dead grass strand. Just beyond, all across the low marsh, squadrons of mud fiddler crabs emerge from their burrows at low tide to spoon up yet more detritus in yet another way.

This wealth of small animal life attracts carnivores from both land and sea, most conspicuously, birds. The bountiful tidal flats of Matagorda Island are a crucial link in the twice-a-year influx of tens of thousands of migrating shorebirds that linger to probe and peck until their fat reserves are replenished. In addition, the association succors the resident shorebird species and all of the waders, gulls, terns, and black skimmers. Clapper rails slink among the taller stalks, and seaside sparrows announce their springtime nesting territories from atop the bushy sea oxeye. Gulf salt-marsh snakes and diamondback terrapins feed on small fishes and crustaceans trapped in the shallows. To this menagerie add salt-marsh grasshoppers, planthoppers, western pigmy blue and great southern white butterflies, tiger beetles, wolf spiders, jumping spiders, salt-marsh mosquitoes, dragonflies, rice rats, and nocturnal forays by raccoons, feral hogs, and white-tailed deer. All of this life is testimony to the amazing productivity of the odorous black ooze where it all begins.

The only specialized habitat worth noting in the tidal flat community is the algal mat that develops on the surface of exposed muddy sand, where conditions are too harsh for rooted plants to take hold. This thin, dark-brown skin is rubbery, smooth, and glistening when the substrate is saturated, but cracks and curls during prolonged dry intervals. In its moist state the quarter-inch-thick sheet is a gelatinous mass of blue-green algae intermixed with green algae, diatoms, protozoa, and bacteria. Multitudes of tiny black shore flies flit and race over the moist surface, mopping up nourishment with their sponge-like tongues and inserting their eggs into the mat. Their tiny white maggots feed on bacteria and decomposing algae in the lower layers and then pupate near the surface. The life cycle of these flies brings flocks of least and western sandpipers to poke avidly into what looks to us like a dead and sterile mess.

Shell Ridge Community

This biotic community develops on the windrow of dead oystershell piled by wind-driven waves on exposed strips of bay shore. A narrow habitat, it occurs intermittently from Ayers Point to the Army Hole. Panther Point, Cedar Point, and the long stretch of Vanderveer Island are all built up of shell.

Mostly, this community begins at the waterline as sand mixed with finely minced shell; it rises abruptly, several feet, over a rounded crest to a plateau of larger shell fragments. The glaring, jagged surface of the plateau is only a few yards wide and the far side drops steeply and ends abruptly, forming a distinct boundary with the adjacent tidal flat community.

The very existence of a shell ridge is due to the exposure of a bank to heavy wave action, which brings dead shell in from submerged oyster reefs. Every ridge is subject to sporadic physical pounding, constant remodeling, continual salt spray, and occasional overwash. In the winter these ridges take the impact of the cold fronts that howl across the bays; in the summer the white shell shimmers and bakes in the glare of the sun. Light reflecting off the shell erases much of the scant shade, and because the ridge lies in the wind shadow of the island, there is hardly a puff of onshore breeze to alleviate the oppressive heat. The shell ridge presents an inhospitable environment, especially for rooted plants, but it offers two benefits: elevation above the usual reach of the bay and drainage in case of overwash. However, both of these features contribute to the most severe limitation of the habitat—the paucity of fresh water. Rainwater rapidly percolates through the coarse, nonabsorbant substrate, and the resulting environment is even more arid than that of the beach and dunes communities. The hard shell and its high calcium content render the ridge community an equivalent to exposed limestone escarpments in the dry stretches of southwest Texas.

Plants survive on the shell by two main strategies. Annuals, mostly the same species found elsewhere on the island, grow and flower during the brief, favorable spring and fall seasons and survive rigorous times as dormant seeds. The others are tough, woody perennials with extensive root systems that allow them to store water and starch. On some larger ridges the assemblage of woody plants and their attendant vines is unique enough to form a distinctive cover called chaparral.

Seashore dropseed, sand saltbush, and clammyweed may eke out an ephemeral existence on the narrow beach of minced shell just above the waterline. On the backslope and in depressions are plants from the higher zones of the tidal flat: bushy sea oxeye, sea lavender, and sumpweed. But the main plateau of the larger ridges is claimed by a dense, head-high thicket of woody species. The dominant and most thoroughly entrenched plant is scrubby mesquite. Coralbean and Carolina wolfberry grow on the perimeter. Scattered through the spreading thorny branches of mesquite, the sharp growth of spiny hackberry and the recurved thorns of wild lime are woven together by the twisted boughs of tanglewood. Here and there clumps of stately Spanish daggers, the tallest plants in sight, rear 20 feet high. Vines—wild snapdragon, ivy treebine, and balsam gourd—wind among the limbs, and sprays of southern dewberry send prickly runners scrambling over everything. In low spots the wind-pruned copse may be broken by a swaying clump of saltcedar; on exposed mounds, Texas prickly pear often takes over. The resultant natural briar patch is interesting to observe but unappealing to venture into.

On the south end, several old shell ridges around Big Brundrett Lake are protected from the bay by the development of younger ridges. There has been time for some soil development atop the shell, and a true chaparral association comparable to the brush country of southern Texas has developed, quite restricted and unique on the island. In the chaparral all of the woody plants of the fringing shell ridges occur, but they are more extensive and are joined by such woody species as Mexican persimmon, brasil, lotebush, Texas torchwood, common lantana, coma, and Berlandier wolfberry. Texas nightshade and dwarf milkweed appear among the vines, and tasajillo cactus is thinly scattered through the association.

The fragmented shell ridge association is too restricted to harbor a distinctive array of animals, but it does have some interesting inhabitants. Those ridges with respectable beaches of pulverized shell and sand support small colonies of ghost crabs, creatures usually associated with the surf side of the island. Beach fleas occur in the strand of dead marine grasses, and a colony of sand fiddler crabs is usually dug-in nearby. The apparently barren strip of larger shell protects a cryptic group of active little creatures, including shore flies, tiny terrestrial crustaceans, small beetles, earwigs, and an abundance of fast-moving, predatory shore spiders. All of these organisms live at hazard among colonies of imported fire ants; the shell ridge is one of the few habitats on the island where the texture of the substrate allows these pernicious invaders to maintain large, permanent populations.

Birds routinely visit the ridges to feed, loaf, and roost, but because raccoons and coyotes can get there, these areas are not used as rookeries. Migrating perching birds feed and seek protection in the woody clumps. Few backboned animals live permanently on the outlying ridges—only a population of prairie-lined racerunners on Vanderveer Island and an occasional horned lizard.

The chaparral harbors several species of ants not found elsewhere on the island, as well as such distinctive insects as walking sticks and wood-boring beetles. A meager array of orb-weaving spiders strings its traps among the branches, and this is the only place known on the island where tarantulas live. Cotton rats are common, and so are western diamondback rattlesnakes. Raptors—black-shouldered kites, white-tailed hawks, and horned owls—hunt and nest here. If, as incidental reports have it, bobcats sporadically occur on Matagorda, they would feel quite at home in the chaparral.

Fresh-water Community

The backbeach, interdune area, and barrier flat swales have been mentioned as natural sites where rainwater collects for various lengths of time. A few of these depressions intercept the hanging aquifer and so become semipermanent sources of fresh water. More important today are the hundred or so "scrapes" that dot the interior grasslands. Most of these shallow basins, excavated to retain water for livestock, serve as rainwater catchments, but some are kept filled by windmills and half a dozen receive runoff from artesian wells. Another permanent source of fresh water is the Military Ditch, an old drainage canal bordering the air base. On the island's south end, many rainfall basins were created by swales deepened with a dragline and a system of dikes built in the adjacent tidal flats. Somewhere on the surface of the island, sufficient fresh water for wildlife is always available, although most of it is not potable by our effete standards.

What lives in and around these fresh-water sites depends on their size, permanence, load of dissolved solids, and their chance of being inundated by overwash from the Gulf or the bays. And, to a certain extent, by the types of predators that inhabit them. Ponds with fish usually harbor fewer invertebrates; a pond claimed by an alligator ordinarily contains fewer fish.

The vegetation around ponds and scrapes is generally similar to that of ponded swales and interdunes. Other than sundry green algae, widgeon grass and muskgrass (also called stonewort) are the only common submerged plants. The shoreline is often dominated by seashore paspalum, which, if the salinity remains low, may send runners with dangling rootlets and emergent tips far out across the surface of the water. Most ponds have fringes of American bulrush and emergent growths of burhead. Cattails and black rush, common around fresh water on the north end, are both rare to the south. On the other hand, tall stalks of coffee bean cover depressions in the central and southern part of the barrier but are seldom seen in the north. Low shoreline plants like Bermuda grass, water hyssop, umbrella pennywort, creeping seedbox, and water smartweed grow sparingly around most scrapes, and many of the larger ponds have an adjacent clump of saltcedars.

Aquatic creatures that can fly, be blown, or incidentally be carried by larger animals, as well as those that lie dormant in dried mud, might be expected in any standing water. So, you will find aquatic bacteria and protozoa; water fleas, ostracods, and water mites; larval midges, mosquitoes, and dragonflies; actively swimming whirligigs, water boatmen, and backswimmers; and any of the four species of aquatic snails known from the island in any pond on Matagorda. The moist margins support mole crickets, staphylinid beetles, small ground spiders, and even a thriving population of earthworms. The resultant rich food base does not fail to attract the notice of larger consumers.

Higher animals in ponds are much more spotty than the small, nearly ubiquitous creatures, and bigger organisms must contrive individual access to each pond. So, blue crabs, which are often the dominant predators in fresh-water pools around the perimeter or near brackish channels, do not frequently occur in isolated interior ones. Frogs and toads breed only in fresh water, and in favorable locations the water is constantly roiled by thousands of tadpoles. Yellow mud turtles live in most ponds and red-eared sliders inhabit the deeper ones. Gulf Coast ribbonsnakes are common around the margins of all such sites. Regardless of pond size, if it is deep enough to reliably hold water most of the year, it is likely to be appropriated by an alligator that feeds there and may nest on its margin.

As one might expect, all of the twenty or so species of fishes that have been seined from fresh-water sites on Matagorda are tolerant estuarine ones that have, by one means or another, managed to invade the inland sites. All must breed in brackish or saline water, so the populations in interior pools have to be maintained by constant immigration. Sheepshead minnow, tidewater silversides, and striped mullet are the most common species encountered in ponds with the lowest salinity.

Almost all of the island's birds, even those usually associated with salt water, drink fresh water daily and many enjoy bathing in it. In addition, both wading birds and shorebirds visit the ponds to feed. When prey is exposed in a drying waterhole, hordes of these birds are joined by clamoring gulls and terns, all seeking their share of the windfall. If there is a saltcedar clump nearby, wading birds frequently use it for resting or roosting. Wintering ducks, grebes, gallinules, and coots make good use of the more heavily vegetated ponds as feeding and watering sites and as secure retreats, while the resident mottled duck's entire life cycle hovers around this fresh-water habitat.

Any of the mammals might take advantage of ponds for drinking water, but foraging raccoons and rooting-and-wallowing feral hogs are probably the prime users.

CHAPTER 5

Vegetation

The vegetation of Matagorda Island is at once biologically important, deeply interesting, and aesthetically pleasing. Green plants, the primary producers, are the beginning point for the terrestrial food web, and they provide cover for the animals while they impede the movement of the perpetually restless sand. Plants have an intriguing array of adaptations and interactions that allow passive sprouts to take root, survive, and reproduce in an open, unforgiving environment. And what could complement the Gulf clouds, the rolling surf, the maniacal gabble of the laughing gulls more perfectly than a sand dune topped by sea oats braced in a supple arc against the onshore breeze?

Despite its vitality and innate charm, the flora of Matagorda is not really remarkable as plant life on Gulf Coast barriers goes. There are no known endangered or threatened forms, and although many of the species are distinctive for the coast, none is unique to the island. There is little diversity, because few kinds of plants can meet the stringent demands of this land of maximum exposure and fickle temperament. The inimical combination of occasional gale-force winds and washover from the sea, continual salt spray, a shifting substrate low in nutrients, an unreliable source of ground water, and recurrent prolonged droughts has proven too rigorous for large-sized, water-profligate perennial woody growth. Most vegetation is low and herbaceous, making smaller resource demands and surviving catastrophe by quick regrowth rather than with stubborn wooden resistance.

The current list of flowering plants growing on Matagorda Island includes about 300 species (excluding a few introduced ornamentals). To put this number in perspective, the Aransas National Wildlife Refuge, an area just about the size of Matagorda on the adjacent mainland, supports 845 native species. The difference can be attributed to the refuge's more protected location, greater variety of habitats, and broader access to dispersing seeds and fruits. But South Padre Island, between the Port Mansfield Cut and Port Isabel, which is nearly the same length as Matagorda, has only 216 kinds of flowering plants;

less rainfall to the south can account for the lower tally. On all three of these areas, the top four plant families, in order of decreasing frequency, are grasses, daisies, legumes, and sedges. Including the goosefoot and mallow families, these six groups account for more than half of the Matagorda Island plant list.

An analysis of the vegetation of South Padre Island suggests that over half of the plant species may have been introduced by humans. There has been no comparable review of the plants on Matagorda. The bulk of the island may appear untouched, but in fact it has been subject to long and extensive exploitation, especially by ranchers and the military. Although it is doubtful if as many as half the kinds of plants on the island were introduced by people, a considerable fraction of the grasses and weeds, and most of the shrubs and trees, owe their presence to deliberate or incidental human activity. Among the ninety-nine plant species thought to be native to South Padre Island, it was judged that their seeds and fruits were introduced mainly by birds, water, and wind. These same dispersal agents probably account for the arrival of Matagorda's native plants.

It is beyond this book to describe all of the plants of Matagorda Island, but the dominant and conspicuous ones of each of the six major communities will be surveyed. Eighty common wildflowers are listed by color, along with their distinguishing traits and normal blooming seasons, in Appendix C, and the serious botanist can consult the flowering plant list in Appendix B.

Beach Community Plants

Although there are no rooted plants on the forebeach, two sorts of floral flotsam are frequently deposited there. Gulfweed (sargassum) is a floating brown alga that grows prolifically in the warm surface waters of the Caribbean, particularly in an area seaward of the Gulf Stream off the east coast of Florida. Through spring and summer, loose streamers of gulfweed ride the current through the Florida Straits into the Gulf of Mexico, and during storms great rafts of it are driven in. This immigrant gulfweed generally remains far offshore, dying and sinking as winter cools the water, to be replenished during the next warm season. Occasionally, winds and currents combine to push masses of living gulfweed ashore; if you are on the beach then, you are in luck!

Gulfweed appears as ragged handfuls of beige, brown, or yellow-brown fleshy branches with leaf-like structures and round, pea-sized bladders. You may find it packed in the strand, scattered over the forebeach, or still rolling in the surf. The best specimens are the fresh-

Gulfweed

est—the ones still in the water. Pick up a clump and note the "leaves" (algae do not have true leaves) with their prickly margins, and the buoyant bladders. With experience, you can distinguish between the two species: The more common *Sargassum natans* has narrow leaves and each bladder is tipped with a small peg-like projection; the less common *Sargassum fluitans* has wider leaves and smooth bladders.

To find out what's so exciting about gulfweed, douse several fresh batches vigorously in a container of seawater; discard the algae and see what you have shaken loose. A menagerie of weird and wonderful things routinely lives among the gulfweed fronds; it would take us too far afield to describe this specialized community, but a brief commentary may encourage you to find out about them for yourself.

If you are really lucky, you will find a sargassum fish. Its fleshy appendages and blotchy coloration make it practically invisible in the gulfweed habitat; the front fins grasp the algal branches like hands and the dangling appendage on its snout can be wriggled as a lure. Like its more widely known relative, the angler fish, the sargassum fish inhales its prey with a sudden, sucking gulp.

Look also for elongate pipefish (straight-bodied relatives of seahorses), crabs of several species, exquisite shrimp with upturned snouts and flecks of electric blue, the sargassum-colored nudibranch (a much modified shell-less relative of marine snails), and sundry flatworms, annelid worms, sea spiders, sea anemones, and no telling what else. Each of these creatures has adapted by color, form, and behavior to its floating algal habitat.

Put some of these animals into a smaller container of water and observe them through a pocket magnifier. (You did bring a pocket magnifier on a beach excursion, didn't you?) Scan the gulfweed for creatures that don't come loose. Check the bladders for *hydroids*—colonial animals that resemble miniature fern fronds or bouquets of stemmed vases. Look on the stems for tiny (though fully grown) sea anemones, clusters of goose barnacles, and crusty growths of bryozoans. Examine one of the white specks on the leaves; it is the coiled shell of a miniscule worm. If you are patient and don't agitate the water, you may see the shy little worm extend its spray of red feeding tentacles.

While other beach strollers are getting bored, you can easily spend most of your visit plumbing a windrow of fresh gulfweed without exhausting its wonders.

Seabeans are among the most interesting and exotic bounties of the sea. Especially on Matagorda Island, where there is not a large variety of shells, a hunt for seabeans can add to the thrill of beachcombing. Like seashells and other wrack, seabeans are regarded as a nonvital renewable resource, so you are welcome to collect and keep them as souvenirs.

"Seabean" is a catchall name for any sort of drifting seed or fruit cast up by the sea. They vary in buoyancy and in resistance to water-logging, but most drift for several months and a few may last several years. Some arrive intact and last indefinitely on the beach; others are in various stages of deterioration. Most lose vitality quickly and seldom germinate when they reach shore after a prolonged voyage; and because most come from the tropics, the occasional sprout quickly succumbs in a temperate climate.

About thirty-five kinds of tropical seabeans have been found on beaches in the Gulf of Mexico. Some are from plants native to Southeast Asia and the west coast of Africa, but almost all of these are now found on lands that rim the Caribbean. They grow on the coast or on inland rivers, from which they wash down to the ocean. Because of the direction of the prevailing winds and the trend of the currents, it is most likely that any tropical seabean you find on Matagorda will have come from the West Indies, the Antilles, the east coasts of Mexico or Central America, or from northern South America. You can also find seeds of some twenty-five temperate species, mostly from rivers on the upper Texas coast or even from the Mississippi.

Winds, longshore currents, and tropical storms conspire to make Padre Island the principal depository for tropical seabeans in the Gulf, but Matagorda Island receives a moderate share of tropicals and a heavy dole of temperate ones. March through early summer is the best time to find freshly beached beans, but durable ones may be found the year-round. The photograph (see photo section) and the following list include the species you are most apt to discover on Matagorda. Check the references in the bibliography for further help in identifying your treasures.

- True seabean (*Mucuna spp.*). Surely anyone would name this some variation on "hamburger bean," because its shape and color so strongly suggest a miniature version of that familiar menu item. The hard bean is bun-shaped, typically 1 inch across and ¾ of an inch thick. It is tan to reddish-brown with a black band, about ¼ of an inch wide, running three-quarters of the way around its middle. The parent plant, a common legume vine throughout Caribbean islands, bears bright yellow flowers. These beans are just uncommon enough on Matagorda for you to consider yourself privileged to find one.

• Sea purse (*Dioclea spp.*). This seed resembles the true seabean, but is flatter, more oval in outline, and the edge, between the ends of the marginal band, is straight; it looks like a little coin purse, about 1 inch wide and ½ of an inch thick. The brown ground color is mottled with black and the thin marginal band is jet black with a narrow yellow border. Despite the similarity in the seeds, this vine, a high-climbing liana from northern South America and the Caribbean, is not related to the true seabean. Its clusters of blue-violet flowers give rise to thick fleshy pods, each containing about half a dozen seeds capable of staying afloat for at least two years. They are rare on Matagorda, but make durable curios and take a high polish.

• Sea heart (*Entada gigas*). Although it is less appealing, this seed might be better called "sea kidney," for it more resembles that organ in shape. The nearly unbreakable sea heart, up to 2½ inches long by ¾ of an inch thick, is one of the largest tropical seabeans that enter the Gulf of Mexico. Most sea hearts are a uniform mahogany brown, and though often encrusted with limey deposit, they take on a luster when cleaned and polished. As befits such large beans, the parent vine is huge and fast-growing, and produces the largest bean pods in the world—up to 7 feet long, with over a dozen seeds. The pod erodes in the sea and is seldom seen on our beaches. The vines are pantropical and the seeds on Matagorda probably come from the Caribbean. Sea hearts are common on Matagorda; they are reputed to be good luck charms, so keep one in your pocket while you search for further treasures.

• Nickernut (*Caesalpinia spp.*). These beans are irregularly ovoid, about ¾ of an inch long, and pale brown or olive-gray. Their distinction is a series of fine concentric lines overlying the ground color. The plants, natives of Southeast Asia, have been introduced into the New World tropics, so those on Matagorda may not have traveled far. The trailing shrubs grow in thickets just above high tide line. They have prickly foliage and yellow flowers, and bear spiny pods. Nickernuts are rare on Matagorda, so consider them prizes.

• Donovan's brain (*Andira galeottiana*). This distinctive disseminule has no accepted name, but, with its wrinkles and a crease dividing it into two lobes, it bears a strong resemblance to a black, shriveled human brain. It is here named after the lead character in a 1953 thriller that offered a riveting view of a bottled brain and incidentally featured a young actress named Nancy Davis (Reagan). Perhaps you will think it more closely resembles a huge raisin. Second largest of the seabeans that enter the Gulf, the 3¼-inch-long by 2½-inch wide by 2¼-inch-thick seed develops inside a shaggy husk, which erodes during the sea voyage. The parent plant is a small tree native to riverbanks in southern Mexico. Brains wash in fairly often, but are not long-lasting on the beach.

• Bay bean (*Canavalia spp.*). Bay beans, rather routine beans in size, shape, and color (brownish to red-brown), come from ribbed pods produced by vines that trail across Caribbean beaches. These unimpressive beans are durable and rather common, but usually ignored. Although never recorded on Matagorda Island, one species, with three-parted leaves and purple flowers, sprouts on Padre Island. There it grows until a cool winter wipes it out.

• Red mangrove (*Rhizophora mangle*). This 12-inch-long, slightly curved, fleshy green torpedo is a seedling. The seed sprouts while still on the tree and drops directly into the ocean. There it bobs along vertically until the heavier lower end strikes the bottom, where it lodges, sets root, and grows into a shrubby mangrove tree with its distinctive cluster of prop roots. Tangles of red mangroves line quiet coastlines throughout the tropics and northward through the Keys onto the southern tip of Florida. Most of those that drift to Texas shores are dead; a rare few have grown on Padre Island, only to succumb to the first light freeze. The beached seedlings are moderately common on Matagorda after storms, but they soon deteriorate.

• Black mangrove (*Avicennia germinans*). The fruit is a flat, fuzzy pod, pale green, ovoid-shaped, 1½ inches long, with a recurved tip. The single seed germinates inside the pod and sends out rootlets whenever it strikes the substrate. Black mangroves grow in dense thickets along secluded tropical coastlines and sporadically up the Texas coast as far as Galveston. Locally, they produce white flowers and numerous fruits, but cold snaps kill them back, so they never manage to progress beyond shrub size. In good years, an extensive thicket of black mangroves grows on the islets between Port O'Connor and the north end of Matagorda Island, and most of the fruits on this beach probably come through Pass

Black mangrove

Cavallo. The seedlings cannot set roots in the unstable beach sand.

- Coconut (*Cocos nucifera*). This is by far the largest of the tropical seabeans that strike our coast. Coconuts drift widely and the trees are pantropical; the fruits that beach on Matagorda probably come from Florida or the Caribbean. Most of these do not look like the familiar grocery store item because they are still encased in their fibrous husks, some even still with the smooth outer rinds. Coconuts are rather common on the island, and stranded ones last for months. Although many may arrive viable, this cold-sensitive and slow-germinating species is not known to sprout here.
- Cocoid palms. Several hundred species of palms from the New World tropics produce fruits and seeds that occasionally make their way into the Gulf of Mexico. Some are round like miniature coconuts, others are about the size and shape of pecans. Most are recognizable as cocoid palms by the characteristic three (sometimes two) basal pores. The fruits of at least half a dozen of these have been found on Matagorda Island.
- Sea coconut (*Manicaria saccifera*). What is commonly found on this beach is the black, golf-ball-sized seed of this palm, with a stem scar and no basal pores. Sea coconuts may be solitary, or two or even three seeds may be welded into a single, lobed fruit. Each seed has a thin, brittle, brown layer and is wrapped in a loose fibrous husk. The whole fruit is covered with an outer shell of close-set, barky scales. The trees grow in the Amazon Basin, and by the time the fruits drift into the Gulf of Mexico they have usually broken into solitary seeds and been stripped of most of their woody scales; you find them in various stages of cracking brownish or dusky layers. These seeds are long dead, and many are punctured and filled with sand.
- Country almond (*Terminalia catappa*). Although not related to the almond of commerce, the country almond does resemble it and even has an almond flavor. Some arrive on Matagorda still encased in their smooth outer rinds, but most are down to a loose fibrous husk or denuded to their corky, straw-colored seedcoats.

These 1½-inch to 2-inch seeds are among the most numerous disseminules on Matagorda. The tall trees are native to Southeast Asia, but have long been planted throughout the tropics for both shade and fruits. Florida or the West Indies are the likely sources of the seeds on Matagorda Island.

• Pecan (*Carya illinoensis*). This fruit is easily recognized, with the outer tough husks intact or just the hard-shelled seed. Pecans are common on Matagorda and they probably have come either from the Mississippi Valley or the local Texas river bottoms.

• Water hickory (*Carya aquatica*). This 1-inch-long nut is flattened, rounded at the base, and abruptly pointed at the apex. The hard, light brown shell is covered with fine, sharp-edged wrinkles. Water hickories grow on riverbanks and in swamps throughout the Southeast, including East Texas, and their nuts are common drift items on Matagorda.

• Black walnut (*Juglans nigra*). This seed is nearly spherical, dark brown, and covered with fine ridges. The nuts are common in the Matagorda strand; most of them probably come from the forests of East Texas.

• Jamaican walnut (*Juglans jamaicensis*). This nut is much like the black walnut but larger (to 1½ inches), paler, and etched with fewer grooves and ridges. The trees are native to the Caribbean.

• Mango (*Mangifera indica*). The pulpy fruit deteriorates rapidly in the sea and only the large (5-inch by 2-inch) seed lasts. These flat, brownish seeds are shoehorn-shaped, covered with downy hairs, and fringed on one edge with longer hairs. The trees are widely planted throughout the tropics, but many of the occasional ones found here may be garbage from the galleys of ships or offshore oil platforms.

Besides all these, you can expect an assortment of morning glory seeds from plants growing on the island, acorns, peach pits, insect-induced galls, and gourds, as well as other items of floral origin such as huge corky prickles from the trunks of kapok trees, the paired thorns of bull's horn acacias, sections of huge bamboo shoots, and an endless variety of worm-bored, barnacle-encrusted, and water-smoothed bits of many-hued woods. Invariably there will be some unknowns, perhaps the most intriguing discoveries of all.

This hostile zone of physical extremes between the strand and the base of the primary dunes is the site of the first battle line in the perennial conflict between vegetation and wind-blown sand, and the wind is winning. Much of the sand is barren of any green shoots; the embattled plants are forced to crouch in wide-scattered, submissive clumps. And the entire area—plants and wind-etched topography— is in constant danger of devastation by the next exceptional tide or tropical storm wave.

The kinds of plants that manage to make it on the backbeach are an unusually hardy lot, determined and resourceful, pioneers in the finest tradition of the term. While identifying them, admire the adaptations that allow them to survive in this rigorous habitat.

All plants on the backbeach are herbaceous, a tacit acknowledgment that deep-seated roots and permanent woody stems can never grow in an everchanging substrate. To minimize wind damage, most species maintain a low profile, either lying prostrate on the sand or having flexible stems. The few shrubby kinds that attempt to resist the wind are noticeably "wind-pruned": growth is inhibited on the windward side, so the plants appear to lean permanently downwind. This inhibition, usually explained as the inimical effect of salt spray on growth buds, has recently been found to be more complicated. The mechanical pressure of the wind activates growth-regulating genes that cause not only the bent-over posture but a sturdier, stockier growth form. Thus, plants directly exposed to the onshore wind may look quite different from individuals of the same kind growing in the wind shadow of a coppice dune.

The ultimate low profile is subterranean stems. A few beach plants specialize in these rhizomes, burrowing horizontally for many yards and producing tufts of roots at intervals, sending up green shoots in favorable spots, and otherwise remaining hidden from the elements. To counter smothering of their leaves by sand, most beach plants release an extra dose of growth hormone when they are partly covered, so their invigorated shoots soon push into the sunshine. In many cases the main biomass of the plant is composed of root and supportive stem tissue, and only a relatively small fraction is green and above the ground. It is this prolific growth of buried stems and roots that makes the pioneer plants such valuable sand binders on the beach and dunes.

Scarcity of fresh water, omnipresent salt (which draws water out of living tissues), drying wind, and intense solar radiation make it mandatory that beach plants be *xerophytes* ('zer-o-fites)—plants that carefully conserve their water. To this end, most have reduced their surface area with leaves that are either very small or have tightly curled edges. Many have drastically reduced the number of microscopic breathing pores on the undersides of their leaves, through which water is lost, and have sequestered the openings of the remaining pores in pits, away from the wind. A few species, especially the grasses, have even modified their photosynthetic metabolism so that they can completely close their pores, effectively holding their breath, during the hottest times of the day when water stress is most severe.

Most beach plants are covered with either a shiny wax film or a dusty, gray coat of hairs. Wax holds in body water and shields the tissues from salt deposits. Hairs not only retard evaporation, they shield the plant from sandblast and their crisscross of minuscule shadows screens greenery against heat and sunburn. Many beach species secrete pigments that protect them from the ultraviolet component of sunshine just as sunscreen protects a human's skin. A few have cells in the surfaces of their leaves that are microscopic lenses deflecting sunlight into special absorptive layers where the potentially damaging energy can be dissipated.

A widespread, rapidly growing root system is an absolute necessity for any plant that inhabits the beach. A meshwork of rootlets seeks out scarce water and nutrients in the dry, infertile sand, and roots are the all-important anchors that secure plants in the shifting substrate. Some species even secrete a thick, sticky mucilage around their roots to enhance their grip.

Most beach plants are succulent: Their inner tissues are juicy with stored water; their leaves thick and fleshy. This moisture can be water greedily absorbed and stashed away after rains or possibly drawn up from the shallow, saline water table. Glands extract and excrete the salt and retain the water; salt crystals on a plant may have been deposited there by spray or they may be excretions from these glands. In severe droughts, beach plants release a special hormone into their tissues for extra stamina against prolonged wilt.

Many beach plants produce small and protected flowers that are, to our eyes, inconspicuous or unattractive, but assure successful seed formation. Ones with larger flowers avoid wind and sun damage by unfurling their petals early or late in the day, and a few species bloom through the night. Seeds that were windborne would be carried away from their beach habitat by the onshore breeze, so most fall directly onto the sand or are carried about by birds, ants, or rodents, and some buoyant ones are transported to other beaches by longshore currents. All of these seeds have exquisite chemical sensors in their external coats that serve as very accurate rain gauges, promoting germination only after the beach has received a heavy rain. Some of the more delicate beach plants are annuals, rapidly sending up their shoots and opening their flowers during a brief favorable period (usually spring or fall), and then dying, leaving the species to survive the harsh seasons as dormant seeds.

If you were to trek the backbeach of Matagorda Island from Pass Cavallo to Cedar Bayou, you would notice occasional local shifts in

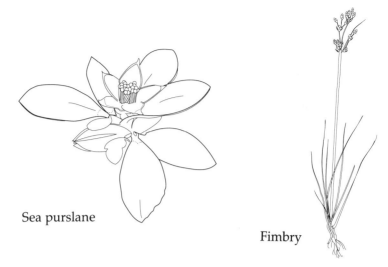

Sea purslane

Fimbry

the composition of the community of plants, but the same dominant species occur throughout. Those described here are characteristic of the backbeach at the end of the shuttle road to the day use/camping beach on the north end of the island. Plants are discussed in their natural sequence, beginning at the strand line and progressing toward the primary dunes.

Sea purslane, also called cenicilla (sen-eh-'see-ya), Spanish for "little ashes," is easily recognized. The numerous, spreading, orange-brown stems with pairs of fat, fleshy leaves form mats up to several feet across. Most of the soft branches lie prostrate on the sand and secure themselves with frequent tufts of roots. Purslane flowers sporadically all year long. Its scattered, ¾-inch, star-shaped blossoms, pale pink with numerous rose-colored stamens, are on short pedicels at the bases of the leaves. A purslane clump, its windward margin partly covered by drifting sand, is the archetypical beach plant, gathering sand into coppice dunes. This plant is more common on Padre Island and continues southward onto beaches throughout the Caribbean.

Quite a few coppice dunes form around the deep-rooted perennial fimbry, a member of the grass-like sedge family. The dense knee-high tufts of very thin, shiny leaves and wiry stalks are topped by loose clusters of brown, cone-like seed heads. Fimbry has no evident flowers; each cone tapers toward its tip and is about ½ inch long.

Three plants that contribute to the beach vanguard are more common toward the south end of the island. Wooly honeysweet or wooly tidestromia (tide-eh-'stroam-me-ya), another mound-forming species, has numerous tiny, fragrant yellow flowers clustered at the bases of the round, hairy leaves. The dense hairs, seen under magnification to be star-shaped, give wooly honeysweet an ashy cast that accounts for another of its common names—ghost plant. As it begins to die in the fall, this annual turns orangey pink. The fleshy annual herb sea rocket is not very common on Matagorda. A member of the mustard family, its brief spray of lavender-white flowers in the early spring is followed by inch-long pods that point skyward like miniature rockets on their launchpads. The fruit is divided into a short basal segment and a longer, pointed terminal segment that eventually turns corky, falls away, and readily floats in the sea. If you know pigweed, you may be able to recognize beach amaranth, another undistinguished member of this group of rank, weedy annuals. Amaranth clumps have leathery, pale green leaves, and female plants bear dense, vertical clusters of tiny greenish flowers and fruits on the terminal branches. The miniscule black seeds are much favored by sparrows and horned larks. Pigweeds are well named; the feral hogs browse the foliage and fruiting stalks.

Among other plants that appear about halfway across the coppice dunes and continue into the primary dunes are four kinds of grasses. Sea oats and gulfdune paspalum, more common on the primary dunes, will be described later. The first isolated clumps of marshhay cordgrass secure themselves here with tangles of thin rhizomes, and become dense in the moist depression at the base of the primary dunes. This tough perennial, one of the most common and widespread grasses on the island, continues over the primary dunes and is an important part of the thick grass cover across the interior. The long, flexible leaves are matte-surfaced, the edges tightly curled so each leaf is scarcely 1/16 of an inch wide. The waist-high tussocks sway with the wind, leaf tips scribing arcs in the sand. In late summer and fall the plants send up thin flower stalks topped by half a dozen widely spaced seed branches.

A favored forage grass, beach panic is relatively uncommon on Matagorda; it has not recovered from years of unrestricted grazing. But the isolated bunches are getting larger and more numerous, and the species may be expected to regain its foothold along the inner perimeter of the backbeach. Several robust, waist-high clumps of panic grow from their extensive rhizomatous bases beside the end of the main beach access road. The flat 1/2-inch-wide leaves have a distinctive blue-green cast. Short, heavy stalks support the dense upright heads of flowers and grain.

The woody-based low shrub called Gulf croton is easy to identify by the silvery sheen of its leaves and its distinctive three-lobed fruit. Train your magnifying lens on the underside of a leaf and observe the

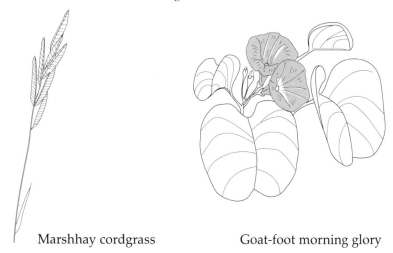

Marshhay cordgrass   Goat-foot morning glory

overlapping shiny scales that give the plant its sheen; they are important waterproofers and sun shields. Where the wind has exposed
them, you can see that each knee-high mound has shallow secondary
roots radiating 30 feet from the central stem. Croton is an important
binder; even when the perennial plants finally die, the black woody
stems and branches continue to hold the sand.

Both of the two species of morning glories may be locally common,
but neither is widespread on Matagorda. They are rather cold-sensitive, and are easily damaged by the trampling of cattle or people.

Goat-foot morning glory is one of the most spectacular members of
the beach and dunes vegetation; you cannot fail to notice and be im-
pressed by its long brown stems (about the diameter of your index
finger) trailing in straight lines across the surface of the sand. At intervals, shiny green clusters of large, leathery leaves with the distinctive outline of a cloven-hoofed animal track erupt on the sand. The
plant is also called railroad vine for the network of ruler-straight
stems across the sand; in fact, in Florida it does grow along railroad
tracks. Vigorous growth soon brings fresh buds to the surface of
drifted sand. After summer rains, this vine puts on an eye-catching
show of large, purple, funnelform blossoms. These open in the evening, attract moths all night, and finally wither early the next morning. The turnip-shaped fruit pods split to release buoyant brown
seeds that are transported by the sea to beaches throughout the tropics. This is another beach plant that is much more abundant on Padre
Island than on Matagorda.

The fiddleleaf morning glory, less common than goat-foot, has
more delicate stems that twist into a mat rather than spreading.

Coast pennywort

Beach evening primrose   Seaside heliotrope

Young leaves are not distinctive, but mature ones, about 1½ inches in length, are lobed at the base, with a vaguely violin-like outline. The funnel-shaped blossoms are bright white, washed with pale yellow in the throat.

You cannot say that you have savored the best of Matagorda Island until you have seen scores of the lovely soft yellow blossoms of beach evening primrose, either at sunset as they unfurl from upright buds or when they glow in the first rays of sunrise. The 3-inch to 4-inch-wide saucers of four petals fade to a rose-colored blush as they close at mid-morning. The low mounds of downy foliage that rise from woody, perennial bases are restricted to the deep sand on the beach and dunes.

In the moist depression at the base of the primary dunes, several species of more delicate plants find suitable habitat. Water hyssop forms small mats of trailing stems with pairs of fleshy leaves and white-lavender, five-petaled flowers. Coast pennywort is recognized by its circular leaves with lightly scalloped margins, which are held at ankle height on central stalks so that they resemble little green umbrellas. The knee-high stems of seaside heliotrope terminate in neatly curled spikes of tiny white flowers. Stiff-stem flax produces ephemeral, five-petaled cups about 1 inch across; each golden yellow petal grades to brassy orange at the base. The five bubble-gum pink and yellow-throated petals of sand pinks are among the most noticeable wildflowers on the island. Just to keep you alert, sand pink flowers are occasionally snow white. Corpus Christi fleabane is a very common daisy on the backbeach and in many inland habitats. Each bright yellow disk with its thick fringe of narrow white petals sits on a stalk above the prostrate plant. The trailing matted stems of frog-fruit are square; roll a stem between your fingers to feel the four corners. Each erect stalk holds a tight purplish globe with a ring of ⅛-inch white flowers at shoetop level.

Sand Dunes Community Plants

Because of wind sorting, the sand of the primary dunes is finer and has less organic content than that of the backbeach. The exposed windward side of the dunes has relatively sparse plant cover while the protected lee side has both more species and more luxuriant growth. Most species of the backbeach manage to at least start up the windward dune face; notice how these variously wax or wane as their root zones get closer to or farther from the water table.

Grasses are significant sand binders on the dunes. We have already met marshhay cordgrass, which forms a dense ring around large dunes and is joined by gulfdune paspalum to completely clothe some smaller ones. On large dunes, where the water table is far away, the more arid-adapted paspalum takes over. This stout perennial has tenacious rhizomes that give it good anchor in the shifting sand. Its tough, blue-green leaves are cylindrical, the margins so tightly in-rolled that you cannot see the seam without magnification. By contrast, the more flexible, paler green leaves of marshhay cordgrass have an evident longitudinal groove. In the fall, paspalum sends up stalks bearing one or, more commonly, two long fingers of seeds. Gulfdune paspalum, one of the dominant grasses on Matagorda, continues down the lee sides of the dunes and across most of the interior of the island.

One grass catches every visitor's eye and has come to symbolize both the romantic and the ecologic aspects of the barrier island environment: Picturesque sea oats swaying atop a dune touches a responsive chord in everyone. Tussocks of sea oats spring up on the backbeach and patches survive on a few secondary dunes, but this plant prefers the risky habitat on the upper windward slopes and open crests of the primary dunes, where it puts down the deep and extensive tangle of roots and rhizomes that simultaneously anchors the grass and holds the dune in place. Where a dune has been breached by wind or wave, you can see an exposure of this massive growth.

Sea oats is a big grass with flat leaf blades over 2 feet long (they may be slightly curled in the heat of the day). After three to five years of growth, it puts up reed-like stalks nearly 6 feet tall with heavy, nodding panicles of flattened fruits. These are an abundant and nutritious food source in the niggardly dunes community; mature grains

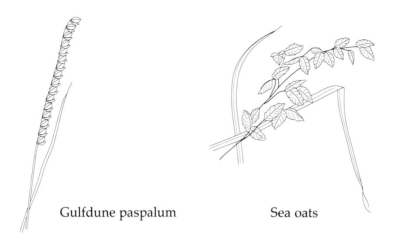

Gulfdune paspalum   Sea oats

sprinkle down all winter long, and everything, from birds and rodents to jackrabbits and ghost crabs, eagerly feeds on them.

Gulf croton, beach evening primrose, and goat-foot morning glory ascend the windward side of the dunes and are usually joined by beach ground-cherry. The blossoms of this perennial herb hang from the branches like little bells, each composed of five green-yellow petals blotched with brown at their bases. The mature fruit is a crisp inflated sac containing a juicy miniature tomato about ½ inch wide. Like the cultivated tomato, the beach ground-cherry is an edible member of the nightshade family.

Over the crest of the dunes new species appear. The very common camphorweed, a waist-high, tap-rooted annual, produces yellow daisy flowers about 1 inch in diameter throughout the warm months. Pinch several leaves and notice their sticky feel and camphor scent, the plant's defense against herbivores. The knee-high clumps of semi-woody stems and dark green foliage of broom groundsel are nondescript most of the year, but in October and November the plants produce abundant, showy, yellow daisies followed by snow white powderpuff fruits. These plants are more common on the island's south end. In the fall, wild buckwheat is easily recognized by its pancake-flat clusters of small white flowers atop waist-high stalks. The pancakes turn an appealing russet as the seeds mature. On the dunes, buckwheat is often stunted, but it stands tall above the grasses in the interior.

The lee side of some dunes is completely captured by a dense growth of partridge pea, a knee-high plant with thin, reddish, woody stems and compound leaves divided into numerous pairs of small

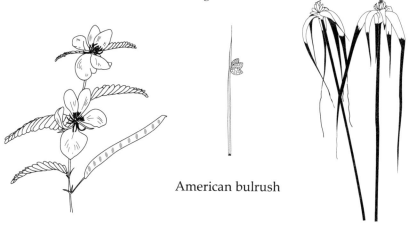

American bulrush

Partridge pea   White-topped umbrella grass

leaflets. The green caterpillars of cloudless sulphur butterflies feed on the foliage and a pair of orange glands at the base of each leaf secretes nectar that attracts ants and wasps. Flowers with five bright yellow petals appear in late summer; four petals have a red spot at the base and the stamens are dark purple. A day's crop of flowers falls by noon. Abundant little pea pods begin to open in October, and soon the sand is peppered with flattened squarish brown seeds that are relished by wintertime sparrows.

In the moist and protected trough of the interdune swale that borders the lee side of the primary dune ridge, life is easier for plants. Unless excessive rainfall has turned it into a temporary pond, the dominant ground cover is a thick sward of marshhay cordgrass marked by head-high stands of American bulrush in wetter spots. These tall sedges are also called sword-grass, or, because their stems are sharply triangular, three-square; feel a stalk to verify your identification. Most of the slender green sabers bear a cluster of brown fruits near their tip. Along with the bulrush you may find clumps of Gulf Coast cattail. This species is distinguished by having a slight gap between the thick, brown cylinder of female flowers and the narrow terminal spike of male flowers.

Of the varied array of nondescript sedges and rushes in the interdune swale, two are worth noting. Dense colonies of waist-high, leafless stalks of black rush are striking even from a distance because of their brooding, blackish green cast. The cylindrical stalks are more slender than those of American bulrush and the stems end in a sharp spine. White-topped umbrella grass is one of the few members of its drab clan that catches the eye of casual passersby. Clusters of the shin-high plants grow in moist spots, each stalk topped by a spray of flat drooping leaves with bright white bases. The small white flowers and fruits are at the center of the rosette of leaves.

If you are out early, you may be treated to the flaring purple funnels of salt-marsh morning glory. The wide-scattered vines twining up bulrushes or cattails are worth a closer look, not only for the ephemeral flower, at over 3 inches long one of the largest on the island, but for the arrowhead-shaped leaves. Another morning bloomer, rarer and equally beautiful, is salt-marsh mallow. This head-high perennial herb has hairy, gray-green leaves, late summer clusters of large rose pink flowers with five flaring petals, and a protruding central column studded with yellow anthers and tipped with five stigmas. The flowers should remind you of cultivated hibiscus; the two are closely related.

Favorable growth conditions in the interdune zone support a variety of wildflowers, including all of those seen on the backbeach. The white lazy daisy blooms nearly year-round, but opens only when the sun is high. It can be distinguished from the similar Corpus Christi fleabane by upright, rather than prostrate, stems and by fewer and longer petals. Indian blanket is a very abundant summertime daisy with a brown central disk and showy red petals with yellow tips. Coast mistflower is a smooth, knee-high perennial herb topped with flat, fuzzy clusters of lavender-blue flowers. Each cluster is composed of many tiny flowers with protruding styles. This very common summertime bloomer is much visited by bumblebees. In moist sites, the occasional dense colonies of yellowstems catch the attention of flower enthusiasts. The leaves of this knee-high plant are in consecutive pairs set at right angles to each other. In the fall, stems are topped with sprays of branchlets, each with an array of small blossoms. Not only the flowers, but the branchlets bearing them, are bright sulphur yellow; especially on cloudy days, they seem to glow with an inner light.

The two large, sky-blue petals of erect dayflower eclipse the third small, white one. One flower a day emerges from each boat-shaped green spathe at the top of the stem. Blue-eyed grass is not a grass and

Indian blanket

its eye is not blue, but this common spring flower does have grass-like leaves, and its flowers, with six purple-blue petal-like parts, has a bright yellow eye. Narrow green flanges on the stems make them look flat; perhaps you can tell by the foliage that this plant belongs to the iris family. Spring and early summer are punctuated by several species of spiderwort, all with three-petaled flowers in shades of lavender to purple. Each 1-inch-wide flower has six shaggy purple stamens bearing bright yellow anthers.

Colonies of the slender, knee-high stems of toadflax are among the earliest spring flowers on the island. The delicate ¾-inch-long, pale lavender blooms are worth stooping to admire. Each flower has two small upright lobes, a large three-lobed lower lip, and a slender tubular spur that curves down from the back. Square, 10-inch-tall stems of skullcap bloom throughout the summer, especially after showers. The ½-inch blue-purple flower is an inflated tube that flares into five lobes, the large lower lobe bearing a white blotch with purple speckles. The "skullcap" is the flat disk on the upper side of the green calyx tube below each blossom. In the knee-high tangle of wiry stems and thin, paired leaves, the flowers of stiff-leaf gerardia (jer-'rar-dee-ah) seem too large. These also have an inflated floral tube and five spreading lobes, but it is larger, about 1 inch long, with nearly equal-sized lobes. It is pinky purple with thin yellow lines and dark purple spots inside the hairy throat.

There are some special delights growing in moist spots across the barrier flat. The 2-inch-wide bluebell flowers are almost tulip-like, with a deep cup of five blue-violet petals with slightly darker centers. You don't go looking for bluebells; you happen upon them. They stand knee-high but are widely scattered in ones and twos. The handsome foliage, coated with a fine white wax, is chalky blue-green and begs to be savored with the fingertips as well as the eyes. Purple pleatleaf, another wild iris, has the typical long, narrow, folded leaves. It also grows shin-high in scattered twos and threes. The 1¾-inch flowers have showy purple, petal-like parts, three large and three small, and a yellow center suffused with brown flecks. The flowers shrivel to a moist wad by midday. Finally, ladies' tresses, Matagorda's only orchid, is fairly common early in the summer and after rains. Shin-high upright stems have a spiral of small white flowers twisting around the stalk. They are not impressive as orchids go, but the realization that you are seeing a bona fide, uncultivated member of this celebrated family should inspire you.

Most secondary dunes support a thick cover of gulfdune paspalum and marshhay cordgrass, perhaps with a lingering patch of sea oats near the peak. If the sand of an open patch is packed tightly, it will

Ladies' tresses

support the pestiferous Gulf Coast sandbur ("stickers"). These grasses are usually laced through by a variety of trailing or twining plants. The most common of these is American snoutbean, with round, heavily veined leaves and slender sprays of bright yellow, bonnet-shaped flowers ⅜ of an inch long that open in mid-morning. The recurved prickles on the sprawling woody stems of southern dewberry can make walking on a secondary dune an ankle-lacerating experience. In the spring they produce five-petaled bright white flowers that transform into berries relished by everything from passerine birds to coyotes and box turtles. Hoary milkpea is a trailing vine with hairy, three-parted, silvery gray leaves and small rose-lavender bonnet-shaped flowers. It has the peculiar habit of driving some of its flowers into the sand, where they develop into one-seeded pods, rather like its kin, the peanut. Indeed, ripe milkpeas taste like peanuts.

Most of the flowering plants on the lee sides of the primary dunes also occur on secondary dunes, especially partridge pea, broom groundsel, and camphorweed. In addition, the lower slopes may have dense waist-high stands of California loosestrife. The many-branched, four-angled stems have ½-inch saucer-shaped rose-purple flowers at the bases of the slender leaves.

Of the three species of sunflowers on Matagorda, the silverleaf sunflower is the most common. Most plants grow about 6 feet high in annual herbaceous thickets on the secondary dunes and on hillocks of sand across the interior grasslands, but tenacious runty flowering specimens hardly a foot tall may infiltrate the lee sides of the primary dunes. The leaves are protected with a distinctive coat of white wooly hairs that give them their characteristic color. The flowers are typical of the group, about 3 inches across, with brown centers and orange-yellow petals. Mourning doves, red-winged blackbirds, bobwhite quail, and sundry rodents all feast on the oil-rich seeds.

Of the four species of cacti on the island, the Texas prickly pear is the one most likely to be noticed. The plants are not especially common, but knee-high clumps occur on the sides of secondary dunes and on sandy rises and openings in the interior grassland, and robust patches grow on shell ridges along the bay side. Prickly pears, easily recognized by their flat, spiny pads, produce lemon yellow flowers in the spring that are eagerly attended by bumblebees and a variety of beetles. By late summer the pear-shaped fruits called tunas ('toon-ahs) ripen to deep purple on the edges of the pads and are pecked open by all sorts of birds, gnawed by rodents, snipped by box turtles, and gobbled up whole by coyotes.

Isolated joints of coast prickly pear can be found rooting on the backbeach, but successful growth is restricted to the sand dunes. Its pads have only a few spines along their margins, and the club-shaped tunas ripen to red. This species hybridizes with the Texas prickly pear to produce plants with contorted pads, variable spination, and intermediate tunas.

Barrier Flat Community Plants

The grassland that covers the interior of the island between the primary dunes and the tidal flat, by far the largest of Matagorda's natural communities, is spread over a low, rolling topography of moist swales and drier ridges. The road from the dock to the beach traverses nearly a mile of this zone; the shuttle road down the island stays within it.

About fifty species of grasses have been recorded on Matagorda, including several kinds of dropseeds, love grasses, such as red love, and windmill grasses, and many species of panics, paspalums, and bluestems. Most of these appear in small stands here and there across the barrier flat, each stand dependent on some unique mix of sand and organic material left by wind and washovers. Although most visitors will not care to identify all grasses, these are listed in Appendix B.

The two dominant grasses of the barrier flat are gulfdune paspalum and marshhay cordgrass; together they cover more acres of the island than any other plants. The two are usually found in combination, but on drier, upland sites gulfdune paspalum prevails, while marshhay cordgrass takes over in the lower, wetter places. Both grow in clumps of long, flexible leaves that tend to lean downwind, and they form a

Seacoast bluestem   Butterfly pea

rippling, knee-deep organic blanket over the substrate. This cover not only holds the sand and collects organic matter, it forms a sheltered hideaway for many of the island's shy creatures, with shade, moist air, and mild, steady temperature.

An area of higher ground in the middle part of the island supports an expanse of seacoast bluestem. This handsome waist-high bunch-grass is spectacular in October and November, with crisp brown foliage topped by many short stalks of awned grains. When these sparkling tufts of hairs are illuminated by the low rays of the rising or setting sun, a stand of seacoast bluestem presents a truly moving scene.

In the fall, when the widely scattered bunches of Gulf muhly ('mew-lee) begin to flower, everyone takes notice. Each slender, knee-high flower stalk holds a wide, lacy panicle of bright pink branchlets and florets. Lit by the morning sun, these glowing, dew-laden gauzes are as eye-catching as any conventional wildflower.

From a window of the shuttle, the interior grassland looks monotonous, but a short walk will reveal many kinds of plants punctuating the sward. Most ridges support the plants that have already been described from the dunes: American snoutbean, southern dewberry, hoary milkpea, beach ground-cherry, and tall stands of wild buckwheat and silverleaf sunflower. Two other twining species may be noticed. The thin stems of butterfly pea, with its three-parted leaves, twines on whatever support it can find; its ⅞-inch violet flowers seem to belong to the supporting plant. The showy flowers open in the morning and fade by mid-afternoon. They are, as on so many legumes, papilionaceous (pap-pilly-o-'nay-she-us), Latin for butterfly-like. The five petals are unequal; there is a large spoon-shaped banner, two smaller wings, and a central keel folded over the stamens. Most legumes hold their banner upright, but the upside down butterfly pea spreads its banner downward. The closely related wild bean twines low through the grasses and its ½-inch creamy pink flowers are less noticeable. They are also papilionaceous, but rightside up, and the keel is curved into a distinctive sickle shape. Both of these vines produce bean pods characteristic of their family.

Any break in the grass may be crisscrossed with the tough stems of sensitive briar, its stems, leaves, and even its pods covered with tiny recurved prickles. If there is a spark of childhood curiosity left, you should need no urging to touch this touch-me-not plant and watch it close its leaflets. Fragrant, fuzzy puffballs are held straight up on the prickly stems. A close look reveals that the fuzz is not petals but a mass of pink stamens, each tipped with a bright yellow anther sac. Yellow puff is a similar, smaller vine that has yellow puffballs; its sensitive leaves close voluntarily at night.

Where the sand has been disturbed by wind or humans or where the effect of overgrazing has yet to heal, the grass cover is dotted with rank patches. Dense, upright stands of dark green yankeeweed bear wands of tiny white daisies in the fall. Closely packed broomweed may cover extensive areas, shutting out most other species. Widespreading branchlets at the top of a stout stem produce green domes that sparkle with zillions of tiny yellow daisies in the fall. Mourning doves and bobwhite quail avidly peck up the oil-packed seeds of the several annual species of goatweed, all with downy, silvery gray leaves, inconspicuous flowers, and globular, three-lobed fruits. Western ragweed has stalkless, lobed leaves and compressed terminal panicles of nondescript greenish flowers, the male blossoms above and the female below. All of these plants are generally considered obnoxious; that is, cattle don't eat them, but they attract insect pollinators and produce seeds eaten by birds, rodents, and ants, so they have their place in island ecology.

In spring, the huge, spiny winter rosettes of bull thistles push their robust stalks up through the grasses. When these hollow, prickly columns are thigh-high, they produce congested flower heads that look like an old-fashioned shaving brush with cream or lavender bristles. Each heavy blossom bustles with a host of pollinating butterflies and beetles, along with their retinue of predatory bugs and ambushing spiders. Later the brushes get ragged and bleach to dirty white as the coastal breeze begins to pick away flotillas of their seed parachutes.

The stem, leaf veins, and even the flower buds of the white prickly poppy are covered with green prickles, and the six broad, white pet-

Bull thistle

als flare to a blossom 3¼ inches across. A wound to a leaf will bleed sulphur yellow latex. The smooth foliage of milkweed bleeds white latex. These knee-high stems with large leaves arranged opposite each other produce groups of stalked flowers of five greenish white petals with folded back tips. The boat-shaped, 3-inch-long fruits ripen and split to release flat seeds that are whisked off on parachutes of fine white hairs. Milkweeds are favorites of the monarch butterflies that migrate along the island in spring and fall.

Spotted horsemint has all the traits of the mint family: four-angled stems, opposite leaves, and strong scent. These common summertime plants have several tiers at the top of the stem; each tier is a ring of eight cream-colored bracts enclosing several yellow-green, two-lipped flowers; the upper lip is finely speckled with maroon.

They are so common on the mainland, it is surprising to find only a few seacoast goldenrods around the air base on Matagorda Island. Perhaps the plants require something that was brought in with the fill for the runways. Their showy yellow, chest-high wands of small daisy flowers make the plants easily recognizable when they bloom in the fall.

The commonest of several species of primroses on the barrier flat is the shin-high, somewhat bushy, yellow primrose. Each plant has several 1½-inch clear yellow flowers with four petals, eight stamens, and a long-stalked, globular stigma. This species is also common on shell ridges. The herbaceous, prostrate cut-leaf primrose has similar but smaller flowers with soft yellow petals and an X-shaped stigma, and it prefers sandy openings in the grassland. The pink evening primrose, with its four rounded rose pink petals forming a showy 2¼-inch saucer is one of the best-known spring wildflowers across the eastern half of Texas. On Matagorda it is restricted to roadsides and substrate with considerable organic content.

The most common spring and summer daisy along roads and scattered across the barrier flat is plains coreopsis, a many-branched annual herb. Each of the numerous flower heads, about 1¼ inches wide, has a central brown disk surrounded by five to seven chrome yellow petals with red-brown bases.

Plains wild indigo grows from a single stalk that branches into a knee-high mound. In March these scattered perennials produce lovely drooping sprays of creamy yellow ¾-inch papilionaceous flowers. Late in summer the black and woody dead stalks snap off at ground level, and, with their inflated pods still attached, roll and bounce downwind, scattering seeds as they go. The large rootstock will yield a weak blue dye, but this is not the source of the original blue-jeans color.

Although it mostly goes unnoticed because it nestles down among the grasses, plains prickly pear is rather common on the island. The clumps of small (2-inch- to 4-inch-long) pads are either prostrate or attain ankle-height; most of the gray spines emerge from the pads at an angle so their tips point down. The yellow flowers with a red blush at the base are followed by reddish, pear-shaped tunas growing conveniently at box turtle level.

Spanish dagger is more at home on the shell ridges, but isolated individuals stand out in the nearly treeless grassland. Well-grown plants may reach 12 to 15 feet, with a stout trunk and one or two stocky branches topped with dense 2-foot to 4-foot globes of radiating leaves. Beware of these stiff spine-tipped daggers; it is amazingly easy to run afoul of the tips, especially at eye level. In February Spanish daggers send up heavy candelabra of waxy white flowers. If pollinated by their special moths, they develop into fleshy pods that eventually turn black and woody. Mockingbirds and loggerhead shrikes use the plants for perches and nesting sites, and the shrikes skewer grasshoppers and an occasional horned lizard on the sharp daggers. Raptors use the tall plants as lookout perches.

The commonest shrub on Matagorda is the groundsel. These much-branched plants seldom grow over 6 feet tall, but they readily interrupt the gaze across the boundless interior grassland. The narrow, 1-inch to 2-inch, olive green leaves have a few low teeth near the tip and the flexible gray-brown stems are striped with pale, low ridges. This is one of the few woody members of the daisy family, and in the fall female plants turn satiny white with thousands of tufts of fine bristles ready for the coastal breeze to carry them off with their loads of tiny seeds. Groundsels can rapidly invade grassland if the native sod is disturbed, as by overstocking, and some areas in the northern half of the island reflect such abuse. Here, deliberate burning (which grasses withstand much better than woody plants) may be necessary to restore the original vegetation.

Southward, from the lighthouse to about halfway down the island, the central portion of the barrier flat is studded with dark mounds of Macartney rose. The stems and leathery, five-part, 3-inch-long leaves are covered with wicked recurved thorns, and the white flowers are typical of wild roses, 2 inches to 3 inches wide with five petals and numerous yellow stamens. The globular fruits (hips), about 1 inch in diameter, are briefly orange and wooly, but soon turn black and woody.

Before the days of barbed wire, this woody, sprawling briar was imported from China to serve as a living fence and later was planted for windbreak and erosion control. It soon escaped to become a problem in the coastal country. Macartney rose was brought to Matagorda Island by the air force to serve as shelter for bobwhite quail, a function it did quite well. Notice that the largest mounds are regularly spaced along the long axis of the island. Although it seems benign, Macartney rose is notorious for its ability to spread and its resistance to eradication. Mounds grow in diameter by rooting at the tips of the drooping branches, and branchlets snagged in the pelts or hooves of cattle, deer, or feral hogs spread it widely. Fortunately, the sandy environment has inhibited, though not entirely prevented, its spread from the original plantings; but the rose bears watching.

Despite its generally open aspect, some trees do grow on Matagorda Island. Historical records mention only live oaks, suggesting that they were the only trees to successfully colonize any of the Texas barrier islands. Spanish soldiers cut down the one motte of oaks that they found on Matagorda so as not to provide cover for hostile force; live oaks have not regrown, but about fifteen other species are now found, mostly on the barrier flat and the shell ridges or in areas of former human occupation.

About half a dozen of these trees are members of the native mainland flora; it is not clear whether any of these were here originally or established themselves, because humans and their livestock have disturbed the natural insular communities. Several other species were brought to the island inadvertently, in cattle droppings, cattle feed, or fill material. The rest were purposely introduced as ornamentals or as shelter for game animals.

Three trees have gotten into the barrier flat community by essentially natural means. Honey mesquite (muh-'skeet) is a distinctive

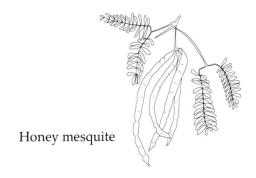

Honey mesquite

tree. Its stout, often contorted trunk and several strong branches are covered with a deeply fissured red-brown bark. The lacy foliage of drooping two-part leaves, each with numerous leaflets about 2 inches long and ¼ of an inch wide, is interspersed with sparse gray thorns, especially on the young growth. Pendant cylinders of small creamy flowers in the springtime are followed by summertime clusters of tan beans about 10 inches long.

Well-grown, robust specimens of mesquite grow on the bay-side shell ridges, and some are scattered down the bay-side margin of the island's midsection, especially in the southern half. On a protected upland on the far south end, where there are a lot of dark delta deposits, they are abundant enough to form a mesquite/bluestem savannah. Others occur between the air base and the J-Hook, where ranching operations were concentrated. Cattle are known to disperse the seeds and to enhance the growth of seedlings, but some mesquites must have reached Matagorda by their own devices. Mesquite has been extolled or damned, depending on the point of view, but since it is apparently incapable of spreading into the climax grassland, on Matagorda it may be regarded as an attribute, providing numerous benefits to wildlife.

Huisache ('we-satch), found sparingly along the main north-south road and between the air base and the J-Hook, seldom grows above head-high on the island. This is another woody legume; its dark green compound leaves have many tiny leaflets scarcely ⅒ of an inch long. The dark bark is covered with shallow fissures and the stems bear numerous pairs of straight white spines about 1 inch long. As early as February, the fragrant, sulphur yellow puffballs appear, and give way to 2-inch, black woody pods containing flat gray beans. Huisache needs more soil moisture than mesquite and is much less tolerant of salt; those on the island are living on the edge.

The third native, Mexican persimmon, is practically confined to the shell ridges, with a few found among the mesquites on the loamy upland south of Shell Reef Bayou. This stout little tree has thin, smooth, silver gray bark that periodically peels off in curls, and leathery, oblong, olive green leaves. The flowers appear briefly in the spring, and on female trees the little white bells with curled back edges produce 1-inch spherical fruits with a downy skin and jet black pulp. Persimmons are relished by every mammal and most birds on the island. Appropriately for a member of the ebony family, the wood is dense and hard.

Saltcedar probably managed to get from the mainland on its own, but was also purposely brought in for windbreaks and wildlife shelter. It is scattered across the interior, especially where water stands; but it is, as the name implies, well adapted to a saline environment, and some trees grow with their roots in bay water. Saltcedars can attain a height of 20 feet or so, and they usually grow in shrubby thickets that sway and hiss in the wind. The smooth brown bark is speckled with raised white dots; the evergreen foliage is composed of stringy, blue-green twigs covered with tiny, overlapping, scale-like leaves; delicate sprays of small pink flowers appear in the summer. A dense grove of saltcedars borders the north edge of the clearing at the lighthouse.

From the lighthouse road you can see occasional head-high Chinese tallow saplings rising out of the grassland, escapees from an experimental plot maintained nearby when the air base was active. In the fall their leaves brighten to yellow or rich red-purple before falling. Several rows of spindly Russian olives, a solitary cherry laurel, and a row of bamboo still survive at the plot. Around the air base and the Wynne lodge a few tall Washington palms linger, lonely survivors of winter freezes that gradually decimated the original plantings. The impressive wild date palm that greets visitors at the boat dock, more cold-hardy than the Washington palms, is readily distinguished from them by its long, fern-like leaves.

Along the north side of the beach road, just past the runway, is a short row of retamas (rah-'tah-mah). These spare little trees are recognized by their smooth green bark. Each long, drooping leaf has a strap-like midrib with a row of tiny leaflets along each side, and a pair of short spines at the base. Frequently the leaflets fall before the ribs, giving the retama a stringy look. These trees were probably brought in with fill material when the air base was established.

If you walk about around the Army Hole campground, you may find the row of stunted cottonwoods planted nearby. One other cottonwood tree is struggling in the barrier flat halfway down the island. The only live oaks on the island are the few planted near the Wynne lodge, and these are succumbing to salt spray. An attempt to establish several mottes of live oaks to recreate the historical stands is under consideration.

So far we have considered plants growing on the drier ridges and hillocks of the barrier flat. In the wetter swales are found most of the plants described from the interdune swale of the sand dunes community. The dominant marshhay cordgrass, intermixed with various rushes and sedges, is joined by bushy bluestem. This handsome perennial bunchgrass has abundant basal leaf blades and stiffly erect culms supporting broomlike flower heads. By the time of the first northers, the seeds are mature and the wind picks apart the shaggy brownish white floc.

The sprawling stems of rough buttonweed have opposite leaves about 1 inch long with a cluster of fine bristles at the base. The small, pale lavender flowers sit among these bristles. Each of the paired fruits is topped with four tiny ear-like projections. Marsh fleabane is a waist-high, much branched annual with lance-shaped leaves and terminal, flattish clusters of small rose-purple flowers. The crushed foliage is aromatic.

By far the most common of three species of senna beans is coffee bean. In early summer, fast-growing shoots of these semi-woody legumes appear in moist places. By midsummer they have grown into lacy green forests, 8 feet to 10 feet tall, with widely spaced, foot-long, compound leaves each bearing seventy or more thin leaflets. By late summer the pendulous clusters of yellow papilionaceous flowers have given rise to stringy pods, nearly 10 inches long but only a scant ¼ inch wide. By the time the mature pods split and scatter the seeds, the plants have died, leaving spare brown thickets.

The border between the barrier flat and tidal flat communities, where the dark clay soil is slightly saline, is the domain of Gulf Coast cordgrass. This zone, from a few feet to nearly 100 yards wide, is covered with coarse knee-high mounds to the exclusion of all other vegetation. Leaves grow straight up from the center of the clump, and as they get longer they are pushed outward and over by new growth, so the outside leaves, maybe 2 feet long, arch over and their tips touch the ground. The cylindrical leaves are flexible, but strong, with tips stiff and sharp enough to prick a finger or pierce trousers legs; a colloquial name is needle grass. Seedheads stand chest-high on stiff stalks, each narrow, lance-shaped head containing fifty or more tightly appressed branchlets of tiny grains. An expanse of dark green mounds of Gulf Coast cordgrass, interlaced with black shadows and deep recesses, presents a brooding, somewhat intimidating aspect.

Tidal Flat Community Plants

The most extensive tidal flats on Matagorda Island cover the old tidal deltas south of Pringle Lake and inland of Ayers Point. Most of Bayucos Island and the edges of the many islets and sloughs from the northern tip of Matagorda around the head of Espíritu Santo Bay are also tidal flat. You can see good examples of this community at the Army Hole and along the bay side directly behind the Visitors' Center.

Although the highly productive tidal flat appears benevolent, a combination of rigors places extraordinary demands on rooted vegetation. The main problem is salt. When the water driven up on the shore by tides or winds evaporates or drains back into the bay, it leaves behind some or all of its salt to accumulate in the mucky clay substrate. For most plants, salt is an outright metabolic poison; for all it presents problems with water balance. In salty soil, plant roots not only have difficulty pulling fresh water in, they must struggle to keep their precious body water from being drawn out. If that happens, vital membranes shrivel, proteins coagulate, tissues wilt, and the plant dies. The only plants that can survive in this watery desert are *halophytes* ('hal-o-fites)—those that have special devices to combat salt-imposed dehydration.

Salt is only part of the problem. The heavy substrate, with its small particles of silt and clay, is already close-packed. When it gets wet, water fills all of the spaces, leaving no air for the plant roots. This is aggravated by a teeming population of microbes that decompose the organic detritus and consume the scant remaining oxygen, leaving a black and malodorous anaerobic zone. Root systems in this layer, closed off from the ready source of oxygen in the air, are left gasping.

Then there is the periodic flooding and baking as tide, wind, and sun conspire to drag the habitat from one extreme to another. During hot weather, water trapped in depressions evaporates rapidly, sending salinities skyrocketing to several times that of ordinary seawater and overwhelming even the crustiest of halophytes. On the other hand, prolonged high tides can drown the vegetation. Germination of seeds and growth of tender seedlings has to be perfectly timed to succeed.

The flats are not exempt from storm overwash from the Gulf, but they are more commonly devastated by the pounding of waves driven by northers, roiling the shallows and carving great chunks out of the banks. All in all, the flats present a risky place to set down roots.

Because of variations in the soil's salt content, the community displays a series of zones parallel to the shoreline, each band populated by plants with a different set of tolerances. This is the same feature exhibited by the beach and sand dunes communities in response to a different constellation of environmental stresses. Where the island slopes gently to the bay, these plant zones may be hundreds of yards wide; where it breaks more abruptly, the bands are correspondingly contracted.

Relatively few species have the adaptations to grow in the tidal flats, but those that can, do so vigorously; biomass is high, but diversity is low.

The only emergent plant along the margin of the island, smooth cordgrass, forms a narrow vanguard. The thick stems stand about waist-high with typical grass blades ½ inch wide. On a low tide most plants will be completely exposed; on a high tide all will be partly submerged. The plant needs this oscillation in water level, so the band of its growth is usually only a few yards wide. This grass lines the bay side at the Army Hole campground and the Visitors' Center.

The adaptive genius by which smooth cordgrass is so well adjusted to its vulnerable life-style is hidden from direct observation. A fairly high concentration of salt in the tissues that lessens the pull of water out, and special root membranes that allow water but not salt to enter, enable cordgrass to extract fresh water from the surrounding salt water. If salt does build up in the tissues, there are glands that remove it and deposit the crystals on the leaves, where they are washed away by the next high tide. Diffusion of oxygen down miniscule tubes running from microscopic pores on the leaves aerates the roots. When the grass is submerged it holds its breath by pinching the breathing pores closed.

Finally, smooth cordgrass secures its position in the oozy substrate with a tenacious mass of perennial rhizomes. Even if severe conditions wipe out the visible plants, fresh shoots soon emerge and reclaim the zone. Seeds are important for starting growth on newly exposed flats, but established colonies are increased and maintained by growth of the rhizomes. Both roots and shoots serve as a buffer, dissipating the destructive energy of wind and water before they strike the shoreline. The plants work into the marine food chains and they provide critical shelter for many freshly hatched and juvenile fish and invertebrates, as well as a hunting ground for everything from clapper rails to purple marsh crabs. A good stand of smooth cordgrass promotes a healthy tidal flat community.

Just above the reach of routine high tide the low marsh begins. On a shoreline with a gradual slope, this is the broadest zone in the tidal flat community. It is always one of the most rigorous. Exceptionally high tides inundate it but do not come round frequently enough to rinse salts back into the bay, and there is seldom enough rainwater runoff to leach salts away. The continued accumulation produces a hypersaline substrate that only confirmed halophytes can tolerate.

Yet, some plants do thrive even here. Low marsh is dominated by squat succulents with such high internal salt concentration that they are capable of osmotically wrenching fresh water from their extremely salty environment. In fact, they have become so adjusted to the severity of their habitat that their metabolism is thrown out of kilter by more amenable conditions; they are obligate halophytes—both plants and seeds require a saline substrate.

The pale brown stems of maritime saltwort trail across the ground or arch up to shin height, growing in such dense tangles that their tough runners make boggy walking in the tidal flats all the more strenuous. The 1-inch-long, yellow-green leaves are so swollen with osmotic water they resemble pairs of jelly beans, stuck opposite each other along the stems. The flowers are inconspicuous, but the lumpy, ⅜-inch yellow fruits dangle from short stalks among the leaves. Perennial glasswort is a shin-high shrublet with a small, woody base and many erect branches scarcely 1/16 of an inch thick growing in dull green, mat-like patches. The fleshy, segmented stems appear leafless because the leaves are reduced to minute scales; less surface area means less water loss by evaporation. Both tiny flower and tiny fruit are recessed into the stem; the only sign of flowering is a yellow dust of pollen in the spring. Perennial glasswort, too, is pumped up with salt water; pop a stem between your teeth and taste its salty sap. The mats make a delicious, juicy crunch underfoot.

In the fall, bright expanses of these dominants, yellow maritime saltwort and reddish brown perennial glasswort, lend Matagorda some seasonal color.

Most low marsh is engraved with a dendritic pattern of salt barrens, depressions that retain such an accumulation of minerals that no rooted plants can grow. Tough annual glasswort makes its stand on the edges of these dead spots. The plants resemble perennial glasswort, but are a lighter green and grow as isolated herbs with segmented, ¼-inch-wide green stalks bearing several stocky upright branches noticeably thickened toward their tips. Runty but deter-

Maritime saltwort

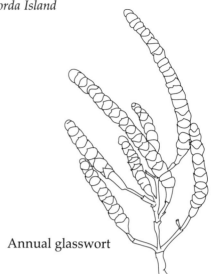

Annual glasswort

mined little plants, encrusted with a heavy rime of salt, can be found struggling on the edge of existence in the salt barrens. All of these plants die in the fall, and by springtime, forests of optimistic green seedlings attempt to recolonize the hostile habitat.

Three other plants are associated with low marsh. Annual seep-weed is an unassuming, shin-high member of the same tough family as the glassworts. Its fleshy 1-inch leaves, flat and narrow, are staggered up the stems. Small green globules at the bases of upper leaves enclose flowers and fruits. Scattered thinly through the low marsh, annual seepweed quietly lives, sets seed, and dies each year; virtually nothing is known of its ecology. In a zone with few showy flowers, even the plain daisies of saline aster catch the eye. Each is about ¾ of an inch across, with a yellow center and lavender-white petals. The plant itself, with its long-tapered, fleshy leaves, slightly overtops the surrounding vegetation.

Black mangrove is a seaside plant of the tropics living on the northern edge of its range in the Coastal Bend of Texas. In favorable years dense stands grow on the islets inside Pass Cavallo, where there is enough salinity and water exchange to meet their needs. Severe winters kill back the exposed growth, and continual regrowth from rootstocks or germination from seeds dooms these potential trees to a perpetually shrubby state. The fruits were described in the beach community section of this chapter; opposing pairs of leaves are shiny green above and gray-green below and often flecked with excreted salt crystals. To avoid suffocation in their mucky substrate, mangrove roots send up numerous, *pneumatophores* (new-'mat-to-fores)—erect, pencil-thin extensions that allow infusion of oxygen directly from the air. Look beneath a mangrove shrub for its attendant forest of gray, woody "soda straws."

High marsh begins where low marsh tapers off. Depending on how abruptly the ground breaks, the boundary between these two bands of vegetation may be gradual or sharp, straight or interdigitated; and the high-marsh zone may be a few yards or several hundred yards wide. The principal environmental change is less frequent inundation by high tides and, consequently, a lower salt accumulation in the substrate. Nonetheless, the high marsh is still a rigorous saline habitat that supports relatively few species of halophytic plants. One shrub and two grasses dominate this zone.

Acres of high marsh on the bay side of Matagorda Island are covered by bushy sea oxeye, a knee-high, sparingly branched shrub with pale gray stems and thickish, gray-green, spatulate leaves arranged opposite each other. A few of the dull yellow daisies at the tips of the branches can usually be found any time of the year, and the spiny brown seedheads cling to the stems for months. Bushy sea oxeye grows in dense stands that effectively sap the energy of waves driven high against the shore by winter storms. Seaside sparrows like to use the plants for shelter.

Shin-high, dark green meadows and fringes of saltgrass are good indicators of high marsh. These perennial plants have a distinctive herringbone pattern of upturned, stiffish, keenly tapering blades. Like the leaves of other halophytes, they usually glisten with excreted salt. The thick mats of rhizomes from which the numerous shoots emerge inhibit shoreline erosion. Saltgrass is grazed by white-tailed deer and provides vital winter forage for geese and ducks—foliage, seedheads, rootstocks, and all. Slight elevations in the high marsh, above all but the highest tides and storm waves, are covered with furry pelts of shore grass, its short, needle-like leaf blades scarcely ½ inch long. Although it is a common soil binder, little is known about its contribution to food chains on the island.

Other less-abundant plants of the high marsh include seashore dropseed, which resembles a delicate version of saltgrass. They can be told apart by their seedheads: seashore dropseed has a ¼-inch-wide, tapering cylindrical panicle of tiny seeds that readily come free when the panicle is rolled between the fingers. Saltgrass does not easily let go of the seeds on its flatter, ½-inch-wide panicle.

Three high-marsh plants have noteworthy flowers. The stalks of sea lavender rise 1 foot to 2 feet from a rosette of broad, leathery leaves, splotched and marked with crimson. The top half of the stalk has many horizontal branches lined on the top edges with numerous papery cups. In the late summer and fall a ¼-inch lavender-blue

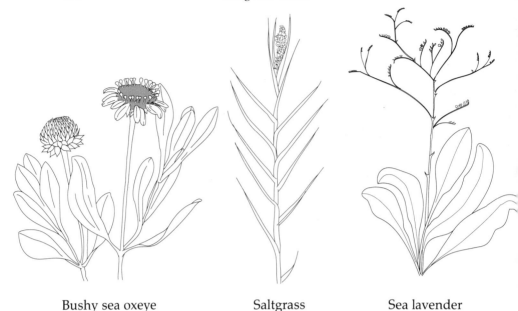

Bushy sea oxeye   Saltgrass   Sea lavender

flower fills each cup. The color of the flower is so intense and the supporting stalks so thin, the spray seems to hover like a will-o'-the-wisp above the somber tidal flat.

Aside from its 1¼-inch yellow flowers, camphor daisy can be recognized by spine-tipped teeth on the leaf margins and by the camphor odor and sticky feel of its crushed foliage. One of the few tidal flat plants that can grow anywhere else, it is occasionally found on the lee side of sand dunes. The pale, woody branches of Carolina wolfberry that droop and trail over the flat are armed with keen thorns. The ½-inch blue-lavender flowers have four petals and protruding anthers; the ovoid crimson berries, which reveal its kinship to the pepper family, are favored food for many birds, including whooping cranes, and for coyotes and raccoons as well.

The boundary between the tidal flat community and the barrier flat community is the low ridge of sand and shell that marks the 5-foot contour along the bay side of Matagorda Island. The changeover is dictated by the shift from a tight, clay-like substrate to a better-drained, sandy-shelly substrate, less subject to tidal overwash and therefore less salty. Scrubby mesquite, patches of groundsel, and low clumps of saltcedar grow along this interface. Marsh elder, a shrub resembling groundsel but with opposite rather than staggered leaves, also grows here. Mounds of Gulf Coast cordgrass may grow immediately inland from these woody plants, but with increasing elevation and protection a dense sward of marshhay cordgrass signals the beginning of the broad barrier flat community.

Shell Ridge Community Plants

Narrow ridges of storm-deposited oystershell rimming exposed sections of the bay-side margin create a unique shoreline habitat. Their elevation, usually no more than 3 feet, is modest but critical, providing sanctuary from all but the most violent storm overwash. The coarse shelly substrate drains rapidly, making for a very dry root zone, but one that does not retain a killing buildup of salt. To grow here, a plant must be a moderate halophyte and an accomplished xerophyte. Carbonates leached from degrading shells mix with rich deposits thrown up from the bay to form shallow pockets of fertile loam in depressions along the ridges. Species with taproots can probe down through the shell to the underlying Pleistocene platform of muddy clay and gain secure anchor and additional nutrients.

Sun-scorched in the summer and norther-blasted in the winter, the exposed shell ridge habitat favors tough, woody vegetation that can withstand the seasonal rigors. But fragile annuals that can take rapid advantage of brief favorable periods and endure the rest of the time as dormant seeds live here too.

On Ayers Point there is a short series of higher ridges, some up to 10 feet. The extra elevation and mutual protection of these shell mounds has allowed the development of an exceptionally thick woody cover complete with an accumulation of organic litter on the ground, an understory of herbs, a tangle of vines, and a wind-pruned profile. These nearly impenetrable brushy copses make up the chaparral, an association that is common on the mainland but rare on a barrier island. This, the most restricted of the communities on Matagorda Island, is the most botanically diverse, but because it is inaccessible to visitors, only the dominant species will be described in detail; others are mentioned to provide a general impression.

A bristly hedge of thorny branches shielding a dark interior gives the chaparral a forbidding aspect. Of the woody plants that make up the bulk of this thicket, the largest and most common are mesquites with heavy, gnarled trunks and twisted, sprawling branches. Their reliable crop of abundant beans is important to the animals that live here—coyotes and mice, mourning doves and bobwhite quail. Dark green wild lime is a shrub-tree with oily, citrus-scented leaves and catclaw thorns. The contorted branches of brasil have twigs tipped with stout, straight thorns and small, sweet, pulpy black fruits that are harvested by raccoons and passerine birds. All this prickly shrub-

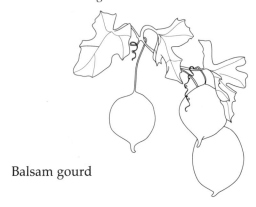

Balsam gourd

bery is laced together by the supple branches of elbowbush and punctuated with the bayonets of Spanish dagger and clumps of Texas
prickly pear. The chaparral is not the sort of place to enjoy an idle
ramble.

Other plants scattered through the community include plains
prickly pear and tasajillo (tah-sah-'hee-yo), a relation of the prickly
pear, but with cylindrical, pencil-thin branches and wicked yellow
thorns. Contributing to the diversity of the chaparral are common
lantana, with clusters of orange and yellow flowers; lotebush, with
strong thorns and blue-black fruits; aromatic Texas torchwood, living
on the northern edge of its range; spiny hackberry, with distinctive
clear orange spherical fruits; coralbean, with showy red flowers that
attract migrating hummingbirds in the spring; Mexican persimmon;
and huisache.

The protection and support of woody branches makes a haven for
vines to scramble and twine up out of the dim understory to the sunlit
canopy. One of the commonest is Texas nightshade, with thin, triangular leaves, ½-inch white flowers, and abundant, spherical red
fruits, like tiny tomatoes. Snapdragon vine has wider triangular
leaves and a summer and fall profusion of 1-inch violet flowers with
a yellow blush at the entrance to the white throat. Although it has
yellow flowers and thick, palmate leaves, balsam gourd is usually not
noticed until fall, when its showy, 1-inch, scarlet gourds are strung
across the canopy. Ivy treebine, the lone representative of the grape
family, has fleshy, three-part leaves and clusters of black, ⅜-inch
fruits; birds eat these nearly pulpless grapes, but they are hardly pal-
atable for people. The diminutive mauve dusters of pink eupatorium
are especially attractive to skippers and swallowtail butterflies. The
large, ornate blossoms of passion flower attract Gulf fritillary butterflies and the red fruits are nibbled by harvest mice, pecked clean
by mockingbirds, or gobbled up whole by coyotes. Add to these

the brambles of southern dewberry, the occasional cascades of tiny winged fruits of the high-climbing madeira (mah-'der-ah) vine, and the parasitic orange twirls of dodder. Finally, although pigeonberry is a shade-loving herb, its slender branches clamber up, vine-like, through the lower strata of the brush. At the tip of each stem is a wand of ¼-inch pink-white flowers topped by several tiny globular red fruits with juice that will stain your fingers if you crush them.

Fresh-water Community Plants

Most of the characteristic plants of this community are shared with the interdune and swale habitats and will not be repeated here. There are only two common submerged plants in the pools and scrapes on Matagorda Island, both relished by winter waterfowl. Widgeon grass forms a tangled mat of thin stems and thread-like leaves just under the surface of the water. This plant is really more at home in the shallow bays and its presence indicates that the water is not strictly fresh. Stonewort is a green alga, but its long, branched stems with rings of thin leaf-like structures at intervals make it look like a higher plant. Stonewort is so-named because of its brittle texture, imparted by a high lime content; it is also called muskgrass for its garlic-like odor.

An ample, fibrous root system anchors burhead in the shallow muddy ooze of depressions and artificial scrapes. It grows either as an emergent or, if the water drops, as a bankside species. Half a dozen slender, knee-high leaf stalks rise from the root mass, each with a spade-shaped blade about 8 inches long. In the summer a flowering stalk grows up, topping the leaves before it branches into a spare panicle of ½-inch, three-petaled white flowers and spherical clusters of bristly, bur-like fruitheads.

Nonflowering Plants

Most fungi demand more moisture than the island affords, but a few species manage by putting on a spurt of growth after rains. Following spring and summer showers, the heavy grass cover of the barrier flat community stays wet enough to succor a respectable show of meadow mushrooms, whose bright pink gills soon age to a deep chocolate brown. Here and there clusters of earthstars crop up, along with occasional puffballs, some directly on the ground and others on thin shoetop-level stalks. Just south of the air base, where cattle have recently been pastured, inkycap mushrooms cluster on cowpies and common stinkhorns pop up from moist depressions. In a really wet year many more species of fungi will surely be recorded on the island.

Because of the general lack of hard substrate, lichens are rare on Matagorda, but the mineral-gray shield lichens do occur on the branches of mesquites and on the trunks of saltcedars.

True mosses usually occur beside streams or in shaded woods; Matagorda Island is no place to expect such a fragile plant. Yet, one species of ground moss spreads its delicate green mat in shaded nooks beneath the dense woody growth in the chaparral clumps on Ayers Point.

Fern habitat is much like that for true moss. To date, no ferns have been found on Matagorda, but the adaptable species called water clo-ver may be discovered on dark soil around the edges of some of the more permanent fresh-water ponds, and mosquito fern may occur in flooded swales.

CHAPTER 6

Mammals

On all of Matagorda there are only nine resident native mammals, which well illustrates the sieve effect that governs immigration of terrestrial animals to islands. This is about a quarter the number of mammals on the Aransas National Wildlife Refuge and only half as many as on Padre Island. And there is no reason to believe that this is due to human interference; it is merely the current result of natural forces.

What are these forces? There has been plenty of time—several thousand years—for potential immigrants to hazard a crossing. Mobile mammals are adept at dispersal and have considerable incentive to roam; for instance, juveniles and bachelor males wander widely in search of suitable terrain and mates. The distance from the mainland is less than 5 miles, and oystershell islets are convenient stepping stones, especially with reefs exposed by low tides. Though development has reduced populations of mainland mammals along most of the coastal prairie, locally, the Aransas National Wildlife Refuge provides a stable reservoir of potential immigrants. So why aren't there more mammals on Matagorda Island?

The colonization of a barrier island by mammals involves the same two steps that other dispersing creatures face: getting there and then surviving there. Apparently getting there is not the main problem for mammals; even barrier peninsulas—strips of land geologically and ecologically like barrier islands, but attached to the mainland (like Matagorda Peninsula, across Pass Cavallo from Matagorda Island)— have meager mammalian faunas despite their ready accessibility. Survival is the problem.

The physical habitat is austere: eternal wind, sliding sand, searing sun, tainted drinking water (and often not enough of that), and occasional total overwash by the sea. Besides, there aren't many places to live—the soil is too sandy for tunnels, and there are no trees, no moldering logs, no rocky ledges, no creek banks. All this limits potential ways of life at the outset. A fox squirrel that managed to make it to the bay-side tidal flats, for instance, might as well be on Mars.

Table 2. *Comparison of resident native mammals on Matagorda and Padre islands and the Aransas National Wildlife Refuge*

	Number of Species		
	ANWR	Matagorda	Padre
MARSUPIALS			
Opossum	1	0	1
INSECTIVORES			
Shrews	2	0	0*
Moles	1	0	1
Bats	4	0	2[§]
ARMADILLOS	1	0*	0
RABBITS & HARES	3	2	2
RODENTS			
Squirrels	1	0	2
Gophers	1	0	1
Rats & mice	7	3	6
CARNIVORES			
Weasels	5	1	2
Raccoons	2	1	1
Dogs	2	1	1
Cats	3	0*	0*
CLOVEN-HOOVED			
Deer	1	1	0*
Javelina	1	0	0*
TOTAL	35	9	19

*Recorded, but probably no viable population.
[§]Some may be migrant only.
Data are from the files of the USFWS, TPWD, and the National Park Service (NPS).

There are more subtle problems. Immigrants must be adaptable. With different and less diverse food chains, they may have to shift to unaccustomed diets and learn to capitalize on seasonal abundance and exploit windfalls from the sea. And while stocking their larders and filling their bellies, they must contrive to evade new predators and put up with new parasites. Finally, even if individuals make homes, find nourishment, and avoid catastrophe, it is useless unless they can locate mates and successfully rear their young.

These impediments to successful colonization are not unique to mammals, but mammals suffer a distinct handicap for the ironic reason that they are so highly evolved. In contrast to a cold-blooded lizard, a warm-blooded mouse represents a state-of-the-art biological machine. The mouse has more efficient circulation, more complex nerves, more diversified muscles, and more sophisticated organs of excretion, respiration, and digestion. The advantage is that the mouse is always ready to perform at peak efficiency; day or night, hot or cold, good times or bad, the mouse is ready to go in an instant. The disadvantage is that this high-tech "mouse-machine" must be continually fueled with lots of food and water. Even at rest the mouse-machine idles at a high metabolic rate and it must be held at a constant internal temperature; to warm up, it scampers about or shivers at the expense of hard-earned calories, and to cool off, it sweats, licks its fur, or urinates, all at the sacrifice of precious body water. The calories it takes to run the fidgety mouse for one summer day would run an impassive lizard for a summer month; the difference is even greater in the winter, when the mouse-machine speeds up and the lizard-machine slows down.

Because of their active life functions, mammals are very demanding of their environment; not only do they need relatively large amounts of food and water, they need them continually. Mammals cannot afford to be stoic; their high-strung bodies do not tolerate prolonged starvation or dehydration, and most cannot lapse into dormancy or take off on migration. Because of this ceaseless consumption of resources, mammals require a lot of elbow room: geographic space to succor their individual needs and social space to satisfy their territorial urges. It is little wonder that immigrant mammals have difficulty carving out niches in the stringent barrier island environment.

Demand for scarce resources fosters intense competition between animals with similar life-styles, another reason the mammalian fauna is not only impoverished but is ecologically spaced out. The gray fox has not become established on Matagorda; once the coyote had claimed the dog niche, there was simply no ecological room for another kind of dog. The white-tailed deer has taken possession of the large grazer niche, the jackrabbit occupies the moderate-sized herbivore niche, and the cotton rat dominates the small herbivore niche. Any late-arriving immigrant with similar niche requirements must not only adjust to the rigors of the island itself but face stiff opposition from the established residents. The combination poses a challenge that few new arrivals can overcome.

Once a species has successfully colonized an island, its numbers increase to the carrying capacity of its insular niche and the population stabilizes around some equilibrium—increasing in good years, decreasing in poor ones, crashing after catastrophes and then resurging. Just because there are few kinds of mammals on Matagorda, it does not follow that there are few individuals. Some, like the white-tailed deer and cotton rats, exist in dense populations, and other kinds are about as common per unit area as comparable populations on the mainland. None of the species of mammals on the island is endangered or threatened.

Resident Native Mammals

Each of the nine species with currently viable populations on Matagorda Island is a member of the native fauna of the adjacent mainland. All could have colonized the island without human help, but two are known to have been purposely introduced, and others may have been inadvertently brought in, thus supplementing ongoing natural colonization.

Rodents

Wherever there are terrestrial mammals, there are rodents. The typical rodent is small, adaptable, and ever-ready for explosive reproduction when conditions are favorable. Geared for harvesting and chewing vegetable matter, they occupy the critical primary consumer level in the community, converting green resources into tempting packets of animal protoplasm, and thus supporting one or more levels of secondary consumers (carnivores). This central role is especially important on Matagorda Island, where rodents have taken well to the extensive interior grassland, and year-round high populations make them fodder for most predators: mammals, birds, and snakes.

Of the three species of native rodents, the hispid cotton rat is the most important. Abundant and widely distributed, it is a staple in the diets of coyotes, badgers, western diamondback rattlesnakes, and all of the raptorial birds, and it is frequently eaten by other species of mammals, snakes, and birds. As their fortunes wax and wane, cotton rat numbers soar and crash, and the effect of these fluctuations ripples through the insular food web; a bad winter for cotton rats is automatically a bad winter for northern harriers, barn owls, coyotes, and badgers.

Medium-sized, plump rodents with short tails, small ears, and grizzled brown coats with coarse black guard hairs, cotton rats do look decidedly more ratty than mousey. Hispid refers to the stiff guard hairs; farmers call them cotton rats because they frequently see them along the weedy edges of their cotton fields.

Hispid cotton rat

This adaptable species occurs throughout Texas, preferring a dense, tall-grass habitat; the luxuriant barrier flat community is cotton rat heaven. They occur throughout the interior of the island and range across the secondary dunes and shell ridges and through the swales; at night, venturesome individuals even forage on the dunes. They avoid only the beach and the tidal flat.

A healthy cotton rat population is indicated by an extensive system of 2-inch wide trailways running beneath the canopy of grass blades. Here in the perpetual gloom cotton rats scurry both day and night, cutting grass, sedges, and sundry forbs and dragging them to special feeding platforms. Unlike many grassland species, cotton rats do not stock food caches, so they are forced into activity the year-round. In the spring and summer as much as a third of their diet is insects and arachnids; they are known to eat the eggs and young of meadowlarks, horned larks, and bobwhite quail, and will probably raid the nests of harvest mice and take a juvenile ghost crab if they get the chance.

Even among the fecund rodents, cotton rats are notably prolific. A female reaches sexual maturity at about two months and for the rest of her short life is continually either pregnant or nursing a litter. In her nest—a globe of shredded grass blades at the end of a burrow among grass roots, in the interior of a bluestem bunch, or tucked beneath surface debris—a female produces a five-pup litter about eight to ten times a year; pups wean at twenty-five days. It is easy to see how in a favorable "rat year" this is by far the most abundant mammal on the island. Numbers typically peak in the spring and again in the fall at a density of seventy-five per acre and drop in the wintertime to about five to fifteen per acre. Your best chance to see a cotton rat bounding across the roads is in the fall, when the vegetation is beginning to die back.

In contrast to the stodgy cotton rat, the fulvous harvest mouse is a charming and even a beautiful little beast. It is house-mouse sized with a long, thin tail, large papery ears, and a pointed face dominated by a twitching nose, a spray of delicate vibrissae, and bulbous black eyes. The smooth coat is a glowing golden-orange above and pale below. Because they are secretive and completely nocturnal, harvest mice are not likely to be seen, but if you look before the wind rises, you should find their dainty handprints among the ghost crab scribbles on the lee sides of the primary dunes.

Harvest mice like grass intermixed with forbs and shrubbery. On Matagorda, they live in the same communities as cotton rats, travel along cotton rat pathways, and eat the same seeds and fruits, tender greenery, insects, and terrestrial crustaceans. But because harvest mice are much smaller and tend to climb, most of their food is found out of the reach of the heavier-bodied cotton rats, so the two do not compete.

Harvest mice excavate burrows among the grass roots and construct cozy nests of shredded grass blades deep inside. They, too, build nests beneath surface debris, and you may uncover a mouse nest, and perhaps a startled occupant. In the summertime, harvest mice build nests a foot or so up in clumps of grass. In these airy penthouses—baseball-sized globes of neatly woven grass blades with a finger-sized entrance hole in one side—the adults rest by day and the females bear their litters of squirmy pink babies.

Harvest mice breed all year long, but the population peaks in spring and again in the fall. There are only about three young per litter, but with short gestation and weaning times, harvest mouse numbers doubtless zoom and crash on Matagorda just like those of the cotton rat. In addition to the same predators that stalk cotton rats, smaller carnivores are also attracted to harvest mice. Surely the massasauga rattler frequently ambushes them in their grassy jungle, and loggerhead shrikes must occasionally pick a wayward individual out of the grass culms.

As its name suggests, the marsh rice rat inhabits moist sites. Common in the swamps and marshes of the coastal plain, it finds flooded rice fields a near-optimum habitat. On Matagorda Island it is at home in the tidal flat and adjacent shell reef communities, and follows ditches and swales into the interior.

This medium-sized rodent with slender build and long, nearly naked tail looks even more ratty than the cotton rat. Its gray coat is flecked with black above and is white below; even the tail is bicolored.

Strictly nocturnal, rice rats are especially active on overcast and rainy nights, moving along surface pathways through the vegetation of the high marsh. When a high tide creeps in, these semiaquatic

Fulvous harvest mouse   Rice rat

rodents slosh along their accustomed trails and readily swim across tidal streams. When pursued, a rice rat is quick to dive beneath the water and swim away.

The main foods of marsh rice rats are greenery, buds, and seeds, but they also take a variety of animal food items: caterpillars, grass-hoppers, wolf spiders, salt-marsh snails, fiddler crabs, an occasional killifish, and even the eggs and nestlings of seaside sparrows and clapper rails. In their turn, rice rats are eaten by coyotes, raccoons, cottonmouth moccasins, massasaugas, night-herons, and especially by their archenemy, the barn owl.

Rice rats occasionally excavate shallow burrows in the high marsh, but they prefer to construct their globular nests of shredded vegeta-tion deep in piles of dead plant material at the bay-side strandline, where they take daytime shelter and bear their young. In the winter, half a dozen adults may share the same nest, with the mutual benefit of a pile of warm bodies.

Hares and Rabbits

One distinction between hares and rabbits is how they bear and rear their young. Mother hares casually scrape out a shallow saucer for their imminent brood of furred babies. The young, which are able to stagger about within hours of birth, soon quit the nest to follow mother and are weaned at one month. Rabbits, on the other hand, construct an elaborate fur-lined hollow for babies that are born blind and nearly naked, are totally dependent on their mother during the first days of life, and do not leave the nest until they are a week and

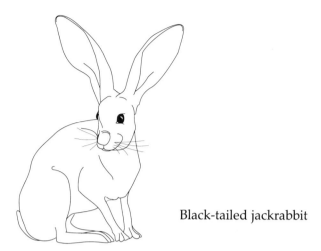

Black-tailed jackrabbit

a half old. Despite the fact that the only member of this group on Matagorda Island is clearly a hare, even biologists persistently call it the black-tailed jackrabbit, and anyone who called it jackhare would be open to ridicule.

This large, familiar hare has enormous black-tipped ears, huge hind feet, grizzled pelage, staring yellow eyes, and a gaunt body streamlined for leaping and bounding. Because jackrabbits rely on speed and erratic dodging to escape predators, they are at a disadvantage in the thick grassland that covers most of the island. This species was much more abundant when the interior was kept open by grazing. Today, jackrabbits thrive only along the roadways and around the air base and the Wynne lodge, and at night they forage into the primary dunes and onto the backbeach. The animals are seen frequently because they live around the public areas, but their small population could be wiped out by a major hurricane.

Jackrabbits prefer to pass a summer day dozing in a shallow scrape in the shade. They become active near sundown and feed throughout the early evening; then they lie up and forage again about daybreak. They are strict herbivores, munching most tender greenery and exploiting grass grains, especially those of sea oats, beach panic, and brome. They hunker in the vegetation to avoid hard northers, but they are active through the entire year.

The jackrabbit's most relentless predator on Matagorda Island is the same one that plagues it throughout its range—the coyote. It is the constant threat of ambush by coyotes that keeps the jackrabbits confined to the scarce open terrain. Western diamondback rattlers probably rank second, for they take the young and quarter-grown animals. Great horned owls can waylay an adult.

You can see evidence of jackrabbits' nocturnal visits to the dunes: loose piles of grass snippets or sea oat husks and tracks in the sand. And they scatter their small, flattened, brown fecal pellets among the dunes and leave yellow urine stains on the sand. You may even spook a resting one from a shady nook on the lee side of the primary dunes. But your best chance to see a jackrabbit is along a road, where they often hump awkwardly along ahead of a vehicle or a pedestrian (only if pressed do they stretch into synchronized high gear) until they finally dart to the side and crouch with ears down, waiting for the source of provocation to pass.

Oldtimers introduced the eastern cottontail rabbit onto Matagorda Island several times, "just to have them around the house," but the animals did not do well. They never spread, and remained rare even at the sites of release, the lightkeeper's house and a nearby ranch house.

The infrequent cottontails seen today around the air base could be immigrants that have rafted from the mainland, but they have never been seen anywhere else on the island, so it is more likely that they are remnants of the introduced population that has hung on and whose persistence hinges on the locally modified environment.

The grassy interior of Matagorda may appear to be ideal cottontail habitat, but they actually prefer open, brushy cover with abundant "edges" around which they can scamper when pursued by their numerous predators. The ranchers blamed the failure of cottontails on rattlesnakes and coyotes, which surely fed on them, as did badgers, hawks, and owls, but a healthy population can withstand severe predation. More likely the dense monoculture of grasses did not fill the cottontails' briar patch requirements, either for optimum dodge-and-run shelter or for diversity in the forbs and twigs that constitute their diet. In addition, cottontails do not thrive on abrupt swings between drought and saturation, and they don't do well on deep, sandy substrate. The sand dunes community is too open and sparse and the tidal flats totally inhospitable; the chaparral sections of the shell ridge community offer the most natural cottontail habitat, but the isolated patches are too small to maintain a population.

Dogs

If you glimpse a medium-sized, bushy-tailed dog streaking across a road or moving at an easy lope across open terrain, you have seen one of Matagorda's coyotes ('ky-yoats or ky-'yo-tees). The animal ranges across the state, including all of the barrier islands and peninsulas.

Coyotes spend the day curled up in the dense grass wherever they finished the previous night's hunt. They rouse near sunset and sing awhile in long, mournful wails to locate comrades, probably a family group composed of a mated pair and the survivors of their last litter. Sometimes, unrelated young animals or perhaps a few bachelor males temporarily team up to form a loose hunting pack. As they gather the animals greet each other with much yipping, tail wagging, facial gesturing, body posturing, and happy cavorting. Soon, stimulated by the movement of a dominant individual, they set off in the gathering dark, each one pouncing on what it can and occasionally coordinating with others to flush or run down game.

On Matagorda Island the staple prey of coyotes is cotton rats, but they will not pass up a harvest mouse or a rice rat. Working together, they bring down jackrabbits, young raccoons, and fawns. Sharp noses sniff out ground-nesting and perching birds and their nests. (The threat of coyote and raccoon depredation is probably the main reason that there are no waterbird rookeries on the island.) In the winter, coyotes fatten on migrant birds, easing out across the shallows to make nocturnal kills on the roost. A favorite daytime tactic is for one or two coyotes to distract potential prey by showing themselves at a distance while other pack members creep up in ambush. In this manner they manage to occasionally bring down geese, and even the wary sandhill cranes, in addition to pelicans, gulls, terns, sundry shorebirds, and ducks.

Though put at the carnivore level, coyotes are in fact consummate scroungers. Between more conventional meals, they fill their bellies with whatever they come across: snakes, lizards, frogs, tadpoles, crickets, grasshoppers, beetles, fiddler crabs, ghost crabs (which they either catch abroad at night or dig from their burrows), blue crabs, fish, and anything else edible from the strandline on Gulf side or bay side. Various plant material goes into their undiscriminating maws and iron guts: prickly pear tunas, southern dewberries, beach groundcherries, wolfberries, mesquite beans, even algae washed up on the beach and an astounding quantity of fresh grass from the barrier flat. And no coyote disdains carrion in any stage of decomposition. When pressed, they will even eat feces.

Mated coyotes form loyal pairs for at least a year, and in their semi-isolation on the island, the bond may last for life. The female digs her whelping lair into the lee side of a dune, where the entrance is well-concealed by thick vegetation. Here, in the springtime, she gives birth

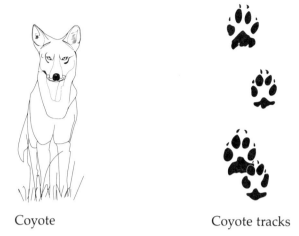

Coyote   Coyote tracks

to about half a dozen pups. The male stays nearby and hunts with his mate while she is nursing. By the time the pups are three weeks old both parents feed them by regurgitating partly digested food. Soon the offspring are allowed to try out their sharp new teeth by dismembering freshly caught prey; by early summer they are catching insects and ghost crabs around the den and running out to meet an adult returning from the hunt. Finally, they begin to follow their parents and to learn all of the wily tricks of the coyote trade. The family may stay together through the winter, but the youngsters will be driven away if they have not wandered off by the time their mother comes into heat in January or February.

Young coyotes occasionally fall prey to hawks, owls, western diamondbacks, alligators, and even to renegade adult coyotes, but the adults, being top carnivores, are not subject to predation. The population is held in check largely by built-in social and physiological controls. These territorial animals scent-mark their domains and challenge interlopers from other packs. The males vie for the females. As the number of coyotes increases they begin to show evidence of stress: Young ones and unattached males emigrate, either to adjacent barriers or toward the mainland. Females begin to skip their annual estrus or produce reduced litters. Scarce food results in malnourished pups that fail to survive. Diseases such as distemper, rabies, sylvatic plague, and canine hepatitis run more easily through crowded animals. Eventually numbers fall to carrying capacity or below, and the coyote population comes back into harmony with its restricted environment.

Coyotes forage through every community on Matagorda, and individual animals are mobile enough to range from one end of the island to the other in a single night, if they cared to do so. In fact, pack territories restrict hunting ranges to designated areas, the boundaries posted with urine and fecal deposits, scratch marks, anal gland secretions, and vocalizations. No one knows how many coyotes normally inhabit Matagorda Island; estimates hover around thirty-five. Because of their remarkable terrestrial mobility and their swimming ability, there is doubtless year-round, intermittent coyote traffic between the island and the mainland.

Raccoons

The masked face, ringed tail, human-like hands, and huge flat hind feet of the raccoon are recognized by everyone. The animal occurs statewide, and although it prefers wooded, moist habitats, it is a most adaptable animal: even in the dearth of trees and fresh water, there is a healthy population of 'coons on Matagorda Island.

Raccoons typically spend the day curled in hollow tree limbs. On Matagorda they make shift with abandoned badger burrows, recesses beneath Gulf Coast cordgrass and the centers of Macartney rose clumps and chaparral thickets. Despite attempts to keep them out, they also take refuge in and beneath the abandoned buildings on the air base and among the dead fronds hanging from the crowns of the palm trees on both ends of the island.

Although raccoons are usually nocturnal, they do forage in the daytime, especially on overcast winter afternoons. Your best bet for seeing one is while playing your binoculars over an expanse of tidal flat.

Raccoons are as good at hustling, as insistent at pilfering, and every bit as inquisitive, opportunistic, and omnivorous as coyotes. If they have limitations, these are that they prefer semiaquatic hunting grounds, have no ability to chase, and are not pack hunters. In the tidal flat habitat, however, 'coons manage quite well. Foraging mostly by night, they rely on acute hearing, a good sense of smell, and sensitive hands to haul in fiddler crabs, blue crabs, marine snails, fishes, snakes, roosting birds, the eggs of birds, turtles, and alligators, and whatever else comes their way. In addition, every raccoon knows that low tide is the time to move onto the mud flats and dig for clams. Raccoons range through all communities on the island, and you can find their handprints around any standing water, as well as at the waterline along the beach and even among the sand dunes. Although they may hole up briefly during severe weather, raccoons are active all year.

Raccoons mate in March. The female retires alone to her chosen lair

Raccoon

and gives birth to about four cubs in April or May. Leaving them only when she needs to forage for herself, she nurses her litter to weaning when they are ten weeks old. Thereafter she begins to take her off-spring on brief sorties. Amid much bumbling, splashing, playing, and twittering, the cute little coonlets eventually get the hang of wresting a living from their surroundings. The family group generally stays together through the coming winter, when the young move out on their own.

Most predation is on young raccoons by coyotes, badgers, alligators, western diamondbacks, and owls. Many juveniles probably starve because they cannot find an unoccupied home range in favorable habitat. When the population rises, disease, emigration, and reduced fecundity bring it back into equilibrium. There is no estimate of the number of raccoons on Matagorda Island, but it must be second only to the number of rodents. Raccoons surely move freely between island and mainland, and individuals live semipermanently on some of the oystershell islets in the bays.

Mustelids (Weasels)

The weasel clan in Texas includes a diverse group of medium-sized, carnivorous mammals, all with a pair of odorous anal glands. The only member of this group confirmed on Matagorda Island is the badger.

Although it has a masked face, a badger can hardly be confused with a raccoon or with any other mammal. Its broad head is flanked by wide stubby ears, and a bright white line along the top of the muzzle continues over the crown of the head and onto the shoulders. The silvery-grizzled coat is coarse and unkempt and the stocky, flattened body is slung on short, powerful legs. Its brief, bushy tail is kept tucked in so that it is hardly noticeable. Although the badger is

Badger

not a particularly pretty beast, either in appearance or in temperament, it is certainly prettily adapted to its way of life.

The badger life-style is *fossorial* (digging); it digs a burrow for shelter and it digs to catch prey. A badger's keen hearing and smell locate
buried food items and its powerful forequarters and long foreclaws
allow it to dig rapidly into the soil. The flattened body with its tapered
edges slides easily into the ongoing burrow. For a relatively large animal, 15 pounds or so, the badger is well fit for subterranean activity.
From the badger's point of view, the deep, sandy terrain of Matagorda Island is made to order.

However, diggable substrate is only half the problem; there must
also be diggable quarry. In the western two-thirds of Texas where
badgers range, they feed on prairie dogs, pocket gophers, ground
squirrels, and kangaroo rats, none of which occurs on Matagorda. So,
the badgers have had to adjust. They have learned to get by on cotton
rats and ghost crabs, supplemented with harvest mice, rice rats, birds
and their eggs, snakes, frogs, lizards, grasshoppers, spiders, carrion,
and whatever they can rummage from the strandline on the beach.

A badger digging out a ghost crab on the backbeach is a model of
concentration and persistence. It detects an occupied crab burrow by
smell and proceeds to dig as only a badger can dig—rapidly and in-
sistently, each alternate swipe from its strong forelegs ending with a
spray of sand thrown rearward several feet into the air. The animal
keeps its nose down where the action is, and its intensity makes it
oblivious to its surroundings. The badger may be out of sight in the
burrow by the time it reaches the crab, and when it does, the contest
is over. Even if it tried, the ghost crab could not outdistance its predator, and its pincers and defensive stance are no deterrent to a hungry
badger. The crab is dispensed with a satisfying crunch and greedily
consumed, hard exoskeleton and all.

Badgers are mostly nocturnal and always shy, so you aren't likely
to see one on Matagorda Island. If you are keen to spot one, quietly
stroll the backbeach on an overcast winter evening. Evidence of them,
however, is not hard to find. The holes they scoop on the backbeach
are frequent and distinctive—wider than deep, fitting the animal's

body shape, and with the terminal end broadly concave and scored by the foreclaws. The removed sand is spread in two fan-shaped piles on either side. A coyote engaged in the same pursuit digs an oval hole that tapers to a pointed end, and the excavated sand is thrown into a single mound.

You might notice the entrance to a badger burrow on the lee side of a primary dune or near the base of a secondary dune. Burrows can be spotted from a distance by the mound of sand beside them; the animal makes no effort to conceal the transverse hole. And badger tracks on the beach are unmistakable. Look for the flat-footed prints, short waddling stride, and especially for the odd toed-in arrangement of the front paws with their prominent claw marks.

Badgers are active year-round, leading solitary lives in their burrow until the local food resource is exhausted; then they move on. The female rears her two to five cubs alone. One mother carrying a youngster cat-like by the scruff of its neck was seen on the north end of the island in late March.

Adult badgers can whip their weight in coyotes and anything else that comes along, but the young occasionally succumb to coyotes, western diamondbacks, and owls. It is likely that juveniles have difficulty finding suitable unoccupied habitat, and they may suffer malnutrition or even starvation.

Longtime residents of Matagorda report that badgers were not among the original natural fauna, but first appeared in the 1930s. The size of the island's current population is not known, but because of their specialized life-style, it is probably no more than several dozen. And because of the scarcity of badgers on the adjacent mainland, immigrants are not likely. A major hurricane might extirpate the species from the island.

Cloven-hooved Mammals

The only native representative of this group is the white-tailed deer, the deer found across Texas. These animals prefer open woods but have adapted to the open terrain of Matagorda by taking up an antelope-like grazing habit, substituting airy distance for wooded retreat. Actually, although they do tend to keep their distance, most of the deer are accustomed to people and are easy to see in the vicinity of the air base, along any of the roads, and around the Wynne lodge.

On favorable range, white-tailed deer are selective browsers, nibbling on the leaves, twigs, buds, and flowers of an array of woody plants and vines; eating the fruits of many of the same species. They are also opportunistic grazers on tender shoots of grasses, sedges,

White-tailed deer

and rushes, and they supplement all this with the foliage of a wide assortment of herbs. On Matagorda Island, deer food sources are severely limited to southern dewberries, mesquite, and scant huisache, brasilwood, elbowbush, wild lime, and Mexican persimmon. Deer staples like live oak leaves and acorns, American beauty berry, greenbriar, yaupon, prickly ash, red bay, and mustang grape occur in insignificant stands or not at all.

The Matagorda herd subsists mainly by grazing the grasses, sedges, and rushes of the extensive barrier flat community. As the seasons turn, they take advantage of the favored greenery of lazy daisy, beach ground-cherry, sensitive briar, western ragweed, bundle flower, hoary milkpea, Louisiana vetch, American snoutbean, partridge pea, amaranth, and tallow weed. When abundant, such herbs make up the bulk of the diet. Deer also occasionally eat prickly pear tunas and even marine vegetation from the strand. Tracks and piles of fecal pellets indicate that deer trek through all of the major plant communities.

Matagorda white-tails follow the usual deer pattern of activity near sunup and sunset, but there is so much individual variation that you are likely to see some deer abroad at any hour. In the summertime they lie up through the heat of the day and forage mostly at night. In the wintertime they may feed intermittently all day long. On very windy days they move about less than usual.

Despite their evident mobility, deer tend to be homebodies. If food and water are adequate, most individuals stay within a mile or so of where they were born, and may spend their entire lives coursing over no more than 25 acres. Occasionally an individual goes exploring, and each fall bucks set out in search of receptive does, but they soon return to their home ranges.

White-tails spend most of the time in small groups of mixed sexes and ages. Each group is socially stratified from the alpha (most dominant) down through an omega (lowest) individual, determined by routine daily interactions that include body odor, eye contact, position of the ears, arc of the neck, a stilted body posture, and a stiff-legged gait, as well as by occasional shoving and hoof-slashing engagements. The animals with the most consistently domineering attitudes, whether bucks or does, gain the highest rank.

The deer's annual cycle, driven by the changing daylength that stimulates the secretion of certain hormones, is affected by herd stress and nutrition. The healthy Matagorda herd enters rut in October, when the bucks begin to lock antlers and to wear themselves out following the does, covering as many of them as they can. This activity peaks in November and rapidly winds down as winter sets in. By February most bucks will have dropped their racks and be either solitary or in small, amicable feeding groups, while the pregnant does with their yearling offspring will form separate feeding herds.

Seven months after conception the spotted fawns are born, usually in April and May. A fawn spends most of its first days curled up in a grassy nook, where it is nursed briefly once or twice a day. The youngster develops rapidly; in about ten days it comes out to meet mama and then to follow her, and it is soon able to keep up wherever she goes. It is weaned at about four weeks but may continue to nurse intermittently throughout the summer. The spotted pattern is lost with the molt of the baby coat in the fall.

Fleshy nubbins begin to swell on the heads of bucks in April. During June and July, when the rapidly developing antlers are still covered with fuzzy skin, the bucks are said to be "in velvet." By August they are polishing the hardened bones of the completed racks against mesquite trees or fence posts. The degree of main beam and tine development is age-related, but is primarily governed by nutrition. Well-nourished bucks produce fine headgear, and the splendid racks on many Matagorda animals attest to the sound condition of the herd.

As the days begin to shorten and the earliest weak northers breathe fresh life into the heat-suppressed barrier environment, hormones begin to bubble through the deer herd, signaling the onset of the rut. Young bucks born the previous spring will feel their oats, but the mature males will keep them from approaching the does. About a third of the young does will mate; the others will begin to reproduce when they are yearlings. First-time mothers bear a single offspring; if they remain in good condition, they usually produce twins thereafter.

Natural mortality in white-tail deer herds falls most heavily upon the young. In many years, nearly half of the fawns succumb before they are a month old, and it is normal for scarcely a third of the newborn to survive to their first winter. What brings them down so harshly? Most effects are indirect and cumulative. Drought through the spring and summer dries up the does and stresses or starves the fawns. Unusually wet conditions make normal foraging difficult and promote the incidence of salmonellosis and other bacterial diseases. Tropical storms and hurricanes can kill the youngsters outright or separate them from their mothers. Common parasites—roundworms, tapeworms, liver flukes—sometimes explode into life-threatening ravages, and hordes of deerflies and mosquitoes and infestations of ticks and lice further wear the animals down. If the deer population is already high, crowding may so stress the does that they abandon their offspring or fail to attend them properly. And wherever there are fawns there are coyotes, their arch predator. This is the stuff on which "the balance of nature" hinges: the weak and unfortunate are eliminated and the population hovers around carrying capacity.

Once through the hazards of its first year, the outlook for an individual white-tail improves. Deer aged three to seven years are enjoying their prime; exceptional ones may live twelve to fifteen years before their teeth wear down and their immune systems fail.

In an isolated ecosystem, the deer are actually their own worst enemy. They naturally respond to a string of favorable years with rising numbers and the potential to overexploit preferred portions of their habitat. Then, when the inevitable bad years come, the crowded animals seriously deplete the range and the herd crashes. Nature will bring about a slow recovery, but the interim is not pretty. For both aesthetic and ecological reasons, human management of such a confined population as the one on Matagorda Island is a reasonable and humane alternative.

As early as the 1950s, air force personnel began a regular helicopter census of deer on the federal end of the island. Then they established a military hunting program that held the population at about 800 animals. By the 1980s the TPWD had assumed supervision of the herd. Using buck/doe ratios, doe/fawn ratios, antler development, and vegetational quality as indicators and continued aerial surveillance to tally numbers, the department determined that a population of 600 animals was desirable.

Supervised public hunts on Matagorda began in 1983, and, to date, have continued, with the goals of providing recreational hunting and population cropping. The actual hunting area is rotated around the Wildlife Management Area in the central part of the island. The number of hunters is adjusted to number of deer by a special permit system, and hunters are shuttled to and from permanent shooting stands. (You may have noticed head-high, pyramidal metal frames here and there in the grassland. During the brief hunting season, seats are fixed atop these for the hunters.) All kills are carefully tallied, and precautions are taken to ensure that endangered species and migratory shorebirds are not disturbed by the hunters. In addition to these special provisions, all routine state and federal refuge licenses and regulations are adhered to.

The management program has worked. After an initial high hunter participation and a significant kill, the operation has been trimmed to maintenance proportions. The deer herd on the northern 44,000 acres of the island is near the target level. The 350 deer on the southern 11,000 acres are judged below carrying capacity, so the USFWS has not subjected them to active management. Give or take, Matagorda Island supports a resident white-tail population of some 800 to 1,000 animals.

It is a matter of record that white-tailed deer were introduced onto Matagorda Island by air force personnel, and this fact has been used to suggest that deer are not native to the island. The population was severely reduced by Hurricane Carla in 1961 and fifty animals were introduced the following year to help bolster numbers. It could be that the extant herd derives entirely from such introductions. However, old-timers definitely hunted white-tails on the island's south end, and these animals surely got there on their own. Deer occur on all of the Texas barriers and peninsulas, and they at least visit the oystershell islets in the lagoons and bays. They readily wade and swim, and the teeming population on the adjacent Aransas National Wildlife Refuge provides a ready source of immigrants. It is likely that there are intermittent deer movements between Matagorda and the mainland during most years. Therefore, the white-tailed deer can be justifiably regarded as native to Matagorda Island.

Introduced Mammals

The mammals in this category are all hangers-on of humans and complete aliens to the natural fauna of North America. Most were deliberately or inadvertently introduced; a few managed to get to the island on their own from other introduction sites. All either currently live on Matagorda Island or are verified to have done so in the past.

Rodents

Of course the house mouse, the archetypical mouse that has hitch-hiked from its Eurasian homeland to become the most ubiquitous of rodents, has made its way to Matagorda Island. Individuals must raft from the mainland occasionally, but in earlier times, numerous vessels docked at the wharves inside Pass Cavallo, and livestock feed has been continually imported, both wide avenues for mice.

Throughout North America, house mice live in or near human dwellings and outbuildings. When they spread to natural habitats they fare best in disturbed areas—abandoned fields, fence rows, roadsides, grazed pastures, or mowed strips that give them an edge over native rodents. Apparently the harsh barrier environment offers house mice no such advantage. Despite their long tenure, house mice have not managed to establish a significant population on Matagorda. In the periodic rodent census conducted by the TPWD by live trapping, the catch of house mice is consistently meager and restricted to the vicinity of the air base. Personnel of the USFWS report no house mice at all from buildings on the south end of the island.

Even more telling than these human observations is the tally of rodent skulls retrieved from hundreds of regurgitated barn owl pellets. An occasional house mouse skull from the air base is found, but none elsewhere. Although they have been reported living afield under driftwood on Galveston Island, house mice on Matagorda remain corralled around the air base; when these moldering buildings are removed or renovated, the mouse population should be further restricted.

"House rats" definitely once occurred in ranch outbuildings, but extensive live trapping and inspection of barn owl pellets present no evidence of a current population on the island. The disappearance of these animals is probably tied to the elimination of a ready supply of livestock feed, stored human foodstuffs, and garbage. Although rats have been reported living in the wild on Galveston Island, the decidedly more arid conditions on Matagorda may have restricted the animals to the vicinity of civilization. But they are consummate dispersers, easily introduced by human activity, and it seems likely that occasional immigrants appear around the docks and buildings on both the north and south ends.

There are actually two kinds of "house rat," both of Asian origin and both now widely distributed in the world. The roof rat, a long-tailed, black rat, is associated with ships, lading, wharves, and urban habitations, and it was almost surely a denizen of the mid–nineteenth-century shipping communities on the northern edge of Matagorda Island. The Norway rat, a larger, shorter-tailed, brown rat, also lives with people, often selecting storehouses and rural settings. It is a less agile climber and a less pernicious invader than the roof rat. Although the two may occur together (often with the roof rat in the rafters and the Norway rat beneath the floorboards), the roof rat seems to be the more common species in the Coastal Bend today. It was likely the kind that pestered the ranchers on Matagorda.

The nutria ('new-tree-ya) is a large, semiaquatic rodent native to the southern half of South America. It resembles a muskrat, but its tail is naked and cylindrical rather than vertically flattened, and its incisors are coated with orange enamel. In 1937, nutria were imported from Argentina to Louisiana to be farmed for fur. Escapees established themselves in the wild, and when it was realized that they fed ravenously on submerged vegetation, more were purposely released at several places along the Gulf Coast, including East Texas, in hopes that they would clear the waterways. (Unfortunately, the animals shunned the most troublesome weedy species.) Today, a vigorous population occupies suitable aquatic habitat across most of the state.

With the object of controlling aquatic vegetation, nutria were released into the ditch that surrounds the air base in the late 1950s. They never prospered but did manage to maintain themselves until the mid-1970s. The failure was probably due to a lack of adequate habitat aggravated by the stress of frequent drought; alligators may have hastened their demise. There is no population of nutria on the island today.

Cloven-hooved Animals

The thriving population of feral hogs on Matagorda Island has a mongrelized ancestry. Throughout South Texas, Anglo pioneers in the middle of the nineteenth century brought in several strains of domestic hogs. Some of these "butcher hogs" were kept penned, but most were allowed to range freely until needed for meat, when they were baited and shot. Inevitably, many of these wary range hogs, avoiding their planned doom, adapted and formed the seed stock for a mixed-breed feral population. On the coast, the tough and versatile feral hogs haunted brackish marshland and readily reef-hopped across the shallow lagoons and island-hopped the smaller passes at low tide. Soon there was an intermittent but extensive migration of feral hog genes back and forth between the barriers and the mainland.

To complicate matters, in the 1930s, wild European, or Russian, boar were introduced onto Blackjack Peninsula (the current Aransas National Wildlife Refuge) as a game animal. This original ancestor of domesticated hogs readily interbred with its newly liberated kin, and injected into the coastal population a dominating measure of sagacity, stamina, and brute ugliness. In short order Matagorda hogs had an invigorating dole of primal boar genes.

So a feral hog living on Matagorda Island today is a patchwork creature, a recent rescramble of several lines tediously extracted and kept separate for a significant part of the eight thousand years that hogs have been domesticated; then this miscegenation was recoupled to its wild progenitor and the motley offspring were tempered in the brine of the coastal marshlands. Little wonder that the survivors are as well adapted to the barrier environment as any member of the native fauna.

No matter its breeding, a hog is a hog, and if you see one hustling through the cordgrass you are not likely to mistake it for anything else, especially since there are no javelinas (also known as the collared peccary) on Matagorda with which to confuse it. The hogs come in all colors, including piebald, and adults reach a body weight of 150 pounds or more. Mostly they are lean, slab-sided versions of domestic stock.

These vigilant beasts are difficult to observe, but you might find yourself downwind of a group. Use your binoculars to see how many wild boar traits they display: a long, unkinked tail ending in a scraggy brush, ears fringed with long hairs, and a mane of coarse bristles extending from neck to rump. The wild boar profile is distinctive: the body stands high on long legs, heavy shoulders slope back to relatively small hindquarters, and a large head accentuates the small eyes, giving the animal a decidedly "pig-eyed" and untrustworthy appearance. The muzzle is unusually long and bears a knobby swelling where the enlarged canines emerge. In males these projecting tusks are visible at a distance. Although formidable in appearance, the animals are extremely shy. Once they detect people, they emit a coarse grunt of alarm and head for the nearest cover.

Feral hogs range through all of the communities on the island but spend most of their time around water. Their trails across the grassy interior generally follow ditches and swales; they routinely slog through the tidal flats, and at night they forage on the beach. Hogs are most active at night, especially in the summertime, but are frequently abroad early and late in the day, and forage contentedly in wet, cold weather. They move about in extended family groups of half a dozen. Each group apparently roams over an extensive home range, but there is no evidence of territorial defense. When ready to farrow, the sow fashions a crude form in a remote, dense stand of grass. Litters are small—two to three piglets—and usually at least some display the watermelon-striped pattern characteristic of their wild ancestors.

Hogs, though mostly vegetarian, are thorough omnivores. In the spring they consume great quantities of freshly sprouted grasses, sedges, rushes, and cattails. As the moistland forbs become available, they feed on water hyssop, coast pennywort, frogfruit, spadeleaf, and burhead. Or they move onto the ridges to crop stemless spider-wort, western ragweed, and beach ground-cherry, or onto the beach for beach amaranth and strandline algae. In summer and winter, when tender greens wither or die back, hogs root more actively for rhizomes and tubers. They are especially fond of the bulbs of yellow nut grass, and will plow up large areas once they discover a patch of these delicacies. They have mesquite beans and prickly pear tunas but are deprived of the live oak acorns, mustang grapes, and the fruits of yaupon and greenbriar that sustain their kind on the mainland.

While rooting for vegetable food, feral hogs quickly snap up any animals they uncover: earthworms, insect larvae, crickets, grasshoppers, ground spiders, scorpions, frogs, lizards, snakes, birds' eggs, and cotton rats. They purposely dig for fiddler crabs along the edge of the tidal flats and excavate the beach for ghost crabs. When the tide is out the hogs move onto the mud flats and into shallow water to grub for razor clams and marine worms and to catch any crabs that scuttle their way. In drying waterholes they consume stranded tadpoles, shrimps, and fish, and they know how to search the edges for turtle and alligator nests. The animals assiduously work the strandline on both the bay side and Gulf side of the island for anything edible—animal or vegetable offal from the sea, human garbage, and unusual concentrations of amphipods or shore fly maggots. They feed on carrion and take special advantage of windrows of fish carcasses beached after kills by summertime red tides or wintertime blue northers.

Although the fifty to seventy-five feral hogs on Matagorda Island seldom form much bacon, by keeping themselves well-stoked, they have a definite impact on the island ecosystem. The omnivorous habits of these large, demanding animals throw them into competition with virtually all members of the native fauna. They are destructive predators of the island's scant list of herptiles, and they ravage nests of reptiles, rodents, and ground-living birds. The animals have a predilection for scarce fresh-water aquatic vegetation, and their rooting and wallowing habits foul drying waterholes, especially in the summer, when fresh water is most critical for other forms of insular wildlife. Although their extensive turning of the soil may promote plant diversity by opening the grass sod, such disturbance can initiate wind erosion in the sand dunes and bank erosion on the tidal flats.

The ecological impact of feral hogs on the island is still being assessed. Meanwhile, individual animals are incidentally shot and occasionally trapped by supervisory personnel, and deer hunters are allowed to take them if they want to. Because they are an alien member of the fauna, there is justification for the complete eradication of feral hogs from Matagorda. Although a dedicated campaign using specially trained dogs might come close to achieving this goal, because of the wary nature of the animals and the continual arrival of immigrants from the mainland, there will probably always be a few feral hogs on the island.

The earliest Anglo landowners brought domestic cattle onto Matagorda Island in the mid-1800s, and until recently there have been cattle there ever since. Even during the war years, cattle remained under a lease arrangement on federal land and in private pasture on the south end. When the Matagorda Island State Park and Wildlife Management Area was established as a unit of the National Wildlife Refuge System in 1982, there was an agreement to retain cattle on the area as a potential land management tool. In 1987, when negotiations were completed for purchase of the Wynne ranch, all livestock was removed from the island's south end. After exhaustive debate, cattle were finally removed from the remainder of the island in June 1991.

At issue is whether a carefully monitored herd of cattle is beneficial or detrimental to the natural ecology of Matagorda Island. Proponents maintain that grazing keeps the interior grassland from becoming a dense and stagnant community dominated by a few species of grasses and populated by only the few kinds of wildlife that are adapted to such a monoculture. Opening up the dense sward, they contend, would allow the invasion of forbs, thus increasing the number and kinds of niches available and ultimately increasing the overall carrying capacity of the land for a more diverse fauna. Opponents question whether these proposed benefits are real and, even if so, whether they come at too steep an ecological price. They suggest that the presence of cattle is attended by a variety of environmental problems. These include wearing down the fertility of an already deficient sandy soil; changing the composition of the vegetation by selective grazing; increasing the likelihood of invasion by alien plant species; promoting the occurrence of external parasites and serving as a potential means of introducing disease; competing with native wildlife for green growth; reducing the natural cover for small animal species important to natural food chains; promoting wind erosion and tidal flat degradation by trailing and trampling; retarding plant growth on the delicate coppice and primary dunes; littering the backbeach and changing its microecology with unsightly fecal droppings; fouling critical fresh-water sites and denuding their banks, especially during critical dry periods. All this necessitates the presence of fencing, holding pens, and assorted human activities in an area set aside exclusively for wildlife.

An avowed goal of island management is the preservation of the natural ecosystem. If the natural climax of the interior grassland is a closed community of low diversity, then "opening" it goes counter to the natural trend. Therefore, grazing by livestock, or any other sort of artificial manipulation, would interfere with the island's normal condition. However, higher priority goals include enhancing the island habitat to favor endangered/threatened species and migratory birds. Opening at least a portion of the central grasslands is viewed as a means of achieving these primary goals. Opponents to grazing as the tool of choice suggest the alternative of periodic burning. They argue that despite the obvious short-term devastation they wreak, deliberate burns are attended by fewer chronic and deleterious ecological side effects than grazing. Burns can be carefully planned, timed, and controlled; can be limited to grassland and excluded from beach, dunes, and tidal flats; are quick and cheap and lend themselves to evaluation and delayed rotation; and do not remove soil nutrients or foul fresh-water sites. When conducted in small strips, burned areas are rapidly repopulated by native wildlife from adjacent unburned areas; after a short period of regrowth, they do provide attractive foraging sites for target species.

So, if some of the barrier flat grassland must be sacrificed for the benefit of certain native wildlife species in jeopardy, burning is regarded as a more nearly natural and less upsetting tactic than grazing.

When pioneer families came to Matagorda Island, they brought not only hogs and cattle but the entire retinue of domestic mammals, including horses, mules, goats, and sheep. Although a few horses were still present until recently, the other animals have been gone since the 1940s.

Dogs and Cats

The residents of Saluria must have kept domestic dogs and cats, and it is known that the keepers of the lighthouse and all of the early ranching families had such pets on Matagorda. Because the animals were free-ranging, they doubtless killed and disturbed wildlife in the vicinity of dwellings, and some dogs were trained for the hunt. During the days when the air base was active, special kennels of well-groomed bird dogs were maintained for quail hunting by VIPs.

Both dogs and cats were removed from the island in the 1970s, and no remnant feral populations exist. Visitors must keep their pets leashed.

Occasional Species

Two kinds of native mammals are observed so rarely on the island that all sightings are thought to involve immigrant individuals rather than the offspring of reproducing residents.

Anyone familiar with the biology of the armadillo would doubt it could either gain access to, or survive on, Matagorda Island. Yet, during the 1980s two live individuals were discovered snuffling along on the north end, and tracks of a third and the skeleton of a fourth were seen on the south end. Although these insectivorous creatures apparently eke out a living in the dense litter beneath the barrier flat grasses and along swales, it is unlikely that they can sustain a population through a series of drought years or that they could survive a major washover. As for getting to the island by natural means, armadillos are quite likely to be among those waifs swept out of the San Antonio/Guadalupe river delta on rafts of flood debris.

Early ranchers agree that bobcats were always rare on Matagorda. Since the 1980s, TPWD personnel occasionally have seen an individual and discovered a few tracks; no evidence of them has been seen on the south end. Because these native cats are so secretive, it is difficult to judge whether there is in fact a sparse resident population. They are certainly adaptable enough to survive in the grassy interior and the chaparral, and they could subsist on the variety of native prey. There is a healthy population of bobcats on the adjacent mainland, and despite the feline reputation for avoiding water, bobcats routinely plod through muck, wade out to ambush roosting waterfowl, swim, and even reef-hop now and then; so their occasional appearance on Matagorda is to be expected.

Marine Mammals

Although none of the species listed in this section is a terrestrial inhabitant of Matagorda Island, the carcasses of all have been discov-

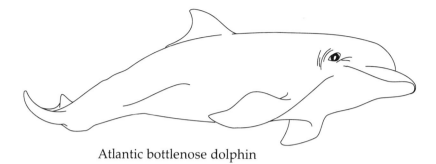

Atlantic bottlenose dolphin

ered stranded on the beach of Matagorda Island or Matagorda Peninsula, and one is commonly observed in the surrounding waters. Bodies that aren't snatched up by the Texas Marine Mammal Stranding Network (TMMSN) to contribute to our scanty knowledge of the biology of marine mammals enter the island food web through the ever alert squadrons of scavengers and decomposers.

It is likely that on your way across Espíritu Santo or Mesquite bays you spotted the graceful black bodies and distinctive dorsal fins of "porpoises" breaking the surface in clean, swift arcs. Because they are the personable stars of television and of aquarium shows, everyone knows Atlantic bottlenose dolphins when they see them, but there is considerable confusion about just what sort of creatures they are and what their proper name is.

Although they have lost their hind limbs and most of their hair, porpoises do have warm blood, they surface to breathe air, and their young are born alive and nurse, so they are clearly mammals, not fish. More specifically, they are small whales, complete with the subcutaneous fat we call blubber, a blowhole (a single nostril atop their head), and a pair of flukes (the flattened, horizontal extensions of the tail), which are whipped vigorously up and down for propulsion. Adults attain a length of 12 feet and weigh about 1,200 lbs.

Dolphins, with a mouth full of conical teeth, are grouped with predaceous toothed whales. Conical teeth distinguish dolphins from the related porpoises, which have blunt snouts and flattened teeth. Despite this technical distinction, along the Texas coast, dolphins are universally called porpoises. If you do otherwise, you will be spotted immediately as a foreigner. True porpoises do not often enter the Gulf of Mexico.

To complicate matters, two species of brightly colored game fish in local Gulf waters are also correctly called dolphins. If you hear anglers say that they have caught dolphins, let's hope they mean the fish and not the mammal. Indeed, it is illegal to harm or harass any marine mammal in the coastal waters of the state, and even their carcasses are protected from molestation.

Where there are shrimp boats, dolphins are sure to be nearby, feeding on fish stirred up by the nets or eagerly harvesting "trash fish" cast overboard as the catch is culled.

Dolphins, on the other hand, are adept predators and don't depend on handouts from shrimpers. Several animals may team up to herd prey into compact schools, and then dash through the milling mass, snapping up as many as they can. Individual dolphins crowd fish against the shore and catch them as they try to break past; they even occasionally slide out onto the bank to snap up fish that have flipped out. Favorite food fish are striped and white mullets, but dolphins will take what they can get: menhaden, black drum, Atlantic croaker, spot, speckled trout, redfish, even flounder. Although they readily eat shrimp, apparently they are not adept at catching them in quantity. Dolphins navigate and detect fish in the turbid bay water by sonar and they also make a variety of audible squealing, whistling, and groaning sounds to each other.

The Atlantic bottlenose dolphin ("bottlenose" refers to the beak) is the only member of its clan commonly living in nearshore Gulf waters. Although most frequently observed in the bays, these dolphins range about 12 miles out to sea. They can often be seen beyond the surf, and they frequent the mouths of the passes at both ends of the island.

Between 1980 and 1990, the TMMSN recorded 155 strandings of dead or moribund marine mammals on Matagorda Island and Matagorda Peninsula; over 90 percent were Atlantic bottlenose dolphins. All recent incidents have involved solitary individuals that were wounded, diseased, weakened by pollutants, or battered by storm; there have been no mass strandings locally. Most stranded animals are dead when discovered; in most cases, the cause of death could not be determined. Attempts to save the live ones have so far failed; the animals are simply stressed beyond recovery.

The other 10 percent of strandings included some interesting creatures. One was a short-snouted spinner dolphin, a species of the tropical Atlantic only known to science since 1981. Two were the peculiar Risso's dolphin, which have toothless upper jaws and a cluster of long teeth at the tip of their lower jaws. Somehow, they use this unusual dentition to catch fish and squid. Some authorities believe that the irregular crisscross of pale scratch-like marks on their gray bodies are actually scars of raking wounds left by the teeth of other Risso's dolphins during social disputes.

Only one pigmy killer whale had been recorded in the Gulf of Mexico before an additional specimen was found on a Matagorda beach. Although this aggressive, 7-foot dolphin is known in most temperate and tropical oceans, it is uncommon or at least very seldom observed. Among other prey, pigmy killers are known to attack the young of other species of dolphins.

Very little is known of the habits of the melon-headed whale, an 8-foot dolphin named for its conspicuously swollen forehead. It is found in tropical oceans, where it usually stays well out to sea, and the discovery of a stranded carcass in the Matagorda area was a total surprise.

In November 1988, one of the very few dwarf sperm whales ever seen in the Gulf of Mexico was found dead on the beach on the south end of Matagorda Island; in March of 1991, a second carcass beached on the north end. This rather sluggish species has a stout, dolphin-like build, a blunt nose with an undershot lower jaw, and small snake-like teeth in the lower jaw (but none in the upper). Adults get about 8 feet long and weigh 500 pounds, far short of the dimensions of their better-known relative, the great sperm whale of *Moby Dick* fame. In March 1991, a live pigmy sperm whale, a species similar to the foregoing one, beached on Matagorda. It was airlifted to Sea World in San Antonio, but soon died.

The discovery of a moribund Minke whale on Matagorda Peninsula in 1988 marked the only local stranding of a baleen whale. The Minke is a scaled-down version of the blue whale, the largest of all animals. The Matagorda specimen was less than half the 30-foot length they can reach. Baleen whales feed by gulping mouthfuls of plankton-laden water and using their tongue as a piston to force the water through the baleen, a series of flattened bony plates suspended from the roof of the mouth. Brushlike fibers on the edges of the baleen snare the plankton and the water is expelled out the corners of the mouth. Then the tongue sweeps the catch into the throat. Agile little Minke whales migrate between cold waters of the North Atlantic and the Antarctic, but a Minke in the Gulf of Mexico must have been off-course.

If you discover a marine mammal on the beach, alive or dead, please inform a park ranger immediately. If the animal is alive, you can render first aid by splashing its exposed parts with water and keeping its blowhole exposed to the air and the gulls away from its eyes. Do not attempt to return the animal to the sea. In the case of a carcass, simply leave it in place. The ranger will contact the regional representative of the TMMSN, and if it is alive or of interest, trained personnel will quickly arrive to try to rehabilitate the animal or process the carcass.

Species of Historic Interest

None of the mammals in this category currently lives on Matagorda Island. There is a sight record for the cougar, but information for the others is too sketchy to warrant more than speculation about their possible early occurrence.

Packs of gray wolves, which were harassing bison, surely passed through the coastal prairie in prehistoric times, but they preferred the open, stony interior. Red wolves, the aboriginal large canids of the eastern third of the state, were thoroughly at home in the fringing marshes and swamps as far west as the Coastal Bend. Their presence on Blackjack Peninsula is well-documented. But there is no specific record of red wolves on Matagorda Island, and gray wolves probably never set foot there.

The solitary report of a cougar on Matagorda Island dates from the early 1940s. Cougars were not uncommon on the mainland in those days—they range widely, and one could have easily made its way to the island if it took the notion.

Although usually associated with the plains, American bison (buffalo) ranged throughout Texas, avoiding only the deepest forests and boggiest swamplands. The name for the local bay derives from the Spanish reference to these wild *vacas* (cattle). Local Indians hunted bison, but using primitive weapons and lacking horses or a topographic advantage, they made scant inroads on the population. However, the mounted and armed Europeans relentlessly and wantonly shot bison until the big animals faded from the Coastal Bend of Spanish Texas, practically without remark. They were probably gone from their lush coastal haunts by the end of the eighteenth century, and the resultant ecological vacuum was rapidly filled by the burgeoning herds of Spanish mission cattle, progenitors of the fabled longhorns. So, even the earliest Anglo pioneers never saw bison on the coastal prairie. Bison were never reported on Matagorda Island. It is unlikely they would have been tempted to risk a crossing, and if they had, lack of drinking water would have curtailed their stay.

Pronghorn antelope ranged out of the plains country into the southwestern half of the coastal prairie as late as the 1850s, but they apparently never invaded the tall grass country east of Corpus Christi. They are not recorded on any Texas barrier, and there is no reason to believe that they ever occurred on Matagorda Island.

There is no record of Caribbean monk seals on Matagorda Island (monk refers to the habit of living in tight-knit social groups), but in Columbus' day they were common throughout the southern Gulf of Mexico, and in the summer, occasionally appeared off the Gulf coasts of Florida and Texas. There are old sight records for Galveston and Port Isabel. These small seals had not been extensively hunted before the arrival of Europeans, and once their slaughter for meat and oil began, the population of the trusting animals plummeted. They had become scarce by the 1880s. The last living monk seal was seen off Jamaica in 1952. Twenty years later, after an extensive aerial search failed to locate a surviving colony, the species was declared extinct. Although there is no record of these seals on Matagorda Island, perhaps in more tranquil days venturesome groups of these gentle pinnipeds spent their summers frolicking in the surf and lolling on the beach where today even the thought of them has vanished.

Even more fantastic is the idea of a manatee roiling through the grass beds in San Antonio Bay. These large aquatic mammals may get up to 14 feet in length and weigh over a ton and a half. With their wrinkled skin, tiny sunken eyes, huge bristly lips, and a spatulate tail, they are unlikely stuff from which to conjure a mermaid myth; they look like nothing so much as enormous, algae-encrusted maggots. Manatees spend their time placidly munching submerged vegetation in warm coastal shallows, estuaries, and river deltas.

The West Indian manatee was once resident along coastlines from Florida and the mouth of the Rio Grande south through the Caribbean Sea and the coast of South America to Rio de Janeiro. From this tropical bailiwick, animals moved north into the luxuriant submarine grass beds of the Gulf of Mexico in the summertime. But humans hunting them for meat and ivory, and more recently, habitat destruction, marine pollution, incidental netting, and frequent collisions with the propellers of powerboats have put the species on the endangered list.

There are no reports of sightings, strandings, or bones of West Indian manatees on Matagorda Island. Indeed, over the past 140 years there have been fewer than a dozen records of the species along the entire Texas coast. Besides one possible 1979 sighting in the Corpus Christi Water Exchange Pass (the so-called "Fish Pass" that cuts across the southern tip of Mustang Island), all live manatees from Texas waters were discovered in the early 1900s in the lower Laguna Madre or in the delta of the Rio Grande. In 1986, a bloated manatee carcass washed up on Bolivar Peninsula near Galveston.

Were there ever manatees around Matagorda? Only the Karankawas knew for sure, and they cannot tell. The alert Spaniards never

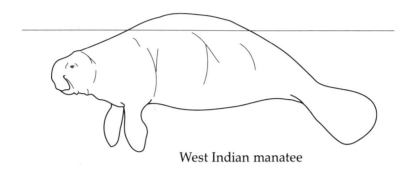

West Indian manatee

mentioned them, nor did the early Anglo seafarers. If these unique marine mammals did occur locally, they would likely have been summer visitors that came up from Mexico to munch on the rich submerged pastures of widgeon grass, shoalgrass, and turtle grass in the bays, and perhaps to work their way up the local rivers. The first hint of falling water temperature would have sent them hying for the tropics.

Other Mammalian Species

Only one of the mammals considered in this section has been reliably documented on Matagorda Island. There are vague references to several of the others. It is interesting to speculate on why these mammals are absent from Matagorda Island; but this list is not merely the pipe dream of armchair biologists. Some of them may actually be part of the native fauna and, because they lead secretive lives or require special techniques for detection, may have escaped discovery. Others might be isolated immigrants that have so far eluded notice. Most of the species are regarded as possibilities either because they live on the adjacent mainland and have dispersal potential or because they have been recorded on other Texas barrier islands.

Biogeography of Matagorda versus Padre Island

Of the several Texas barriers, the mammalian fauna of Padre Island has been most completely surveyed. Because Padre has many species that do not occur on Matagorda, it is useful to begin by comparing the biogeography of these two islands.

1. Natural assemblage of mammals on the adjacent mainland: The two islands are exposed to different reservoirs of mainland

stocks. Padre Island borders the Tamaulipan biotic province, a vast expanse of semi-arid brush country that grades into the desert Southwest and bears the stamp of Old Mexico. Tamaulipan mammals, adapted to open, scrub terrain, readily take to the barren wastes of Padre Island. Matagorda Island lies offshore of the Texan biotic province, the mesic terminus of the great grassland that sweeps down from the Central Plains. In addition, the Coastal Bend occurs on the western fringe of the Austroriparian biotic province, which harbors species characteristic of the pine and hardwood forests and the tall grass meadows of the Southeast. The life histories of Austroriparian mammals hover around the dense sward of waist-high grasses with their dank accumulation of ground litter.

2. Access: Although the two barriers are of the same geologic age and origin, they have experienced very different degrees of isolation.

Until the dredging of the Gulf Intracoastal Waterway in the 1940s, Padre Island was frequently connected to the coastline at several points by exposed tidal flats across Laguna Madre, and these were natural highways for the spontaneous dispersal of all local terrestrial mainland animals. Before the jetties were built at Brazos Santiago Pass, the southern tip of Padre was not consistently separated from the lower coast. Nor is the northern end of the island cleanly disjunct from Mustang Island (intervening Corpus Christi Pass is often filled with sand). Padre Island has been repeatedly visited by Europeans since the ranching days began in 1760, and since the 1950s, two causeways continually busy with heavy traffic have linked the island to the mainland. The hundreds of thousands of vehicles and their multifarious loads, and even the causeways themselves, all provide ingress for animals. The direct connection to heavily developed Mustang Island opens additional avenues.

By contrast, Matagorda Island has apparently always been separated from the adjacent coastline. Even at extreme low tide, the chains of oystershell islets never formed a complete bridge over which mammals could wander. Although there was a brief flush of civilization on Matagorda before the Civil War, this was soon snuffed out and eventually totally erased by hurricanes. For almost a century, the island had minimal human traffic, and to this day the only access is by water or air. Other than by natural rafting, terrestrial mammals of the coastal prairie have had scant opportunity to get onto Matagorda.

Although the ephemeral nature of Cedar Bayou renders St.

Joseph and Matagorda islands a single biogeographic unit, this composite barrier is bounded on the south by Aransas Pass and on the north by Pass Cavallo, two of the most durable passes on the Texas coast. Neither has ever been known to fill with sand, and Aransas Pass is now jettied. Therefore, unless they were displaced by rough weather, there has been scant chance for terrestrial mammals to island-hop from Padre–Mustang islands to St. Joseph–Matagorda islands.

3. Human modification of the island environment: Aside from the 70-mile segment preserved as the Padre Island National Seashore, both the north and south ends of Padre are heavily developed with resort motels, high-rise hotels and condominiums, urban centers, residential streets, mercury vapor lights, landfills, and all of the traditional spinoff designed to attract tourists, fun seekers, and permanent residents. On popular holidays the sea of humanity on the island is awesome. The direct connection with Mustang Island simply adds another bustling 18 miles of strand, a thriving urban center, busy docks, and a heavily used vehicular ferry access point. While most native mammals have retreated before the glitter and the stampede, some with camp-follower inclinations have adapted and taken advantage of the diversity of new habitats and food sources.

By contrast, Matagorda Island has retained most of its natural features. Hurricanes wiped out the early townsites and military establishments. Livestock suppressed the vegetation, but this is in the process of reclamation. The air base was a serious local disruption, but the bustle of mock war has long since faded and natural communities now exist right up to the edges of the cracked runways and shell roads. The master plan for the current state park and for the Wildlife Management Area stipulates very few modifications for the convenience of visitors. Daytime sounds on Matagorda are still dominated by the wind and the sea; the night is not held back by artificial illumination. The mammals on the island pulse to age-old, natural rhythms.

Potential Matagorda Mammals

Because the durable Virginia opossum, an omnivore with the ability to survive in a variety of habitats, is common in the Coastal Bend, it is surprising that there is not a thriving population on Matagorda Island. Yet, no records exist of individual sightings. Opossums do occur on Padre and Mustang islands, but they are recent additions to the fauna and flourish only in the vicinity of human habitation.

Seldom-noticed shrews are a common and important component of the fauna of the coastal prairie. No shrew has been collected on Matagorda Island, but this may not mean that they are absent. Special pit-fall sets, which catch shrews more effectively than live traps set for rodents, have not been tried on Matagorda.

The most likely shrew to expect on Matagorda Island is the common and adaptable least shrew. These voracious little predators live in shallow burrow systems or beneath surface debris on forest edges, in grasslands, and even on slight elevations around the edges of tidal flats. They are particularly at home in dense stands of tall bluestem grasses, where they scamper in protected seclusion along cotton rat runways in their incessant search for insects, arachnids, and crustaceans. Although these energy-demanding little creatures would be hard-pressed to survive several foodless days adrift in order to reach the island, once there, they would find the extensive barrier flat community an ideal habitat.

But there is convincing evidence against the occurrence of least shrews on Matagorda Island. Barn owls are acknowledged experts at catching shrews, but among the hundreds of rodent skulls extracted from barn owl pellets collected on the island there was only one least shrew skull. This suggests two things: Least shrews do not occur on Matagorda; barn owls make occasional flights between the mainland and the island.

The eastern mole is common on sandy and loamy uplands in the Coastal Bend, and there is a vigorous population on Blackjack Peninsula. On Texas barrier islands, moles have been reported only from leaf litter beneath the few hummocks of live oaks on the north end of Padre Island.

Two bits of evidence confirm the lack of moles on Matagorda: The quite evident ridges of soil that moles make while feeding just beneath the surface have not been observed; the island's ever-vigilant barn owls, which somehow manage to consistently catch moles wherever they are available, have left no telltale mole skulls in their regurgitation pellets.

Despite their evident mobility and relative abundance as both residents and migrants in the Coastal Bend, only four species of bats have been recorded on the Texas barrier islands and none on Matagorda. This may be due as much to lack of observation as to any scarcity of the animals. Bats might be incidentally noticed in flight, but they are best-documented by systematic searches of potential daytime roosts and winter hibernation sites and by setting specially made, finely woven mist nets. Such investigations have not been conducted on Matagorda Island.

Mexican free-tailed bat

The two species of bats regarded as most likely to feed or roost on Matagorda Island are the Mexican free-tailed bat and the eastern pipistrelle. The Mexican free-tail, a local summer resident in the Coastal Bend, readily uses buildings for roosts, and large migratory flights of this bat pass through in spring and fall. The little pipistrelle, a common resident seen fluttering erratically in the twilight, is active throughout most of the year and remains in the Coastal Bend during the winter. Both of these species have been found roosting on Padre Island. Since the musty odor and heaps of guano usual from Mexican free-tail roosts have not been noticed by supervisory personnel, it is possible that these large bats do not stop over on Matagorda.

Although nocturnal and not often seen, the swamp rabbit is common in moist terrain throughout the eastern third of Texas. In the Coastal Bend, where these rabbits reach the western edge of their range, they prefer wooded river bottoms and sloughs to the sparse tidal flats, and there is a healthy population in the palmetto-studded delta of the Guadalupe River directly across from Matagorda Island.

Swamp rabbits readily pad through shallow water, and they are strong and determined swimmers, even submerging to avoid predators. As they are among the commonest mammals seen adrift on flood debris, it seems likely that an occasional one would be cast ashore on the bay side of the barrier islands. Yet, there is no record of the species here or on any other Texas barrier.

The fact that Matagorda Island has only three species of native rodents is testimony to its natural isolation and relatively light human traffic. Rodents, with their natural dispersal ability, have been most successful at colonizing the Texas barrier islands. They are adaptable and small enough to hitchhike in human conveyances. In addition, their potentially explosive reproductive capacity allows them to quickly exploit human modification of the natural environment.

Mexican ground squirrels are part of the Tamaulipan fauna sweeping in from the Southwest to its eastern limits in the Coastal Bend. They once occurred in the open pasturelands of Blackjack Peninsula but disappeared several decades ago with the encroachment of live oaks and associated woody plants. Apparently they were never able to migrate to Matagorda. This species does occur in the dunes on South Padre Island.

Spotted ground squirrels, a related southwestern species, are common among the sand dunes on North Padre and Mustang islands and inhabit sandy areas southward down the coast. These quick, shy, little squirrels give their thin whistles of alarm and scamper into their burrows at the slightest sign of danger. They are well adapted to the barrier and feed on fresh greenery, the abundant seedheads of sea oats, and insects. If they had ever managed to cross Aransas Pass, spotted ground squirrels doubtless would be characteristic of the dunes habitat on St. Joseph and Matagorda islands today.

Although the thirteen-lined ground squirrel occurs sporadically in the grassy interior of the Coastal Bend and the adjacent Blackland Prairie, it avoids the deep sands of the immediate coastline and has never been recorded on a Texas barrier island.

There are reliable accounts of pocket gophers around the Wynne ranch buildings in the 1950s, but the population was severely reduced by Hurricane Carla in 1961 and extirpated by Hurricane Celia in 1970. Neither gophers nor the sandy mounds that betray their presence have been seen elsewhere on the island.

These gophers present several mysteries. If they came from the adjacent mainland, as seems most likely, they would have been Attwater's pocket gophers, which occupy the coastal prairie between the Brazos and Nueces rivers. However, if they came by island-hopping northward from the well-established populations on Padre and Mustang islands, they would have been South Texas pocket gophers, which occur in sandy soils south of the Nueces River. Because the two species look and behave very much alike, the issue is only of academic interest.

Why were pocket gophers limited to the south end of Matagorda when the whole island is an apparent gopher's paradise? The simplest answer is that they were recent immigrants and had not had time to spread. Why were these gophers wiped out by hurricanes that other resident rodents survived? Gophers live in subterranean burrows vulnerable to floods, and the highly specialized animals flushed to the surface are totally out of their element. So they are more susceptible to sudden overwash than surface-living rodents that can scramble to high ground and eke out a living until better times. Then why, despite hurricanes, are there still gophers on Padre and Mustang islands? Together, these two barriers stretch for many miles down the Texas coast. Even a major storm would be unlikely to inundate all insular pocket gopher colonies, and the survivors could rapidly reclaim their former domain.

Finally, why have gophers not become reestablished on Matagorda Island since 1970? Aransas Pass (both the salt-water pass itself and its heavily developed south bank) is probably an insurmountable barrier to northward migration of gophers from Mustang Island. Successful natural rafting and such circumstances as barge loads of fill material in which gophers from the mainland could be carried do not occur frequently. Perhaps there has simply not been enough time for potential immigrants to bridge the gap.

Three rodents—the silky pocket mouse, the northern grasshopper mouse, and the Gulf Coast kangaroo rat—all occur on Padre Island but not on Matagorda Island. All are southwestern species that probably crossed the Laguna Madre flats but could not get over Aransas Pass. The two mice are rare on Padre, but the kangaroo rat is an abundant and characteristic inhabitant of the sand dunes community, though seldom seen because it is strictly nocturnal. If Mother Nature would improve on Matagorda Island, it might well be by the ingress of the delightful and well-adapted kangaroo rat; the ideal habitat awaits it.

The hispid pocket mouse occurs on Padre and Mustang islands as well as on the mainland in the Coastal Bend; yet, this species does not inhabit Matagorda Island. It is a slow-moving, easily stressed, and rather dim-witted rodent that apparently lacks both the inclination and the ability to survive a salt-water crossing. If immigrants ever do gain the island, they could presumably establish themselves along the boundary between the barrier flat and the sand dunes communities, where numerous plants would furnish them the seeds upon which they mainly subsist.

The northern pigmy mouse is still expanding its range from Mexico through the eastern half of Texas. These gray midgets are abundant in grassy habitats throughout the Coastal Bend; they are uncommon in the sparse grass cover on Padre Island. It is surprising that these opportunistic little mice have not gained access to Matagorda Island. If they ever do, they should find in the spacious interior grassland everything a pigmy mouse desires.

Although the white-footed mouse is one of the most widespread rodents in Texas and in the Coastal Bend, it has a distinct predilection for woody cover. The species has not been recorded on any Texas barrier island, probably because occasional immigrants cannot establish populations in the open, sandy terrain. Live traps set in the chaparral community and within Macartney rose hedges on Matagorda have failed to take specimens. Even the island's ever-alert barn owls have coughed up no white-foot skulls.

The geographic ranges of two species of woodrats (popularly called pack rats) meet along the Guadalupe and San Antonio rivers across the bay from Matagorda Island. The southern plains woodrat is a charter member of the Tamaulipan fauna characteristically associated with mesquites and prickly pears in the dry brushland. The eastern woodrat belongs to the Austroriparian fauna of the southeast and haunts bottomlands, swamps, and the wooded edges of salt marshes. Both of these large rats, though shy and nocturnal, reveal their presence by the mounds of sticks, leaves, and debris they habitually pile up over den sites.

There is a vague reference to "pack rat nests in prickly pear patches" from the early ranching days on Matagorda Island; when livestock kept the barrier flat more open, it may have been suitable habitat for southern plains woodrats. But neither rat has been definitely recorded on any Texas barrier. Today the species would likely be restricted to the chaparral community, but den sites have not been discovered there. The island environment is probably too open, dry, and herbaceous for eastern woodrats.

Though everywhere rare, the long-tailed weasel is one of the most widespread predatory mammals in the state. Even when these slender, low-slung, nervous animals are present, they are difficult to detect unless special traps are set for them. Weasels swim, but, preferring upland terrain, are not likely to be caught adrift and so are improbable migrants to the offshore islands. The long-tailed weasel has not been recorded on any Texas barrier.

Mink range through East Texas and reach their western limit along the Guadalupe River across San Antonio Bay from Matagorda Island. Although they live along the edges of salt marshes on the upper coast, in the Coastal Bend they forego the sparse tidal flats for the wooded banks of creeks and sloughs in the bottomlands. Because of their semiaquatic habits, a mink might get swept seaward during a major flood. However, the species has not been recorded on any Texas barrier. If a migrant mink made landfall on Matagorda, it could probably substitute fiddler crabs for its favored crayfish prey, but the absence of directional fresh-water flow, woody cover, and banks with tangles of roots for den sites would doubtless weigh against prolonged survival.

The river otter, even more aquatic than the mink, also reaches its western boundary in the Coastal Bend. Most at home along wooded stream banks, in East Texas, river otters forage deep into salt marshes to feed on mullet and blue crabs. Otters are rare locally, but one of these strong swimmers could make it to Matagorda Island, especially on the outwash from a heavy flood. An otter should be able to feed itself in the tidal flats, but it would surely find the environment too open for permanent occupation. The species has not been seen on any Texas offshore island.

Early ranchers report that skunks were absent from the barrier, and none are known to exist there today. But there is one reference to the need to "control skunks around the air base" during its active years on Matagorda Island. If skunks did live there, they were probably striped skunks, which might easily have been introduced during the massive movement of personnel and materials that attended military occupation of the site. Presumably, the eradication attempt was successful.

The striped skunk is one of the most common, abundant, and adaptable medium-sized mammals in Texas; there is a healthy population along the Gulf Coast. Skunks might survive rafting across the bays, but a more likely means of introduction is as stowaways or pets. Striped skunks have recently appeared on Padre and Mustang islands, but they avoid the natural environment and live around human habitations. Striped skunks should flourish in the grassland interior of Matagorda Island, easily subsisting on rodents, ground-nesting birds, herptiles, and insects; they would doubtless become a devastating predator.

The handsome gray fox ranges nearly throughout Texas, but it is so alert and shy that it is seldom observed, even when it chooses to live near human habitations. This trim and agile little canid certainly possesses the dispersal ability to move from the mainland to the barriers by swimming and islet-hopping, but it has never been recorded as a migrant. Although foxes show a definite preference for broken and wooded terrain, they could probably make shift in the insular grassland and dunes environment, where they could subsist on rodents, insects, land crabs, and sundry fruits. However, the occasional gray fox that might venture onto Matagorda or any other Texas barrier would be rapidly detected, run to ground, and killed by resident coyotes. The mainland environment is varied enough for foxes to avoid such a confrontation; on a barrier not even the center of a chaparral clump would offer them safe retreat.

Javelina (hava-'leen-ah; also called collared peccaries) are characteristic inhabitants of dry brushlands of the Southwest. The population on Blackjack Peninsula is near the eastern limit in coastal Texas for these native pigs. Although a rare individual has been reported on Padre Island, none has been observed on Matagorda. Javelina are mobile and can swim, and coastal animals readily muck through brackish shallows. However, it is doubtful that a pack of half a dozen or so (a minimum number for these highly social creatures to set up a resident population) would attempt the crossing to Matagorda voluntarily. If they did manage to get access, they would find all but the widely scattered patches of chaparral unsuited for their food and shelter needs. Beyond those scant, brushy limits, they would be in direct competition with feral hogs for all pig amenities.

CHAPTER 7

Birds

Excerpts from a Matagorda Birder's Notebook

"We were in the right place at the right time today. Brackish pool near Pringle Lake just after dawn, sun at our backs. More ooze than water; fish, shrimp, and bugs trapped. Birds just found it and already in a feeding frenzy, nearly oblivious to us. What a tumult of snapping bills, flapping wings, and dancing legs amid a cacophony of squawks, gurgles, and groans! Everybody here: white ibises; roseate spoonbills; American avocets; wood storks; great, snowy, and reddish egrets; great blue, juvenile little blue, tricolored, and even two black-crowned night-herons; two pairs of mottled ducks dabbling in the murky middle; juvenile laughing gulls, lesser yellowlegs, willets, black-necked stilts, two Wilson's plovers, a black-bellied plover, a killdeer, and a scattering of western and least sandpipers around the edge. Everybody doing their thing at high speed—spearing, stabbing, snatching, scything, sieving, stealing, scavenging, pecking, picking, probing; pausing only to swallow gluttonously. Some organization in the confusion: white ibises in a line across the pool walked the length in solid front, each switching partly opened beak 'til it caught some morsel; gobbled it down without losing step and quickly back to work. Ibis rank marched up and down the pool with other waders falling in behind, snapping up what was roiled to the surface.

"A prime example of commensal feeding—the foraging behavior of one species incidentally adding to the feeding success of another. The ibis beaters attracted a passel of wading followers. And the whole lot of them had attracted us. After a solid hour behind the binoculars we were pleasantly exhausted.

"Discovered a well-kept secret of the sanderlings this morning. For a bird's eye view, we lay down on the opalescent, sunrise-lit beach just above a calm surf and immediately noticed dark flecks among the countless sparkles—shadows of minuscule irregularities in the sand. The slightest movement shifted the pattern of dark-and-dazzle. A lot of subterranean mini-bustle in the back-wash of every wave, all faithfully registered by a change in surface sparkle. Sure enough, from sanderling-eye level and with sanderling wave timing, we used a hand sieve to scoop up mole crabs and sand digger amphipods almost as reliably as the birds themselves. Later, watching a flock of sanderlings dash back and forth in perfect synchrony with the waves, we smiled knowingly.

"Cedar Bayou in dying light, a flock of avocets settling down on a tiny spit of sand. More birds than sand; some, shouldered off into the tidal current, fly to the upstream end, settle down, and jostle others loose. Tide rising; how will they ever make the night? Imagine standing all night completely exposed, wet feet, maybe nudged into dark water. Do they not comprehend?

Hard norther roared in last night; temperature 21° F at dawn; wind chill unthinkable. Back to pass. The sand spit gone; surely engulfed by the first surge of wind tide. Did avocets sense it and chance the dunes or tidal flat rather than cling to their doomed islet? Or, surprised and confused in the bitter darkness, were they swallowed up before they could make a move?

We never found out, but as we shivered on the edge of the wind-whipped pass we had a deep and somber feeling of what it takes to be a survivor in Nature.

"Perhaps there really is protection in numbers. Driving down the beach. Loafing flocks of ring-billed, laughing, and herring gulls; Caspian, Forster's, sandwich, and least terns; sanderlings; turnstones, and a few piping plovers, taking off as we neared, flapping out, banking, settling behind us. Fifty yards ahead a solitary adult sandwich tern crouched and took off but never really got fully airborne. A feathered bomb zoomed down, smashed in, instantly crumpling the tern into a lifeless mass of feathers and sinew. Peregrine! Truly 'swifter than arrow from Tartar's bow', gone over the dunes before we could close our mouths and raise our binoculars. Waited; waves nudging the ruffle of feathers that once was the tern, but the falcon never returned. Maybe the spectacular stoop not driven by hunger at all, but by the appearance of an irresistible, solitary dark target moving against the glaring sand. Peregrine responded elegantly to the urge to test its mettle; tern paid the final measure for its interlude of uncustomary reclusiveness; and we felt richer for having been there.

"Island food chains interlink in strange ways. Spooked two double-crested cormorants off muddy bar in Cottonwood Bayou. One unloaded half full gullet as it labored into air. Two ring-billed gulls immediately on the pile of liquified silversides for a smelly second harvest. One snapped up several fish in its bill and took off. Gull climbing when a dark male magnificent frigatebird appeared out of nowhere. Gull spotted it; leveled off for speed; hopeless. The man-o'-war came on in high gear, zoomed a feather's-width over gull's back, adroitly wheeled on bent wing and forked tail for return. But ring-bill had had enough. Dropped its fish. Frigatebird instantly swooped, flicked beak, grabbed fish in midair. Suddenly it caught a thermal and rose like a kite. Within seconds, a speck in the sky. There, among high drafts above Matagorda, the well-traveled silversides doubtless dissolved inside this most spectacular air pirate, completing a lofty third harvest.

"Walking toward the beach; took short cut across the grassland east of air base; a mistake. Mosquitoes horrendous; ravening clouds at every step. Finally regained the road. Glanced back at a strange sight: for 75 yards, every nuance of our backtrail marked at waist-level by line of fluttering swallows—a mix of tree, barn, and rough-wings. Mosquitoes we flushed had attracted the migrating birds. Hundreds couldn't put a dent in jillions, but grimly satisfying to see them try.

"We've done it! We've witnessed one of the fabled Matagorda fallouts. The dark line of thunderstorms heralded an April norther that put the migrating passerines down in saltcedar and rose clumps. A cascade of bright colors, restless twitters, twitching bodies: indigo and painted buntings; blue grosbeaks; scarlet and summer tanagers; orchard and northern orioles; gray-cheeked thrushes and blue-gray gnatcatchers; bobolinks and yellow-headed blackbirds. And, of course, the warblers: blue-winged, orange-crowned, black-and-white, Nashville, yellow, chestnut-sided, black-throated green, prothonotary, hooded, Wilson's, American redstarts, and more. As an indication of the action, at one point I spoke breathlessly into my tape recorder: 'I have nineteen, no make that twenty-two, indigo buntings in the field of my binoculars simultaneously; the effect is simply overwhelming. I half expected the illusion to be gone when I took my glasses down, but the birds were still there; and with my wider field of vision I could have tripled the count if they had only perched long enough for me to tally them accurately.' If what we saw was a fair sample of the number of grounded passerines on the island that afternoon, the extrapolated total must have been truly dumbfounding.

"Sitting atop a dune idly watching the surf when a line of six brown pelicans came gliding silently along a trough between the breakers, not moving a muscle yet maintaining speed and perfect formation a feather's breadth above the surface of the water. Perfect symmetry, inherent beauty, unconscious perfection; unplanned, unsolicited, unanticipated; the indelible stuff of which lifelong memories are forged, haikus written, and souls recharged."

Birds, certainly the most evident, most diverse, and most ecologically significant segment of the vertebrate fauna of Matagorda Island, are also among the most popular attractions. Bird-watching ranks, in terms of visitor hours, just behind fishing and beachcombing. Indeed, when the U.S. Congress appropriated the funds that brought Matagorda Island into total public ownership, it mandated that the barrier be dedicated first and foremost to the protection of the endangered and migratory species of birds that occur there.

To date, 314 bird species have been recorded on Matagorda Island. This compares with 495 for the Coastal Bend, over 350 for the Aransas National Wildlife Refuge, and 333 for Padre Island National Seashore. The Matagorda bird list counts all but one of the seventeen kinds of large wading birds that inhabit the United States, all nine of the American rails, three-quarters of the thirty-five kinds of ducks, and two-thirds of the twenty-seven kinds of raptors. Sixteen gulls and terns, thirty-five shorebirds, thirty-two wood warblers, and twenty-five sparrows routinely set down on Matagorda during part of their life cycles. There are eleven endangered/threatened bird species.

With so many highly visible birds living on or passing over the island during the most active seasons, exciting observations are almost commonplace. Since a bird is counted as occurring in an area if one reliable person has ever seen it there, more birders visiting Matagorda means the island's species list will doubtless grow. It is only a matter of time before Matagorda Island is recognized as a premier birding spot in the number one state in the nation for native bird diversity (about 540 species).

There are no birds unique to Matagorda Island. Except for lack of woodland forms, the kinds of birds on the barrier are about the same as those on the mainland, although the abundance and date of appearance of certain species are often quite different. No physical barrier prevents any local birds from getting to Matagorda Island, though some, like wrens and chickadees, have significant behavioral barriers that keep them from freely flitting out across the open bay. Many kinds of birds use Matagorda only as a temporary stepping stone on long-range journeys, and a few pelagic species occasionally wander over or are blown upon the island.

You can enjoy birds without knowing one from the other, but a modicum of spotting skill may add to your appreciation of them. (Fifty-eight species were mentioned in the previous excerpt; how many of them can you recognize in the field?) Experienced birders will know the many field guides available; some of our favorites are listed in the bibliography at the end of the book. It is beyond the scope of this book to describe and discuss all of the birds that touch Matagorda Island; a complete list of documented species, along with their preferred habitats and seasonal abundance, is available at the TPWD office in Port O'Connor and at the Visitors' Center on the island. Check off the ones you have already seen on the island and extend your list with each visit. If you see an unusual species, try to get independent verification from other birders; take a photo if you can, and by all means tell a park employee. New bird listings frequently trace to an observation by an alert visitor.

Rather than an aid to identification, this will be a commentary on bird ecology, stressing the two interrelated facets that dominate the lives of birds on the Gulf islands: migration and food chains. Matagorda Island will be the focus, but much will be applicable to any Texas barrier.

We will also weave in a rationale for the conservation of our vanishing birdlife. In fact, this is a good time to mention one aspect of conservation often overlooked—unintentional harassment of birds by birders trying to get a better look. It may seem like a minor irritation for such easily mobile creatures, but every time birds must take flight or change their normal behavior patterns, they are using energy and suffering psychological stress. On refuge areas visited by a lot of people, like Matagorda Island on a sunny spring weekend, the wildlife may be tormented by continual disturbance. This issue is absolutely critical for nesting birds and endangered species. Judicious use of binoculars and telescopes can keep birding the noninvasive activity most birders imagine it to be; one that satisfies the birder without unsettling the bird. Try to set a good example and help spread the word.

Migration

Matagorda Island lies in a narrow bottleneck on the great Central Flyway that links North America with Central and South America via the wingbeats of hundreds of thousands of passing birds. Shorebirds, waterfowl, gulls, terns, raptors, and a host of passerines make up the bulk of these biannual voyagers. Some are long-distance champions; if you recognize a flock of Baird's sandpipers on the edge of a tidal pool, give these nondescript little birds the respect they deserve.

They will have just come nonstop from the high Arctic; when they take wing, they may not come down again until they reach Bolivia, 4,000 miles to the south; after a brief respite they will push on another 3,000 miles deep into Patagonia. In the spring some of these same intrepid individuals might reappear at the very same tidal pool, this time bound for the Arctic.

It is not widely appreciated that many migratory birds spend nearly three-quarters of their lives on the move, vulnerable to weather, accident, predation, drifting off-course, fatigue, drain of stored fuel, and—increasingly these days—usurpation of their customary stopover points by human development. It is obvious that birds must successfully nest and rear young to maintain their kind, but unless enough potential parents arrive safely on the breeding grounds, the question of brood survival is moot.

Awareness that the migratory phase is just as important as the nesting phase in a bird's life cycle has led to an enlightened view about the importance of sites like Matagorda Island as staging areas—resting and refueling stops habitually used by migrating birds. In addition to providing the shelter, food, and respite they absolutely require, the site may have a traditional hold on some species. Banding records reveal that individual migrants show amazing site fidelity, returning to the same specific spots year after year for as long as they live. If their customary staging area is destroyed, birds may not be able to switch, even if an acceptable substitute is available. Throughout the world, conservationists are currently highlighting the important and irreplaceable nature of staging areas for migratory birds.

Matagorda Island is a conveniently situated and bountiful staging area for long-distance migrants between the Americas. It is the terminus for winter residents and a welcome landfall for spring migrants that launch from the Yucatan Peninsula and traverse 700 miles of open Gulf on their way north. Finally, it lies directly in the narrow corridor bounded by dry highlands on the west and the perilous Gulf of Mexico on the east, which serves as a natural pathway for migrating birds from all over eastern and central North America.

At least a few migrants are shifting along this ancient route during every month of the year, but each spring and again each fall, the frenzy builds, the clamor rises, wings roar, numbers swell, and the ages-old miracle is wrought anew. Up to 100 million birds make their biannual passages through the region, putting on such shows of grim determination, uncanny navigation, efficient marshaling, and sheer biomass as to confound and amaze all who witness them. And Matagorda Island makes a significant contribution to the spectacle.

Only about twenty species of birds are year-round residents on

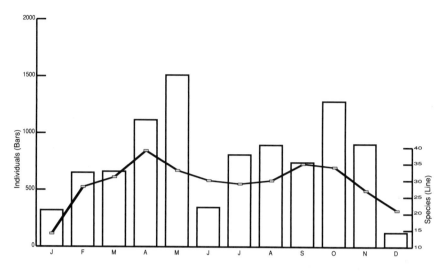

Figure 5. Number and diversity of birds on Matagorda Island beaches. Migration accounts for spring and fall highs (Data from the USFWS, 1989–1990).

Matagorda; all others vary in their occurrence. Some, like the green-winged teal, arrive in the fall, stay the winter, and depart in the spring. Others, like semipalmated sandpipers, breeze through each spring and fall. Black-necked stilts nest on the island, only drifting down the coast during the middle of winter. Great egrets can be found in every month of the year, but become scarce in April when most move to the offshore islets to nest. Wood storks spend only the summer on the island. Northern mockingbirds and eastern meadow-larks are among the permanent residents; they nest on the island and never leave en masse.

To understand Matagorda's birdlife one must comprehend Matagorda's seasons. From the viewpoint of the birds, the seasons are spring (March to May), summer (June and July), fall (August to October), and winter (November to February). Figure 5 shows that spring migration peaks during April to May; fall migration peaks from August to September; winter residents are on the island from November through February, and summer is the slack time for bird diversity.

Long before the doldrums of summer have lifted off the coastal country, birds far to the north have fledged their young and begun to feel the urge to be on the wing. By late July and early August the first blue-winged teal begin to splash down on the fresh-water ponds and tidal pools and the earliest nervous flocks of long-billed dowitchers, dunlin, greater and lesser yellowlegs, and semipalmated sandpipers show up on the mud flats of Matagorda Island. Ruddy turnstones and an early wave of sanderlings appear on the beach, along with increasing numbers of royal and Caspian terns. Long-billed curlews arrive to stalk the edges of the tidal flats and the interior grasslands. Activity picks up steadily as August progresses: more of the above, along with increasing numbers of "peeps"—least, western, pectoral, and white-rumped sandpipers; and groups of marbled godwits, throngs of American avocets, and clusters of black-bellied plovers.

Through September and October the activity continues in high gear, with fresh waves of birds arriving from the north and early flocks departing southward. Shorebirds dominate the scene. Swarms of peeps, many semipalmated, piping, and snowy plovers, a great flush of sanderlings, larger flocks of long-billed dowitchers and dunlin, occasional clumps of red knots, and fast-moving stilt and buff-breasted sandpipers filter through. Herring and ring-billed gulls arrive on the beach; overnight, thousands of double-crested cormorants appear on the shell reefs and pilings. Early in September the vanguard of ducks begins to show up: American wigeon, gadwall, northern shovelers, green-winged teal, and a scattering of pintails. By late October most wintering ducks, including the open-water diving species, will have arrived in the Coastal Bend, as well as sundry grebes and rails. Geese are in the vicinity by late October, but they do not usually visit the island immediately. Early in October the first sandhill cranes, osprey, and northern harriers arrive; later in the month peregrine falcons appear atop the dunes, and eventually the earliest whooping cranes are sighted in the tidal flats. Meanwhile, almost unnoticed amid the bustle of larger birds, a thin but steady stream of transient passerines passes through: flycatchers, thrushes, tanagers, sparrows, and warblers.

By November the birds are in place. Species that will do so have moved on south; those that will stay the winter have located their favored feeding and roosting sites. The northers that began in October increase in frequency and sting through November and December. Although it will be interrupted by frequent warm intervals, winter has come to Matagorda Island. Winter resident shorebirds, waders, and waterfowl steal the show: herons, egrets, ibises, spoonbills, avocets, peeps, dowitchers, dunlin, plovers, dabbling ducks, diving ducks, grebes, gallinules, loons—all are highly visible as they seek their daily fare. Reduced gull and tern diversity is made up by numbers of individuals. Rafts and mounds of white pelicans dot the tidal inlets and crowd the muddy bars. Sandhill cranes and whooping cranes can be reliably found at their preferred feeding sites. Sometime late in December a few snow and Canada geese leave the well-gleaned grain fields on the mainland and settle in the saltgrass zone on the bay side of the island.

The nearest Audubon Christmas Count, centered on the Aransas National Wildlife Refuge, takes in only the tidal flats on the extreme southwestern end of Matagorda Island. Appendix D gives some idea of winter-resident diversity and numbers in this small part of the island.

Although intermittent cold weather continues through February, groups of ducks begin to haul out of the Coastal Bend in late January. By late February many ducks are gone and a northbound flow of shorebirds has begun. The number of herring and ring-billed gulls and of sandwich, Forster's, royal, and Caspian terns rises as birds begin to move up from southern beaches; black skimmers begin to reappear.

The gusty winds of March herald the peak of spring shorebird movement. This passage is always more hurried than in fall. Still, as many as ten thousand birds may be seen crowding the tidal flats, stoking up on marine worms and crustaceans before the long flight north. The geese begin to leave and by mid-March, even as all the geese and ducks start northward, the first legion of barn swallows comes zooming in low over the tidal flats and grasslands.

Anyone who has watched waterbirds through the winter will notice changes in their color and demeanor. The heads of avocets turn rusty; reddish egrets brighten to a brassy-pink; bills of Caspian terns turn blood red; the snowy egrets' necks get shaggy and their filmy plumes wave in the breeze; spoonbills turn a fluorescent carmine-pink; and here and there the birds dance, flutter, chase, and lock bills. Clearly, the breeding season is upon them. And now all birders' eyes will be turning to the saltcedars, the mesquites, and rose clumps, where they will soon delight to the arrival of the first wave of perching birds.

Throughout April and May northbound birds pass swiftly over the island. Swallows fill the air: tree, bank, rough-winged, cliff. Almost as abruptly as they arrived, the double-crested cormorants are gone. The flush of shorebirds dwindles rapidly, and the mud flats finally stand nearly vacant. The sandhills are already gone and the whoopers leave by mid-April; the island is strangely quiet without these two buglers. Herons, egrets, ibises, and many gulls and terns are moving to the offshore islets and reefs to nest. Kettles of raptors and a fast-moving front of ruby-throated hummingbirds pass through. But late April and early May belong to the passerines: buntings, tanagers, orioles, flycatchers, kingbirds, kinglets, thrushes, vireos, and, of course, warblers galore. If heavy weather puts the exhausted migrants down for a day or two, birding on the island has to be experienced to be believed. Even professionals must keep their field guides handy to sort out the riot of bright colors that suddenly enlivens every woody refuge.

Finally, by June, the phenomenon is finished. There are still plenty of birds around, but most are preoccupied with nesting and raising young. The resident waders, gulls, terns, and brown pelicans rear their broods on oystershell islets in the bays; by late June the adults and their begging fledglings begin to appear on the island. Meanwhile some thirty-four species of birds will have nested on Matagorda, including white-tailed hawks, black-shouldered kites, crested caracaras, common nighthawks, loggerhead shrikes, horned larks, and seaside sparrows. By this time magnificent frigatebirds and wood storks will have come up from the south. At last, the oppressive, humid heat of late June and July suppresses all enthusiasm beyond gular-fluttering survival.

Some birds follow elliptical migration routes, passing across Matagorda Island in considerable numbers on only one leg of their journey. The most common situation is fall migrants from the eastern Atlantic Seaboard that ride favorable winds across the open ocean to the West Indies and to Central and South America. On their return trip in the spring, these birds avoid exhausting headwinds by detouring up the continental margin and then through the central United States. These species—lesser golden plover, Hudsonian godwit, white-rumped sandpiper, and several of the thrushes and wood warblers—appear on Matagorda Island mainly as spring migrants.

This general pattern varies in details from year to year. Numbers of participating birds depend on breeding success and survival on the wintering grounds, which, in turn, depend on good weather, normal rainfall, sufficient food; in general, the continued integrity of the habitat. Timing en route is very much weather-dependent; unusually warm weather holds up fall migrants, while early cold snaps hasten them on their way. Southbound birds use rapidly moving cold fronts as convenient tailwinds, but northbound spring migrants are temporarily grounded by such weather. Severe storms wreak havoc on birds caught in the open. Amount of waste grain left in the fields, the well-being of crucial staging areas, occurrence of abnormal tides, accumulation of fresh water, incidence of water-borne avian disease, and hunting pressure all influence the arrival and departure of migrants.

Although aspects of the same cycle, spring and fall migrations are not mirror images. For most species, the spring journey north is more urgent; the birds leave, regardless of the weather, according to the cue of changing daylength, and they do not dally along the way. Their hormones and their instincts drive them relentlessly northward, for the long, balmy days full of thronging insects are ephemeral. Neither early nor late arrivals at the nesting grounds fare as well as those that synchronize their reproduction with the brief boreal time of plenty. So spring migration on Matagorda Island is swift and concise; the birds have urgent business elsewhere.

The southbound fall migration, if not quite leisurely, is certainly more relaxed than its counterpart. The birds are simply shifting down to more tolerable latitudes, and if not pressed by cold weather, many tarry at hospitable spots. Tired and hungry, adults usually leave the breeding grounds first, and so make up the bulk of the early fall migrants. Later come juveniles bedecked in fresh plumage. By the time the young birds filter through, the adults have molted and moved on, avoiding competition between experienced parents and their inexperienced offspring. Fall migration on Matagorda Island is gradual, prolonged, and somewhat obscured by the fact that for many birds (winter residents) the island is the end of the line.

It is not uncommon to see a few migratory shorebirds on Matagorda Island in the summertime. For sanderlings, this is a regular occurrence; the lingerers are mostly first-year birds that will migrate in their next season. For black-bellied and semipalmated plovers, long-billed dowitchers, and long-billed curlews, occasional perverse individuals simply do not follow the flocks to the breeding grounds.

Resource Partitioning

Even during the excitement of courtship, the brief orgy of mating, and the nonstop flights of long-distance migrants, the day-to-day activities of birds center mostly on the search for food. In our efforts to comprehend this aspect of avian ecology, we have devised such abstractions as food chains, food webs, feeding strategies, and feeding guilds. There is much to be learned here, and most of it can only be discovered by standing still and quietly observing wild birds in the field, for hours and hours.

One of the most intriguing aspects of the feeding biology of birds is the means, conscious and unconscious, by which several species divide a common food source or separate from each other on a common feeding ground so that competition between the several species is minimized. This we call resource partitioning. If you know what to look for, you can observe this universal precept on any tidal flat or stretch of beach on Matagorda Island where a mixed group of shorebirds is feeding. Notice that different species forage in different ways. Some kinds work the shoreline, others wander the shallows, and a few stalk through deeper water. Some are active spookers, others are deliberate stalkers. Some peck, some probe, some sieve. Mud, sand, shell, ooze—each substrate attracts a different coterie of avian hunters. It is logical to assume that in their different habits they harvest different prey. With a good telescope you might be able to see what the birds are actually eating.

Sooner or later you will notice that for each species, behavior and anatomy are neatly meshed. The birds that work in deeper water are those with longer legs, necks, and bills; the little shoreline peeps have quick feet and nifty pick-'em-up bills; birds that sieve the bottom muck have bills with intricately crenulate margins. Surely it will dawn on you that all this is one grand scheme: behavior, anatomy, size, food, niches—life; something that is beautiful to watch, fascinating to study, and challenging to ponder. If you are not careful, you may become a confirmed birder!

On a barrier island, competition for food among shorebirds is somewhat reduced by the fact that all tap the bountiful sea. No matter how many hungry birds arrive, there is no absolute shortage of marine worms, bivalves, and crustaceans to feed them. The point of contention is not food but feeding space—a chance to get at the rich resource while sun, tide, wind, and weather allow its exploitation. For an apt analogy, consider the noon hour on a routine urban workday. Restaurants have plenty of food; the hassle is in finding a parking place, getting through the lines, finding a table, and eating before the allotted lunch time is up. So it is with the shorebirds during the rush hours of migration.

Just how pressed is a shorebird? A bird refueling on migration must consume at least a third of its body weight a day to survive and to lay aside a fraction of a gram of body fat. A western sandpiper, for instance, searches out such miniscule prey items that it needs about 40,000 of them. With a maximum pecking efficiency of 70 percent, the bird must make at least 60,000 pecks a day to satisfy its demand. You only blink your eyes about 9,000 times a day; no wonder that western sandpipers are up early and move frenetically. They can ill-afford to wait in line when the tide goes out and uncovers the food counter. Focus your binoculars on an actively feeding sandpiper and watch it for 5 minutes; then do some simple arithmetic to extrapolate from your observation.

The intriguing puzzle for the birder is how all the birds manage to find their places. How do a large number of several different kinds of ravenous birds apportion what appears to be a rather uniform stretch of shoreline? Ecological separation is managed by devious ways; the more you watch, the greater the variety of subtle tactics you will discover. Most involve passive avoidance rather than aggressive usurpation. Fighting wastes energy, and even the victor might suffer debilitating wounds. The birds are surely aware of each other, but they seem driven more by the ingrained wisdom of their genes than by conscious motives. Here are some tactics to watch for.

To return to our lunch hour analogy, the worst of the crowds can be avoided by going out to lunch a little before or a little after noon. So it is with shorebirds, but with less leeway; they must feed when local conditions make their prey most available. Because of the press of the seasons, especially in the springtime, shorebirds cannot all wait their separate turns to utilize a staging area. But even at the height of migration, birds pass through in successive waves, some species definitely preceding others. There is always overlap, but these pulses keep peak numbers of potential competitors from coinciding.

A good example of this timing can be found among the common, small, nondescript little sandpipers with similar feeding habits that birders call peeps. Most of the semipalmated sandpipers pass through before many least sandpipers arrive. And the leasts begin to leave just as the main mass of western sandpipers comes in. Assuredly, at times, all three appear at every Matagorda banquet table, but all three kinds are never in hordes simultaneously.

Shorebirds feed when their prey is most accessible, usually in the daytime, on a rising or falling tide. A few, like the black-bellied plover, red knot, and sanderling, feed extensively at night, especially on a favorable tide, while others, like the willet and black-necked stilt, stalk about at midday when other birds are resting. These birds, like shiftworkers, avoid rush-hour traffic because they can feed efficiently at off-times.

A city full of people can have lunch at noontime because they don't all go to the same restaurant. They spread out, each seeking the places they know and can reach quickly, places with food they like and can afford. Shorebirds, too, spread out, separating according to their abilities and preferences. Knowing this, birders go to specific habitats to look for certain birds. The inference is that a bird prefers a habitat because it is the place to get its preferred prey. A hungry oystercatcher alights on a shell reef rather than on a sandy beach because mussels live on oyster reefs. You could say that prey organisms choose the habitat and the predator simply follows their lead. Regardless of the sequence, it comes to the same thing: all kinds of shoreline are not equally used by all kinds of birds.

Couplings between habitat and specific shorebirds on Matagorda Island are rather clear cut: sandy beach (sanderlings, snowy plovers); bare mud flat (long-billed dowitchers, dunlin, peeps); vegetated tidal flat (clapper rails); saline barren (Wilson's plover); shell reef (American oystercatchers, ruddy turnstones); tidal pass (American avocets, lesser yellowlegs); fresh-water pond (black-necked stilts, common snipe). None of these species is restricted to its favored habitat, but each occurs most frequently and in greatest numbers where its food requirements are most easily satisfied. Unusual conditions often force birds out of their common haunts. During unfavorable tides, rough water, or high winds, you may find bay-side birds on the beach or vice versa. And birds from all over the island congregate around a particularly productive shallow saline pond in the tidal flats.

Just as a restaurant attracts customers by offering good food at affordable prices, a productive stretch of shoreline lures in many birds because it harbors abundant prey that are easily accessible. Of the several shoreline habitats, the bare mud flat, the one that seems least appealing to human eyes, is the most attractive to shorebirds. The mud flats that line so many miles of its twisting bay-side margin are one of the main reasons that Matagorda Island is such an attractive staging area for migrating shorebirds.

What is so alluring about a mud flat? The smell and the color of the nasty stuff, although repulsive to us, hint of rich detritus, jillions of bacteria, and continual decay. This is food for a multitude of filtering, sucking, and nibbling worms, clams, snails, and crustaceans. With the odorous ooze transformed into appealing packets of protoplasm, the birds come to dine. There is no scarcity of nutrient-laden tidal mud, and marine invertebrates reproduce prolifically, so a mud flat is a natural restaurant with a full and varied menu. Although it closes when the tide comes in, it reopens with fresh vigor on a regular schedule, and the birds know its hours; they arrive before the doors are fully open. The fine, moist sediments of a mud flat accommodate all sorts of table manners—probing, pecking, noodling, slurping. The ambiance is pleasant—quiet water, firm footing (for a bird, at least), and an unobstructed view that promotes peace of mind while dining. If you want to see shorebirds en masse on Matagorda Island, visit the mud flats at low tide during the migration rush hours.

As a feeding site, the beach definitely ranks behind the mud flat in shorebird popularity. Although you see a lot of shorebirds on the beach, the numbers are misleading because they are so visible here,

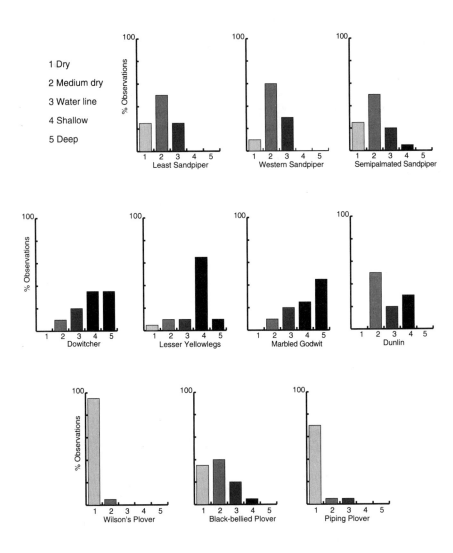

Figure 6. Resource partitioning among birds in the mud flat habitat.

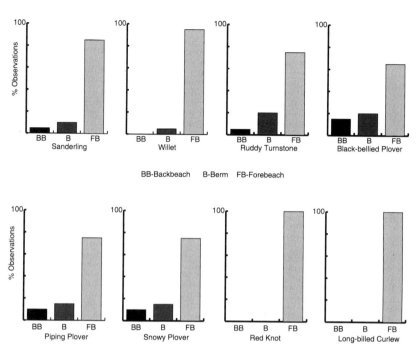

Figure 7. Resource partitioning among birds in the beach habitat.

and many of them are not feeding but taking advantage of the open terrain to rest and preen. On the beach, the detrital food base is less concentrated, the shifting sand is too abrasive for many soft-bodied prey organisms, the surf is often too high, and the bottom drops off too rapidly for most shorebird species. Yet, if one knows what sanderlings know about mole crabs and coquina clams or if one is plover-quick and can peck up amphipods and beach flies, then the strip of sand is a well-spread buffet. Of course, for different sorts of diners like gulls and terns, the beach and surf are more attractive than the mud flat.

Shell reefs attract specialists like oystercatchers and turnstones, and shorebirds that routinely peck in crevices, like willets and black-bellied plovers. A shell reef is a poor hunting ground for probers. Flocks of shorebirds on shell reefs are usually there for a secure roost.

Here our analogy falters; once at a restaurant, there is little we can do to speed things beyond ordering the daily special or using the drive-up window. Shorebirds segregate within a habitat, as though they can detect some tables that command bigger portions. Many pleasant hours in the field can be spent in close observation to divine what cues they follow.

The surface of every habitat can be divided into zones of differing productivity. For the shore habitat, the waterline is a convenient index for marking out parallel feeding zones.

The waterline is where food is most plentiful for many shorebirds. The oscillating front of water creates a wave of disturbance that lures tiny organisms to the surface to feed and to mate. Worms squiggle, amphipods skitter, and clams reposition their siphons. Many creatures get stranded on a falling tide, and their death throes do not go unnoticed. Here sharp-eyed birds line up to feed.

Above the waterline the substrate gradually dries out and its texture changes. The moist zone is still productive, especially for probing birds; some species prefer it, and it is a satisfactory alternative for others. As the substrate becomes drier, pecking birds fare better. Those that can exploit special spots like piles of moist seaweed or crusts of blue-green algae find good pickings free from competitors.

As the waterline moves with the tides, the extent of the feeding zones changes. On a falling tide the birds have room to separate; on a rising tide they crowd together when the preferred zones narrow or even vanish. Prolonged high tides or sudden wind tides can play havoc with feeding schedules. Sustained low tides, though they expose a lot of feeding area, aren't good, either; when the substrate dries, the invertebrates retreat down out of reach.

Depth, both of the water and within the substrate, is an important factor in the distribution of prey organisms and in their accessibility to the birds.

Whether the substrate is submerged or exposed, most shorebirds feed from its surface or by poking their bills into it. All will take swimming prey if they can catch it, but few are specialized for sieving.

On and within any open shore or submerged bottom there is a definite layering of prey organisms. At any level, the kinds and densities of creatures are geared to the requirements of each for water, salinity, substrate texture, and food: Shore flies and shore bugs flit over the bare surface of a sunny flat. Amphipods stay tucked in moist crevices. Microcrustaceans live in the froth at the waveline. Nematode worms squiggle in the skim of detritus on the shallow bottom. Small annelid worms burrow just beneath the surface of submerged mud; bigger worms dig deeper down; some clams and ghost shrimp go deeper yet.

To birds, the main importance of the water column that is added to the layering of prey on and in submerged bottoms is the constraints it places on seeing and getting at the food items. This is where anatomy gives various advantages to some species. The long pipe-stems of a black-necked stilt will take it where a stumpy-legged red knot could never go; no dunlin can probe to the depth that a godwit can reach.

Figures 6 and 7 indicate how birds slice up the mud flat and beach habitats according to horizontal and vertical zonation. See, on the mud flat, how close, and therefore competitive, the three sandpipers are. (The black-bellied plover, which forages beside the sandpipers, seeks larger prey.) Notice the subtle separation of dunlin and dow-itcher, and the relative isolation of the marbled godwit from all the rest. On the beach, the foreshore attracts most of the birds, but there is also differential use of the berm and backshore. This is the raw stuff of which resource partitioning is made.

Just as we dine with friends, birds of a feather tend to flock to-gether. Birds of a species flock because, having identical food require-ments and habitat preferences, they follow the same environmental cues and they use their fellows as indicators of good foraging sites. Migrants stick together because their hormones have set them into the same clumping-and-traveling mode. These gatherings have other advantages beyond companionship; individuals in flocks can relax their vigilance to concentrate on feeding, relying on mutual alertness to spot predators and confusion-in-numbers to thwart them.

Sometimes these principles work to bring birds of different species together. Mixed flocks of long-billed dowitchers, western sandpipers, and dunlin constitute a common feeding guild on Matagorda mud flats in the wintertime. Sometimes birds of one species are attracted to another species for some specific foraging benefit, as when sander-lings follow ruddy turnstones along the beach, pecking up items the turnstones expose but scorn.

When the menus go around the table, people order what strikes their fancy. Shorebirds are less individualistic, but different species have definite preferences.

Within the limits of their abilities, shorebirds are opportunists—if food is generally abundant, most will take what is easily obtained: bivalves, snails, polychaete worms, amphipods, crabs, isopods, os-tracods, shrimps, fishes, the eggs of worms and crustaceans, shore-side insects, even bits of vegetation and seeds; and most birds will peck at carrion. When there is something especially abundant, like an influx of juvenile crabs into the tidal flats or killifishes trapped in a drying pool, all the birds seem to develop a fix on the abundant prey and pass over other sources as they congregate for a feast. If they can appease their appetites quickly, they have more time to preen, rest, and watch out for predators.

It is when food gets short that shorebirds focus on the kind of prey that they can get more easily than their competitors, and each species stays within the zone with the greatest concentration of its speciality. Now least sandpipers scamper after amphipods and ostracods, long-billed dowitchers slurp worms, sanderlings pop mole crabs, and long-billed curlews surprise ghost shrimp; each with its own sort of deadly precision.

When they are pressed, the birds not only harvest specific prey organisms, many of them select specific sizes. For instance, two plovers eat amphipods, but the little semipalmate chooses ones about $\frac{1}{16}$ of an inch long, whereas Wilson's prefers those at least five times larger. So the two can feed simultaneously on the same resource, while the difference in prey size reduces direct competition between them. This is so for many other shorebirds: the prey of least sandpipers is generally less than $\frac{1}{4}$ of an inch long, that of dunlin between $\frac{1}{4}$ inch to $\frac{1}{2}$ inch; willets easily take items between $\frac{1}{2}$ inch to 1 inch, and long-billed curlews can gulp down ghost shrimp several inches in length. In general, larger birds take larger prey, but sometimes they hedge. American avocets are so efficient at snatching the tiny creatures they disturb by stirring up the bottom muck with their curiously curved bills that they can maintain a relatively large body on a high volume of quite tiny prey. The roseate spoonbill is another interesting similar variant.

Being at the right place at the right time with the right equipment and the right behavior all converge while birds seek, find, and catch prey. Different foraging techniques are among the most important ways species with similar food habits avoid competing with each other. Merging distinctive feeding strategies with temporal and spatial variations gives us a basis for describing a unique feeding niche for each kind of shorebird.

It is implicit that birds with different feeding tactics tap different segments of the food base. But when there is plenty of food and ample feeding opportunities, most shorebirds forage by whatever means brings in the greatest bulk. When times get hard, each kind of bird shifts to its special mode of hunting. So feeding niches broaden in good times and constrict in bad times, having much to do with resource partitioning and thus survival, especially during the harried, crowded migratory seasons.

Observing birds actively pursuing their prey is a fun part of bird-watching. Here are some behavioral patterns to be alert for among shorebirds.

Most shorebirds can be categorized as either peckers or probers, and their category is easy to determine by watching them search for food.

Peckers hunt by sight, usually along the shoreline or in very shallow water. These birds are usually small, and their prey are more likely to be insects and crustaceans than worms and clams. When a pecker spots prey, it hustles after it, stopping and starting and making erratic twists and turns. These active hunters frequently startle their prey into detectable movement and so are also called "spookers."

Finally, there is a quick peck with the bill, which, if it is successful, picks a morsel off the surface or plucks prey from its retreat. Some birds peck once and move on; others characteristically "machine gun" their prey with a rapid series of pecks. Peeps and plovers are classical peckers; watch a busy least sandpiper for a good demonstration. If you observe a piping plover for a while you will notice some distinctive plover traits: a repetitive stop-and-go gait, an occasional foot wiggle that stirs up prey, a peculiar "tilting at the ankles" body posture on pecking that makes up for not having a flexible neck.

Probers never see their prey; they have sensory nerves in the tips of their bills and in their tongues that allow them to locate and recognize food items by an exquisite sense of touch. Probers are more deliberate feeders, choosing soft substrate at the waterline or in the shallows, where they walk forward, randomly pushing the bill into the soil. They usually plod along at a fairly constant rate and direction, pausing only when they happen onto an especially productive spot. These birds tend to be somewhat larger than peckers, and tend to take larger prey, mostly worms, clams, and burrowing crustaceans.

In the probe, the partly opened bill is pushed into the substrate, often to its limits (sometimes beyond that, right up to the eyeballs; if a deep-seated delicacy is encountered, the entire head). Some birds probe once and withdraw. Others "noodle," probing rapidly in one place with a vibratory action. Most probers can swallow prey without fully withdrawing the bill from the substrate or clearing the surface of the water, making it difficult to tell when the bird has made a successful strike. Watch for a quick swallowing movement.

To observe probers at work you cannot find better examples than long-billed dowitchers or dunlin riddling a mud flat. Marbled godwits work the same in deeper water but with a twist; recognizing a promising worm burrow by sight, they ease up and stab into it with their long bill, frequently coming up with at least half of a juicy worm. Long-billed curlews use the same sight-and-probe strategy to catch unwary fiddler crabs and ghost shrimp.

Once you have determined that a shorebird is a pecker or a prober, notice how consistently it follows this feeding technique. Some species seldom change their foraging style; piping plovers, for instance, are stereotyped peckers. Although they take a variety of prey, it is always caught in the characteristic plover-pecking manner. Dowitchers are stereotyped probers, ill-equipped for, and disinclined to do, much pecking. Dunlin, on the other hand, are plastic probers, primarily probing, but readily shifting to pecking if that will bring in more food.

A shorebird that can take a wide array of prey by a variety of methods is called a generalist. Such opportunistic species are found in almost any habitat, foraging in whatever way brings in the most edibles. The willet is the most common generalist among Matagorda's shorebirds, probing, pecking, and scavenging throughout all of the popular feeding zones. On the other hand, American oystercatchers are specialists—they have a restricted diet and a small repertory of feeding habits. Look for oystercatchers on shell reefs and watch them open oysters or twist loose hooked mussels with their bills.

Bird species with similar food preferences and foraging strategies are the most likely to interfere with each other if they occur together; a worm-prober will compete more with another worm-prober than with an amphipod-plucker. If those kinds of birds with the most similar food niches are the ones most likely to compete with each other on a common feeding ground, then extend that logic. Think of a mud flat. Of all the birds present, those with the most similar food niches will be members of the same species. As far as competitors for food are concerned, dowitchers, for example, are dowitchers' own worst enemies because their food niches are identical. Individuals of the same species seek precisely the same resource in precisely the same way in the same place at the same time. So how do they stay out of each other's way at the dinner table? Watch them and see. Enter the bewildering world of bird body language, vocal communication, instinctive mannerisms, and territoriality.

From the pirouette of a Wilson's phalarope and the methodical sweep of a roseate spoonbill to the pin-point stab of a black-necked stilt and the anxious noodling of a dunlin—feeding strategies of birds can be appreciated as important manifestations of the birds' food niches and still enjoyed as entertainment. You can look for comparable patterns in other groups of birds and in other kinds of creatures on the island; the opportunities are endless and the pursuit can last a lifetime. Marvel at the intricacy of resource partitioning while you feel the delight of having discovered some of its details for yourself, and you will have savored some of the best fare that Matagorda Island has to offer; hopefully it will pique your palate for more.

Matagorda Island Birds

Here we briefly mention the common, conspicuous, and noteworthy birds with emphasis on migration, feeding habits, and specific places to look for each kind.

Loons

Watch for wintering common loons in the open bays on your way to and from the island during October through April; a few linger into summer. Dark and sleek, these solitary birds usually ride low in the water. Loons dive frequently, with an abrupt forward spring that makes hardly a ripple. They remain under for a minute or more, swimming rapidly with wings and webbed feet. With eyes especially adapted for underwater vision, they are expert at catching fish, mostly schooling fish like striped mullet, bay anchovies, scaled sardines, Gulf menhaden, and rough silversides. They take prey with their heavy straight bill and often swallow it underwater. It requires a surface pattering effort for a loon to get airborne, so they usually dive when approached by a boat. The eerie, mournful calls for which loons are renowned are made during the breeding season. Alas, while in Texas the birds are almost always silent.

Grebes

Of the four species of grebe (pronounced greeb) recorded on Matagorda Island, only the eared and the pied-billed are common. Highly specialized for aquatic life, with legs positioned to the rear, lobed toes, longish neck, streamlined body, short wings and tail, and dense, waterproof plumage, grebes are awkward on land and unremarkable fliers that must patter across the water to take off. They catch their food, mostly small fish, underwater, but also take crabs, grass shrimp, and snails in the bays and a variety of aquatic insect larvae, tadpoles, and small crustaceans in fresh-water ponds. They also habitually consume a considerable quantity of their own feathers, which apparently protects their stomach lining from the needle-sharp bones and bits in their food. It is commonplace to see a grebe dive, but not everyone gets to see one sink. When it is suspicious but not overtly

Common loon

Pied-billed grebe

threatened, a grebe may slowly disappear into the water by compressing its feathers and squeezing air out of internal sacs.

Eared grebes are fairly common winter residents in the Coastal Bend. Watch for them alone or in small flocks in the bays or rocking on the waves just beyond the breakers. Pied-billed grebes are most often seen in vegetated fresh-water ponds. (Be sure to distinguish them from coots and moorhens.) Although they nest on the adjacent mainland, the ponds on Matagorda are not reliable enough to attract breeding birds.

Pelicans

As everyone interested in the coastal environment knows, Texas almost lost its brown pelicans during the pesticide decades of the 1950s and 1960s, and the species went on the endangered list in 1973. Happily, conservation efforts have been rewarded with a recovering, although by no means secure, population. The species remains endangered.

For many visitors, these droll birds symbolize the Gulf coast. Throughout the warm months they may be seen atop pilings in the bays or flap-gliding over both bay side and gulf side of the island, and they frequently rest on the J-Hook. In the wintertime most birds drift south along the coast to Mexico.

Brown pelicans feed by spectacular dive-bombing into schools of fish (Gulf menhaden, rough silversides, and bay anchovies are favorites). The gular pouch works as a net from which they quickly drain

Brown pelican

the water before swallowing their catch and laboring back into the air. Young pelicans have to learn their trade. We once watched a juvenile make sixteen unsuccessful dives before it flapped off, exhausted and still hungry. Brown pelicans now nest with fair success in the Coastal Bend on natural islets and spoil banks; but even there nesting colonies are subject to multiple hazards, and human disturbance is at the top of the list. Don't get closer than binocular-range to a pelican rookery.

The ecology of the American white pelican is quite different. They feed from the surface, often working together in flocks to corral schools of small fish in the shallows. These pelicans are accomplished scoop-netters, splashing with their wingtips to concentrate the fish and improve their efficiency. After a successful haul they quickly drain their pouch, gulp down their catch, and return to business. In the vicinity of the island they prefer the brackish water of bay-side inlets and also use fresh water on the mainland.

Most American white pelicans nest on large lakes in the western states and as far north as Canada. The only breeding colony on the Texas coast is in the Laguna Madre opposite the Padre Island National Seashore. No one knows what proportion of Matagorda birds fledge locally. A different habitat and consequent differences in their food chain allowed white pelicans to avoid the pesticide buildup that decimated their brown relative. Despite that good fortune, their population seems now to be declining in the Coastal Bend.

White pelicans are scarce on Matagorda Island in the summer, but common during the rest of the year. The most spectacular sightings are in the winter, when great numbers of bright white pelicans rest beside equally numerous black cormorants on the shell reefs and beaches and around the mouths of the passes. Now and then you may see a flock of white pelicans take advantage of a rising thermal to spiral up into the blue. Although they are large, white, and have black wingtips, don't confuse these soaring birds with whooping cranes.

Cormorants

These large, dark water birds have slightly shaggy heads, an expanse of yellowish unfeathered skin on the face, a compressed gular pouch, and a long, hooked bill. When they ride the water the bill is held at a distinctive slight incline. Though their inner feathers are waterproof to keep their skin dry and warm, cormorants' outer feathers are not oiled and so get wet during dives. This lubricates the streamlined body for submarine swimming and counters a tendency to bob to the surface before the bird is ready. However, when cormorants are done feeding, they must dry the soggy feathers. So they spend a lot of time drying out by preening and standing with slightly drooping wings spread wide.

Double-crested cormorants are voracious submarine fishers, diving from the surface and using wings and webbed feet to pursue any of the common schooling fish of the bays. They bring their catch to the surface to carefully juggle it into headfirst position and gulp it down their expandable throat. Although a bird will occasionally catch and swallow a foot-long fish, most prey are 5 inches or less.

Large feeding flocks of these gregarious birds float in the bays, and aggregations haul out to rest on spoil islands, shell reefs, and the beach. Fast-flying groups occasionally are seen winging across open water in ragged formation; a crook in the outstretched neck gives a cormorant head an upward tilt. Banding records indicate that Texas birds hatch in Canada and the northern tier of midwestern states. They arrive in the Coastal Bend en masse in October and abruptly depart in March. If the double-crested cormorants are here, you probably will not miss seeing them.

Neotropic cormorants prefer the fresh-water sloughs of the mainland, where they nest. After raising young, they become more common along the tidal inlets on the backside of the island. If you see cormorants on Matagorda in the summertime, check your field guide; it takes a careful eye to distinguish the slimmer neotropic cormorant from the double-crested.

Magnificent frigatebird

Frigatebirds

This is one of Matagorda's specialties. Magnificent frigatebirds begin arriving from the Caribbean in late May, and for the next few months are just common enough for a birder to anticipate a sighting but fickle enough to keep you guessing; keep your eyes open. Many roost on pilings and channel markers in the bays and on posts in the water near Bray Cove on the island's south end. They are late risers, so watch for them on posts if you come over early in the morning; later they will be high-floating specks in the sky. Presumably you will notice any dark, gliding bird with a deeply forked tail and a 7 and a half-foot wingspan that happens within range of your binoculars.

Large internal air sacs, hollow bones, and long wings make the spare-built frigatebirds the lightest of all birds in proportion to their size. Their gravity-defying gliding makes even soaring turkey vultures look awkward. Although they are seabirds, frigatebirds never enter the sea. Indeed, if they get wet, these ultralight flying machines lack the power to lift their bodies from the water's surface. The incredible flying prowess, though sometimes spent on bouts of playful aerobatics, is primarily to obtain food. They skim over the waves, using their long, hooked bills to pluck fish, jellyfish, and crustaceans from just beneath the water's surface, or they harass gulls and terns into dropping their catch and then retrieve the purloined loot in midair. Frigatebirds deliberately work the busy feeding lanes along which gulls and terns travel to bring food to their nestlings.

The Spanish called these pirates frigatebirds and man-o'-wars after their own light and maneuverable warships. Old timers in the Coastal Bend astutely called them hurricane birds.

Herons and Bitterns

Twelve species of this group inhabit North America, and Matagorda Island hosts them all. Because most are easy to spot and are fairly abundant, and only a few migrate, a visitor can aspire to seeing over half the species by working their favored tidal flat and fresh-water pond habitats. This is one of the few groups of birds that is well-represented on the island during the slack summer season.

Herons (a catchall term that includes egrets) and bitterns are keen-eyed, long-legged, stalking spear fishers that fly with the neck folded and the legs outstretched. They are often seen in statuesque pose at the water's edge or slinking through quiet shallows. Their forte is an intent, slow stalk culminating in a sudden strike as the neck extends and the rapier bill plunges on the prey—a small fish or other aquatic life. Some birds impale larger prey, but most grasp it with the tip of the bill. Small creatures are immediately gulped down; larger ones may be manipulated or even carried ashore and beaten or dismembered before being swallowed. Because their habits and haunts are so similar, herons make interesting subjects for a study of resource partitioning.

From late February through mid-March, the herons and egrets get ready for breeding, with filmy plumes, neck crests, lacy epaulets, brightened colors, and prancing and bill sparring behavior. All but one of these birds are Coastal Bend residents, but because of potential predation by raccoons and coyotes, few nest on Matagorda Island. When they are at their resplendent best, most move to traditional nesting sites on shell reefs and spoil islands in the surrounding bays; a few travel to fresh-water swamps and sloughs on the mainland.

From April through June all activity is centered on the rookeries, with the adults flying the congested feeding lanes to and from the Matagorda tidal flats to stuff their gullets with food, return, and empty them into their ravenous offspring. During this period a bleak and nondescript acre-sized hump of oystershell is transformed into pandemonium. There is life and death, murder and mayhem, health and disease, unbridled vigor and hunkered hopelessness, fecal plops and regurgitated food boluses, egg shells and tiny carcasses, heat and putrescence, and movement in every plane; all set to an unworldly cacophony of grunts, squeals, squawks, bill pops, and raucous cries. All directed to somehow fledge offspring.

It is a critical, vulnerable time, open to natural hazards ranging

Table 3. *Waterbird breeding colonies, Texas Coastal Bend, 1989*

Species	# Nests Observed
American white pelican	250
Brown pelican	575
Neotropic cormorant	112
Great egret	1,219
Snowy egret	734
Reddish egret	352
Cattle egret	12,523
Great blue heron	700
Little blue heron	93
Tricolored heron	2,214
Black-crowned night heron	174
White ibis	9
White-faced ibis	756
Roseate spoonbill	826
Laughing gull	18,991
Gull-billed tern	495
Caspian tern	254
Royal tern	5,334
Sandwich tern	8,194
Forster's tern	237
Black skimmer	10,331

Data are from the files of the TPWD.

from parasite epidemics to storm overwash. The most serious pre-
ventable threat is human disturbance. Rookeries are intriguing, but a
close approach by people sends the adult birds into a frenzy and ex-
poses eggs and young to fatal heat and lurking predators. The most
prudent way to observe a rookery is aboard one of the commercial
tour boats that ply out of the Rockport-Fulton area during the height
of the season. These professionals know how to keep their distance
while still providing an excellent viewing experience.

The great blue heron, largest, most widespread member of the
group, is also the most reclusive and grumpiest. They mainly haunt
the bay side and the fresh-water ponds and swales, but are seen occasionally in all the insular communities. If forced by an intruder to
leave their humped rest atop pilings or snags, they often express their
displeasure with a series of guttural croaks and maybe a fecal dump.

Even in a clan noted for voracious appetites and catholic tastes, the
great blue heron stands out as a glutton. Its primary prey are fish and
especially blue crabs, but it pecks up almost anything that presents

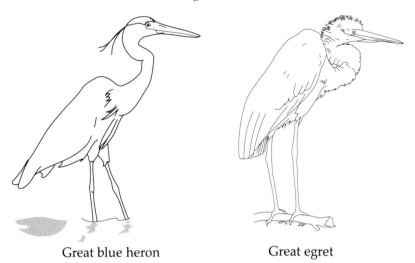

Great blue heron   Great egret

itself: shrimp, snails, fiddler crabs, small ghost crabs, frogs, tadpoles, watersnakes, young alligators, hatchling turtles, aquatic insects, and nestling or fledgling rails. Away from the shore herons are alert for rice rats and cotton rats, grasshoppers, nestling meadowlarks and quail, and snakes. An expandable gular fold and gullet allows the bird to wolf down anything that it can catch and subdue. We once watched nearly 45 minutes while a determined great blue killed, manipulated, and—after repeated attempts—finally swallowed a huge flounder. The heron's potent digestive juices can transform a fish into circulating nutrients and a liquefied squirt in less than an hour.

There are clusters of great blue herons nesting in most island rookeries, and isolated nests can be found on many channel pilings and oil platforms. A few heap their ragged piles of sticks atop the poles along the abandoned powerline on the north end of the island. They are not long-range migrants, but in the wintertime there is an influx of individuals to the Coastal Bend from across Texas.

Both little blue herons and tricolored herons are medium-sized spear fishers. Tricolored are common residents that nest on island rookeries. Little blues are fairly common on the island except in the spring, when they are nesting on the mainland. In the fall you can spend much time trying to distinguish the new generation of white juveniles from immature snowy egrets and white-phase reddish egrets. Study bill and leg color traits in your field guide.

The chunky little green-backed heron is seen only occasionally on Matagorda. It prefers a thickly vegetated fresh-water habitat on the mainland, where it also nests.

Egrets are plumed herons, not ecologically distinct, but tending more to flocks. Stately, white great egrets, with their long black legs and keenly-tapered yellow bills, are most often seen in loose groups, plying their trade in tidal inlets. The largest members of this sub-group, their size sets them off from other white herons. Eager begin-ners can save themselves potential embarrassment by thoroughly re-viewing the field traits that distinguish great egrets from whooping cranes.

Common the year-round on the island, snowy egrets are always dainty and pretty; at breeding time their fleecy plumes make real showpieces. Although they are on the state threatened list, reddish egrets are delightfully numerous on Matagorda Island. They have brassy-pink breeding colors and are best known for the lilting, clown-like antics they use to scare up small fish in the shallows. A white phase of this species is just common enough to be considered if you have trouble identifying a medium-sized white heron.

Few of the generalizations about herons apply to cattle egrets. They are gregarious birds, feeding, roosting, flying, and nesting in large flocks. Although they nest and roost on islands or in swamps for protection from predators, these are not water birds; they feed almost exclusively on insects gleaned from grasslands, mostly grasshoppers in the Coastal Bend. They characteristically hang around cattle, catch-ing insects scared up by the grazing animals; they have learned to patrol the freshly turned earth behind tractors in the fields, and are attracted to flooded ground and freshly burned prairies.

Despite great success in colonizing the coastal prairie and using the island rookeries, cattle egrets are not especially common on Mata-gorda Island. Elimination of cattle may make them scarcer still, but rotational burning may attract more. With the onset of winter, the bulk of the population moves southward down the coast.

Cattle egrets are distant Old World relatives only recently arrived in North America. From their homeland in Africa they immigrated to South America and worked their way north. The first sighting in Texas was on Mustang Island in 1955; a few years later they were nesting in the Coastal Bend, and since then have spread into favor-able habitats up both coasts and through much of the interior of the United States and southern Canada. They have exploited an appar-ently vacant niche, so their advance was, happily, not at the expense of native birds.

Night-herons are stocky birds with short legs and thick bills. They spend the day hunkered in shaded recesses and go abroad at twilight. Flushed from rest in a clump of saltcedars, they flap off in all direc-tions, popping their bills and making disgruntled "quoks." Night-herons hunt along the waterline in tidal inlets, swales, and vegetated ponds. As they move in a slow crouch, their huge eyes miss nothing and their powerful bill easily grasps and subdues small aquatic life. Crabs are a staple, but they also take small fish, insects, frogs, snakes, and young rice rats, and are known to swallow unprotected nestling birds.

The black-crowned night-heron, the more common species on Matagorda, is a year-round resident, nesting on the mainland and in the island rookeries. The yellow-crowned night-heron is more at home in mainland fresh-water bayous, where it nests, but quite a few birds roost and feed on the island. In their preferred swamplands yellow-crowns are notably secretive birds; in Matagorda's open environment you have a good chance to add this species to your life list.

Birders know that you do not go looking for bitterns; you happen upon one. These birds steal quietly through the heavy vegetation of fresh-water marshes and escape detection because camouflaged plumage and a peculiar, frozen stance render them nearly invisible among the reeds. During their spring and fall migrations, you may flush an American bittern from among the cattails and bulrushes around any pond, ditch, or swale on the island, but their favored habitat is too limited for more than a few to linger here through the winter. Least bitterns are common enough on the mainland, where they nest, but they seldom brave the flight over open water to reach Matagorda.

Ibises, Spoonbills, and Storks

Ibises are set off from other long-legged waders by a large, cylindrical, down-curved bill that is used to grope for aquatic prey. They typically walk through the shallows, often in ranks, sweeping their partly open bills from side to side and snatching any swimming creatures that they stir up. On Matagorda Island ibises "pig out" on juvenile white and brown shrimp, grass shrimp, and killifish in shallow tidal inlets and pools.

White ibises, by far the more common of the two species found on the island, are year-round residents but move to the oyster reef rookeries in the spring. You will likely find groups of these gregarious birds feeding or roosting in the tidal flats; or you may spot them flying low in picturesque lines with necks outstretched and distinctive bills well-displayed. They fly with several rapid wing beats and then a short glide. The white, red-faced adults are unmistakable, but juveniles are brownish above and first-year birds are mottled brown-and-white.

White ibis   Roseate spoonbill

The white-faced ibises prefer fresh-water marshes and are only occasionally seen on the bay side of the island. But in spring some move into the Coastal Bend from the south and nest on the mainland. They will look uniformly dark, but you can recognize them as ibises by their bills, and if you get a good viewing position you will see flashes of brassy purple, chestnut, and metallic violet and green. The white-faced ibis is on the state's list of threatened species.

No one needs to be shown a roseate spoonbill; if one is in view, its resplendent color catches and holds the eye. Lines of flying spoonbills reflecting the rays of a low sun are among the unsurpassed highlights of a trip to Matagorda Island.

Look for small groups of spoonbills feeding in the tidal flats. They move like ibises, humping over while moving deliberately through the shallows, swinging their bills to and fro to intercept small fish, shrimp, and aquatic insects. Spoonbills sweep more vigorously; their bodies sway with the effort. The unique spatulate bill is soft and loaded with sensitive nerve endings that allow detection of prey, while the expanded tip makes a good grasping implement.

It is hard to imagine, but a spoonbill's colors brighten in March; the pink gets pinker and a rush of deep carmine drips down the upper wings. At this time they move to islet rookeries and the mainland to nest.

In the late nineteenth century, roseate spoonbills were among the most sought-after species in the plume trade, and by 1900, they had become extremely rare in Texas; all known breeding colonies had been wiped out. In 1923, a few birds were found nesting on the Second Chain of islands, a series of oystershell reefs between Matagorda Island and the mainland. Since then they have gradually recovered. Today there are over two thousand breeding pairs in the state, mostly concentrated in the Coastal Bend.

In the summer, large flocks of wood storks, several hundred adults and juveniles, move to Matagorda Island from their breeding grounds in Mexico. They feed on fish and shrimp trapped in drying tidal pools, foraging somewhat like ibises, but with a less-rhythmic motion and more erratic stabbing as they snap at their prey. Storks also shuffle their large feet through the ooze to roil aquatic creatures to the surface. After feeding, the dour birds retire to a convenient mud flat to preen, and then stand motionless with the heavy bill pressed against the breast. More peculiar than pretty, a flock of wood storks with their vulturine heads and humpy gait adds a grotesque garnish to the tidal flats. Before cool weather sets in, most of them head back south. The species is on the state threatened list.

Geese

Coastal Texas is a mecca for wintering geese, with more than a million birds, over 80 percent of the traffic on the Central Flyway, finding their way into the state each fall. But the barrier islands get only a belated, marginal share of this influx.

The haunting sky calls of migrating geese are first heard in the Coastal Bend in late September, when the earliest white-fronted geese pass over or settle down briefly en route to their major wintering grounds in Mexico. They rarely appear on the island. During the first two weeks of October, major flights of snow geese and Canada geese move in, but most settle in the rice fields southwest of Houston, harvested, but still laden with waste grain. Here the birds feed heavily and retire to surrounding shallow ponds for night roosts. When this favored food is exhausted, they disperse more widely, shifting to corn, sorghum, and soybean fields. Finally, in December and January, geese are down to natural forage in brackish coastal marshes; this is when small flocks of snows and Canadas appear on the bay side of Matagorda Island.

Geese are almost exclusively vegetarians, but they divide into two fairly distinct feeding styles. Snow geese are "grubbers" that use their heavy bills to scoop into the mud and dislodge tubers and rhizomes, which they consume along with the foliage. These geese usually return to a site until everything is eaten, often leaving the ground laid bare. Canadas and white-fronts are more delicate "grazers" that strip seed heads and snip greenery. Although they are known to use over thirty species of coastal plants, at least two-thirds of their diet derives from grasses. On Matagorda Island, all of these geese feed on marsh-hay cordgrass, bulrush, seashore paspalum, saltgrass, Bermuda grass, glasswort, and assorted sedges.

In early March the geese begin to haul out; by the middle of the month they are gone, and with them goes a special part of the magic of the Coastal Bend.

Ducks

All of the fifteen or so species of ducks that routinely visit the Coastal Bend have been documented on Matagorda Island. A wintertime visitor who works the bay-side inlets and inland ponds, visits one of the passes, and sweeps a telescope beyond the breakers along the beach can hope to see at least a dozen kinds.

Populations of this important group of waterfowl have suffered lately from drought and from development in their northern breeding grounds, and much conservation effort has gone into accommodating wintering flocks. About 350,000 ducks move into the central Texas coast each year. Although the barrier islands do not have extensive stands of favored feeding habitat for many of the shallow-water ducks, the islands and associated bays are important as protected refugia for these species and as principal stopover sites for the kinds that prefer brackish or saline open water.

The general traits of ducks, essentially those of the semi-domestic birds in any city park pond, are familiar enough to most people. Birders recognize two major groups of ducks based on their anatomy, behavior, and ecology.

Dabblers, or puddle ducks, prefer fresh-water marshes, well-vegetated ponds, and estuarine shallows. Because they are widely dispersed in small flocks near shore, they are the most frequently observed species. On Matagorda the most common members of this group include gadwall, American wigeon, green-winged and blue-winged teal, northern shoveler, northern pintail, and mottled duck.

Dabblers are primarily vegetarians. They feed by skimming the water's surface or by tipping tail-up, often with much paddling to hold their position, and finding food on the shallow bottom. The legs, like

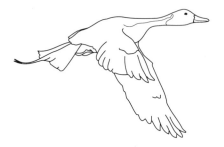

Northern pintail

those of all ducks, are positioned to the rear of middle, an advantage for swimming, but it makes for a waddling walk. Still, most species in this group can move readily in marshy meadows and fallow fields; pintails and green-winged teal, for instance, glean much of their winter fare from waste grain.

When flushed, dabblers leap vertically into flight and accelerate rapidly. This strong takeoff is made possible by a relatively broad, powerful wing. When setting down, they circle warily a time or two and then drop straight down onto the water. These habits probably grew from a need to maneuver in the emergent vegetation that typifies their shallow aquatic habitat. Dabblers rest out of the water on a mud bank or protected shoreline, and they have a speculum—a bright patch of iridescent feathers—on the trailing edge of the wing.

Divers, or bay ducks, prefer the open waters of bays, the nearshore Gulf, and large inland lakes. Many feed and rest near shore, but distant feeding or sleeping flocks are often visible only as dark rafts or bobbing flashes of color. The common members of this group around Matagorda Island are lesser scaups, redheads, ruddy ducks, common goldeneyes, and buffleheads.

Most diving ducks feed extensively on animal prey supplemented with what plant material is available. From their floating position they execute a quick forward spring and dive all the way to the bottom, where they noodle energetically for food. Texas bays are seldom over 15 feet in depth, so these ducks can easily reach the bottom anywhere and come bobbing back up in less than 30 seconds.

To go along with more aquatic habits, the legs are situated further astern than in the dabblers, giving better propulsion in the water, but a weak and awkward walk. The three forward toes are more webbed and the back toe has a lobe that aids in dives. Although they are strong fliers once in the air, the narrow wings provide less lift, so diving ducks must patter over the water's surface to get airborne. They usually avoid this labor by diving, rather than flying, when threatened. When they alight on the water, these birds splash down heavily on their breasts and skid to a stop. Divers characteristically rest and sleep on the water in aggregations called rafts. The wings lack a speculum.

Except for the resident mottled duck, all of the ducks that use Matagorda Island, divers and dabblers, are migratory. Migration begins in late August when the first blue-winged teal pass through. The major influx comes in October; wintering populations then hold steady through January. Many, especially redheads, move south into the Laguna Madre in midwinter. The earliest pintails begin to leave in late January, and the main exodus follows in February. By mid-March northbound blue-wing teal pass over, and by the end of the month most ducks have left the Coastal Bend.

Although all kinds of ducks have their feeding preferences, most are opportunists in search of bulk. Local abundance, accessibility of food and fresh water, and severity of the winter determine whether wintering ducks hold up or move on.

Despite differences in feeding behavior, most ducks have the same sort of broad, soft bill terminated by a hard, hooked nail. The soft part is packed with nerves that sense taste and touch, so a duck can find food without seeing it. The edges of the bill are intricately shaped with grooves and fine teeth that mesh to form a sieve and the fleshy tongue has a fringe of fine papillae. By rapidly vibrating the upper and lower mandibles and using the tongue as a piston, a duck can filter tiny seeds and minute crustaceans with great efficiency. Or it can snip and tug at vegetation, gather floating foliage and algae, or use the hard tip to gouge the bottom. The bill of fish-eating mergansers has a saw-toothed edge for holding on to prey caught underwater.

What, exactly, do the hundreds of wintering ducks find to eat in the vicinity of Matagorda Island? Surely the extensive submarine meadows of widgeon grass and shoalgrass (neither a true grass) with their streamers of attached algae account for more daily pounds of biomass consumed than all other plants combined. Dabblers in brackish interior ponds and tidal inlets graze widgeon grass; dabblers and divers further out in the bays eat shoalgrass. Some species snip the foliage, others include the seeds, while many dig up the rootstocks. Eventually the birds will reduce the submerged meadows to stubble, but the prolific plants quickly regrow after the ducks depart.

Coastal ducks are known to use about fifty other plants, but only a few are staples and not all are abundant on Matagorda Island. Some important and available ones are the foliage and seeds of sago pond-weed and smartweed; submerged tufts of naiad, common poolmat, and muskgrass; skeins of floating algae; the seeds of sedges and bul-rushes; the greenery of glasswort, coast pennywort, and water hys-sop; the fresh shoots and seeds of saltgrass, marshhay cordgrass, and a variety of other wetland grasses.

Those ducks that take significant animal prey, mostly the divers, rely largely on molluscs (several kinds of marine snails and many kinds of small clams); crustaceans (small crabs, grass shrimp, seed shrimp, water fleas, and amphipods); aquatic insect larvae (especially those of sundry kinds of shore flies and water beetles); and small fish (killifish, mosquito fish, and silversides).

The various kinds of ducks specialize; for instance, 90 percent of the diet of gadwall is greenery and this is mostly the foliage of wid-geon grass and masses of attached and floating algae. Because this is a low-nutrient diet, gadwall spend over two-thirds of their time eat-ing, including many hours at night. Pintails and green-winged teal are mainly seed eaters, and this concentrated food source more quickly satisfies their demands, so they spend considerable time loaf-ing. Ruddy ducks dive for mouthfuls of bottom ooze, from which their guts extract the protoplasm of thousands of midge larvae and nematode worms. Goldeneyes dive for mud crabs and small clams; they crack the shells and eat the soft meat. Buffleheads also dive for clams but swallow them shell and all; their gizzards grind up the shells and their guts process the remains within half an hour. Lesser scaups are more versatile, diving for clams, crustaceans, and shoal-grass rhizomes. Red-breasted mergansers specialize in the submarine capture of small schooling fish. Redheads feed almost exclusively on shoalgrass, and before winter is over most of these birds move to the

Lesser scaup

more extensive meadows in the Laguna Madre. Shovelers use their enormous, boat-shaped bills to skim seeds and microcrustaceans from the surface of the water. Wigeon not only dabble for widgeon grass, they have learned to wait while scaups and other divers root up the plant, then they harvest bits that float to the surface.

This brief survey of the feeding habits of ducks should remind you of the resource partitioning described for shorebirds. This is, indeed, something you can watch for while observing this group of birds. Aside from the food source, important environmental features that segregate feeding ducks include depth of the water, openness of the habitat (presence and height of emergent vegetation), and texture of the bottom. Especially when food is abundant, there will be overlap and mixed flocks, but when food gets scarce, ducks definitely are selective in their feeding sites.

Look for mottled ducks and green-winged teal in shallow water with many emergent plants. A bit deeper, but still among water plants where seeds and microcrustaceans collect near the surface, shovelers and blue-winged teal will be sieving. American wigeon and pintails tip up further out, over widgeon grass beds. Gadwall like it a smidgeon deeper and ruddy ducks are beyond them. Redheads and lesser scaups prefer the deep shoalgrass beds in open water, and way out, goldeneyes and buffleheads dive for animal prey. Red-breasted mergansers torpedo after fish in the bay; hooded mergansers do the same in narrow tidal inlets. See what other patterns you can recognize.

Vultures

There are always opportunities for scavengers at the edge of the sea, and on Matagorda Island, turkey vultures join the gulls, crabs, and flies. On most days, at least a few vultures can be spotted, lazily riding the thermals or battling a stiff north wind as they scan the island for carrion. They often rest atop sand dunes or on the beach, where they have a wide view and an unobstructed takeoff. Local birds fly to the mainland to roost and nest, and do not migrate.

Turkey vultures feed on any sort of dead animal matter. On Matagorda they routinely work the beach strand for assorted dead creatures cast up by the waves. After a fish kill by red tide or a cold snap, vultures feast for days on the bay-side strand of fish carcasses piled up by the wind. They also congregate with gulls and waders at drying pools, pecking up fish and tadpoles trapped in the mud. In the springtime vultures visit the island rookeries, where they consume the mounds of disgorged fish that miss their intended mark, scavenge dead birds, and, occasionally, turn predator and swallow nestlings left unguarded.

Black vultures often associate with turkey vultures on the mainland, but seem little inclined to visit the island.

Diurnal Raptors

The daytime birds of prey find good hunting across Matagorda's open terrain. We mention the more common and conspicuous species; others are occasional. Because migrating hawks prefer to soar, they avoid the open Gulf and follow the coastline, where the updrafts that hold them aloft are more reliable. Matagorda Island lies directly in the narrow corridor used by hawks migrating between North America and points south. The fall migration of raptors, from late September through early October, pulsates with the passage of cold fronts; the more impressive spring migration lasts from mid-March to mid-April. During these intervals hundreds, even thousands, of mostly broad-winged hawks, and Swainson's hawks, with occasional large flights of Mississippi kites, pass over the island in silent, swirling kettles and miles-long streams. Because of a lack of roosting sites, few hawks set down here, but isolated individuals of these and other migrant species can be seen on snags, poles, and dune tops.

Three species of diurnal raptors nest on Matagorda Island. The buoyant black-shouldered kite, one of the avian showpieces of the island, should be looked for over the interior grassland; it is more common on the south end, where there is more woody vegetation. These gleaming white birds are at their best when they hover (kite) on long fluttering wings, intently watching for movements in the grass below. When a cotton rat or harvest mouse is spotted, they suddenly fold their wings upward and drop straight down, talons extended. Although a pair of kites stakes out a hunting territory, the birds roost communally in mesquites and nest there or in the canopy of chaparral clumps. One spring a pair obligingly built its nest in a small oak beside the Wynne lodge.

Matagorda Island is one of the few places where a buteo ('byou-tee-oh—a large, broad-winged, round-tailed hawk) is as likely to be a state-threatened white-tailed hawk as the more generally common red-tailed hawk. White-tails are at home over the open coastal grasslands and nest in the mesquites on the south end of the island. Along with black-shouldered kites, they are attracted to burning grassland, where disabled and disoriented rodents and flying grasshoppers are easy to catch.

Black-shouldered kite

The crested caracara (locally called the Mexican eagle), with its brown head crest, orange-red facial skin, creamy breast bib, and long, chicken-like walking legs, is an eye-catching raptor. These birds scrounge a wide variety of small ground-living prey, and frequently share carrion with turkey vultures. Look for them gliding on flat wings, perched on posts, or striding along on the ground in the barrier flat community. Caracaras nest in the chaparral or in niches in isolated Macartney rose clumps.

Matagorda Island routinely hosts two notable pass-through raptors: the osprey and the peregrine falcon. From late September through October, ospreys stop over on Matagorda on their way to Central and South America, and pass back across in March and April. These long-winged, baleful-eyed "fish hawks" are most often seen hunched on snags or flapping over the bay shallows and tidal inlets. When it sights a fish, an osprey makes a rapid, slanting stoop, striking the water talons first, with the body and wings canted backward. It quickly labors back into the air and, if successful, will have a fish clutched in its ice-tong talons to carry back to its perch and tear into.

Matagorda Island is one of the most important of the handful of staging areas used by the endangered peregrine falcons on their long journey between the high arctic regions and South America. Especially in the fall, these sleek birds may linger for several weeks to enjoy the abundant shorebird and waterfowl prey in unharassed security. From late September through October, peregrines are often seen perched on driftwood along the backbeach or swiftly winging over beach and dunes. (Do not confuse them with the smaller merlins, which have similar habits and pass through at the same time.) Peregrines seem to be able to bring down shorebirds, terns, and waterfowl almost at will, and it is a memorable experience to witness this most expert of avian dive-bombers crumple a fleeing bird in midair.

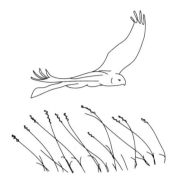

Northern harrier

The American peregrine falcon was one of the hallmark species consigned to the federal endangered list during the tragic pesticide years. Most of the peregrines that pass across Matagorda belong to the tundra (or arctic) race that nests in Alaska, Canada, and Greenland. These birds, remote from most sources of pesticides, suffered less decimation and are "merely" threatened. No matter the designation, all peregrines are fully protected, and in today's pressured environment they can nowhere be taken for granted.

Two kinds of diurnal raptors routinely winter on Matagorda: the northern harrier and the American kestrel. Early harriers arrive on Matagorda by late September, and stay the winter. The first kestrels may beat the first harriers.

No raptor is more supremely adapted to the open coastal country than the northern harrier. One of the most graphic winter observations on Matagorda Island is a long-winged harrier stolidly battling a gusting norther as it banks low over the windswept grassland, quartering back and forth in a systematic search of every square foot of turf. Guided by both keen sight and acute hearing, the bird frequently drops into the grass. When it catches a cotton rat, meadowlark, or bobwhite quail, it consumes it on the spot, then takes wing again and continues its maneuvers. Now and then a harrier puts on enough speed to strike a savannah sparrow or a heedless mourning dove, and the panicky reaction of shorebirds and waterfowl to a harrier passing overhead is proof enough that this raptor occasionally takes their kind.

You are virtually guaranteed a sighting of the handsome, robin-sized American kestrel on any wintertime trek through the island's interior. They perch on fence posts or streak rapidly across the sky uttering their high-pitched "killy-killy-killy" alarm call. Kestrels (most people call them sparrow hawks) climb 30 feet into the air, turn into the onshore breeze, and hover while they search the grass below for harvest mice and insects. If they spot movement they often drop half-way and hover again before a final descent. Grasshoppers are their principal wintertime prey on Matagorda.

Owls

These birds take up where the diurnal raptors leave off. Although six species have been documented on the island, it is unlikely that you will see a single one. But you could happen upon a short-eared owl flapping slowly along behind the dune ridge in the wintertime or spook a great horned owl from its patch of gloom in a motte of salt-cedars. The most common species on the island, the barn owl, almost never appears in the daytime unless flushed from a roost deep in the bowels of a deserted building or one of the concrete bunkers.

When it is fully dark, barn owls take off to hunt with deliberate, utterly silent flaps of their rounded wings. Occasionally from a high soar they make a harsh, wheezy squawk that will raise hairs on the neck of those who are not familiar with it. Although they flash ghostly white in the dark, they are truly beautiful birds, feathered above with burnt orange attractively sprinkled and blotched with old pewter.

American kestrel

Barn owl

Barn owls are nature's perfect mouse catchers. Aside from their silent wings, fierce talons, and sharp hooked beak, it is their exquisite sense organs that elevate them to super status. They see well enough to navigate in what would to us be complete blackness; on ordinary nights they suffer no visual impairment at all. But, experiments have shown that barn owls can detect and catch a mouse in absolute darkness, when even their remarkable eyes are of no use. They can do this because their hearing is also remarkable. They have a large acoustic receptor area in the brain, and the finely tuned cochleas receive sounds from an accessory locator system. The wide, dished face is a precisely engineered parabolic reflector that funnels faint sounds directly to the ears. Whisker-like feathers around the facial rim can alter the contour, even rendering half the face slightly out of kilter with the other half. In addition, one ear hole is higher than the other. These combined asymmetries allow the owl to pinpoint a sound source both horizontally and vertically. When a barn owl is in the vicinity, being merely quiet as a mouse is no defense.

Most birds of prey swallow their meals whole and regurgitate the indigestible parts in compact pellets. These are a gold mine for the biologist interested in the birds' diets. Dissection of 100 barn owl pellets retrieved from nest and roost sites on Matagorda Island revealed the skulls of 293 cotton rats, 71 harvest mice, 28 rice rats, 1 house mouse, 1 meadowlark, 1 boat-tailed grackle, and 5 unidentified small perching birds.

Grassland Birds

Two species deserve special mention here: bobwhite quail and eastern meadowlark.

Northern bobwhites, the common native quail of the coastal prairie, are native on all the Texas barriers. Additional birds were introduced onto Matagorda by military personnel; the north end of the island was managed to provide a huntable population. The remnant stand of Russian olives, the spaced clumps of Macartney rose, the scattered remains of over six hundred wire and frame shelters, and the concrete foundations of bird-dog kennels between the main dock and the Army Hole are all vestiges of this avid interest in quail hunting.

Quail do best in a habitat dominated by weedy growth and fare poorly when this is replaced by grasses; the dense stand of climax grasses provides little food and hinders mobility. So, although associated with the interior grassland, quail are actually restricted to its edges—along roadways, near mowed areas, on sparsely grassed sandy hillocks, and across the lee sides of the dunes. Bobwhites are usually common on the island; you are most likely to spook a covey or to hear the distinctive "bob-bob-white" of calling males along the roadways and around the air base.

Quail use about fifty species of insular plants, but most of their needs are supplied by a few. They eat green shoots and emerging insects in the spring, shifting later to ripening seeds and adult insects, and the usually prodigious quantities of weather-resistant seeds of ragweed, partridge pea, Gulf croton, and silverleaf sunflower tide them through the winter. Quail peck up whatever insects they can get and readily consume ground spiders and juvenile ghost crabs, but grasshoppers make up the bulk of their animal prey.

All of the larger diurnal and nocturnal raptors prey on bobwhites, and coyotes routinely ambush coveys. Snakes feed on quail eggs and nestlings, as do coyotes, raccoons, badgers, and cotton rats. Even the innocuous box turtle sometimes destroys a clutch of quail eggs when it clambers heavily into what it perceives as a ready-made shady shelter. In addition, bobwhites are plagued by an assortment of bacteria, roundworms, lice, and ticks, and nestlings are sometimes attacked by imported red fire ants. Despite all these depredations, it is still the weather—mainly through its effect on food supply and cover, and indirectly upon the health and exposure of the birds—that keeps four out of every five bobwhites from experiencing more than one breeding season.

The melodious, lilting songs of eastern meadowlarks are as evocative of Matagorda Island as the muffled roar of the surf. These calls of the males are announcements of ownership: "no trespass" signs on their particular 3 acres of ground. When you hear a song, scan weed-tops or sandy hillocks in the vicinity for a shining yellow breast marked with a dark chevron. If you locate several birds, they will be neatly spaced out across the grassland. Along a disputed boundary two males may engage in a musical duet supplemented with bill tilting, tail flashing, and assorted posturing. All of this is to assure the attraction of a female, or several of them; for a male may service up to three females, all of which will nest within his domain.

Female meadowlarks conceal their neatly woven domed nests in clumps of bluestem grass. These are usually oriented with the opening downwind of the onshore breeze so that the swaying grass tends to cover the entrance. The female incubates the eggs and brings in most of the insects for the nestlings. Males give highest priority to singing and courtship and are less enthusiastic about helping to feed their assorted offspring.

Meadowlarks, their eggs, and nestlings fall prey to the same pre-

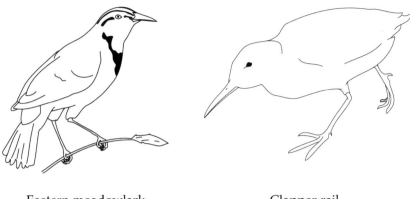

Eastern meadowlark   Clapper rail

dators that ravage bobwhite quail, and they bear the additional burden of nest parasitism by brown cowbirds.

Three other kinds of ground-living grassland birds were introduced
onto Matagorda Island. The air force released fifty hooded African
black guinea fowl, but these failed to survive. The military also consistently brought in Rio Grande wild turkey, planted food plots, and
constructed twenty-two roosts for them. A free-ranging flock of about
100 birds was finally established. About twenty remnants of this effort still survive and reproduce in the vicinity of the Wynne lodge.
Mr. Wynne kept a group of Indian chukar in the clearing at his lodge.
Since taking over the land, the USFWS has left these birds to their
own devices and by 1991, the flock had dwindled to a single pair.

Rails, Coots, and Gallinules

All nine North American species of this group have been documented
on Matagorda Island, but even a dedicated birder is unlikely, without
determined effort and considerable luck, to see more than two or
three of them. Several prefer fresh-water habitat and are scarce on the
island; most of the others adhere to the family tendency to keep a low
profile; only coots unabashedly show themselves.

On Matagorda Island, the clapper rail is the most common member
of its secretive clan. It has a chicken-like body, medium-length legs
with long toes, a rather small head, a long, slightly down-curved bill,
and a short tail that is often cocked upright. These "marsh hens" are
most often seen at dawn or dusk, especially on a low tide, walking
deliberately along the edge of a dense stand of smooth cordgrass

searching for salt-marsh snails, fiddler crabs, and insects. They are common in this habitat around the main dock on the north end of the island. A glance is usually all a human observer is allowed; a disturbed rail quickly darts into the depths of the vegetation. Even when pressed, they prefer to slink rapidly through the vegetation, or even to dive, rather than fly. If one is startled into flight, it flaps heavily for a short distance with legs dangling awkwardly, and quickly drops back into its protective habitat.

In March and April, you can detect the presence of clapper rails by the dry "kek-kek-kek" territorial calls of the males. The clap-like notes are repeated about a dozen times, accelerating in frequency and then slowing near the end. At the height of their ardor they even call at night. You can sometimes elicit this call by whistling or clapping your hands. By June you can watch for a female being followed by three or four fuzzy black chicks tripping along on pipestem legs.

Both yellow and black rails winter on Matagorda, and a quick look at either one is a real prize for any birder. These sparrow-sized rails scamper mouse-like through the vegetation in swales and around the margins of ponds. They are not rare, just rarely seen. Your best bet is to visit the island after heavy winter rains. Then slosh briskly across the flooded grassland between the beach road and the lighthouse. Several watchers, spaced out in a row, will enhance your chances, and everyone will stay enthusiastic if you don't see a massasauga rattler. Tuck your binoculars away and just keep both eyes open; an abrupt flutter is all you can hope for.

American coots are most numerous on the island in the winter, when loose rafts of these dark, duck-like birds ride the choppy bayside waters. Even at a distance, you can recognize them by their shining white, chicken-like bills. Coots are omnivorous, feeding on algae, widgeon grass, green sprouts on the bank, snails, killifish, small clams, crabs, and whatever else presents itself. Their huge lobed toes allow them to swim, dabble, and dive with ease, as well as trek across tidal ooze (hence their common name, "mud hen"). However, getting airborne is hard work for a coot; it has to patter and splash for some distance before it can lift off. The birds often choose to swim or dive, rather than fly, when threatened.

If you are startled by a series of squawks, clucks, yips, croaks, toots, and maniacal cackles issuing from the depths of bulrushes and cattails around one of the inland ponds, you have probably been detected by coots, possibly in company with a common moorhen and a purple gallinule or two. All of these birds winter on the island, and all leave in the spring to nest in fresh-water marshes on the mainland.

Cranes

The sandhill cranes that come to Texas belong to the mid-continental flock, which nests in the tundra and subarctic in Alaska and across Canada and stages on the Platte River in Nebraska en route south each winter. During the first two weeks in October they begin to arrive in the Coastal Bend. The wintering population peaks at about thirty thousand in November and December and they depart abruptly in mid-March. Matagorda Island routinely hosts about 400 to 700 of these stately birds. They are most frequently seen in small groups feeding in moist swags in the grassland or winging low on powerful wingbeats down the interior of the island. They are alert and wary, so have your binoculars ready.

Sandhill cranes are handsome birds bedecked in steel-gray plumage and sporting a patch of bright red skin on the forehead. They have a typical crane build, with long necks (held outstretched in flight), long, striding legs, a stout dagger-like bill, and a feathery bustle over the tail. They are quite vocal, talking to one another while feeding, and almost always producing their loud, throaty musical rattle when in flight. It is true avian soul music, inimitable, haunting, steeped in wildness; the sort that you can never get enough of.

Most sandhills in the Coastal Bend make long flights inland each day to feed on waste grain in the fields, but the ones on the island stay put. They roost together in several shallow inlets on the bay side but spread out at dawn, in feeding groups of about six to twenty-five, across the interior of the island. They prefer moist meadows with fresh, green growth or recently burned areas where rhizomes and tubers are exposed. There the birds stalk along, alternately gouging in the ground with their strong beaks and pausing to peer across the landscape for any sign of approaching danger. It is nearly impossible to approach them unseen.

Vegetation makes up over 80 percent of their diet; they eat the subterranean bulbs and rootstocks of nut grass (actually a sedge), purple pleatleaf, wild iris, wild onion, stemless spiderwort, wood sorrel, and spadeleaf. They dig energetically, sometimes to a depth of 6 inches, using the stout bill like an ice pick. Any small animals, earthworms, crickets, caterpillars, grasshoppers, snails, beetles, ground spiders, ribbonsnakes, ghost crabs, and an occasional cotton rat are also eaten.

The whooping crane, archetypical endangered avian species and the bird that put the Aransas National Wildlife Refuge on the map, is a routine visitor to Matagorda Island. Its periodic presence was one of the driving reasons for the incorporation of the area into the National Wildlife Refuge System.

Whooping crane   Sandhill crane

Whoopers are impressively big birds; mature males stand 5 feet tall and have a wingspan of 7 feet. The adults sport snowy-white plumage gathered into the typical crane bustle in the rear. Their black wingtips show only in flight. Crimson skin studded with black, bristlelike feathers covers the face and crown. The bill is a heavy olive dagger. Their long legs and large feet allow whooping cranes to stalk with ease over boggy and tangled terrain. First-year birds are cinnamon brown and become mottled as they shift to adult plumage. If you see a group of three, scan them carefully. In all likelihood, two are adults—a female and slightly larger male—and one, with cinnamon plumage, is their chick. Three or more white cranes together are probably unmated second-year birds that have formed a temporary group.

Being less social, whooping cranes are not so prone to call as sandhill cranes. A bird on the ground (usually the male) that has been agitated by the sight of another crane or by the approach of a human observer, especially one on foot, will often sound off, and when one bird bugles, it usually sets off a similar outburst from its mate. In contrast to the prolonged, sonorous, rolling calls of sandhill cranes, the whooping crane emits a shorter, more explosive, strident, trumpet-like sound climaxing in almost a shriek, and it is sometimes repeated several times in quick succession. Once heard, it will not be forgotten.

The whooping cranes that visit Matagorda Island are part of the only self-sustaining wild flock in existence. These birds hatch in May in the cold swamplands of Wood Buffalo National Park in the Northwest Territories amid dwarf willows, alders, and swamp birches. By the time the solitary chick is four months old, it is ready to accompany its parents on the 2,600-mile journey to the Texas Gulf Coast. They set off in October and, stopping frequently, take several weeks to make the trip, arriving in Texas by early November. They soon sort themselves into territories on the tidal flats in the vicinity of San Antonio Bay, and there they remain for the winter. The lengthening days of late March and early April are the signal to begin hauling out, back to the nesting grounds. If you want to be on Matagorda when the whoopers are there, come between mid-November and the end of March.

Whooping cranes mate for life, and each pair stakes out a nesting territory in the north and a wintering territory in the south. Usually the same birds reestablish themselves on the same piece of real estate year after year. They defend their boundaries by gesturing and trumpeting at rivals, but they never come to blows. Wintering territories are several hundred acres in extent and always in the tidal flat community. Currently, about thirty-five to forty whoopers use Matagorda Island, and their domains are strung out down the bay side from Pringle Lake to Bray Cove. Your best chance to see these birds is from the overlook at Army Hole or from the shuttle.

Except for drinking water, which they obtain from inland ponds, whoopers on Matagorda Island satisfy all their requirements in the tidal flats. There they slosh through the vegetated shallows all day long, feeding on blue crabs, razor clams, marine worms, striped mullet, salt-marsh snails, fiddler crabs, spiders, grasshoppers, caterpillars, Carolina wolfberries, and the tips of glasswort. Occasionally they grub for assorted bulbs and tubers in moist spots along the edge of the adjacent grassland. At night they roost, standing, in shallow tidal inlets. If the weather turns foul, these hardy birds either plod along unconcerned or wait it out on the lee side of a shell ridge. Born only 400 miles south of the Arctic Circle, they are unfazed by a Texas norther.

When the plight of the whooping crane was fully appreciated in 1937, it was noted that some birds occurred on both Matagorda and St. Joseph islands, as well as on Blackjack Peninsula. In that year the Aransas National Wildlife Refuge was created, thus assuring that the existing flock of fewer than twenty cranes would have a safe wintering haven in the tidal flats bordering the peninsula. Through the ensuing years, as the whoopers battled back from the edge of extinction,

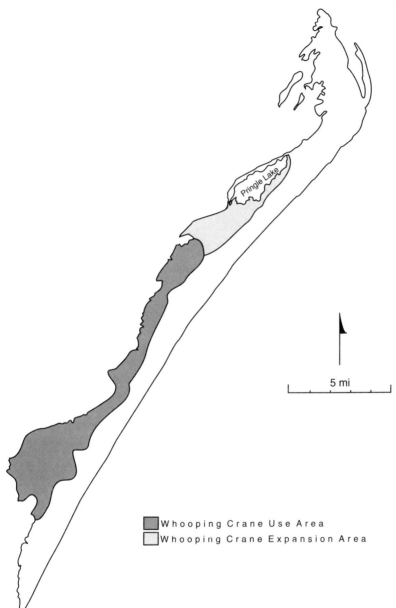

Map 10. Whooping crane habitat in the Matagorda tidal flat community.

up to a dozen birds were seen on aerial surveys over the adjacent barriers. By the 1980s the Wood Buffalo flock numbered over seventy individuals and the resultant crowding on Blackjack Peninsula was forcing cranes all around the perimeter of San Antonio Bay. Matagorda Island was routinely hosting twenty to thirty birds. Today, Matagorda is looked upon as the prime area for continued expansion of the population. It has the necessary natural resources plus the prime requisite of whooping cranes—isolation from undue human disturbance. USFWS officials believe that, with proper management, the Matagorda flats can handle fifty pairs of adult cranes plus an assortment of juveniles and subadults. We can hope that happy circumstance is one day realized.

Shorebirds

This category includes a number of small- to medium-sized birds that forage at or near the water's edge. Most of them wade, at least occasionally, and the entire group is distinguished from the herons because shorebirds are short-legged waders. They share migratory habits; an inherent gregariousness that results in flocks, sometimes of mixed species; roosting on the ground or in shallow water; repetitive, unmusical calls; and young that follow their parents immediately after hatching but find their own food. Some members prefer fresh-water habitats, and we restrict our discussion to those that frequent the marine and estuarine shores of the barriers. Shorebirds are strict insectivores on their boreal nesting grounds, but on Matagorda their prey also includes marine worms, clams, snails, crustaceans, the eggs of sundry invertebrates, small fish, and carrion.

The migratory behavior of shorebirds is notable. Among them we find some of the most phenomenal of long-distance flyers, and their spring and fall hordes rank among the truly spectacular concentrations of birdlife. These broad ranges and dense aggregations make shorebirds both vulnerable to human depredation and difficult to conserve. Some species (Eskimo curlew, lesser golden plover, red knot) still have not recovered from unbridled market and sport hunting of the last century. Most kinds cross international boundaries on their biannual flights, making conservation agreements complex and legal protection difficult. The birds' coastal feeding and staging sites and some breeding grounds are under constant threat of development, and ingrained site fidelity makes birds resistant to change, even if other locations are available. Shorebirds are especially susceptible to the effects of marine pollution, succumbing directly from oil spills and indirectly from fouled habitats and disrupted food chains. It was one of the highest priorities of the U.S. Congress that Matagorda Island be managed for the well-being of migratory shorebirds.

Numbers wax and wane with the seasons, but, year to year, shorebirds account for a large part of the avian biomass on Matagorda Island, and they hold a central position in the insular food web. In addition, they constitute one of the most conspicuous and appealing segments of the barrier bird fauna. Certainly, Matagorda would not be the same without shorebirds.

Of the thirty-eight species of shorebirds that routinely nest or migrate along the Atlantic coastline of the United States, Matagorda Island hosts thirty-five. Six of these nest on the island. One (the piping plover) is on the federal endangered species list. Some of these were mentioned in the early part of this chapter. Here we mention only the main groups and a few of the more common species.

The American oystercatcher is so distinctive that it is placed in a subgroup all its own. These stocky birds with bold black and white plumage and a straight, orange-red bill are seen in twos and threes around the passes and on shell reefs. Their speciality is using the strong, vertically compressed bill to pry open or hammer apart various bivalves, especially bent mussels and young oysters; they also probe the mud between oyster clumps for worms and mud crabs. Oystercatchers are residents and nest sparingly on the islets in the bays.

Stilts and avocets both have a rather slender build, long neck and legs, and a keenly tapered bill. Both produce incessant, noisy alarm cries when disturbed. The bill of the black-necked stilt is a fine, straight stiletto used for precision pecking of aquatic insects (especially shore flies and shore bugs) and small crustaceans. The stilt's slender red legs are so long in proportion to its black and white body as to render the bird grotesque, yet these namesake appendages give it extra "reach" after its quick-flying prey. This species drifts south in

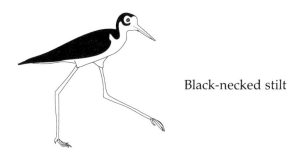

Black-necked stilt

the wintertime but returns to feed and nest on the tidal flats. American avocets are most common on Matagorda in the wintertime, but some occur the year-round and a few nests have been found on the J-Hook and elsewhere. Resting flocks of 400 birds jam the sandbars at Cedar Bayou in cold weather. Feeding shoulder to shoulder in tidal pools, avocets use a scything motion to pick up organic matter and tiny worms and crustaceans with their exquisitely tapered, upturned bill. In March the birds' silvery necks and heads begin to turn cinnamon-pink.

Plovers generally have short bills, necks, and legs. They work the shoreline with a characteristic stop-and-start gait. They walk a few steps, pause, agitate the substrate with a trembling foot, tilt the entire body forward to peck up prey, and walk again. Three species of ringed plovers—small, dumpy birds with a white neck collar and, usually, a dark breast band—nest on the island: the snowy and Wilson's plovers and the killdeer. The endangered piping plover migrates through, and a few winter. Great numbers of semipalmated plovers pass through in spring and fall. Although the larger, nonringed black-bellied plovers do not nest on Matagorda, a few can usually be found the year-round on the beaches and tidal flats. Northbound individuals, already in striking silver and black breeding plumage, move across in late March and April.

Sandpipers, mostly small birds with slender, probing bills, work the waterline and patter through the shallows. All nest in northern latitudes. Ten species have been documented on Matagorda, including the several small kinds collectively called "peeps." The least and western sandpipers are the most common wintering species; in spring and fall the very similar semipalmated sandpipers arrive to contribute to the nervous confusion of peeps.

The most consistent winter probers on the mud flats are long-billed dowitchers and dunlin. Small groups of migrating marbled godwits appear in the fall. Except in the spring when they go north to nest, long-billed curlews can always be found on the tidal flats and the forebeach or stalking over moist sites in the grassy interior and in mowed areas around outbuildings. They use their fantastic down-curved bills to tweezer up insects, to probe in mud and moist soil for worms and insect larvae, and to pluck fiddler crabs and ghost shrimp from the depths of their burrows. A curlew often twists its head upside-down as its long bill follows prey backing down its burrow. If you spook a bird, listen for its fluting "cur-leee" and watch for its cinnamon wing linings.

The relatively large willets are year-round residents and nesters on Matagorda Island. A stout, unspecialized bill allows these generalists

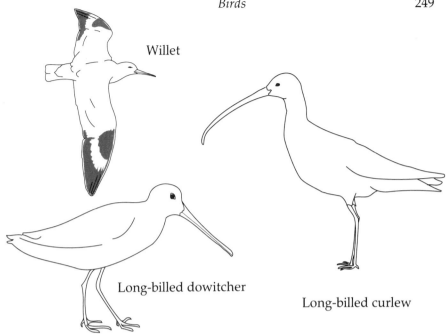

Willet

Long-billed dowitcher

Long-billed curlew

to peck, probe, surface-feed, turn surface debris, search shell reefs, and pluck at carrion with equal ease. Willets are somber and generally solitary birds, but during courtship in April the males soar high and then spiral down on rigid, down-curved wings, joyously proclaiming "will-will-willet" until the whole world is tired of it.

Less versatile than the willet, greater and lesser yellowlegs are also pecking-and-probing omnivores that feed in tidal pools and at the passes in the wintertime. Both species are long-legged and long-necked and both teeter and tail wag nervously as they walk. If you are a novice, find the two species together to compare the subtle difference in their bills and body size.

Wilson's phalaropes pass rapidly across Matagorda in May and again in August. If you've never seen these birds spinning in the water to raise aquatic prey, time your visit especially for them and trek the tidal flats.

Of all the birds in the large and heterogeneous shorebird group, the sanderling probably best typifies the beach inhabitant on Matagorda Island. Although they nest in the north and the majority winter farther south, a few sanderlings can be found in any month of the year comically chasing the waves in their perpetual search for mole crabs and sand digger amphipods. They are occasionally joined on the beach by wintering or migrating groups of red knots and ruddy turnstones. Sanderlings frequently join in pecking up the wildly hop-

Sanderlings   Laughing gulls

ping beach fleas that are exposed when turnstones flip patches of algae.

Gulls, Terns, and Skimmers

Gulls and terns are as characteristic of the coast as the shorebirds. They have short legs and webbed toes and spend a lot of time on the wing. Gulls generally are noticeably larger than terns; they have a bill with a hooked tip and although they sometimes splash down onto the water, they do not dive-bomb as the straight-billed terns do.

Matagorda Island hosts five species of gulls. For most people, the laughing gull is *the* sea gull of the Texas coast. It is a common year-round resident and the only gull that nests locally. One nesting colony uses a shell islet in Pringle Lake.

Laughing gulls are the ones with the insane cackling laugh, the black-headed gulls that follow in the wake of shrimp boats, perch atop pilings, and nimbly hawk after handouts pitched aloft by visitors on the beach. These social birds watch each other constantly, and when one finds a good food source, a hungry, squabbling flock quickly materializes. Like all their clan, laughing gulls pass through a series of juvenile and wintering plumages that make identification confusing at times; in the wintertime, for instance, the adults lose their black head feathers.

From September through May, the beaches of Matagorda are populated with mixed groups of resting herring and ring-billed gulls. These omnivores cruise the coastline, frequent the bay edges, walk the beach, and float beyond the surf or at the passes, ever alert for fish, crabs, shrimp, carrion, or any sort of edible windfall. Both species are white-headed in all plumages. Bill and leg traits distinguish the adults, and the herring gull is much the larger, but beware of confusing juveniles.

Bonaparte's gulls are erratic winter visitors. Look for these buoyant birds with pale heads and a black dash behind the eye at the passes, fluttering above the water with legs dangling and dropping low to pluck small fish from the surface. Franklin's gulls pass across Matagorda Island during their spring and fall migration. They can be confused with laughing gulls; your field guide will describe their "wing windows" that help distinguish between the two.

Terns, more airy and graceful fliers than gulls, have straight bill tips and often, forked tails. Their hallmark is their dive-bombing means of catching fish. A hungry tern flies low over the water with bill pointing downward, watching intently for a school of fish near the surface. When it locates prey, it hovers briefly and then abruptly folds its wings and plunges into the water, bill first. The bird emerges and rises into the air almost immediately, lightly flicking water from its feathers, and, if successful, clutching a wriggling fish in its bill. With a deft maneuver, it flips the fish into position and swallows it on the wing.

Ten species of terns have been seen on Matagorda Island, but only five of these are common. The most widespread and numerous are the resident Forster's terns. The tail is deeply forked and the adults' black caps are reduced in the wintertime to a black eye dash . In addition to routine dive-bombing, Forster's terns also swoop and pluck fishes from the surface without entering the water.

Caspian and royal terns are both large and black-capped; the royal has a white forehead and an orange bill; the Caspian has a black forehead and a blood red bill. Although these birds commonly rest on the beach, they mostly feed in the quiet waters of the bays, and are often seen in twos or threes, flying high and fast on their way to a favored fishing ground. Both nest on local island rookeries.

Mixed flocks of terns on the beach usually include a few sandwich terns, recognizable by their shaggy black crowns and dark, yellow-tipped bills. They are more pelagic, working the troughs between the breakers and diving well out beyond the surf zone. They lay their eggs in bare scrapes on shell reefs in the bays, often in company with nesting royal terns.

Caspian terns

The dainty least tern is indeed the smallest of its clan. This little butterfly of a bird forages like its relatives on smaller fishes. During their aerial courtship in the spring, the males have the appealing habit of seducing their mates with an offering of fish. These birds nest on sandy beaches, and throughout their range many colonies have been lost because of human disturbance of their favored sites. Nesting least terns are one of the many reasons for the prohibition on free-running dogs on the J-Hook on Matagorda Island. A colony of least terns routinely nests on one of the abandoned runways near the Visitors' Center; the site is cordoned off each spring until the young have fledged.

Black skimmers are neither gulls nor terns. They are, in fact, black skimmers, and there is nothing else quite like them. These gull-sized birds have long wings and are boldly decked in black and white plumage. However, what renders the skimmer unique is its huge orange bill with a black tip. This bill has such a seemingly absurd shape that it looks broken, and it goes with a strange means of fishing.

The upper mandible of the skimmer's bill is unremarkable, but the lower mandible, which is an inch or so longer than the upper one, is shaped like a blunt-tipped knife blade. When it feeds, a skimmer opens its mouth wide and flies at a precise altitude so that its lower mandible cleaves the water edge-on like a plow tip while its upper mandible is clear of the water. When the moving blade touches a small fish or shrimp, the bird clamps its bill closed with a character-

Black skimmer

istic downward jerk of the head. The prey is immediately swallowed; the skimmer re-cocks its mandibles and continues, cruising back and forth parallel to the shore. Because small fish and crustaceans rise to the surface at night, and because the water is often quieter then, skimmers habitually feed after dark, and cat-eyed pupils that enhance night vision add to their oddity. They make soft, dog-like barking calls to each other.

Skimmers move south in the winter, but return to lay their eggs in shallow scrapes on bare sand or shell on the local islands and on shell spits. They are gregarious birds, and sometimes rest in large flocks on the sandbars at Cedar Bayou and on the J-Hook at Pass Cavallo.

Passerine Birds

This very large and diverse group of small- to medium-sized perching birds includes all of our familiar songbirds, from swallows to flycatchers, mockingbirds to warblers. We can do little more than mention a few highlights here.

Six passerines are resident nesters on Matagorda Island and should be seen by most visitors at any time of the year. Mockingbirds, the state bird of Texas, and cardinals are common wherever mesquite trees, rose clumps, or chaparral offer food and shelter. Loggerhead shrikes, colored somewhat like mockingbirds, but with a black mask and a hooked beak, are open-country birds. They perch in mesquites or on sunflower stalks to survey their domain for small prey, almost exclusively grasshoppers. Shrikes impale extra catch on mesquite thorns or the tips of Spanish daggers, thus earning the name "butcher bird." Although they do occasionally feed on it, their skewered prey is mostly a grisly means of advertising territorial boundaries and for attracting mates.

In the springtime, the gurgling territorial calls and bright red epaulets of male red-winged blackbirds energize the bulrushes, cattails, and mottes of saltcedars.

Horned larks are common on Matagorda Island all year and, although not documented, surely nest there. In winter they move in flocks, but during the warm months horned larks travel in pairs over the saline borders of the tidal flats or along the windswept backbeach, pecking insects and the tips of glasswort. On casual glance, these sand-colored birds are nondescript, but binoculars will reveal a yellow breast with black bib, face, and eye mask. Unless you happen on a courting male, you are unlikely to see the horns, a pair of black feather tufts on his crown.

Look for seaside sparrows in bushy sea oxeye along the bay side and bordering tidal inlets. The best time to find these symbols of the tidal flat is when the males sit atop clumps and energetically emit their buzzing territorial call. They spend much time in the fringe of smooth cordgrass, feeding on seeds, insects, and amphipods. Rice rats are a major predator on their eggs and nestlings.

Although there will be others about, the common dark swallows seen zipping low across the grassy interior hawking small flying insects are barn swallows. They come in late February or early March to plaster their mud-and-grass nests beneath eaves on both ends of the island, and stay around until fall.

In late March the matchless scissor-tailed flycatchers arrive to put the entire island in a good mood with their cackling and cavorting. Wherever there is woody vegetation they build their nests, twiggy cups lined with a cushion of milkweed down. They head for Venezuela when the first northers arrive.

Two passerines are common winter residents on Matagorda Island. When sedge wrens have arrived in the fall, you are greeted by an insistent, dry chatter from the bulrushes and cordgrasses around ponds and the inner margin of the tidal flats. If you stand still and scold in return, the pert little denizen may get curious enough to show itself. Savannah sparrows are the common wintertime sparrows on Matagorda. All you need to do to see them is trek along the main road or over the grasslands, especially through weedy spots and forests of dead sunflower stalks.

Then there is the unbelievable melange of fidgety, colorful passerines, what can only be called an ecstasy of small birds that passes across Matagorda Island each fall and spring. For reasons explained earlier, the spring migration is generally the more concentrated one, and unsettled weather can cause a truly spectacular fall out. Overnight, the island comes alive with movement and color: hummingbirds, flycatchers, kinglets, thrushes, vireos, wood warblers, tanagers, grosbeaks, buntings, orioles. They come in exhausted and ravenous, yet so hyped up that they cannot sit still nor remain for long. For a month the waves pass through, but individual flocks generally stay less than a week. Then the little birds are gone and Matagorda girds for the long hot summer.

They move by day and by night, high in the sky, making wispy calls to keep together. Reckoning by stars, sun, wind direction, and magnetic fields, they flutter along ageless routes invisible to our senses. Hurried by hormones, pressed by the seasons, buffeted by wind and weather, confused by clouds, and dealt harsh odds by chance, they run on fractional grams of fat reserves, making up for small size with sheer grit. The navigational programs wired into their brains are not enough; to arrive safely, specifics must be added from experience. By instinct, intellect, and luck, each bird manages not just to find its way, but to reappear in the same shrub at predictable time intervals. Of course, many never make it. We must not forget that what is to birders merely a breathtaking spectacle is to the birds a serious and hazardous business.

Where have they been? North to nest and south to winter, and therein lies their current problem in conservation. Their semitropical and tropical wintering grounds are being razed; their critical intermediate staging sites are not fully protected from human disturbance; their temperate breeding habitats are fragmented, their food chains splintered. Unfortunately, successful conservation of migrating passerines cannot be achieved piecemeal or on one end of their range and not the other. For them it must be all or none, and their dwindling numbers suggest that we have not yet done our part. Enjoy them, but temper your euphoria with concern and voice your opinion where it will be heard.

Two other birds nest on the island and are common enough to be expected on any summer visit. In the winter, mourning doves by the thousands gather on Matagorda to feed on the abundant crop of weed seeds. Throughout the warm months, common nighthawks ply the twilight, hawking flying insects and emitting their wheezy calls. By day they hunch atop fence posts or tree limbs. In the springtime the male engages in aerial displays that terminate with a dramatic dive accompanied by a loud whirring boom of the wing feathers. The female lays two well-camouflaged eggs in a slight depression in open sand or shell, usually where the parent birds are obliged to withstand extremes of heat, wind-blown sand, and bright sunshine to protect their clutch and brood.

Rare Birds

Every birder likes to add an exceptional species to his or her life list, and Matagorda Island provides a lot of opportunities. Birds that exist in low numbers or that have wandered or been blown out of their normal ranges show up occasionally. Of course, to see them you have to be at the right place at the right time. You can get an edge through a birders' "hot line," by preparatory reading so you know what to look for, and by frequent visits, but nothing beats dumb luck.

So, don't anticipate but do be alert for a sooty or roseate tern, a shy group of masked ducks, a visiting flock of swallow-tailed kites, a misplaced white-tailed tropic bird, a confused band-tailed pigeon, a hurrying springtime buff-bellied or Allen's hummingbird, or winter flocks of bobolinks and yellow-headed blackbirds. And when the dark clouds gather and the sea winds roar, rather than hightail it for cover, watch along the surfside for pelagics (birds of the open sea): masked boobies, northern gannets, surf scoters, pomarine jaegers, and who-knows-what-else blown in from their usual haunts where there is nothing but water and sky joined all around by a distant horizon.

CHAPTER 8

Herptiles

Herptile, from the Greek *herpeton*, meaning "creeping-crawling thing," applies pretty well to both amphibians and reptiles. As these two groups are quite small, compared to mammals or birds, the study of both is usually lumped together into herpetology, and the animals together are called herptiles.

We are still in a phase of discovery and documentation of herptiles on Matagorda Island; Table 4 indicates their current status. Diversity of herptiles on the island is low compared to the Aransas National Wildlife Refuge just across the bay: only a quarter the number of kinds of amphibians and less than half as many reptiles. The numbers for drier Padre Island are comparable to those for Matagorda. This reflects both the difficulty these animals have in getting across the barrier of salt water and the severe demands placed upon them by the barrier environment. The reptiles, as might be expected, have met these challenges more effectively than the amphibians.

Amphibia

No frog or toad can tolerate even brief submergence in salt water. How, then, did these sensitive herptiles ever get to Matagorda Island? Almost surely they rafted here on debris washed out of rivers during floods. At such times the bays stay fresh for days. Amphibians frequent streamside habitats, where they are apt to be swept up by flood water. Prevailing currents from the modern San Antonio/Guadalupe watershed push drift against the southern end of Matagorda Island; prehistoric currents probably did much the same. Major floods have been recorded frequently in historical times, and must have occurred throughout the several thousand years of Matagorda's existence. It remains unverified, but the rafting hypothesis is credible.

Once ashore, immigrant amphibians, facing a daunting environment, do what they can to avoid the drying out that is a continual threat to their wet-skinned bodies. They stay near ponds and swales or deep in the recesses of the barrier flat grassland, coming out at night or on dew-sopped mornings, and retreating to their damp

Table 4. *Comparison of number of species of herptiles on Matagorda and North Padre islands and the Aransas National Wildlife Refuge*

	ANWR	Matagorda	North Padre
AMPHIBIA			
Salamanders	3	0	0
Frogs & toads	14	5	4
REPTILES			
Alligator	1	1	0
Nonmarine turtles	5	5	3
Lizards	8	4	6
Snakes	32	11	13
TOTAL	63	26	26

Data are from the files of the TPWD and the USFWS.

nooks when the air gets dry. They spend much time hunkered down with eyes closed and limbs tucked close, holding in body water and waiting for better times.

These tactics work for adult amphibians, but water takes on special importance for reproduction. Laying of eggs and survival of larvae require uncontaminated fresh water for several weeks or even months. Amphibians meet this recurrent difficulty with opportunistic, explosive breeding; when the rains come, they breed ecstatically. Even then, if the water dries up or gets salty, all the broods die and there can be no new additions to the population. But if things go well, thousands of froglets and toadlets hop hopefully away from the ponds. On this boom-or-bust basis, the populations have managed to maintain themselves.

Amphibians' lack of internal control over their body temperature meshes neatly with their water regimen. They must limit activity to times of amenable temperature, which is mostly at night during the moist spring and summer, and must remain dormant when it is hot or cold, in the dry fall and winter. The upside of this part-time, cold-blooded existence is that much less energy is required to keep the body going. All herptiles have relatively low food demands and can survive long intervals without eating at all. When times get tough, they can simply huddle down and wait.

The question of where amphibians fit in the eat-and-be-eaten scheme on Matagorda Island is complicated by their two profoundly different life phases. The whole existence of the completely aquatic larvae (tadpoles) is dedicated to voracious consumption, rapid growth, and continual development, while the biological goal of the semiter-restrial adults is simply to live long enough to reproduce. Each phase has distinctive adaptations to cope with its particular habitat. Like caterpillar and butterfly, were it not for the fact that one leads into the other, a tadpole and a frog would surely be regarded as unrelated animals.

Tadpoles have a soft, globular body with a meager cartilaginous skeleton and a muscular tail bordered by broad fins. These aquatic eating machines are in nearly constant motion—rasping with the rows of horny teeth and chopping with the horny beak over algal surfaces and rooting through bottom debris. They are suspension feeders—the fleshy lips suck in mouthfuls of water from which the organic particles are extracted by a sticky membrane in the throat. The filtered water is then forced across the gills and out an exhaust port on the side of the body. The ravenous little creatures engulf any-thing edible and much that is not: algae, protozoa, microcrustacea, bacteria, decaying plant and animal matter, animal feces, sand, and muck. The long, coiled gut absorbs nutriment as the ingested me-lange twists to the end, where a continual stream of undigestible ma-terial is squirted back into the water.

Adult frogs and toads are opportunistic insectivores using their sticky tongues to pop up whatever wriggling creatures they come across. In addition to roaches, crickets, planthoppers, beetles, flies, grasshoppers, maggots, and caterpillars, they feed on ground spiders, scorpions, terrestrial isopods, juvenile fiddler crabs, newborn ribbon-snakes, and even recently metamorphosed amphibians, of their own or other species. After rains, when termites and ants swarm and hordes of moths emerge, the frogs and toads enjoy rare gluttony.

But at a slightly larger scale, amphibians themselves are of that hap-less group of rather passive animals that is harassed at every turn by predators. The tadpoles and the froglets and toadlets take the brunt of the assault.

Tadpoles are routinely eaten by killifish, mud and red-eared turtles, blue crabs, ribbonsnakes, and juvenile alligators, and occasionally even by foraging ducks. Among the least appreciated but most deadly predators on tadpoles are aquatic insects: the larvae of dragonflies, diving beetles, and water bugs, and adult diving beetles, water bugs, and water scorpions. Tadpoles are especially vulnerable when they are crowded into squiggling masses as their pools begin to evaporate. Then they are gobbled up by any predator that happens along. Num-bers of herons and egrets and flocks of boat-tailed grackles avidly peck up the helpless tadpoles by day; at night raccoons rake in their share, and feral hogs swallow mouthfuls of ooze along with its squirming bounty.

Life does not get safer after metamorphosis. Snakes, birds, mammals (even cotton rats), larger amphibians, even wolf spiders find the disoriented froglets and toadlets easy picking. The same host of predators pursues the adults. Great blue herons and great egrets are especially efficient at spearing frogs; all of the hawks and even owls will take them when they can; ribbonsnakes, massasaugas, and an occasional western cottonmouth moccasin exact their toll; hognose snakes specialize in eating toads; badgers and coyotes join the raccoons and hogs as incidental predators. The fact that the life of amphibians is so hazardous suggests their importance in the island's food chains.

The southern leopard frog is the most abundant and widespread of Matagorda Island's six amphibians. Moderate-sized, with a typical frog anatomy, it can be immediately recognized by its bold pattern of dark blotches on a green or brown background. Leopard frogs move easily on land and are especially active during rainy weather, when they are frequently seen crossing roads or hopping along pond margins. They are rather tolerant of environmental extremes, and are found not only around all fresh-water sites but throughout the barrier flat community, but because their larval stage is long (two to three months), they breed only in relatively permanent pools and ditches. Cool-weather breeders, from December through February the males congregate after rains at ponds, where they sprawl on the surface of the water to call. With the aid of a pair of inflated vocal sacs, they produce a series of chortles and groans. This weird serenade, sounding rather like wet fingers rubbed over a balloon, attracts the females, and eventually fist-sized masses of fertilized eggs are left attached to submerged vegetation. Tucked in their jelly layers, each of the several hundred black specks is now launched on its perilous course toward froghood.

Rio Grande leopard frogs are very similar to southern leopard frogs in appearance and behavior, but are somewhat larger and much less common on the island.

The appealing green treefrog is typified by its expanded toe pads and protruding eyes, as well as by its spring green color. They are most commonly seen in their daytime poses, hugging the stem of a cattail or bulrush or huddled under the eaves of buildings at the air base or on the shaded side of a sign. When the early summer rains begin, nights and cloudy days ring with the bell-like "quonk, quonk" of the males, which sit in emergent vegetation of the pools and ditches. Soon the night is filled with a swelling crescendo as hun-

Green treefrog

Southern leopard frog

Gulf Coast toad

dreds of voices join the sonorous chorus. The mated pairs leave inconspicuous platforms of eggs floating on the pond surface.

A robust body with stumpy legs (the classical "hop-toad" anatomy), warty skin, and large gland behind each eye distinguish Matagorda's only true toad (family Bufonidae), the Gulf Coast toad. Adults are up to 4 inches in length, with a brownish body marbled with straw-yellow and marked by a thin yellowish stripe down the backbone. Because their thick skin allows them to conserve body water, toads are more terrestrial than frogs. This is the only amphibian that routinely ventures into the inland perimeter of the sand dunes community. Toads are confirmed summer breeders; only when the water reaches a comfortable 70° F do the males begin to emit their throaty trills from the banks of temporary pools and swales. Clasped pairs lay and fertilize two parallel strands of eggs, which are left wound indiscriminantly among submerged plants. Because their larvae are exceptionally tolerant of high temperature and modest salt concentration, and they hurry through development in about a month, Gulf Coast toads can breed in ephemeral pools.

The eastern narrow-mouthed toad (family Microhylidae) is hardly ever seen or even suspected on Matagorda Island until the males begin to produce their distinctive buzz-like mating calls from grassy pools in the summertime. Even then the sounds are taken for those of insects. Looking carefully seldom helps; the grape-sized brown toads (they are called toads despite their thin, smooth skin) crouch in the submerged bases of the grass with just their little pointed snouts above the water. Only if a flashlight beam happens to shine on the white bubble-like vocal sac of a calling male will the songster be spotted. They are seldom captured, for these little toads are adept at scurrying mouse-like through the vegetation. Their larvae, too, are peculiar. Shaped like animated frying pans, they hang by their funnel-like mouths to the underside of the surface film and suck in organic material collected there. Adult narrow-mouthed toads range throughout the barrier flat community. They are most often found beneath surface debris, and they probably move through rodent and spider burrows. Their principal food items are termites and ants.

The most reclusive of Matagorda's amphibians are the eastern spadefoot toads (family Pelobatidae). These pudgy creatures spend most of their lives hunkered beneath the sand, coming up to feed on insects after rains. It takes a violent summer downpour to put them in the mood to breed. Once a deluge begins, male spadefoots quickly collect in flooded swales, where they float out into the water and begin to produce the peculiar, grunt-like yawps that lure in the females. After a night or two of unleashed ecstasy, the adults disappear underground, using unique horny flanges on their hind feet to excavate burrows. Spadefoot eggs hatch quickly and their tadpoles proceed to metamorphosis in a few weeks. If evaporation threatens their survival, the tadpoles turn to cannibalism to hasten the development of a lucky few.

There may be several more kinds of amphibians on Matagorda that have escaped verification to date. Two possibilities are near lookalikes of mentioned species: the Great Plains narrow-mouthed toad and Couch's spadefoot toad. Four other species—Strecker's chorus frog, spotted chorus frog, northern cricket frog, and Woodhouse's toad—have been reported on the island, but as they have not been observed recently, their populations may be extirpated. Finally, bullfrogs, probably introduced by military personnel, did once occur in the ditches and larger ponds on the north end of the island. This population apparently no longer exists.

Reptilia

Like the amphibians, most of the resident reptiles on Matagorda Island probably arrived by rafting. A greater species diversity reflects important advantages reptiles enjoy that promote their dispersal to, and establishment on, the barrier.

The scaly skin of reptiles is not only dry but waterproof. This skin holds in vital body water and protects the tissues from salt imbalance, so reptiles could make the journey across the salty bay with impunity; once on the island, they would suffer less from dehydration. They also have an efficient kidney that allows them to void crystals of uric acid rather than watery urine. And they have broken the age-old bond with water as a medium for reproduction. The female is inseminated directly and lays shelled eggs on land (a few species bear live young); even aquatic reptiles must leave the water to deposit their eggs. This relative independence of water and general mobility allow the reptiles to explore and colonize all of the major communities on the island.

Because they are more diverse, it is harder to generalize on how the reptiles fit into insular food chains, but, except for a few turtles, they are confirmed carnivores. Some are specialists but most are opportunists that take any moving prey that they can catch and overcome. Lizards chew their catch slightly before gulping it down; snakes laboriously swallow their prey whole; alligators bolt most food items and crudely dismember the larger ones; only the turtles display any etiquette at mealtime.

Although a big alligator, sea turtle, or diamondback rattler may be crusty enough to exist at the end of a food chain, most reptiles are linked with higher predators, including members of their own clan. Sometimes the connections are unexpected. Raccoons, for instance, are a menace to alligators because the 'coons pilfer alligator nests. Great blue herons are another threat, skewering juvenile alligators when they can. Large snakes eat toads; large toads eat small snakes. Lizards eat spiders; large spiders eat small lizards. Blue crabs occasionally catch young ribbonsnakes, and diamondback terrapins occasionally catch young blue crabs. Box turtles compete with coyotes for prickly pear tunas and with ghost crabs for beach ground-cherries. Ground skinks compete with narrow-mouthed toads for termites and with scorpions for terrestrial isopods. And so the reptilian strands play diverse and often significant roles in the island's food web.

Crocodilia

The American alligator, the one reptile on Matagorda Island that needs no description, was once an important component of the natural fauna of the coastal plain of Texas. Habitat destruction and indiscriminant hunting brought alligators to grief throughout their range in the United States, and they were charter members of the list when the Endangered Species Act was passed in 1973. Under protection,

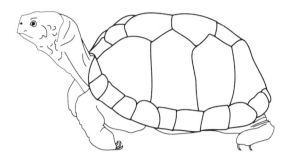

Western box turtle

numbers rallied quickly, and by 1983, the reptiles were reclassified in Texas and carefully regulated hunts were begun. Alligators are not hunted on Matagorda Island, and probably never will be; the standing population of thirty or so adults does not call for management.

These large reptiles can easily navigate the bays between island and mainland, and there probably is intermittent traffic between the two populations. On the island, they seek out the fresh-water ponds and ditches. (It is suspected that they can smell favorable habitat.) They are only occasionally seen in the bay-side tidal flats, where the salty water is too shallow and the terrain too open for their liking; and the rare 'gator spotted on the gulf side is surely on his way elsewhere.

Once it chooses a fresh-water site, an alligator generally usurps any smaller 'gators and settles down to a solitary, sedentary existence. On a bank with favorable exposure to the sun there will be a bare spot where the creature routinely hauls out to bask. Most individuals excavate a deep tunnel in the bank at water level to which they retire during dry or unusually cold weather. 'Gators are able to make-do in amazingly small bodies of water, some hardly large enough for the animals to stretch out. For weeks or months an alligator can be found in its customary hole; then it abruptly disappears, sometimes temporarily, sometimes for good. It is presumed that they move about at night, especially during warm, wet weather, in search of mates or better hunting grounds. Or perhaps they are just obeying some obscure and ancient wanderlust.

Although their favored habitat is widely scattered on the island, these great beasts do manage to get together. Good spring and early summer rains promote nesting attempts. The female drags several bushels of bankside mud and vegetation into a knee-high mound about 4 feet across. Here she scoops a cavity with her hind legs and lays her clutch of thirty or so leathery eggs, covering them carefully. She remains in her nearby pool for the next two months while sunshine and the decaying organic matter incubate her brood. During this time she actively guards her nest against marauding raccoons and hogs, and will even menacingly approach humans who come too close. When they start to hatch, the little 'gators make gulping grunts that alert the female to scratch into the nest and release them. The 9-inch hatchlings join their mother in the home pool, where they may remain for months before dispersing.

Alligators are opportunistic carnivores; what they eat depends very much on the size of the 'gator. Babies and juveniles feed mostly on adult and larval aquatic insects, grasshoppers, and dragonflies that fall into the water, killifish, crabs, grass shrimp, frogs, ribbonsnakes, and small turtles. As they grow larger, they grade up to mullet, adult turtles and snakes, blue crabs, birds (ducks, coots, and herons are common prey), and whatever mammals they can surprise on the bank (raccoons, and the young of feral hogs and white-tailed deer). Alligators take advantage of drying pools to feed on whatever is crowded into accessibility and to lie in wait for other predators that come to share in the harvest; they also eat carrion.

Despite the vigilance of the females, raccoons and feral hogs manage to get an occasional clutch of eggs. Hatchling and juvenile 'gators are food for great blue herons, raccoons, and larger alligators and possibly for adult blue crabs. Juveniles dispersing across the barrier flat must surely run afoul of coyotes and badgers, and many young die because they cannot find a suitable unoccupied pond. But adult alligators are immune to attack by natural predators.

Routine counts indicate about ten adult alligators on the northern half of Matagorda Island and perhaps twice that many on the southern half, where there are more habitable sites. Your best chance of seeing one is to watch at sizeable fresh-water pools for the distinctive set of two knobby eyes and a nostril protuberance that indicates a 'gator suspended just beneath the surface, watching, but ready to submerge if it feels threatened. The military ditch is a good place to look. You can also ask at the Visitors' Center about recent sightings. If you are on the south end, you might persuade a ranger to introduce you to "Charlie Brown" or to "Jaws," who can usually be found in their respective ponds.

In any case, don't get too close. Although alligators usually shun contact with people, there are special circumstances. First, you might inadvertently approach a nest and provoke the guardian female. Second, the 'gators on the island are used to people and therefore less shy, which increases the likelihood of a close encounter with unpredictable consequences. This familiarity is worse on the south end, where they were routinely fed fish offal. They learned—and still remember—to approach people on the bank for a handout. So keep your distance; let binoculars or a telephoto lens narrow the gap.

Turtles

If you spot a turtle head above the surface of a fresh-water pond, it will surely be a red-eared slider, the most evident kind on the island. The red-ear (there is a red dash behind the eye) is very tolerant of both temperature extremes and moderate salinity. In wet periods it readily travels overland, so it has colonized all of the island's deep, reliable pools. These turtles feed on a variety of aquatic invertebrates and what little aquatic vegetation is available, and in times of stress they make do with bottom muck. They are preyed upon by alligators; raccoons and wading birds eat the young, and raccoons dig up and pilfer their jug-shaped bankside nests.

Although mud turtles are rather common in ditches and swales, they are nocturnal and secretive and so are seldom seen. Perhaps you will notice a movement in shallow water and glimpse a brown shell about the size of a bar of soap rapidly disappearing into the submerged vegetation. That is all you will see of a mud turtle unless you happen upon one crossing a road during rainy weather. If you pick it up you will discover that it has left a foul odor on your hands. These are bottom-dwelling turtles that feed mainly on aquatic insects, crustaceans, and snails. They work their way down into the muck to escape winter cold and summer drought.

There are two kinds of mud turtles on the island, the yellow mud turtle and Mississippi mud turtle. Only a herpetologist can easily distinguish them. No one knows how the two species interact ecologically.

The personable western box turtle is rather commonly seen plodding methodically on stumpy legs down any road through the barrier flat. "Box" refers to the high-domed shell that can be closed, by folding up the front and rear halves of the lower shell, so tightly not even a coyote can get into it These terrestrial turtles spend much of their time sequestered in the tall grass or down animal burrows in an immobile "turtle daze." They sally forth in the spring, after summer showers, or on lazy fall afternoons in search of fresh greenery, Southern dewberries, beach ground-cherries, and prickly pear tunas to rip into with their strong beak and stout forelegs. Despite their

Texas diamondback terrapin   American alligator

cumbersome gait, they can strike quickly enough to harvest some of the island's bountiful grasshopper fodder. Juveniles are almost never seen; it is presumed they keep to the dense grass cover or lead a subterranean existence.

The most enigmatic of Matagorda's turtles is the Texas diamondback terrapin. These are handsome animals, up to 9 inches long, the scutes deeply etched with concentric grooves and ridges, suggesting a faceted gem. The limbs, head, and neck are olive gray and the head is thickly freckled with jet black dots. They favor the brackish water of the bays, and on high tides, move onto the tidal flats, up estuaries, and along the margins of islets and oyster reefs to forage for clams, snails, crabs, and marine worms. The fact that they are readily lured into crab traps baited with cut mullet suggests that they also scavenge.

These turtles are almost never seen on Matagorda, and what little we know about them is inferred from studies of a related variety in the Chesapeake Bay. Eggs are reportedly laid in sand above the high-tide line, but no local nesting sites are known. No one knows where the local terrapins go in the wintertime, although they are said to burrow into the shallow bay mud. Do they eat submerged marine vegetation? What are their natural predators? These are questions without answers.

Terrapins were abundant here until around 1900, when, in the spate of market hunting that decimated so much of the state's marine life, they were nearly extirpated. Although a census of the population has not been taken recently, it is certain that they are uncommon and on the decline. Incidental capture and drowning in shrimp trawls and crab traps, as well as general degradation of their favored bay-side and estuarine habitats, seem to be the principal reasons the turtles are in trouble. Despite the pressures working against them, diamondbacks have not been classified for protection; they probably merit it.

You are not likely to see a diamondback terrapin on your visit to Matagorda. They must be left among the intriguing portion of the island's fauna—creatures we can best enjoy in contemplation, satisfied in the knowledge that a few at least are somewhere close at hand and hopeful that somehow they will manage to take advantage of the refugium that was created for the ecosystem of which they are an integral part.

Four species of sea turtles have been recorded on the Matagorda Island beach: Atlantic loggerhead, Atlantic green, Atlantic hawksbill, and Atlantic ridley. Unfortunately, all recent sightings have been of dead or dying specimens. Every year, over a dozen carcasses of these large turtles are discovered washed up on the beach. Because most strandings coincide with the offshore shrimping season, it is strongly suspected that the turtles were incidentally snared and drowned in the shrimp trawls. In 1990, amid controversy and protest, turtle excluder devices were mandated for the shrimping fleet. Routine beach patrols are currently monitoring the effect of this attempt to reduce the carnage.

Sea turtles live in the bays or over the shallow continental shelf, feeding on a variety of marine invertebrates and grazing submerged grass beds and algal masses. Each species annually congregates offshore to mate; then the females come in to lay their eggs on sandy beaches. Hatchlings head directly to the sea. All four species listed here range throughout the warm waters of the Atlantic Ocean. The

Atlantic ridley

Atlantic ridley is most closely restricted to the Gulf of Mexico, but the loggerhead is the commonest species in the Gulf and the one most frequently stranded on the Matagorda beach.

For a variety of reasons, all of the sea turtles are in ecological trouble. Incessant, wholesale human raids on their nests and persistent market and subsistence hunting of the adults have been the most devastating factors. Loss of traditional nesting beach to development is another; the animals do not easily shift to alternate sites. The turtles must run the seasonal gauntlet presented by the nets of commercial fishermen and shrimpers. Ingestion of discarded plastic materials, which often causes disability or death, is a significant additional problem. The general degradation of the nearshore marine environment due to multifarious human activities has surely weakend the food chains on which these turtles depend. To these human pressures natural mortality must be added, especially nest predation by coyotes and raccoons, hatchling predation by shore crabs and gulls, and heavy attrition of the juveniles at sea.

Attempts to save the sea turtles have so far achieved little more than a holding action, and for some species, not even that much. The protective classifications definitely help, but international agreements have not been achieved across all the turtles' last strongholds in tropical seas. Even where there are laws, illicit exploitation continues. Turtle excluder devices, prohibitions on dumping plastics at sea, manufacture of artificial tortoise-shell wares to compete with the natural resource, and research programs designed to rehabilitate decimated populations are all working to the turtles' advantage. As always, however, the ultimate answer must be education designed to change attitudes. If you already appreciate the plight of the sea turtles, you are part of that answer. Act accordingly and help pass the word, beginning with your children.

Because of their former local abundance, it is presumed that green turtles, and probably loggerheads, did nest on the Texas barrier islands as late as the close of the nineteenth century. The hawksbill may have always been a more tropical nester, but ridleys reportedly nested on South Padre Island in historic times. The only recent documented nesting on the Texas coast has been three ridleys (1976, 1990, 1991) and one green (1987), all on Padre Island. Despite rumors, there is not a single verified record of any species of sea turtle ever nesting on Matagorda Island. The massive rehabilitation effort begun in 1979, designed to establish a nesting colony of ridleys on Padre Island, has so far not been successful.

There have been reports of snapping turtles on Matagorda. The species is retiring and it can withstand brackish water; its presence,

though still unverified, would not be surprising. A fifth endangered
sea turtle, the leatherback, is observed occasionally in the open waters of the Gulf of Mexico and there have been beach strandings along
the Texas barriers, but it has never been sighted, alive or dead, on
Matagorda Island.

Lizards

Lizards, at least ground-living forms, would seem well-adapted to
establish themselves in the barrier island environment. But although
there is no lack of prey, most species require relatively open ground
for foraging and escape maneuvers, so the grassy central barrier flat
is closed to them. That leaves just the beach and the roadsides, and
only four kinds of lizards are known to occur on Matagorda.

The first lizard you see on Matagorda Island will likely be a prairie-
lined racerunner, easily recognized by narrow longitudinal pale stripes
and a long, tapering tail (they are sometimes called whiptails). The
males have a flush of mint green on their heads and forequarters.
They are common around the air base, the roads, and the shell ridges,
and they infiltrate the stabilized sand among the dunes. Streamlined
for rapid movement over open ground, racerunners are well-named.

These alert lizards are active during the hottest part of bright sunny
days. They characteristically move in spurts, pausing to test the
ground with their tongue, apparently to locate subterranean prey
such as termites and ants. Racerunners also feed on grasshoppers
and other surface insects and arachnids. Coachwhip snakes and
hawks rank high among their predators. If you approach a racerunner
it will be gone in a flash, often to the safety of its burrow; find a patch
of shade and let your binoculars do the work.

Although it is on the decline over most of its range in Texas (and so
is on the state's list of threatened species), the Texas horned lizard
seems to be holding its own on Matagorda Island. Even more than
prairie-lined racerunners, horned lizards are creatures of open, barren ground and bright hot days. They are inactive when it is cloudy
and retire into dormancy with the first cool weather of fall. Also called
"horny toads," their pancake body and horn-like scales make them
instantly recognizable. They are fairly common around the air base
and along roadways, but do not inhabit the loose sand of the dunes.
They feed on ground-living insects, with a preference for ants. Despite their armament, these lizards are frequently preyed upon by
loggerhead shrikes, coachwhip snakes, kingsnakes, and probably by
the large raptors as well. The island's native population may have been
supplemented by the introduction of specimens by military personnel.

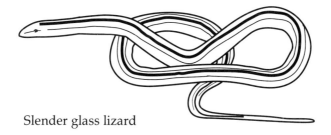

Slender glass lizard

Because they are inhabitants of the dense grassland that covers the central part of the island, slender glass lizards are mostly seen on the roads, where they come in the cool of the morning to soak up heat. These legless creatures look like snakes, but bony plates make their movements less sinuous. Experts distinguish them from snakes by the presence of eyelids and ear openings. Straw-colored, with thin, black, longitudinal stripes, they blend well with their grassy habitat. Adults are about 1½ feet long, two-thirds of it tail. When grasped by a predator, this "glass snake" squirms violently, causing one or more sections of its tail to break loose. The tail fragments writhe energetically, distracting the predator long enough for the lizard, with vital organs intact, to slip away. Rapid vessel constriction prevents undue loss of blood and the tail soon begins to regenerate. The frequency of individuals with regenerated tails (regrown tails are a distinctive brown color) suggests that the ruse is often successfully employed.

The most secretive of Matagorda's lizards is the ground skink. On the mainland these little lizards are at home in moist leaf litter and among rotting logs; on the barrier island they must make shift with storm-deposited debris behind the primary dunes. So far, they have been found only on the northern end of the island, which may mean that they were introduced there with the establishment of the air base. Adults are about 3½ inches long, including the long tail, metallic brown above, with a thin black line down each side. Ground skinks feed on any of the soft-bodied insects, arachnids, and isopod crustaceans that share their habitat. The young are so tiny that they are preyed upon by jumping spiders and wolf spiders, and they may be eaten by ghost crabs.

Five other species of lizards merit brief mention. Both the green anole and the Mediterranean gecko were reported on the air base as late as the 1970s. The former (called a "chameleon" locally for its ability to change its color between green and brown) is easily introduced with human goods or transported as a pet; the latter entered Texas in 1955 and has readily taken to living in and around human habitations, especially on the coastal plain. Neither species has been seen on the island recently.

It is surprising that neither the southern prairie lizard nor the keeled earless lizard inhabit Matagorda. The southern prairie lizard is very common on the Aransas National Wildlife Refuge, where it seems well-adapted to habitats similar to those on Matagorda. The keeled earless lizard is the most distinctive reptile of the sand dunes on Padre and Mustang islands. Why it has not made it up St. Joseph to Matagorda is a mystery.

Finally, the Texas spotted whiptail, closely related to the prairie-lined racerunner, occurs on the adjacent mainland, but not on Matagorda. Perhaps it could not survive here in competition with the racerunner, or maybe it just never lucked across the bay.

Snakes

Snakes, though subject to the same general ecological restrictions as the closely related lizards, are considerably more tolerant of moisture and darkness; some species are nocturnal, some are semiaquatic, and some spend nearly all of their time underground. Their main anatomical distinction is the lack of legs, but this apparent deficiency has hardly reduced their mobility. Using special musculature attached to the tips of their ribs and the edges of transverse scutes on their bellies, snakes can slither, swim, burrow, and even climb with agility. They make up for the lack of an external ear by being highly sensitive to vibrations in the substrate. Their slender forked tongue is continually flicked out to taste the air by carrying airborne chemicals to a special organ in the roof of the mouth. Several species have a heat-sensing organ to help locate warm-blooded prey.

Most kinds of snakes take only live prey, and movement is essential to excite the reptile to attack, but some also eat the eggs of reptiles or birds. At least some species are rather stereotyped, interested only in a narrow range of prey, while others go for anything of the right size. And the right size may be surprising. The two halves of a snake's lower jaw are loosely connected by an elastic ligament, allowing the animals to swallow whole prey much larger than their own head. Powerful digestive juices dissolve nearly all body tissues.

Because most snakes lead secretive lives and their populations are not high, individuals are encountered only occasionally. Those that inhabit the extensive grassy interior of the island are most often seen

Gulf Coast ribbonsnake

when they cross the roads. To date, only eleven species have been confirmed on Matagorda Island, three of them poisonous to humans.

The Gulf Coast ribbonsnake is the most abundant species on the island, the one visitors are most likely to see, because it is abroad in the daytime and frequents grassy banks around fresh-water pools and roadside ditches. These slender snakes, marked with three yellowish stripes on a dark background, are well named. The young, brightly colored miniatures of the adults, are born alive. Adults may get over 2 feet long and be almost all dark, but most are smaller and brighter. They swim readily and frequently take refuge amid submerged vegetation. Ribbonsnakes are avid predators on all small aquatic and semiaquatic life in their moist habitat: killifish, tadpoles, freshly metamorphosed frogs, insects and their larvae, spiders, and grass shrimp. They are in turn preyed upon by juvenile alligators, larger fish, blue crabs, leopard frogs, Gulf Coast toads, birds of prey, raccoons, feral hogs, and even cotton rats. Newborn ribbonsnakes are small enough to be taken by the larger wolf spiders that frequent the same habitat.

Texas brown snakes lead ribbonsnake-like lives along the edges of the tidal flats. These harmless little serpents (adults are seldom over a foot long) are pale brown with two rows of dusky blotches along the sides. They spend most of their time beneath debris or in moist vegetation, where they search for insects, arachnids, and terrestrial crustaceans, and they probe the damp soil for earthworms. Texas brown snakes are taken by almost every carnivore that stalks the island.

The western coachwhip is a large (3 to 4 feet) snake of the interior grassland. The uniform tan color of the body allows the pattern of smooth scales to dominate, giving the impression of a braided whip. These alert snakes are strictly diurnal and prowl through the grass with their heads held several inches off the ground, hunting by keen eyesight. They readily climb shrubbery in search of insects and bird nests. Their specialty is prairie-lined racerunners, lizards that can only be caught by a high-speed chase, but they also consume large numbers of grasshoppers, and are important predators on the eggs and hatchlings of meadowlarks, the young of harvest mice, and on small lizards and snakes. Coachwhips are nervous and ill-tempered; if cornered, they hold their head high, watch their tormentor closely, strike repeatedly with wide-open mouth, and vibrate the tail ominously against the surrounding vegetation. Despite their show, the bite is little more than a cat scratch. The vigorous population of coachwhips on Matagorda is noteworthy; the species is rapidly declining on the mainland.

Although a bit less irritable, the eastern yellow-bellied racer is much like the coachwhip in behavior and ecology. This thin serpent is olive above and yellowish below. It seldom gives the visitor more than a glance before it disappears into the grass.

The speckled kingsnake is surely one of the most handsome snakes on Matagorda Island. An enamel-yellow spot in the center of each glossy black scale produces a sparkling effect and yields the animal's colloquial name: salt-and-pepper snake. These relatively large snakes, commonly over 3 feet long, range across the grasslands and onto the fringe of the tidal flat, but apparently not onto the loose sand of the dunes. Although diurnal, they are usually encountered coiled beneath surface debris. Like all kingsnakes, they are powerful constrictors, feeding mostly on harvest mice, cotton rats, and rice rats. They will take eggs of birds, lizards, and turtles and they occasionally catch adult birds and lizards. The kingsnakes are immune to both rattlesnake and cottonmouth moccasin poison, and occasionally catch and squeeze these reptiles to death like any other victim and swallow them down.

The Mexican milksnake, a second species of kingsnake, has a showy pattern of bright rings: narrow black, narrow yellow, broad red. The belly and the tip of the snout are black. Freshly shed specimens are truly resplendent in bright colors with a soft bluish luster. Adults get about 2 feet long. This very docile species is seldom seen abroad, but is found beneath debris either behind the primary dunes or above the high tide line on the bay side. Milksnakes feed on mice, snakes, and lizards; the ones on the bay side may have learned to catch the abundant fiddler crabs.

The eastern hognose snake has a remarkable defense behavior. It coils, inflates with air, raises and flattens the front third of the body in cobra-fashion, emits a wicked hiss from a huge gaping mouth, and strikes repeatedly. All this has earned it the names of puff adder and spreading adder. If the menacing display fails, the snake flops over on its back, writhes about with tongue dragging limply in the sand, and finally comes to rest, dead, apparently, until the coast is clear. The display is impressive to a human observer and presumed to be at least disconcerting to a would-be predator. These creatures are also called hognose snakes because of the upcurved scales on the tip of the snout, which are used to shovel in the sand. These interesting snakes prefer sandy, vegetated areas and are not often encountered on the island unless seen as they cross a road. Their principal prey is the Gulf Coast toad, but they also feed on frogs and insects. Adults are about 2 feet long and are yellow-brown with prominent black blotches.

More than any other species, the Gulf salt-marsh snake specializes in the brackish water habitat of the low marsh. Although they are common enough, with nocturnal habits and mucky surroundings, these snakes are seldom seen. Like all members of the watersnake clan, they are quick to take refuge beneath the water and are bad-tempered when cornered. The rather thick-bodied adults, about 2 feet long, are patterned with four longitudinal dark stripes on a straw-yellow ground color. Although no one knows for sure, it is presumed that this species feeds on small fish, crabs, and whatever moderate-sized creatures it comes across in the tidal pools.

When disturbed, the western cottonmouth moccasin throws its head back and opens its mouth wide, showing the bright-white lining; thus, its name. This display is usually accompanied by vigorous vibration of the tail and is apparently meant to indicate danger to any passerby. It is no idle warning. Although individuals vary in their temperament, many cottonmouth moccasins are pugnacious and prone to hold their position rather than retreat. They will strike repeatedly if approached closely. Their venom is toxic enough to require immediate attention if they bite a person. Although on the adjacent coastal prairie this thick-bodied species is quite common around fresh-water sites, it is not often seen on Matagorda Island, perhaps because it keeps to the heavily vegetated swales. Unlike cottonmouth moccasins in Florida, the local variety does not inhabit the tidal flat, or at any rate, it is seldom seen there. These snakes are noted for eating virtually anything: fish, frogs, tadpoles, young alligators, birds, rice rats, other snakes, crabs, even (very unsnakelike) freshly dead fish and frogs in drying puddles. To avoid cottonmouth moccasins, watch where you step on the margins of pools and ditches.

Although some may find it hard to regard any snake with a rattle on its tail as pretty, the western massasauga (mass-ah-'saug-ah—a

Western massasauga

corruption of an American Indian name for a related variety in Canada) deserves that distinction. These little rattlers (adults rarely exceed 2 feet in length) are steel-gray with a series of bold dark-brown, rectangular blotches down the back. They are rather abundant on the island, but because they stay beneath the dense grass cover of the barrier flat, are seldom seen except when they are crossing a road. When surprised, a massasauga does not retreat but "freezes." The snakes are feisty; if approached, they will coil and raise their rattle to produce an insect-like buzz, and if further provoked, will strike energetically. Like that of any rattlesnakes, the bite of a massasauga demands immediate medical attention.

Massasaugas prefer moist, well-vegetated sites such as the grassy swales on the barrier flat, but wander more widely after rains in their pursuit of harvest mice, frogs, other snakes, and whatever small birds come their way. Like other rattlers, they are pit vipers, with sensory pits that help locate warm-blooded prey. With cold-blooded creatures like frogs and snakes, and with birds, they usually strike and maintain their grip; but when catching mice, which are apt to deliver a nasty bite in return, they strike and release. Then, while the venom takes effect, the snake uses its sensitive tongue to follow its quarry's final short and futile race for life. Once upon the fresh carcass, flicks of the tongue determine the front end, where the process of swallowing will begin. Soon the massasauga, with a comfortable bulge in its midsection, crawls off to a dark recess to digest undisturbed.

For Texans, the western diamondback rattlesnake is "the" rattlesnake, and Matagorda Island is usually reported as "crawling with 'em." Certainly the species occurs on the island, but estimates of its abundance seem to be exaggerated. It takes few encounters with rattlesnakes to impress the imagination and affect recall. Early ranchers tell of killing twenty rattlers a day while working cattle. This is probably an exceptional figure, but in the past there were more rodents on the island, and with the grass cropped by livestock so that visibility was increased, people abroad from sunup to sunset probably did encounter more rattlesnakes. Today it is unlikely that a visitor will see one unless it is crossing a road. Nevertheless, commonsense precautions are in order. Always watch where you (and your children) step, especially around deep grass tussocks, surface debris, dewberry brambles, rose hedges, or cactus clumps; be especially careful on the shell ridges, a habitat rattlers seem to favor. You are gambling if you trek about at night without a flashlight.

Diamondback rattlers are active throughout the warm months, and on sunny days, even in the dead of winter, some emerge from their retreats to coil in the sun. During the summer, they are mostly nocturnal, but in the spring (April), when they move out of their winter quarters beneath Gulf Coast cordgrass clumps and in sundry holes, they are diurnal and especially active. After several months of fasting, they are hungry, and spring is when they seek out mates. In August, the females give live birth to over a dozen 9-inch-long babies, diminutive copies of the adults, complete with venom apparatus and the instinct to use it. The newborn even vibrate their tails vigorously if provoked, but the natal prebutton doesn't make a sound; that capacity comes only after the second molt.

The western diamondback, by nature irritable and prone to stand its ground when threatened, is responsible for more venomous snakebites in the United States than any other species. The spectacle of an aroused adult diamondback, viewed from a safe distance, is a memorable experience. The lower half of the snake's body lies in a flattened anchor coil, with the end of the tail raised vertically in the center or

Western diamondback rattlesnake

to one side; the vibrating rattle making a loud sizzling hiss. The forward half of the body, angled upward (the height varies with the size of the snake—6 to 8 inches in adults), terminates in a tight S-shaped crook in the neck so that the broad head can be kept pointed directly at the source of provocation; the black tongue, with its forked tip flipping slowly up and down, is extended. The nerve-wracking sibilation of the rattle is enhanced by a strong hissing as the inflated reptile exhales.

The rattlesnake's potent venom is stored in glands behind the upper jaw. Each gland is connected by a duct to the base of a fang in the roof of the mouth. The fang is hollow, with a small hole on the front edge at its tip. As the fangs are imbedded during a strike, muscles are contracted around the glands, forcing venom through the fangs into the tissues of prey or threat. But this is not automatic; the snake can choose to release venom through one, both, or neither fang, and its degree of irritation and individual temperament dictate the result.

The venom of the western diamondback causes shock, hemorrhaging, and rapid tissue destruction (advance digestion) in its prey. Although its use in defense is secondary, it is obviously equally potent against any creature the snake considers a threat. Rattlers are immune to the effect of their own venom. Because of its long fangs and potential to inject a large volume of poison, when this snake bites a human, it is always considered a medical emergency.

The rattler's fangs are more than passive hypodermics. Each fang is attached to a movable bone set well forward in the roof of the snake's mouth. As the mouth is closed, fleshy sheaths are drawn over the fangs and they are rotated upward and backward to fold against the palate, with the tips pointing toward the throat and the curved shafts nestled in grooves in the floor of the mouth. During a strike the sheaths are retracted and the tooth-bearing bones swivel so that the fangs come erect as the mouth is gaped. At the instant of contact, the upper jaw is nearly vertical and the fangs point directly at the victim. Both the force of the forward motion and a quick snap with the lower jaw drive the fangs home. With fangs nearly ½ inch long, a direct hit by an adult rattler can pierce ordinary trousers or tennis shoes, but not leather. Retraction and recocking is nearly as rapid as the initial strike. These special teeth and their mobile bones are also used as grappling hooks to draw prey into the mouth during swallowing, and the fangs are shed and replaced periodically.

The rattle, unique to the rattlesnake clan, is a series of hollow, interlocking segments made of the same horny material as the scales. The sound is produced when muscles in the tail contract and relax at the rate of about fifty times per second; this sets the rattle segments into motion, and they rapidly click against each other to make the characteristic hissing sound. The rattle is used only to amplify the threat display; rattlers don't rattle at their prey, to prospective mates, to their young, or for any other reason. The real adaptive value of the sound is to reduce the likelihood that the snake will have to protect itself by biting—always a risk to the all-important feeding apparatus.

All rattlesnakes are pit vipers, with a pair of special heat-sensing organs in cavities that can be seen, in a close-range photograph, below and behind each nostril. Experiments have shown that these organs sense the infrared radiation given off by all warm bodies, and that the snake can actually perceive a crude image of its prey and determine its distance, position, and size. Even in the dark, a rattlesnake can "see" a mouse at a little over striking distance.

These snakes will take any mammal up to the size of a quarter-grown jackrabbit; no systematic analyses have been made, but their principal food on Matagorda Island is almost surely cotton rats. They also feed on ground-nesting birds and their eggs (on the island, mainly meadowlarks and bobwhites). Young rattlers will eat frogs and grasshoppers. An adult feeds only about once every two weeks, fasts during the cool months, and makes up for lost time in the spring.

Large adult diamondbacks are essentially immune from natural predation, but smaller ones, and especially the young, have their enemies. Among birds, hawks and great blue herons are important. Coyotes are nimble enough to kill small rattlers without being bitten. Badgers routinely feed on these snakes. Feral hogs are reputed to eat snakes, and a layer of subcutaneous fat would seem to afford them some immunity from bites, but their degree of predation is not known. Both speckled kingsnakes and cottonmouths eat rattlers. Although they can hardly be considered a predator, female white-tailed deer with fawns are apt to flail at a rattlesnake with their front hooves until the reptile is either killed or manages to escape.

There is a lot of rattlesnake lore, much of it myth. See what you think.

- Rattlesnakes can strike a distance equal to their body length, and a bit more if they leap forward slightly.

  No way. They can strike about half their body length. The rest of the body stays coiled for stability. No species jumps, although a belligerent individual may advance between strikes.
- A rattlesnake can't strike unless it is coiled and ready.

  A rattler can strike from a simple crook in its neck. It can bite any time it can get its mouth on something.

• Rattlesnakes always rattle before they strike.

Most do, but don't count on it. Hungry rattlers coiled in ambush may only click the rattle lightly several times. If it seems an intruder has not detected them and may pass by, a rattler may remain quiet. The lower the temperature, the less likely a snake is to use its rattle. Temperaments vary.

• Snakes can sting with their rattles; dust from the rattle can cause poisoning, if inhaled.

Definitely not. It's the other end of the serpent that is dangerous.

• Snakes can sting with their tongues.

No. The tongue is a delicate organ of taste/smell.

• The rattle is used to attract a mate.

Hardly. Rattlesnakes are deaf to airborne sound.

• Rattlesnakes can mesmerize birds, causing them to approach within striking distance.

Try this instead. Birds of several species, when they spot a snake (rattlers as well other species), cluster around and scold. Occasionally a naive or careless bird gets too close to an immobile snake and must pay the price. Snake gets bird, but not by a mystical device.

• Male rattlesnakes carry their rattle string flat above the ground; females carry theirs edge-on (or vice versa).

Not so. Both sexes hold the rattle string edge-on, slightly elevated above the ground.

• You can tell the age of a rattlesnake by counting the segments in its rattle string.

No; a segment is added at each molt of the skin, but this may occur several times a year, thus increasing the apparent age of the snake. Also, terminal segments are frequently broken off, thus decreasing the apparent age.

• When her young are in danger, the female rattlesnake swallows them for temporary security.

It makes a good story, but no herpetologist has ever seen it happen. There are many reasons to accept the professional judgment: (1) Mother and young separate permanently within a day or so of birth. This doesn't negate the notion, but it severely limits its time of occurrence. (2) In captivity, at least, harassing the young elicits no response whatsoever from the mother. (3) Young snakes, purposely forced down a female's gullet, quickly succumb to her digestive juices. (4) It is not difficult for a surprised and excited observer to imagine young snakes appearing to pass into the female's mouth when they disappear into the vegetation or down a

hole beside her head. (5) Finally, there is the "conclusive" evidence of cutting open a freshly killed rattlesnake and having a dozen live and squirming babies come tumbling out. Rattlers are live bearers, so this observation can be easily explained by the adult carrying a brood near term; observing that each snakelet is enclosed in a membranous sac would clinch the explanation.
- Rattlesnakes will not cross a hair rope.
  How gullible are you?
- Then there was the man who died from snakebite when a fang pierced his cowboy boot. Later his son and then his grandson suffered the same fate when scratched by the same fang still lodged in the boot. Or how about the man who ran over a rattler as he drove up to his garage one night. Later he went back out in the dark and cut off the rattles to show his wife. Next day he noticed the dead rattler still had its full string!
  Everyone enjoys tall tales.

Various references indicate that Matagorda Island falls within the general range of no fewer than twenty additional species of snakes. This does not mean that these reptiles occur on the island; difficulties in dispersal and in contending with the specialized habitats may preclude their presence. However, snakes lead cryptic lives, and systematic observations on the island have only been going on for about fifteen years. For several of the following species, there are incidental specimen records, and populations of at least some of them might yet be discovered.

Both the checkered and the eastern garter snakes prefer about the same habitat as the very common Gulf Coast ribbonsnake. However, they are also diurnal and rather easily observed, so they may not be on the island. The marsh brown snake closely resembles the Texas brown snake, and its range might extend onto Matagorda. Even if it is present, this little serpent might be overlooked.

The Great Plains and the Texas rat snakes are hardy species common on the mainland, and both can raft and swim. The former especially should find the rodent-filled grassland to its liking; the latter would be at home on the larger shell ridges. There is one island record for the Great Plains rat snake.

At least three species of watersnakes—the green, blotched, and diamondback—might easily make the journey across the bay from the mainland. It is amazing that there is not a single documented record of any species of this hardy group from the fresh-water sites on the island.

An assortment of moderate-sized harmless snakes—Texas long-nose snake, prairie kingsnake, and Texas glossy snake—are all adapted to grassland.

The western mudsnake, if it could shift from its mainland diet of sirens (eel-shaped amphibians) and crayfish to an insular diet of fiddler crabs, would find the tidal flats a good haven. There is one island record for this species.

The rough green snake is an adaptable species and one often transported purposely or inadvertently by man. Once into the grasslands and dewberry brambles, it should prosper; but it has been reported only once on the island.

A group of small, obscure, mostly burrowing species are possibilities: Texas patchnose snake, rough earth snake, flat-headed snake, and Texas lined snake.

Two additional venomous species, although possible, are not very likely. The western pigmy rattlesnake prefers a more wooded environment. The Texas coral snake might be on the island, but it is more likely that early references were observations of the Mexican milksnake or possibly the rare Texas scarlet snake.

CHAPTER 9

Fish

 Many visitors come to Matagorda Island loaded with fishing gear and conversing about whether the bull reds are running, where the specks are holed up, and how well Hoagie's swimming shad—the chartreuse lure with green tail—is pulling them in. Others may see an occasional mullet leap above the waves as they boat across the bay, but they seldom observe or think about other fish while they are on the island. Yet, the bays and the Gulf teem with fish living out their lives in a submarine world governed by factors that barely touch our lives—tides, currents, salinity, dissolved oxygen—and by calamities like hurricanes, red tides, and oil spills. While the fish's world is indeed an alien one, it is not disjunct from what goes on in ours. Aquatic food chains emerge from the shallows and fuse into the terrestrial food web that succors the ecosystem of the island. Fish are important links in this pipeline of energy from the water to the land.

Direct food chains joining sea and island are everywhere: brown pelicans dive-bombing Gulf menhaden beyond the surf and reddish egrets spearing bay anchovies in the tidal flats; a raccoon waylaying a striped mullet along the bay shore; a Gulf Coast ribbonsnake swallowing a mud-encrusted sheepshead killifish in a drying tidal pool; a blue crab methodically using its powerful pincers to tear apart a tidewater silverside at the edge of a tidal inlet; occasional dead fish washing ashore or windrows of thousands of carcasses piling on the strand—brought in by blue northers or red tides—all carrion fodder for ghost crabs, turkey vultures, gulls, feral hogs, and coyotes, and a basic resource for beetle larvae, fly maggots, and bacteria.

Indirect links are less evident but equally important. These surface links are based on a maze of underwater food chains, of fish eating fish and of fish eating a plethora of marine invertebrates, plankton, and organic muck. After all, a great blue heron cannot continue to spear juvenile black drum unless the drum can find plenty of dwarf surf clams, and without a continual source of suspended organic matter there would be no surf clams. So, the livelihood of the heron is deviously but definitely dependent upon the fertility of the water

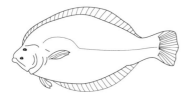

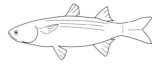

Striped mullet

Southern flounder

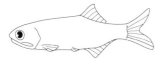

Gulf menhaden

Bay anchovy

through which it wades. Thus, Matagorda Island and San Antonio Bay fuse into a single ecological entity.

Over four hundred species of fish are known from local brackish and marine waters, making them the most diverse group of back-boned creatures in the ecosystem. Ask anglers to name the important fish in the bay and they will unhesitatingly list red drum (redfish), spotted seatrout (speckled trout), southern flounder, and black drum, probably in that order. "Important" to them means the kinds that are a challenge to catch and good to eat. But, the anglers' "Big Four" are all top predators, existing in relatively small numbers at the ends of their respective food chains. Ask ecologists the same question and they will name a different "Big Four": Atlantic croaker, bay anchovy, striped mullet, and Gulf menhaden, in that approximate order. "Important" to the ecologist means biomass—huge numbers near the bottoms of food chains; fish that not only feed other fish but that manage to work their way into the terrestrial food web as well.

To give you an idea of some other kinds of fish in the nearby bays, Table 5 lists the species seen in greatest numbers in the bay-side strand along the island after a killing green tide (a high concentration of toxic, oxygen-consuming algae) occurred in the summer of 1990. Many of these fish live on, in, or near the bottom, where oxygen depletion is most severe during an algal bloom.

Not all kinds of fish are common; life-styles vary and not all are present throughout their life cycles. One prominent life pattern emphasizes the use of the inlets and bays as nurseries where juvenile fish feed and find shelter during their tender months; as adults they spawn in deeper water or in the Gulf, with its stable temperature and

Table 5. *Common fish from Matagorda bayside strand after green tide, summer 1990*

Common Name	Latin Name
Bay whiff	*Citharichthys spilopterus*
Black-cheek tonguefish	*Pogonias cromis*
Black drum	*Symphurus plagiusa*
Blackedge cusk eel	*Lepophidium graellsi*
Gulf flounder	*Paralichthys albigutta*
Gulf toadfish	*Opsanus beta*
Hog choker	*Trinectes maculatus*
Inshore lizard fish	*Synodus foetens*
Lined sole	*Achirus lineatus*
Naked goby	*Gobiosoma bosci*
Pigfish	*Orthopristis chrysoptera*
Pinfish	*Lagodon rhomboides*
Sea catfish	*Arius felis*
Southern flounder	*Paralichthys lethostigma*
Speckled worm eel	*Myrophis punctatus*
Striped mullet	*Mugil cephalus*

Original data from authors.

salinity. Fish in the bays move with the local conditions, following gradients of salinity and temperature, depth and bottom substrate, and the density of favored food organisms. Killifish stick close to shore. Atlantic croakers prefer deeper water. Spot, bay anchovies, and juvenile menhaden are more common at lower (brackish) salinities, while black drum, redfish, and speckled trout prefer higher saltiness. Gulf kingfish, Atlantic threadfins, and Florida pompano disport in the heaving surf. Redfish and southern flounder move to the Gulf to spawn in the wintertime, as do mullet, spot, and Atlantic croakers. Speckled trout spawn only in the bays, but they may move to the Gulf in cold weather. Black drum spawn in both bay and Gulf. Killifish lay their eggs in shallow tidal pools and almost never venture into the open bays, let alone the Gulf of Mexico.

How do fish get from the bays to the Gulf and back again? Through the passes—Pass Cavallo and Cedar Bayou. The many bird and fish predators, as well as knowledgeable human anglers, know about these busy seasonal highways. Egg-laden females, mate-seeking males, and jillions of tiny, hopeful fish larvae routinely make the journey, with peak traffic riding flood and ebb tides. In the 1950s personnel from the TPWD erected a barrier across Cedar Bayou to direct all fish using the pass into holding cages where they could be identified

Table 6. *Most-common fish trapped in Cedar Bayou*

Common Name	Latin Name	% of Catch*
Atlantic croaker	*Micropogonias undulatus*	70.4
Sea catfish	*Arius felis*	10.3
Bay whiff	*Citharichthys spilopterus*	3.4
Sand trout	*Cynoscion arenarius*	2.5
Silver perch	*Bairdiella chrysura*	2.3
Pinfish	*Lagodon rhomboides*	1.8
Spotfin mojarra	*Eucinostomus argenteus*	1.1
Gulf menhaden	*Brevoortia patronus*	< 1.0
Speckled trout	*Cynoscion nebulosus*	< 1.0
Ribbonfish	*Trichiurus lepturus*	< 1.0
Total		94.8

*Percentage based on grand total of 281,948 fish of 90 species. The remaining 5.2 percent was divided among 80 other species.
(TPWD data, modified from Simmons & Hoese, 1959)

and counted before being released. Even though the barrier was in only intermittent use, in a little over one year it caught more than a quarter of a million fish of ninety different kinds! Peak movements were at night from April through September. As Table 6 shows, ten species accounted for over 90 percent of the catch.

The fish that haunt the shallows, either as juveniles or adults, are the ones that make the greatest contribution to the terrestrial food web because they are most accessible to birds. When you see Forster's terns diving, white pelicans scooping, and tricolored herons spearing in a shallow bay-side inlet, what sorts of fish are they getting? Dragging a 50-foot minnow seine through the water gives a good idea. In the spring and summer, several seine hauls will bring in about thirty species of small fish. Table 7 presents the top ten kinds taken in a series of samples from the backside of Matagorda.

The isolated pools that dot the tidal flats are of special significance for fish eaters. These pools, irregularly filled by rainfall, drainage from the shore, flooding by high tides, and overwash during storms, present grim habitats. After rains the water they contain is nearly fresh, but as it evaporates the salt concentration rises steadily until it may be two to three times that of natural seawater. These shallow potholes sometimes freeze over in the winter, while in the summertime they are hot to the touch. Almost all of the dissolved oxygen is driven from such warm water, and it becomes fetid. Eventually most of the ponds transform into sumps of rank ooze and then dry up

Table 7. *Most-common fish taken with minnow seine from bay shallows near Matagorda Island, summer 1990*

Common Name	Latin Name	% of Catch*
Striped mullet	*Mugil cephalus*	30.6
Sheepshead killifish	*Cyprinodon variegatus*	19.4
Bay anchovy	*Anchoa mitchilli*	15.2
Inland silverside	*Menidia beryllina*	6.9
Gulf menhaden	*Brevoortia patronus*	5.8
Spot	*Leiostomus xanthurus*	4.8
Gulf killifish	*Fundulus grandis*	3.7
Pinfish	*Lagodon rhomboides*	2.9
Long-nosed killifish	*Fundulus similis*	2.7
Silver perch	*Bairdiella chrysura*	1.6
Total		93.6

*Percentage based on grand total of 6,242 fish of 30 species collected with a ¼-inch mesh, 15-foot minnow seine used along the edge of Matagorda Island bordering San Antonio and Mesquite bays. Remaining 6.4 percent was divided among 20 other species.

Original data from authors.

entirely, leaving depressions of a cracked, salt-encrusted clay and mud mixture littered with fish scales and bird droppings and tracked by raccoons and feral hogs.

These tidal pools, rather than being barren, harbor an amazing biomass of hardy aquatic creatures. Bacteria, nematode worms, polychaete worms, snails, insect larvae, juvenile shrimp, and an array of microcrustaceans all feed on the rich detritus, the films of blue-green algae, and each other. About a dozen kinds of durable little fish, oblivious to the likelihood of being trapped there, take advantage of high tides to escape their usual predators in the bays and invade these bountiful pools. Of these the killifish are the most remarkable. They can stand water that is saltier, hotter, colder, more anaerobic, and downright nastier than any other kind of fish. If the water lasts, their schools of speck-sized fry begin to appear in the pools, and soon the population of killies will weigh down a light net passed through the soupy medium.

Among this tough clan, the sheepshead killifish displays the most grit. These chunky, minnow-sized fish thrive on adversity. They maneuver in water so salty that the muscles of lesser species are paralyzed; they burrow in the muddy bottom when the water freezes; they gulp air when the dissolved oxygen is gone; they turn sideways

Sheepshead killifish

Table 8. *Most-common fish taken with minnow seine from tidal pools on Matagorda Island, summer 1990*

Common Name	Latin Name	% of Catch*
Sheepshead killifish	*Cyprinodon variegatus*	42
Striped mullet	*Mugil cephalus*	21
Inland silverside	*Menidia beryllina*	16
White mullet	*Mugil curema*	9
Gulf killifish	*Fundulus grandis*	4
Gulf menhaden	*Brevoortia patronus*	3
Long-nosed killifish	*Fundulus similis*	2
Spot	*Leiostomus xanthurus*	< 1
Pinfish	*Lagodon rhomboides*	< 1
Bayou killifish	*Fundulus pulvereus*	< 1
Total		98

*Percentage based on grand total of 1,606 fish of 30 species collected with a ¼-inch mesh, 15-foot minnow seine used in typical tidal pools on the bay side of Matagorda Island.

Original data from authors.

and slide along when there is not enough water to swim upright; they lie immobilized in the thick ooze for several days awaiting a reprieve, until even their amazing resistance is finally overwhelmed.

The tidal pools are always favorite fishing spots for birds, and they become especially attractive when they shrink enough to render the trapped aquatic life easily available. A well-stocked pool in a late stage of evaporation will attract hundreds of avian waders and scavengers to participate in an uninterrupted feeding frenzy for several days. Raccoons, coyotes, feral hogs, cottonmouth moccasins, and alligators all join in the gluttony and occasionally manage to ambush some of the other diners. One feast ends when the ooze has been picked

Table 9. *Fish from inland ponds on Matagorda Island, 1983*

Common Name	Latin Name
Atlantic croaker	*Micropogonias undulatus*
Bayou killifish	*Fundulus pulvereus*
Black-cheek tonguefish	*Symphurus plagiusa*
Darter goby	*Gobionellus boleosoma*
Fringed flounder	*Etropus crossotus*
Gulf killifish	*Fundulus grandis*
Gulf menhaden*	*Brevoortia patronus*
Inland silverside	*Menidia beryllina*
Mosquitofish	*Gambusia affinis*
Pinfish	*Lagodon rhomboides*
Rainwater killifish	*Lucania parva*
Red drum	*Sciaenops ocellata*
Sailfin molly	*Poecilia latipinna*
Sheepshead killifish*	*Cyprinodon variegatus*
Skipjack	*Elops saurus*
Southern flounder	*Paralichthys lethostigma*
Spot*	*Leiostomus xanthurus*
White mullet*	*Mugil curema*

*The most common species
Data are from the files of the TPWD.

clean, but another orgy will already have begun at another tidal pool. Table 8 lists the common fish taken in nets from tidal pools on Matagorda Island.

Ponds, ditches, and swales in the grassy interior of the island get their water from rainfall and from the shallow aquifer. Although these may be nearly fresh, all contain a high level of dissolved solids and are subject to contamination from salt water during storms. Many of these pools are too isolated or too ephemeral to harbor fish, but some have up to half a dozen species. As you might expect, the fish in these sites come from the tough tidal pool coterie that can withstand (though usually not breed in) fresh water. In 1983, the TPWD surveyed the inland ponds on Matagorda and found the twenty species listed in Table 9.

In 1970, the air force, ever hopeful, tried stocking several ponds with catfish, bass, and sunfish. None of these survived.

CHAPTER 10

Invertebrates

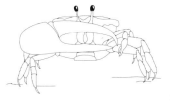 People can feel a brotherhood with most mammals and birds, and a distant kinship with reptiles; some can even find a remote relationship with fish. But, like a closed family of immigrants, we float, isolated, in a vast sea of invertebrates, that myriad of relatively small creatures without backbones we lump carelessly, even derisively, into "bugs." Our culture, our heritage, our very religion teaches us to regard invertebrates as insignificant, annoying, or downright evil. They are too important and too diverse for catchall attitudes; they deserve better.

Ecologically, this group is important because of sheer numbers and because of the diversity of niches they fill; their cumulative biomass works its way into every food chain. When you see a thousand western sandpipers busily pecking on a mud flat, a cloud of barn swallows darting over the low marsh, squadrons of dragonflies patrolling a swale, a prairie-lined racerunner eyeing movement in a grass clump, or a raccoon methodically feeling in every nook along an exposed oyster reef, you are observing ever-hungry predators in search of invertebrate prey. If a western coachwhip snake ambushes the racerunner or an American kestrel outmaneuvers a dragonfly, energy from invertebrate protoplasm moves up a notch in the food web. Your imagination can suggest ramifications: How might a grasshopper be a link in a chain that ends with a great blue heron? In what devious way could a mole crab help nourish a peregrine falcon, a shore fly maggot stoke a massasauga, or a sand roach nourish a coyote?

If you think that invertebrates are uninteresting, it is probably because you have never paused to observe them. If you have noticed, how can you fail to be curious about the semaphore language of fiddler crabs, the peculiar little trails of parallel dots that meander across the sand dunes, the ear-splitting, rasping, metallic whistle that emanates from sea oats clumps in the heat of a summer afternoon, or the finger-sized holes in the sand where the waves lap against the beach? You will have missed some of the best that Matagorda Island has to offer if you ignore the antics of shell-swapping hermit crabs, or the frantic reburying of a cluster of coquina clams after exposure by a breaker, or the exquisite timing of a ghost crab as it snaps each peri-scope eye into its protective groove a fractional instant before disap-pearing sideways into its burrow. You can read about these things or see them on television, but nothing compares with discovering for yourself; that's what a visit to the island is all about.

And what about the annoying habits of many invertebrates? Salt-marsh mosquitoes do bite as though driven with a vengeance, beached jellyfish sting, chiggers itch, and oystershells are razor-sharp. Such irritations should be welcomed as evidence that this is not a theme park groomed specially for your visit, but a natural eco-system, getting along perfectly well without humans. Although you need not ignore these aggravations, you should be able to tolerate them if you appreciate that they are a valid part of your personal ex-cursion into nature. It may be an unusual and educational experience to find that, for a change, our kind is regarded as nothing special among the many life forms that surround us. Can you grin and bear it when you lack the option of flipping the channel if things are not going your way?

In addition to the welter of insects, there are arachnids (spiders, scorpions, and their kin), myriapods (millipedes and centipedes), and, on every seaside, many kinds of crustaceans, either along the shoreline or with a semiterrestrial life. Other invertebrates are en-closed in a limy shell—snails with a single shell and clams with a hinged pair of shells. Then there are the many different kinds of worms, and a whole array of tiny creatures that makes its contribu-tion to the ecosystem beneath the notice of all but those who know how to seek them out. We cannot do justice to all of the kinds of invertebrates that inhabit Matagorda Island, but must limit our dis-cussion to the more common ones an ordinary visitor might see, or at least see evidence of. Let's take a stroll along the beach, traipse across a sand dune, and walk beside the tidal flat, keeping an eye out for critters without backbones.

Beach Invertebrates

We have already looked at the seabeans and the piles of gulfweed, now let's concentrate on the seashells. These are the remains of mol-luscs that live in the Gulf or in the nearby bays. Coiled shells with a single opening belonged to snails. Dish-shaped shells were originally hinged in pairs (you may find fresh specimens still intact) and en-closed clams. Inspect the snail shells you collect, they are usually oc-cupied by hermit crabs. The spidery legs and stalked eyes of the crabs often show in the opening, but sometimes they retreat too deep. If you hear your shells clunking around in your collecting bucket, you'll know you've picked up a hermit crab; it is best to return inhabited shells to the beach; you will be doing the crabs a favor and saving yourself from the distress of killing a creature, not to mention the appalling odor of decay when you get your treasures home. Check your children's treasures, too.

Table 10 lists thirty-seven of the most common kinds of shells that you might find on the Matagorda beach. Some of these are shown in the photograph section. We recommend using Jean Andrews' *Sea Shells of the Texas Coast* to identify your finds.

Over 95 percent of the shells on the beach are from clams, and most of these are among the nine kinds listed at the beginning of the table. The group called arks (from the Latin *arca,* a chest or box) is especially prominent. Intact pairs of ark shells do in fact resemble sturdy ribbed chests joined inside by a straight hinge etched with many comb-like teeth. The incongruous ark (so called because one shell is larger than its mate) and the ponderous ark (with very heavy shells) are the two most common seashells on the Matagorda beach. The incongruous ark, along with alternate tellins, disk shells, and giant Atlantic cockles, are found along the length of the island, indicating that the animals live in the troughs just offshore, beneath the breakers. Since the shells have not been moved very far, pairs are often found with the hinge intact. Ponderous arks, blood arks (one of the very few clams with red blood), and transverse arks live in the depths at the mouth of Pass Cavallo, and the longshore current does not move their heavy shells far from this source, so they are much more common on the north end of the island and are easily found near the main beach access road.

The other two members of the "Top Nine," the eastern oyster and the brown rangia ('range-ee-yuh), are inhabitants of the bays, and their shells must be carried out through the passes before they can be deposited on the beach. But most of the rangia and many of the oystershells are discolored and eroded; these shells are probably hundreds of years old and did not come from the modern bays, but have been washed out of Pleistocene deltaic deposits that now lie offshore. They date back to the infancy of the island, so, when you pick one up you are handling a genuine antique.

Though small, the ¾-inch-long coquina clam ('ko-keen-ah, Spanish for cockle) deserves special mention. These sturdy, wedge-shaped shells come in an array of pastel colors from yellow and pink to rose and salmon and from pale blue to purple, and are often marked with a rayed pattern. Generally, coquinas are most common in August and they tend to cluster on cusps where the beach slopes abruptly, but

Table 10. *Common seashells of Matagorda beach**

Common Name	Latin Name	Abundance
MOST-COMMON BIVALVES		
Alternate tellin	*Tellina alternata*	C
Blood ark	*Anadara ovalis*	C
Brown rangia	*Rangia flexuosa*	O
Disk shell	*Dosinia discus*	A
Eastern oyster	*Crassostrea virginica*	C
Giant Atlantic cockle	*Dinocardium robustum*	A
Incongruous ark	*Anadara brasiliana*	A
Ponderous ark	*Noetia ponderosa*	A
Transverse ark	*Anadara transversa*	C
ADDITIONAL BIVALVES		
Angel wing	*Cyrtopleura costata*	O
Atlantic surf clam	*Spisula solidissima*	O§
Bay scallop	*Argopecten irradians*	O
Channeled duck clam	*Raeta plicatella*	O
Clench's chione	*Chione clenchi*	R
Coquina clam	*Donax variabilis*	O
Cross-barred venus	*Chione cancellata*	R
Dwarf surf clam	*Mulinia lateralis*	O§
Lady-in-waiting venus	*Chione intapurpurea*	R
Mossy ark	*Arca imbricata*	R
Ribbed mussel	*Geukensia demissus*	R
Sawtooth pen	*Atrina serrata*	O§
Spoon clam	*Periploma inequale*	R
Thick lucine	*Phacoides pectinatus*	O
Tulip mussel	*Modiolus americanus*	R
Yellow cockle	*Trachycardium muricatum*	R
UNIVALVES		
Atlantic moon snail	*Polinices duplicatus*	O
Common baby's ear	*Sinum perspectivum*	R
Common slipper shell	*Crepidula fornicata*	O
Common sundial	*Architectonica granulata*	R
Eastern murex	*Muricanthus fulvescens*	R
Lettered olive	*Oliva sayana*	R
Lightning whelk	*Busycon contrarium*	O
Pear whelk	*Busycon spiratum*	O
Purple storm snail	*Janthina janthina*	R§
Rock shell	*Stramonita haemostoma*	R
Salle's auger	*Hastula salleana*	R
Scotch bonnet	*Phalium granulatum*	O

*Bayside shells not included.

A = abundant; C = common; O = occasional; R = rare; § = abundant after storms their numbers vary seasonally and from one year to the next, and they are unaccountably patchy in occurrence. On Padre Island these little clams can often be scooped up by the double handfuls, but possibly because of subtle differences in the texture and slope of the beach, they are seldom so numerous on Matagorda.

Coquinas live just beneath the sand in the swash zone and follow the tide up and down the beach to stay in the most favorable position for filtering diatoms and other algae from the surf. You may see a patch of the beach seem to come alive when a group of coquinas, exposed by a receding wave, hastily rebury themselves before they are spotted by one of their many predators. The life of a coquina is hazardous: sanderlings, willets, and black-bellied plovers swallow them whole; ghost crabs, blue crabs, and speckled crabs crush them with their pincers; lettered olive snails smother them; moon snails bore a hole through their shell; shimmy worms snatch at their exposed parts; and black drum pulverize them with their strong, cobblestone teeth.

The only thing more delightful than holding a handful of wet beach sand filled with coquinas and feeling their probing bodies tickle your palm is watching the face of a child who is discovering the same sensation.

Sawtooth pens and Atlantic surf clams live just offshore and are washed up in great numbers during storms. The large, prickly, pale brown pen shells are iridescent on their inner face. Thousands of these light and brittle shells are often deposited in windrows along the strandline, while the heavier Atlantic surf clams remain piled on the forebeach. A heavy surf also commonly deposits shells of dwarf surf clams on the forebeach. Since this is a bay species, its small, sturdy, half-inch white shells have probably been exhumed from offshore Pleistocene sands.

Two of the most fragile shells on the beach are those of channeled duck clams and angel wings. Channeled ducks live on the bottom beyond the breakers; angel wings live in burrows inside the passes. Both must be transported some distance before being washed up onto the beach, so perfect specimens are rarely found.

The checkered shells of Scotch bonnets are also quite fragile. These plump snails live just offshore, where they cruise the troughs in search of sand dollars and heart urchins, which they overcome with a dose of sulphuric acid. Beachcombers covet intact Scotch bonnets; a high surf sometimes throws up hundreds of these treasures.

Whelk shells are heavy and durable, so you can almost always find one on the backbeach. Two kinds of these large predatory snails live in the sandy bottoms beyond the surf. (They are even more common in the bays; many beach specimens may be reworked from offshore Pleistocene deposits.) Their shells differ most conspicuously in handedness. To distinguish a left-hand snail from a right-hand snail, hold the shell with your thumb on the coiled tip and wrap your fingers around the body and into the opening of the shell. If you can do this with your left hand, it is a left-handed snail—a lightning whelk; if you can do it with your right, it's a right-handed snail—a pear whelk.

Both kinds of whelks prey on clams, which they grasp with their muscular foot and wedge open with the awl-like projection of the shell. Roomy whelk shells are favorites of hermit crabs, so check your specimens carefully. The chains of squarish, horny chambers occasionally found on the beach are the egg capsules produced by these snails. The lightning whelk, incidentally, belongs alongside the bluebonnet, pecan tree, and mockingbird; it is the official state shell of Texas.

Watch for shallow furrows meandering across the swash zone and see if you can follow one to a small hump at its end and uncover a live snail. It will be either the bullet-shaped lettered olive snail or the round Atlantic moon snail, both relentless predators on clams and other small creatures in the surf. The olive moves easily through the sand by coating its streamlined shell with a veil of mucous-covered tissue, which it also uses to wrap and smother its prey—coquina clams, dwarf surf clams, and mole crabs. Moon snails also move through the sand with their body outside the shell, but when they find prey (favorites are coquinas, disks, and tellins), they sit on it and use a rasping mechanism to bore a neat hole in the shell through which to insert their mouthparts, release digestive juices, and suck up the liquified mass. See how many of the shells in your collection bear the telltale countersunk hole of a moon snail.

If you are lucky, you may find one of the real jewels of Matagorda—a purple storm snail. These globular, fragile shells have a relatively large opening and grade from lavender on the spire to royal purple below. The living animals are pelagic—they live in the open Gulf—where they float at the surface, hanging below specially made rafts of bubbly purple mucus, and feed on other floating creatures, including the Portuguese man-o'-war. Your best chance to find storm snails is just after storms or prolonged strong southeast winds.

Everyone knows and collects the chalky wafers called sand dollars, actually the endoskeletons, or tests, of keyhole urchins, which live in great numbers beneath the surf, in the third trough and beyond. In life, the test is covered with a reddish brown felt of movable projections by which the urchins slide sideways beneath the sand and collect diatoms and bacteria to convey to their mouth, the hole at the center of the flat, bottom side. The flower-like pattern of small holes on the upper, rounded side leads to the breathing organs. The five slots through the test help the urchin maintain its position in the heaving surf. As it digs into the bottom, sand oozes up through the slots, and if a wave flips it out of the sand, water passes through the slots and the urchin rapidly settles back onto the bottom. Keyhole urchins are preyed on particularly by Scotch bonnet snails and starfish.

Heart urchins are related to keyhole urchins, but are much less well-known. Heart urchin tests are more common on the south end of Matagorda, and after a high surf hundreds of them may be found on the beach near Cedar Bayou. They are very fragile, and even the ones found whole will soon fall apart. The test is a chalky globe about 1¾ inches long, in shape vaguely reminiscent of a heart. The slotted mouth opening is at one end of the flattened bottom side, the pinhole anus higher up on the other end. Five deep creases, comparable to the petal marks on the sand dollar, mark the upper surface. The living animal is covered with a golden fur of hair-like projections. (The positions of these projections are revealed by the delicate engraving on the surface of the test.) Heart urchins live in burrows in soft silty bottoms like those found at the mouths of the tidal passes.

After rough weather the strand is often littered with cylinders of minced shell fragments, about 3 inches long and ⅜ inch wide. Inspection reveals that these are parchment tubes to which the shell bits are cemented. They belonged to the plume worms that live abundantly among the offshore troughs and thinly up to the water's edge. The worms (their "plumes" are red gills behind the head) live in vertical parchment tubes down in the sand and extending several inches above; the exposed end, to which the shells are stuck for stiffening, is usually curved like the handle of a walking cane. A heavy surf snaps off the upper sections to wash ashore and mystify beachcombers; they are soon replaced by the worms.

Several creatures that live in the swash zone along with the coquina clams can be caught with a mesh about the gauge of screen wire; an old kitchen strainer will do nicely. The best place to try is a few inches below the upper limit of the waves. Scoop through the sand while a wave is actively receding across your feet. Wash out the sand and see what you've got. Don't expect a creature every time, but keep trying, or keep encouraging the kids, until you have luck.

The most common catch are skittery, egg-shaped creatures up to ¾ inch long—mole crabs—highly modified for their precarious existence in the teeth of the surf. They have no pincers, so you can handle them with impunity; roll one around with your finger for closer in-

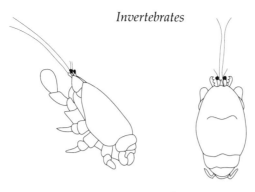

Mole crab

spection. The little pearl-gray animal is smooth on top, and keeps its legs and tail tucked beneath its carapace. Give it a dollop of wet sand in your palm or drop it back into shallow water and watch it quickly burrow backward out of sight.

All of this crab's legs, and even its tail, are modified for shoveling sand; the tail is also an anchor. Like all crustaceans, mole crabs have two pairs of antennae, but these are very specialized. One pair forms a breathing straw so water can flow around the gills when the crab is buried in the sand; the second pair is festooned with delicate hairs that form a basket fine enough to sieve algae and bacteria from the water.

Mole crabs position themselves just beneath the sand in the upper part of the swash, facing the sea, with their heads slightly inclined. They lie quietly as a wave washes in, and then stick up their antennal baskets to sieve the backwash. They move up and down with the tide like coquinas and are plagued by the same predators. In the summertime you may catch a female with bright orange eggs clutched under her rear end. These little creatures are appealing, but they absolutely require not just salt water, but well-aerated, moving salt water with microscopic food in it. You can't keep them alive in an aquarium.

If you keep at the sieving long enough, you may get a surf crab. These little flattened creatures have a life-style very like that of mole crabs, but they are not nearly so common.

Occasionally you will spot in your sieve a white wiggly about ⅛ of an inch long that you take for a baby mole crab, but look closely. This may be another type of crustacean called a sand digger amphipod. Like other denizens of the swash, their plump, white bodies and numerous legs, some spade-like for digging and others covered with spines to keep sand out of the gills, are specially modified. These little creatures draw a stream of water beneath their bodies and filter out suspended organic matter. Because they are numerous and delec-

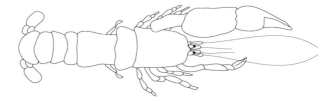

Ghost shrimp

table, sand diggers are important members of the swash food web.

Two kinds of marine worms may appear in your sieve. Thread worms are red, very long, and very slender, and break easily. Shimmy worms, about 5 inches long, with a bright-red vein along the back and numerous leg-like appendages along the sides, are named for the frenzied movements that propel them through the sand or water. These predaceous worms feed on most other members of the swash community.

A third kind of worm lives abundantly at the upper edge of the swash zone and deep in the damp sand of the forebeach. Palp worms are too tiny for study, but you might notice the thin traceries of dry sand they leave at the surface. Each worm extends a pair of sticky tentacles (the palps) into the water stream where, like other suspension feeders, they snatch food from a receding wave.

One abundant and important denizen of the swash is almost never seen, but most visitors notice its half-inch holes, especially when jets of sand and water indicate subterranean activity. These are the entrances to the burrows of ghost shrimp, actually crabs related to the hermit, but they look more like ghostly crayfish with one large pincer. Adults get to about 3½ inches long. They spend their life in an extensively branched, mucous-lined burrow, which they ceaselessly maintain against the erosive powers of the surf. With a series of piston-like appendages beneath the abdomen, they pump a current of water from which fine hairs on the legs sift diatoms, bacteria, and detritus. Now and then a reverse flow sweeps the burrow clean, and produces the sand plume at the entrance. Several surface holes usually connect to the same burrow system.

You can dig into a ghost shrimp burrow if you like, but you will almost certainly not see the creature; it is very sensitive to pressure on the surface, and if disturbed, descends into the lower reaches of its tunnel, 3 feet or more under the sand.

Although few surface predators other than an occasional willet or long-billed curlew can snatch a ghost shrimp from its burrow, these crustaceans play an important role in the swash community. Their numerous burrows aerate and mix the bottom sediments, and the steady stream of fecal pellets, once softened and reworked by bacteria, are transformed into nutritious detritus to be strained out and consumed by the filtering organisms in the sand. Ghost shrimp themselves take advantage of this microbe-enriched second harvest.

Although you will see carapaces of several species of crabs in the strand, only two kinds live in the swash zone. The speckled crab, a thoroughly typical member of its kind, has a flat, palm-sized body, with a spiny margin, a pair of large pincers in front, and a pair of paddle-like swimming appendages in back. Its light brown carapace, thickly sprinkled with pale flecks, provides excellent camouflage in its sandy habitat. Speckled crabs haunt the offshore troughs and shallows, where they lie in ambush just beneath the sand, with only their eyes and antennae protruding. They are predators on all of the other swash fauna, and they also feed on bits of vegetation and carrion. Several kinds of hermit crabs live in the swash, but the beach hermit crab is the typical resident species. These small white crabs with fuzzy antennae labor along the waterline and through the shallows, dragging, as though in penance, the abandoned shell of a moon or lettered olive snail. The purloined shell protects the soft abdomen, but the crab must be continually on the lookout for bigger shells to accommodate growth. You may encounter a "swap meet"—several of these little crabs climbing over each other as they gauge their neighbors' shells for a possible trade. When the opportunity arises, they can switch in the blink of an eye. Beach hermits make their living by scavenging along the waterline.

As you move away from the swash and up the forebeach, you will scare up the tiger beetles mentioned in Chapter 4. At the strandline, turn over some of the larger objects or masses of algae; you will almost surely cause exposed beach fleas to explode in frenzied skittering as they seek another sheltered nook. These quarter-inch amphipods, related to the sand diggers, are adapted for a semiterrestrial existence. They require high humidity but drown in water, so they are limited to surface debris on the strand and forebeach. Beach fleas are most active at night, when they move over and through the strand in search of decaying vegetable and animal matter. If you want to appreciate the dexterity of a snowy plover, try catching and holding a slippery beach flea with two fingers.

Leaving the strand and progressing across the backbeach, you enter the domain of one of the most characteristic members of the beach

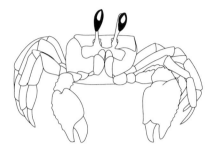

Ghost crab

community—the ghost crab. You may have already gotten a glimpse of a cryptic shape scuttling across the sand and noticed holes with nearby piles of crumbling pellets of moist sand and a fan of scribble-like tracks. Such evidence becomes more common in the coppice dunes. Experienced beachcombers will associate these signs with "sand crabs," but few appreciate either the abundance or the ecological significance of the army of crustaceans lying quietly a foot or so beneath the daytime bustle on the beach.

An inhabitant of Atlantic beaches from New Jersey to Brazil, the ghost crab is well-named for its pale, fleeting appearance and its even more spectral disappearance—either by halting instantly from headlong flight or by darting into a burrow. Its Latin name, *Ocypode quadrata*, (oh-'sip-po-dee qua-'drah-tah) is descriptive: "fast-footed square." The distinctly quadrangular ghost crab is the fleetest of terrestrial crabs; in a hurry it can skitter sideways at 10 feet per second. The squarish, sand-gray body, about 4 inches across in an adult, sports eight hairy, yellowish walking legs, a pair of strong, warty, white pincers and a pair of dark, bean-shaped eyes on fold-down stalks.

Tropical ancestry makes ghost crabs more sensitive to cold than to heat; they are active in the warmer months and remain in their plugged burrows from December to March.

In the summertime, the ghost crab's daily cycle begins just about dark, when crabs appear in their burrow entrances, flicking out accumulated sand or sitting quietly, cleaning appendages, polishing eyes, and gesturing to each other with their pincers. By 10:00 P.M., most individuals have moved down to the water. There they spend the rest of the night, foraging for food and dashing back and forth with the waves while wetting their gills and dancing lightly about when they come in contact with each other. On a summer night the beam of a flashlight reveals the beach filled with hundreds of glistening, active bodies.

As daylight approaches, the crabs move inland in search of a moist retreat. By marking individuals, biologists have learned that a crab seldom uses the same burrow two nights in a row. During nocturnal foraging it may drift along the beach for several hundred feet, and when it turns inland it will either dig a fresh burrow or find one of the proper size. A larger crab will evict a smaller one and take over its burrow. If the fit is not just right it will do a bit of remodeling; the crabs always enter sideways, so the critical dimension is body length, not width. Displaced owners appropriate the burrows of yet smaller crabs, and the shuffling continues down the hierarchy until, by the time the sun is high, everyone is settled in for the day, one crab to a burrow.

Its burrow is the ghost crab's main means of coping with the demanding environment; here it takes refuge from glaring sun, drying wind, and baking temperatures. Manipulating sand to plug or unplug the entrance, a crab can keep its retreat within tolerable limits.

The burrow is also important in the reproductive cycle. In late spring males sit at their burrow entrance and gesture suggestively to passing females. If she responds, a female is crowded into the burrow for copulation. At the height of the season she is sometimes roughly flipped on her back and mounted on the beach. When the female is heavy with eggs, she plugs her burrow and remains underground about two weeks while her clutch ripens. When some inner sense tells them that the full moon has drawn up an exceptionally high tide, all of the ripe females dig out and head for the surf. As soon as they hit the water, their thousands of eggs break free. This highly synchronized ritual occurs in April and again in August, and is rarely observed, but it serves as an inviolate reminder that the sea is where the ghost crabs came from and where they must return to begin life afresh.

Within hours, the eggs hatch and the scad of larvae begins a sojourn among the nearly microscopic plankton. After a hazardous six weeks, the match-head-sized ghost crabs that have made it to the final larval molt strike the beach, where their speckled carapaces make them nearly invisible on the wet sand.

Little-bitty ghost crabs dig little-bitty vertical burrows only a few inches deep just above tideline. Larger crabs dig deeper burrows further up the beach. Adult animals excavate the deepest retreats among the coppice dunes and further inland. Burrows of older crabs are J-shaped or Y-shaped, with two entrances, and usually slant down at a

45-degree angle. The crabs do not necessarily dig to the water table, but they must reach moist sand; so burrows in or beyond the dunes may be over 3 feet deep. By pressing tufts of special setae against the moist sand lining their burrows, crabs can absorb water; special glands in their gills allow them to maintain their salt balance. Large ghost crabs living perhaps 100 yards inland from the beach can thus satisfy their water requirements without a nightly trip to the surf. Except for reproduction, crabs living in and beyond the primary dunes lead a truly terrestrial existence, and they routinely return to the same burrow after a night's foraging.

The most obvious value of the ghost crab's burrow is a quick refuge from danger. Crabs that wander about in the daytime retain a keen memory of their burrow location, and they make a beeline for it when they feel threatened. If you happen to get between a crab and its burrow, the animal will dodge adroitly in a single-minded effort to get to its shelter. In a pinch, a crab will pop into the nearest hole it will fit into, but an owner at home may force quick eviction. Experiments have shown that the animals memorize surface landmarks; altering the shape of the sand surface and surrounding vegetation confuses the crab.

The larvae of ghost crabs suffer the same decimation that is the lot of all plankton. Once ashore, tiny crabs are picked off by shorebirds, but their biggest threat is larger ghost crabs. Cannibalism of the young is routine, and it appears to be an effective means of population control. Adult crabs abroad in the daytime can ably defend themselves from birds, and it is presumed that these agile animals can avoid most nighttime assaults by beach-hunting coyotes and raccoons. The main predation on adults occurs after the animals have darted into their burrows. As any visitor will notice, the backbeach is often pocked with arm-deep holes. These are the excavations of the three principal predators on the crabs: badgers, coyotes, and feral hogs. A keen nose and rapid digging make this profitable for these mammals, but crab numbers suggest their population can easily withstand such depletion.

Ghost crabs are opportunists, taking whatever edibles come their way. Besides eating any crab smaller than themselves, they use tactile and taste sensors on their pincers to locate mole crabs and coquina clams in the swash. Crabs living inland catch crickets, moths, and any other small creatures they come across. Mainly, ghost crabs are scavengers, working the strand and waterline for dead and dying creatures thrown up by the sea. If they find a large carcass, they dig in nearby and feast on it for several days. The crabs are fond of goose barnacles that cling to driftwood; they diligently pick through clumps of gulfweed; they consume bird droppings, and they sample all manner of human refuse. When the wet sand is tinted green with microscopic algae, ghost crabs become deposit feeders, scooping up globs of sand and deftly sifting out the algae with their mouthparts. Crabs living inland eat fresh greenery, and fruits such as beach ground-cherries and seeds, including the fallen or low-dangling seedheads of sea oats.

Sand Dunes Invertebrates

As you climb onto the primary dune ridge you leave behind all the invertebrates of the beach except ghost crabs and tiger beetles, and you enter a dry and sandblasted community dominated by insects. Within a few steps you should startle the first of many dunes grasshoppers into flight. These well-camouflaged, inch-long insects are nearly impossible to spot until they burst from the sand on pale yellow wings. If you can follow the short flight with your eye, note the little spread-eagle track a grasshopper makes where it lands. Unless you see it happen, the isolated imprint would be a total mystery. You might enjoy watching these grasshoppers with your binoculars; they gesture to one another and display the soft rose color on their hind legs. Dunes grasshoppers are masters at seeking just the right mix of sunshine and shade to maintain their body temperature at a tolerable level, even in the middle of a glaring summer afternoon.

Among the neatest denizens of the dunes are the sand wasps. Look for gregarious clusters of them only after the sun is well up, buzzing in rapid curlycues just above the surface of the sand on the lee side of a dune. Individuals are about ½ inch long and have greenish-yellow abdomens banded with black. It is the females that attract attention. Each one, after many false starts, finally begins to dig rapidly with her forelegs like a terrier, kicking out a steady spume of sand beneath her upraised abdomen. After disappearing into the dune, she periodically backs out, dragging more sand beneath her body, until she has completed an unbranched, sloping tunnel about 4 inches long. Then she plugs the entrance with sand and zooms off.

If she is hungry, the sand wasp sips nectar, but she is really on a hunting sortie, and the flowers she visits attract the several kinds of flies that are her prey. With a quick jab from her stinger, she paralyzes a fly, tucks it beneath her body with her middle legs, and zips back to her burrow, finding it by memorized landmarks. Back home, the wasp hurriedly unplugs her burrow, carries in the fly, and deposits one egg, then exits and recloses the tunnel. The haste is to reduce the opportunity for a variety of parasitic flies and wasps to lay their own eggs in her brood chamber. The several false burrows she digs around the real one are thought to distract and discourage such parasites. In an odd turnabout, several of the very kinds of flies that the sand wasp feeds to her larva are among the parasitic species that hatch their eggs internally and deposit their live maggots in the sand wasp's tunnel to feed on her larva.

For most kinds of digger wasps, the job would be done once the tunnel is stocked and sealed, but the sand wasp is a doting parent. Over the next five days she repeatedly returns to the burrow with fresh flies for the rapidly developing larva. When it finally pupates, she plugs the tunnel for the last time; not long afterwards the metamorphosed offspring digs its way out into the world. Meanwhile, mom has been busy with other burrows.

When the summer sun beats down and heat waves transform the sand dunes into a weaving mirage, a shrill hissing whistle begins to emanate from a clump of sea oats. This first sound elicits others, and the stimulus passes rapidly until the air pulsates with a unified sizzling shriek like a warning from an overheated pressure cooker. Mercifully, the sound passes its crescendo and rapidly dies away; but after a short pause the din is repeated and repeated, for the rest of the afternoon. These are the songs of male dunes cicadas; each one, perched on a vertical stalk of sea oats, is trying to lure a female. If disturbed, the insect abruptly flies off with a startling buzz that causes even experienced naturalists to momentarily think they have aroused a rattlesnake.

Dunes cicadas have an inch-long, bullet-shaped brown body with a thin white collar, and their clear wings, leaded with veins, extend half an inch beyond the abdomen. Their widely spaced bulbous eyes give them a frog-like face. Like others of their kind, dunes cicadas use their sharp proboscises to pierce plant stems and suck sap. Females insert their eggs into the growing tip of a twig. This causes the twig to die and fall off so that when the eggs hatch, the nymphs can burrow into the sand. There they spend the next five to six years, sucking sap from roots to support their growth and gradual transformation. Finally the humpbacked nymphs dig out, climb up plant stalks, and shed their exoskeletons to become members of the year's crop of dunes cicadas.

Adult dunes cicadas only live one year, and even this brief life span is frequently cut short by their principal predator, the cicada killer. This large yellow-and-black wasp specializes in cicadas, paralyzing and hauling them off to provision its brood chamber dug deep into a sand dune. Aside from the wasp, the dry, chitinous cicadas do not appeal to many appetites. As fall approaches, moribund individuals

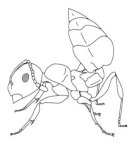

Pyramid ant   Valentine ant

are snatched from their stems by bobwhite quail, early arriving kestrels, cotton rats, and ghost crabs. Finally, ants glean what little is left, and the brittle cicada carapaces remain to rattle across the dunes before the season's first norther.

Although the island supports only a few kinds, ants play their important ecological roles as small but efficient predators and scavengers. Pyramid ants are the species best-adapted to the barrier, seemingly unaffected by the difficulty most ants have in maintaining tunnels in dry sand. Their nests, frequent on open sand, are marked by smooth, ankle-high mounds, with the nest entrance in a central crater. The workers are about ⅛ inch long, with dusky heads, pale yellow bodies, and exceptionally long legs that allow them to stride easily over the sand. They are alert and quick-moving, actively foraging for caterpillars, termites, insect eggs, small or wounded insects, and any windfall, like fresh carrion or feces, from which they can extract nutritious fluids. Because they are so widespread and numerous on the island, pyramid ants are an important item on the menu of the ant-loving horned lizards.

Imported red fire ants invaded the Coastal Bend in the 1960s, and Matagorda Island was not spared this pernicious species; but fortunately, they do not fare well in loose dry sand or saturated sand. Consequently, they occur mostly on dikes, levees, shell ridges, and the packed ground around buildings and roads. If you have not learned to avoid their nest mounds, be forewarned—they are called fire ants for good reason. The rapidly proliferating colonies of these invaders from South America overwhelm many kinds of native ants, including native fire ants. This is probably why the several kinds of indigenous fire ants on the island are most common in the sand dunes, where their imported cousin cannot follow. Around the bases of the dunes plants there are occasional nests of southern fire ants and tropical fire ants. Both species will sting if molested, but they have smaller colonies and individuals are less pugnacious than the imported variety. Their workers forage tirelessly for any type of small, soft-bodied creatures they can overcome. Sequestered beneath drift are occasional colonies of minuscule fire ants, too tiny to sting people and too cute to pass without comment.

Worker valentine ants have reddish bodies and black, heart-shaped abdomens that they stick up in the air when disturbed. Although they can bite and sting, they rarely do so. Large colonies of valentine ants line the interior cavities of their nests (which are inside pieces of rotted driftwood and dead sunflower stalks) with papier-mâché from chewed vegetable matter, wood bits, and soil glued together with sugary saliva. These ants feed on honeydew from aphids and upon soft-bodied insects. A few colonies of Texas leafcutting ants are scattered through the center of the island around secondary dunes, but they do not invade primary dunes. With its bountiful crop of grass seeds, Matagorda Island would seem to be a paradise for the seed-eating red harvester ants that are so common on the mainland; but this species cannot excavate its massive granaries in loose sand.

Small insects in the dunes are in mortal danger from ant lions. These fat, quarter-inch-long creatures, familiar to children everywhere as "doodle bugs," are the larvae of a flying insect resembling a delicate but clumsy dragonfly. The larvae are fierce predators, lying buried at the bottom of sandy craters with their ice-tong jaws open and ready for some small creature to step onto the steep side of the pit and slide down within reach. Pyramid ants are favored prey. Eventually the ant lion pupates in the sand.

In the miniaturized world of insects, robber flies play the role of falcons. These inch-long, streamlined flies with stiletto abdomens perch on stem tips, continually turning their big-eyed heads to watch for flying prey. They zip off faster than the eye can follow and use their bristly legs to snare small insects in midair, then return to their perch to suck the fluids from their victim. Squatty bee flies are black and hairy, like a bee; the black wings are clear on the tips. Adults visit flowers for nectar, where they are frequently zapped by a sand wasp. Not to be outdone, a bee fly that locates an open sand wasp burrow zooms down and deftly flicks an egg into the entrance; the egg soon hatches and a tiny maggot wriggles down the tunnel to parasitize the wasp larva. Bee flies use the same tactic on tiger beetle larvae in their tubes.

Look twice at any bit of white fluff whisking across a sand dune. On closer inspection, it may still look like fluff, but if it has six scurrying legs and a pair of dark eyes, it is a thistledown velvet ant. This half-inch-long, exceptionally hairy insect is a wingless female wasp.

She sips nectar now and then, but spends most of her time searching for bumblebee and sand wasp nests in which to lay an egg. There her parasitic larva can mature. Even among the tough insects of the sand dunes, velvet ants are noticeably immune to heat and glare (their long hairs insulate them), racing about throughout the day. Have a care; although they are not aggressive, these fuzzy wasps pack a potent sting.

The most common large bees on the island are the bumblebees you see during all the warm months visiting whatever plants are in flower. These bees nest underground, with the entrance protected by a southern dewberry bramble or a clump of seacoast bluestem. You are not likely to run across them unless you wander off the trails, but if you hear the muffled droning of many wings at your feet, back off at once. An angry mob of bumblebees is serious business. Yellow jackets, red paper wasps, and a variety of smaller bees and wasps also visit flowers, but most of these hide their nests away where visitors seldom encounter them. For sheer beauty and exquisite sculpturing, look closely at one of the little metallic green-and-coppery halictid bees (ha-'lick-tid) you can find curled among the anthers of Corpus Christi fleabane blossoms in the spring.

If you like to watch insects, visit the sand dunes in late summer when partridge peas are in flower. A myriad of wasps, bees, flies, bugs, and beetles visits both the blossoms and the nectar glands on the leaf stalks, and praying mantids, assassin bugs, and spiders come to ambush the nectar feeders. Large butterflies are scarce because they can't fly well in the wind and because there aren't many favored larval host plants. Among species that do breed on the island are buckeye, dog-faced sulphur, cloudless sulphur, variegated fritillary, Gulf fritillary, and grey hairstreak. Pipevine swallowtails visit the island's wildflowers, but individuals must arrive from the mainland, because the pipevines on which they lay their eggs are not known to occur on the barrier. If you are in the dunes in the spring or fall of a good year, you may find yourself awash in a silent flutter of hundreds of migrating monarch butterflies.

Early in the morning, before the breeze has erased the night's tracks, you can find sinuous trails of two parallel lines of dots, the traces of foraging sunflower seed beetles. Although their black bodies are somewhat larger, they are shaped after their namesake; the patter of their six feet makes the dots. The beetles hide beneath surface debris during the day and search the sand for vegetable detritus by night.

There are several kinds of roaches on Matagorda, but the one best-adapted to the dunes is the sand roach. The male looks rather like any

Dog-faced sulphur butterfly   Sand roach

household roach, but the inch-long female is peculiar. She is wing-less, flattened, and nearly round. In searching for wind-deposited vegetable debris, she easily pushes her thin body edge-on just be-neath the surface of the sand, leaving a little humped trail that resem-bles a miniature mole run.

Strong, steady winds make construction and maintenance of large spider webs difficult, and most possible anchoring places whip vio-lently in the wind, ripping up any attached web. Still, on a quiet foggy morning the island is festooned with sagging, beaded webs of small to moderate size. These were spun during the evening, used through the night when the breeze is gentle and the air is alive with flying insects, and dismantled just after dawn or left to the mercies of the rising onshore wind. Three kinds of small brown spiders account for most of these webs: humpbacked orb weavers, starbellied spiders, and arabesque orb weavers. In addition to these orb webs, morning dew or fog reveals thousands of webs spread like handkerchiefs on the ground and low grasses. Each flat web has a small funnel at one corner where its maker—a grass spider—lies in wait for roaches, crickets, or grasshoppers.

A flashlight beam will raise a constellation of green-white sparkles around the bases of grass clumps, the reflective eyes of the several kinds of wolf spiders that patrol the ground by night, ready to pounce on any small soft-bodied creature they can overcome. The burrowing wolf spider waits at the entrance to its deep retreat. When prey wan-ders within reach, it is snatched with a lightning-quick move, and the spider drops with it to the bottom of the vertical shaft to leisurely suck the juices. These spiders are seldom seen, but the entrances to their burrows in the interdune association are easy to recognize. Look in well-packed sand around the bases of grass tufts for a little chimney about ½ inch tall, composed of grass snippets and silk surrounding the ⅜-inch hole.

Bull thistles are likely places to look for flower spiders. Several kinds of these spiders—with flattened bodies and long, incurved, crab-like legs—crouch on flowers waiting for pollinating insects. Most of them can change their color, over a day or so, to match the blossom where they lie in ambush. Look closely at any small butterfly with its wings askew; it may be in the clutches of a well-camouflaged flower spider.

There are several kinds of jumping spiders on the island, but the most noticeable is the emerald-jawed jumping spider. This relatively large, active species is covered with black hairs and patterned with white dots and streaks on the abdomen. It frequents the stalks of flowering plants and is especially at home on the pads of prickly pears. These spiders have good eyesight, and they usually look directly at you as they back away to shelter. If the sun is at the right angle while the spider is peering at you head-on, you should notice its brilliant metallic-green mouthparts. Emerald-jawed jumping spiders are voracious and powerful predators; it is common to see one clutching a struggling insect as large as the spider itself.

There is a healthy population of black widow spiders on Matagorda, but it is confined to the undersides of driftwood, so most visitors will never encounter this poisonous species. If you do lift pieces of surface debris, you might also see a variety of other cryptic invertebrates: brown centipedes; an occasional scorpion; fast-moving terrestrial isopods that resemble pillbugs (but do not roll up); field crickets; a colony of termites; a wriggling grubworm (the larva of a June beetle); German, oriental, and fulvous wood cockroaches; and bombardier beetles, which release a puff of gas (harmless to people) with an audible "ffffttt" when they are disturbed.

Tidal Flat Invertebrates

Most of the mollusc shells you can find along the bay shore north of the Visitors' Center will be different from those on the Gulf beach. Among the snail shells are the sturdy, sharp-spired marsh periwinkle and the brown-banded salt-marsh snail; both live in the smooth cordgrass. Other snail shells washed in from the submerged beds of widgeon grass and shoalgrass are the distinctive striate and paper bubbles, fragile shells with elongate openings; long-spired plicate horn shells; and tiny dwarf and grass ceriths. There will be occasional lightning whelks; bay-side specimens are often over a foot long, and some are discolored and badly eroded, indicating that they have been washed up from Pleistocene deposits hundreds of years old. At least some of the snail shells you pick up will contain striped hermit crabs.

Bay scallops are often very common in the shallows during the

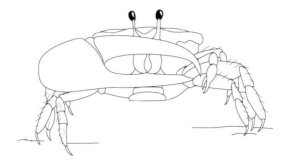

Sand fiddler crab

summertime, and northers blow their deeply corrugated shells with the distinctive "ear flaps" onto the shore in large numbers. Other common clams—thick lucines, bay tellins, jackknife clams, and cross-barred venuses—live close to the shoreline, either on the bottom or slightly buried in the sediment. Two other clams, angel wing and the razor clam, bore into the bay mud; their shells are extracted by rough weather. Of course, the most common shell of all is that of the eastern oyster, which accumulates in windrows from the reefs scattered around the margins of the bay. Like those of lightning whelks, some oystershells are stained black and have been worn smooth from long entombment in lagoonal sediments.

Fiddler crabs are among the most distinctive denizens of the bay shore. Armies of these personable, squarish little crabs with pop-up eyes and one out-sized pincer can sometimes be found scuttling along the timbers of the dock at the Visitors' Center, and a stroll along the fringe of cordgrass at low tide will provoke an eerie rustle caused by hundreds of retreating, sidestepping feet. There are two common species on Matagorda: the mud fiddler, with a metallic green carapace, prefers the soft mud near stands of smooth cordgrass; the pale brown sand fiddler frequents more open shoreline of muddy sand. Even if the crabs are not abroad, their numerous 1/2-inch burrows are readily evident.

Fiddler crabs spend much of their time in L-shaped burrows that descend about a foot to the water table. At low tide they come out to feed in gregarious throngs. Fiddlers are accomplished sediment sifters. They scrape up a dollop of material from the surface of the substrate, deposit this into their mouth, and mix it with water from their gill chambers. Light particles of organic matter, bacteria, and algae float free and are collected with a sieve of fine hairs, while the granules of soil are packed into a pellet and discarded. The mouthparts of mud fiddlers allow them to handle mud, while those of sand fiddlers are fitted for sifting sand, so the two species do not compete with each other for food. If you observe a fresh fiddler crab burrow, you will notice two sizes of pellets around the entrance. The fewer large ones result from burrow maintenance; the many small ones are the cast-off feeding pellets.

Perhaps the most interesting aspect of fiddler crabs is the "fiddle"—the enlarged pincer of the male (the female has two equal-sized pincers). A male fiddler stands at the entrance to his burrow and uses his enlarged appendage as a semaphore to signal other members of his colony. To other males his energetic waving means "this is my territory; you stay away"; to any passing female it means "please come into my bower where we can make love." If a female shows interest in his rhythmical, jerky waving, the male abruptly increases his tempo, raps his pincer against the ground, and begins to bow and curtsy to hold her attention. If you are patient enough to watch awhile through binoculars, you can detect subtle differences in the courtship movements of mud fiddlers and sand fiddlers.

Fiddler crabs play important ecological roles in the tidal flat community. Their ceaseless burrowing and sifting turn over a large volume of sediments, while the animals themselves are an important link near the base of the food chain. They are favorites on the menus of blue crabs, clapper rails, willets, long-billed curlews, gulls, and raccoons. Feral hogs often dig up long stretches of bay shore in search of fiddlers.

Open stretches of moist sand near the bay shoreline are often sprinkled with numerous small piles of tiny sand pellets. Though easily mistaken for earthworm casts, these are produced by spiny-legged rove beetles, cylindrical, cream-colored insects hardly ⅜ of an inch long. The beetles dig vertical galleries about 6 inches deep into the sand, where they feed on detritus and diatoms trapped in the substrate. In their cumulative thousands, rove beetles annually mix, cleanse, and aerate a significant fraction of the heavy bay-side sediment.

Most of the numerous kinds of insects and arachnids in the tidal flat community occur in parallel strips in accord with the distinctive tiers of vegetation. There is, for instance, a characteristic bustle of life among the emergent stems of smooth cordgrass. This is the domain of the cylindrical, ½-inch-long cordgrass bug, which passes its entire life cycle within and upon its chosen host, sucking the briny sap.

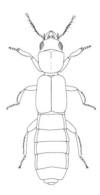

Spiny-legged rove beetle

Mixed groups of juvenile and adult bugs with black bodies and brown wings can usually be found squirreling adroitly around cordgrass stems and seeking shelter at the bases of the leaves. Here also are the webs of starbellied spiders, banded orb weavers, and elongate stilt spiders, strung up to catch the clouds of midges and shore flies. Predaceous mantis flies perch on the grass tips and hawk freshly emerged horseflies and deerflies, while sundry small jumping spiders stalk the stems in search of plant hoppers and larval grasshoppers. A species of valentine ant risks establishing its colonies in the hollow core of dead cordgrass stems. Three species of brackish-water dragonflies cruise methodically back and forth above the tips of the cordgrass, suddenly darting to scoop up small flying insects in their spiny leg baskets. Occasionally the males meet in wing-clattering jousts, and the females dip down to peck eggs into the water with the tips of their abdomens.

The low marsh is home to one of the real gems of the tidal flat—the western pigmy blue butterfly. With a wingspan of only ⅜ of an inch, this is the smallest of our butterflies; so small that you can easily walk through a stand of its favored glasswort without noticing the silent flutter of little butterflies about your shins. The white-edged wings shift from coppery at the outside to brilliant ultramarine blue near the body. If you have ever yearned to be with fairies, squat down among a sparkle of pigmy blues.

Great southern white butterflies float above the blossoms of bushy sea oxeye in the high marsh, and bristly black wooly bears (salt-marsh caterpillars) munch on leaves of coast mistflowers. From there the welter of small animal life continues: planthoppers and leafhoppers suck sap; myriads of small shore flies sponge up assorted fluids, from the cleanest and sweetest to the rankest and most fetid; grasshoppers, katydids, field crickets, and walking sticks munch plant tissues; beetles, bugs, wasps, and ants fill all manner of specialized niches; and spiders and predaceous insects prey on the herbivores. From this humming-and-buzzing melange most visitors notice only two kinds of creatures—mosquitoes and deerflies.

Every barrier occasionally cringes under the sustained whine of swarms of mosquitoes, and Matagorda Island is no exception. Following heavy rains or exceptionally high tides, these biting insects emerge in such numbers as to become not only a nuisance, but even a deterrent to people and a menace to wild creatures that cannot avoid them. However, as with other members of the fauna, mosquitoes have their place in the ecosystem of the island, and we must grudgingly admit that they are supremely adapted to their pestiferous way of life.

No systematic survey of the mosquitoes of Matagorda Island has ever been conducted, but overpowering clouds of these insects are usually composed of one or more of three dominant species. If you care to observe before you swat, the golden salt-marsh mosquito and the black salt-marsh mosquito are similar: small, dark, with a white ring around the middle of the proboscis, white rings on the hind legs, and a bronze smudge on the back. The golden salt-marsh also has a silvery white stripe down the middle of its abdomen. The purple rain mosquito is large and dark, with a golden patch on its back and flashes of blue and purple iridescence on its dark proboscis and legs. Salt-marsh mosquitoes fly rapidly with a perceptible whine and their bite produces an unpleasant sting; rain mosquitoes fly more slowly and nearly silently; they pierce the skin so painlessly that they are often not noticed before they are heavy with blood.

All mosquitoes pass through four stages in their life history, each stage serving a specific biological purpose and filling a slightly different ecological niche. The egg, the beginning point of development, can withstand seasonal extremes intolerable to other stages. All three mosquitoes scatter their dark eggs singly in moist depressions in the soil; the two salt-marsh species use the tidal flats, while the rain mosquito chooses swales and pot holes in the grassy interior. The eggs can withstand dehydration, heat, and cold for weeks or even months, yet they are ready to hatch within ten minutes of being flooded by a good rain or a surging tide. Although they are more responsive when it is warm, a few eggs can be stimulated to hatch at any time of the year. Mosquito eggs are eaten by fiddler crabs and beetles and many are destroyed by fungi.

The mosquito larva, or wiggler, is the eating-and-growing stage. From hatching until its final molt, about four days, these bristly aquatic insects hang beneath the surface film, breathing air through a siphon on their rear end and voraciously feeding. They create minuscule swirls in the water and filter out the suspended food items—bacteria, protozoa, microcrustaceans, nematodes, algae, and detritus—with special brushes of hairs around their mouths. Because of their intimate association with the surface film, mosquito larvae must live in quiet water; they cannot survive in the wind-whipped bays.

When conditions are favorable, shallow tidal pools and swales become black and vibrant with millions of mosquito larvae, and they attract a host of predators. Startled wigglers abruptly descend to the bottom with characteristic kinking movements, but this is scant defense against most pursuers. All of the small fish, especially killifish, mosquito fish, and sailfin mollys, feed avidly on mosquito larvae; it is thought that the habit of laying eggs in isolated depressions is the mosquitoes' way of securing their larvae from fish. Concentrations of wigglers also attract ducks, which skim them up by the mouthful. Shorebirds and small sandpipers join in the feast. But their most persistent predators are other small denizens of the aquatic community: dragonfly nymphs, water spiders, and diverse members of no fewer than seven families of predaceous water bugs, four groups of diving beetles, and five types of aquatic fly larvae. Wigglers also suffer from sundry viral and bacterial diseases. A lot of mosquito protoplasm is funneled off into diverse food chains before it can mature to the vexatious stage.

Wigglers that manage to reach full growth split out of their larval skins as black, comma-shaped pupae ('pew-pea). Destined to last only a day or two, the pupal stage does not feed, but busies itself with the remarkable internal reorganization leading to the adult. Pupae do respond to shadows and water vibrations, swimming jerkily and descending to the bottom in a series of somersaults; yet many of them succumb to the same predators that gobble up wigglers. If the pool dries up, this works to the advantage of the mosquitoes, which can complete their transformation in the mud while their aquatic predators either die or move elsewhere.

Less than a week after an egg hatches, an imago (im-'may-go), or adult, mosquito laboriously pushes its way out through a slit in the back of the pupal skin. It rests from its labors while its wings inflate and new exoskeleton hardens, and then it is ready for its destiny—to reproduce its kind. The first stop is at a flower to tank up on nectar, and soon the two sexes meet in mating swarms, where the males achieve their goal and leave the remaining burden to the impregnated females. It is the horde of females that now become a threat to any creature with blood in its veins; they can kill unprotected nestling birds, sap the strength of everything from fawns to coyotes, and drive human beings to utter distraction.

Compelled by the need for protein to complete the development of their eggs, the females sally forth in the evenings or rise in ravening swarms any time they are disturbed from their rest in damp vegetation. Although they can see movement in the daytime, mosquitoes mainly home in by their antennae, following chemical, temperature, and moisture cues. The final approach is quick, and at the last moment they usually duck to the downwind side of an animal's body, where they can make a secure and stealthy landing.

It only takes a moment for a mosquito to work the tip of her proboscis into a capillary and begin to swell her abdomen with blood. When finished, she lifts off heavily and seeks out a dark nook to rest while her eggs mature. A few days later she will be busily sprinkling several hundred speck-sized eggs in moist hollows. If she is fortunate enough to live out her life span of a few weeks, a female mosquito will take several blood meals, producing a fresh batch of eggs after each.

Mosquitoes deal us much misery while sucking our blood, but both the females and the innocuous males serve as a ready food source for many creatures. Small hemipteran bugs and flower spiders ambush mosquitoes seeking nectar. Strategically placed spider webs sag under the weight of captured mosquitoes. The sluggish, blood-engorged females are dispatched by ants. Dragonflies snatch mosquitoes to eat on the wing. Birds—swallows by day and nighthawks by night—scoop mosquitoes from the air, while black-necked stilts, semipalmated plovers, and least sandpipers meticulously peck up resting mosquitoes one by one. Froglets and toadlets tongue-pop their share, and bats gorge on swarming mosquitoes. So, even though it may not satisfy your personal vendetta against them, mosquitoes do pay their dues and ecological justice is ultimately served.

Slightly larger than houseflies, deerflies have large, flashing green eyes and swept-back wings with a mottled black pattern. As with mosquitoes, the female has the lust for blood, especially that of cattle, horses, or deer; unfortunately, she readily accepts a human substitute. She circles her intended victim several times at high speed and suddenly darts in and settles gently. A flick of a tail or the wave of a hand sends her into flight again, but she resettles almost immediately. Perhaps because she homes in on the odor of perspiration, a favored site on people is the back of the neck or the hairline near the ears. Her bite, geared for thicker hides, produces a sharp sting and elicits a violent swat, so unless they occur in large numbers, deerflies seldom get much blood from humans. They are usually nothing more than occasional nuisances along the edges of the tidal flats. Both robberflies and sand wasps prey on deerflies.

Matagorda Lighthouse

Keepers of the Light

1852–?	Captain James Cummings
?–1878	Records lost
1878–1885	William Chichester
1885–May 1888	Horace W. Crockett
October 1888–1913	Joseph Forestier*
1913–1918	Theodore O. Olsen*
1918–1946	William Heinroth
1946–1966	Arthur Barr

Lighthouse Chronology

1847	$15,000 appropriated by U.S. Congress for construction.
1848	Land is acquired on northeastern edge of Matagorda Island from long-time resident and seaman, Captain James Cummings. This original site is now submerged inside the J-Hook.
March 1852	Assembly begins by Murray and Hazelhurst of Boston.
September 1852	Captain James Cummings is named first keeper of the light.
December 21, 1852	Matagorda Light, with a reflector light atop a 55-foot tower, becomes the first operational lighthouse on the Texas coast.
1854	Lighthouse rides out its first severe hurricane.
July 1859	Tower height raised to 79 feet, and tower daymarked in horizontal bands of red, white, and black; lantern is 96 feet above sea level. Light has third-order Fresnel lens and colza oil fuel, flashes every 90 seconds, and is visible 16 miles at sea.

December 1862	Confederates remove and bury the lens, and damage the tower while attempting to demolish it ahead of Union occupation.
1865	Tower is dismantled and salvagable pieces stored; temporary light with fifth-order Fresnel lens erected nearby.
1872	U.S. Congress appropriates $32,000 for renovating and reassembling tower and installing a new third-order lens.
September 1, 1873	Lighthouse becomes operational at its second (current) site, using kerosene fuel. Flash and visibility are about the same as the original; exterior is daymarked solid black.
September 1875	Lighthouse rides out fearful hurricane.
August 1886	Part of lens is blown out when a devastating hurricane shakes the tower.
1902	Conversion is made to IOV (incandescent oil vapor) light, a brighter and whiter light fueled by vaporized kerosene, with 1,300,000 candlepower. It is visible for 45 miles.
August 1942	Hurricane puts 7 feet of water inside the tower; sweeps the assistant keeper's residence away.
1943	Conversion is made to battery-powered electric light, which is visible for 45 miles at sea.
1946	Arthur Barr becomes the last keeper of the light, and in so doing confers a rare distinction upon his wife, Ruth: her maternal grandfather (T. O. Olsen), her father (William Heinroth), and her husband were all keepers of the Matagorda Light.
1952	Just as it was the first, so the Matagorda Light becomes the last functional lighthouse on the Texas coast when the Port Aransas lighthouse is officially closed.
1956	Switched to electrical lines serving Matagorda Air Base, the Light now only uses batteries and generators as backup. Light and flashing mechanism are fully automated; the keeper now merely maintains the system. Light rotates inside lens to give 2-second flash every 20 seconds.

September 1961   Hurricane Carla sweeps over most of
                 Matagorda Island, but only puts 8 inches of
                 water in the tower.
1966   Last keeper is discharged. U.S. Coast Guard
                 takes over maintenance and quarterly checking
                 of automatic system and maintenance of
                 surrounding 116 acres.
1977   Light is extinguished; lens is removed and
                 eventually deposited at its current site, Calhoun
                 County Museum in Port Lavaca. The coast
                 guard considers dismantling the tower.
1984   Matagorda Light renovated by the coast guard
                 for entry into National Registry of Historic
                 Landmarks.
February 1986   Conversion is made to special 250 millimeter
                 plastic lens with electrical bulb powered by
                 20-watt solar panel (visible on gallery); there is
                 no rotating device, and the light is regulated by
                 an electronic flasher unit. Bulb beams out over
                 the Gulf, 2 seconds on, 6 seconds off. It is
                 visible for 18 miles; maintained by the coast
                 guard unit out of Port O'Connor.

Lighthouse Cemetery

Joseph Forestier   ?–August 20, 1913; keeper of the light,
                          1888–1913. (Grave bears no stone.)
Adeline Forestier   March 1, 1854–May 13, 1901; wife of
                          Joseph.
William Henry Forestier   November 4, 1885–September 1, 1888;
                          son of Joseph and Adeline.
Theodore O. Olsen   November 16, 1864–December 15, 1918;
                          keeper of the light, 1913–1918; a
                          daughter, Ruth Elizabeth, married
                          William Heinroth, the succeeding keeper
                          of the light.
Mary Ann Collins Hawes   1855–1892; wife of assistant keeper
                          H. W. Hawes.
*Buried in lighthouse cemetery.

Flowering Plants of
Matagorda Island

Family	Latin Name	Common Name
Aizoaceae	*Mollugo verticillata*	Indian chickweed
	Sesuvium erectum	Purslane
	Sesuvium portulacastrum	Sea purslane
Alismataceae	*Echinodorus rostratus*	Burhead
Amaranthaceae	*Amaranthus greggii*	Beach amaranth
	Froelichia gracilis	Slender snakecotton
	Philoxerus vermicularis	Silverhead
	Tidestromia lanuginosa	Wooly honeysweet
Amyrillidaceae	*Allium canadense*	Wild onion
	Cooperia drummondii	Drummond rain lily
	Nothoscordum bivalve	False garlic
Apocynaceae	*Nerium oleander*	Oleander
Aquifoliaceae	*Ilex vomitoria*	Yaupon
Asclepiadaceae	*Asclepias oenotheroides*	Milkweed
	Cynanchum angustifolium	Thin-leaf milkweed vine
	Cynanchum barbigerum	Dwarf milkweed vine
	Sarcostemma cynanchoides	Milkweed vine
Avicenniaceae	*Avicennia germinans*	Black mangrove
Basellaceae	*Anredera scandens*	Madeira vine
Bataceae	*Batis maritima*	Maritime saltwort
Boraginaceae	*Heliotropium curassavicum*	Seaside heliotrope
Cactaceae	*Opuntia engelmannii*	Texas prickly pear
	Opuntia leptocaulis	Tasajillo
	Opuntia macrorhiza	Plains prickly pear

Family	Latin Name	Common Name
	Opuntia stricta	Coast prickly pear
Capparidaceae	*Polanisia dodecandra*	Clammyweed
Chenopodiaceae	*Atriplex arenaria*	Sand saltbush
	Atriplex matamorensis	Matamoros saltbush
	Chenopodium ambrosioides	Wormseed goosefoot
	Chenopodium berlandieri	Pitseed goosefoot
	Salicornia bigelovii	Annual glasswort
	Salicornia virginica	Perennial glasswort
	Suaeda conferta	Seepweed
	Suaeda linearis	Annual seepweed
Commelinaceae	*Commelina erecta*	Erect dayflower
	Tradescantia hirsutiflora	Hairy-flower spiderwort
	Tradescantia subacaulis	Stemless spiderwort
Compositae	*Ambrosia psilostachya*	Western ragweed
	Aphanostephus skirrhobasis	Lazy daisy
	Aster spinosus	Spiny aster
	Aster tenuifolius	Saline aster
	Baccharis halimifolia	Groundsel
	Borrichia frutescens	Bushy sea oxeye
	Chaetopappa asteroides	Least daisy
	Cirsium horridulum	Bull thistle
	Coreopsis tinctoria	Plains coreopsis
	Croptilon divaricatum	Scratch daisy
	Erigeron myrionactis	Corpus Christi fleabane
	Eupatorium betonicifolium	Coast mistflower
	Eupatorium compositifolium	Yankeeweed
	Eupatorium incarnatum	Pink eupatorium
	Eupatorium odoratum	Fragrant boneset
	Euthamia leptocephala	Prairie goldenrod
	Euthamia pulverulenta	Prairie goldenrod
	Flaveria brownii	Yellowstems
	Gaillardia pulchella	Indian blanket

Family	Latin Name	Common Name
	Gnaphalium pennsylvanicum	Cudweed
	Helenium amaurum	Bitterweed
	Helianthus annuus	Common sunflower
	Helianthus argophyllus	Silverleaf sunflower
	Helianthus debilis	Coast sunflower
	Heterotheca subaxillaris	Camphorweed
	Iva angustifolia	Narrow-leaf sumpweed
	Iva frutescens	Marsh elder
	Machaeranthera phyllocephala	Camphor daisy
	Palafoxia hookeriana	Showy palafoxia
	Palafoxia texana	Texas palafoxia
	Pluchea purpurascens	Marsh fleabane
	Pyrrhopappus carolinianus	False dandelion
	Ratibida columnaris	Mexican hat
	Ratibida peduncularis	Gulf Coast Mexican hat
	Rudbeckia hirta	Brown-eyed susan
	Senecio riddellii	Broom groundsel
	Solidago sempervirens	Seacoast goldenrod
	Sonchus oleraceus	Common sow thistle
	Thelesperma filifolium	Greenthread
	Verbesina encelioides	Cowpen daisy
	Xanthium strumarium	Cocklebur
	Xanthocephalum dracunculoides	Broomweed
Convolvulaceae	*Cressa depressa*	Seacoast cressa
	Cuscuta cuspidata	Dodder
	Cuscuta indecora	Showy dodder
	Dichondra carolinensis	Ponyfoot
	Ipomoea pes-caprae	Goat-foot morning glory
	Ipomoea sagittata	Salt-marsh morning glory
	Ipomoea stolonifera	Fiddleleaf morning glory
	Stylisma villosa	Hairy stylisma

Family	Latin Name	Common Name
Cruciferae	*Cakile lanceolata*	Sea rocket
	Lepidium virginicum	Peppergrass
Cucurbitaceae	*Cucurbita texana*	Texas gourd
	Ibervillea lindheimeri	Balsam gourd
Cyperaceae	*Cladium jamaicensis*	Sawgrass
	Cyperus elegans	Sticky flatsedge
	Cyperus esculentus	Yellow nut grass
	Cyperus ovularis	Flatsedge
	Cyperus polystachyos	Flatsedge
	Cyperus surinamensis	Tropical flatsedge
	Dichromena colorata	White-topped umbrella grass
	Eleocharis albida	White spikesedge
	Eleocharis cellulosa	Gulf Coast spikesedge
	Eleocharis montevidensis	Sand spikesedge
	Fimbristylis caroliniana	Fimbry
	Fimbristylis castanea	Fimbry
	Scirpus americanus	American bulrush
Ebenaceae	*Diospyros texana*	Mexican persimmon
Elaeagnaceae	*Elaeagnus angustifolia*	Russian olive
Euphorbiaceae	*Croton capitatus*	Wooly goatweed
	Croton glandulosus	Tropical croton
	Croton punctatus	Gulf croton
	Croton texensis	Texas croton
	Euphorbia ammannioides	Ingall's euphorbia
	Euphorbia maculata	Spotted euphorbia
	Phyllanthus polygonoides	Leaf flower
	Sapium sebiferum	Chinese tallow
Fagaceae	*Quercus virginiana*	Live oak
Gentianaceae	*Eustoma exaltatum*	Bluebell
	Sabatia arenicola	Sand pink
Gramineae	*Andropogon glomeratus*	Bushy bluestem
	Andropogon virginicus	Broomsedge bluestem
	Aristida intermedia	Plains triple-awn
	Bothriochloa ischaemum	King Ranch bluestem

Family	Latin Name	Common Name
	Bothriochloa laguroides	Silver bluestem
	Bromus texensis	Texas brome
	Cenchrus echinatus	Southern sandbur
	Cenchrus incertus	Gulf Coast sandbur
	Chloris cucullata	Hooded windmill grass
	Chloris latisquamea	Nash windmill grass
	Chloris petraea	Stiff-leaf chloris
	Cynodon dactylon	Bermuda grass
	Dichanthium annulatum	Kleberg bluestem
	Digitaria adscendens	Southern crabgrass
	Digitaria diversiflora	Crabgrass
	Digitaria texana	Texas crabgrass
	Distichlis spicata	Saltgrass
	Eragrostis oxylepis	Red love grass
	Hordeum pusillum	Little barley
	Leptoloma cognatum	Fall witchgrass
	Limnodea arkansana	Ozark grass
	Monanthochloe littoralis	Shore grass
	Muhlenbergia capillaris	Gulf muhly
	Panicum amarum	Beach panic
	Panicum hians	Gaping panic
	Panicum lanuginosum	Wooly panic
	Panicum oligosanthes	Heller panic
	Panicum ovinum	Sheep panic
	Paspalum monostachyum	Gulfdune paspalum
	Paspalum notatum	Bahia grass
	Paspalum plicatulum	Brownseed paspalum
	Paspalum setaceum	Thin paspalum
	Paspalum vaginatum	Seashore paspalum
	Phalaris canariensis	Canary grass
	Poa annua	Annual bluegrass
	Schizachyrium scoparium	Seacoast bluestem
	Setaria geniculata	Knotroot bristle grass

Family	Latin Name	Common Name
	Setaria leucopila	Plains bristle grass
	Spartina alterniflora	Smooth cordgrass
	Spartina patens	Marshhay cordgrass
	Spartina spartinae	Gulf Coast cordgrass
	Sphenopholis obtusatum	Prairie wedgescale
	Sporobolus indicus	Smut grass
	Sporobolus pyrimidatus	Whorled dropseed
	Sporobolus tharpii	Padre Island dropseed
	Sporobolus virginicus	Seashore dropseed
	Trachypogon secundus	Crinkleawn
	Uniola paniculata	Sea oats
	Vulpina octoflora	Six-weeks fescue
Hypericaceae	*Hypericum pauciflorum*	Saint-john's-wort
Iridaceae	*Alophia drummondii*	Wild iris
	Eustylis purpurea	Purple pleatleaf
	Sisyrinchium biforme	Blue-eyed grass
	Sisyrinchium exile	Small-flower blue-eyed grass
Juncaceae	*Juncus bufonius*	Toad rush
	Juncus interior	Inland rush
	Juncus marginatus	Grass-leaf rush
	Juncus megacephalus	Cherry-coke rush
	Juncus roemerianus	Black rush
	Juncus validus	Roundhead rush
Labiatae	*Monarda punctata*	Spotted horsemint
	Scutellaria muriculata	Skullcap
	Teucrium cubense	Coast germander
Leguminosae	*Acacia farnesiana*	Huisache
	Acacia tortuosa	Huisachillo
	Amorpha bushii	Indigobush
	Baptisia leucophaea	Plains wild indigo
	Cassia fasciculata	Partridge pea

Family	Latin Name	Common Name
	Cassia occidentalis	Coffee senna
	Centrosema virginianum	Butterfly pea
	Desmanthus brevipes	Bundle flower
	Erythrina herbacea	Coralbean
	Galactia canescens	Hoary milkpea
	Indigofera miniata	Scarlet pea
	Indigofera suffruticosa	Anil indigo
	Medicago lupulina	Black medic
	Medicago polymorpha	Bur clover
	Melilotus indicus	Yellow sour clover
	Mimosa strigillosa	Powder puff
	Neptunia pubescens	Yellow puff
	Parkinsonia aculeata	Retama
	Petalostemum emarginata	Wedge-leaf prairie clover
	Prosopis glandulosa	Mesquite
	Psoralea rhombifolia	Round-leaf scurf pea
	Rhynchosia americana	American snoutbean
	Schrankia latidens	Sensitive briar
	Sesbania drummondii	Rattlepod
	Sesbania macrocarpa	Coffee bean
	Sesbania vesicaria	Bladderpod
	Strophostyles leiosperma	Wild bean
	Stylosanthes viscosa	Pencil flower
	Vicia ludoviciana	Louisiana vetch
Liliaceae	*Yucca tenuistyla*	White-rim yucca
	Yucca treculeana	Spanish dagger
Linaceae	*Linum alatum*	Wild flax
	Linum rigidum	Stiff-stem flax
Loasaceae	*Mentzelia oligosperma*	Stickleaf
Loganiaceae	*Polypremum procumbens*	Polyprim
Lythraceae	*Lythrum alatum*	Lance-leaf loosestrife
	Lythrum californicum	California loosestrife
Malvaceae	*Abutilon incanum*	Indian mallow
	Abutilon lignosum	Woody mallow
	Hibiscus laevis	White rose mallow

Family	Latin Name	Common Name
	Kosteletzyka virginica	Salt-marsh mallow
	Malvastrum americanum	Rio Grande false mallow
	Malvaviscus arboreus	Turk's cap
	Sida ciliaris	Bracted sida
	Sida lindheimeri	Showy sida
	Sphaeralcea lindheimeri	Wooly globe mallow
Meliaceae	*Melia azedarach*	Chinaberry
Moraceae	*Maclura pomifera*	Bois d'arc
Nyctaginaceae	*Boerhaavia coccinea*	Scarlet spiderling
Oleaceae	*Forestiera angustifolia*	Elbowbush
Onagraceae	*Calylophus australis*	Yellow primrose
	Gaura filiformis	Tall honeysuckle
	Gaura parviflora	Small-flower honeysuckle
	Ludwigia glandulosa	Creeping seedbox
	Oenothera drummondii	Beach evening primrose
	Oenothera kunthiana	Pink-net evening primrose
	Oenothera laciniata	Cut-leaf evening primrose
	Oenothera speciosa	Pink evening primrose
Orchidaceae	*Spiranthes vernalis*	Ladies' tresses
Oxalidaceae	*Oxalis dillenii*	Yellow wood sorrel
	Oxalis drummondii	Purple wood sorrel
Palmae	*Phoenix sylvatica*	Wild date palm
	Sabal sp.	Palmetto palm
	Washingtonia robusta	Washington palm
Papaveraceae	*Argemone albiflora*	White prickly poppy
Passifloraceae	*Passiflora foetida*	Passion flower
Phytolaccaceae	*Rivina humilis*	Pigeonberry
Pittosporaceae	*Pittosporum crassifolium*	Pittosporum
Plantaginaceae	*Plantago hookeriana*	Tallow weed
	Plantago rhodosperma	Red-seed plantago

Family	Latin Name	Common Name
Plumbaginaceae	*Limonium nashii*	Sea lavender
Podocarpaceae	*Podocarpus macrophylla*	Japanese yew
Polemoniaceae	*Gilia incisa*	Split-leaf gilia
Polygalaceae	*Polygala verticillata*	Whorled milkwort
Polygonaceae	*Eriogonum multiflorum*	Wild buckwheat
	Persicaria punctata	Smartweed
	Rumex chrysocarpus	Dock
Portulacaceae	*Portulaca mundula*	Shaggy portulaca
Potamogetonaceae	*Potamogeton pectinatus*	Sago pondweed
Primulaceae	*Samolus ebracteatus*	Coast pimpernel
Rhamnaceae	*Condalia hookeri*	Brasil
	Zizyphus obtusifolia	Lotebush
Rosaceae	*Prunus caroliniana*	Cherry laurel
	Rosa bracteata	Macartney rose
	Rubus trivialis	Southern dewberry
Rubiaceae	*Diodia teres*	Rough buttonweed
	Diodia virginianum	Virginia buttonweed
	Hedyotis nigricans	Prairie bluets
	Richardia brasiliensis	Mexican clover
Ruppiaceae	*Ruppia maritima*	Widgeon grass
Rutaceae	*Amyris texana*	Texas torchwood
	Zanthoxylum clava-herculis	Prickly ash
	Zanthoxylum fagara	Wild lime
	Zanthoxylum hirsutum	Prickly ash
Salicaceae	*Populus deltoides*	Cottonwood
Sapotaceae	*Bumelia celastrina*	Coma
Scrophulariaceae	*Agalinis fasciculata*	Beach gerardia
	Agalinis strictifolia	Stiff-leaf gerardia
	Bacopa monnieri	Water hyssop
	Linaria texana	Toadflax
	Maurandya antirrhiniflora	Snapdragon vine
	Stemodia tomentosa	Silverstems
Solanaceae	*Lycium berlandieri*	Berlandier wolfberry
	Lycium carolinianum	Carolina wolfberry
	Physalis pubescens	Downy ground-cherry

Family	Latin Name	Common Name
	Physalis viscosa	Beach ground-cherry
	Solanum americanum	American nightshade
	Solanum eleagnifolium	Silver-leaf nightshade
	Solanum triquetrum	Texas nightshade
Tamaricaceae	*Tamarix chinensis*	Saltcedar
	Tamarix gallica	Saltcedar
Typhaceae	*Typha dominguensis*	Gulf Coast cattail
Ulmaceae	*Celtis pallida*	Spiny hackberry
Umbelliferae	*Centella erecta*	Spadeleaf
	Hydrocotyl bonariensis	Coast pennywort
	Hydrocotyl umbellata	Umbrella pennywort
	Limnosciadium pumilum	Dogshade
Urticaceae	*Parietaria floridana*	Pellitory
	Urtica chamaedryoides	Stinging nettle
Verbenaceae	*Lantana horrida*	Common lantana
	Phyla nodiflora	Frogfruit
	Verbena halei	Texas vervain
	Verbena quadrangulata	Four-angle vervain
Vitaceae	*Cissus incisa*	Ivy treebine
Zannichelliaceae	*Zannichellia palustris*	Common poolmat

Eighty Common Wildflowers of Matagorda Island

Species (grouped by color)	# Petals	Width*	Community**	Bloom	Comments
WHITE					
Coast germander (*Teucrium cubense*)	5	½	BF,SR	Mar–Nov	long lower petal
Coast pennywort (*Hydrocotyl bonariensis*)	5	⅛	B,FW	Mar–Nov	round, umbrella-like leaves
Coast pimpernel (*Samolus ebracteatus*)	5	½	B,BF	Mar–Nov	basal-leaf rosette
Corpus Christi fleabane (*Erigeron myrionactis*)	many	1	B,SD,BF	Feb–Dec	narrow petals
False garlic (*Nothoscordum bivalve*)	6	⅝	BF	Feb–Nov	no onion odor
Fiddleleaf morning glory (*Ipomoea stolonifera*)	5	2	B	May–Sep	petals in trumpet
Frogfruit (*Phyla nodiflora*)	4	⅛	B,BF	Apr–Nov	flowers in dense heads
Ladies' tresses (*Spiranthes vernalis*)	3	¼	BF,SD	Apr–Jun	flowers in spiral
Lazy daisy (*Aphanostephus skirrhobasis*)	many	1¼	BF,SD	Feb–Nov	yellow disk
Macartney rose (*Rosa bracteata*)	5	2¼	BF	May–Jun	catclaw thorns
Peppergrass (*Lepidium virginicum*)	4	¼	BF	Feb–May	weedy
Seaside heliotrope (*Heliotropium curassavicum*)	4	⅛	B,TF	Mar–Nov	flowers in curl

Species	Petals	Size	Habitat	Bloom	Description
Southern dewberry (*Rubus trivialis*)	5	1	BF,SR	Mar–May	stems with prickles
Spanish dagger (*Yucca treculeana*)	6	2½	BF,SR	Mar–Apr	spine-tipped leaves
White prickly poppy (*Argemone albiflora*)	6	3¼	BF	Mar–Jul	prickly foliage
Wild buckwheat (*Eriogonum multiflorum*)	6	⅛	BF,SD	Sep–Nov	flowers in flat clusters
LAVENDER-WHITE					
Prairie bluets (*Hedyotis nigricans*)	4	⅜	BF,SR	Apr–Nov	leaves opposite
Rough buttonweed (*Diodia teres*)	4	¼	BF	May–Nov	narrow leaves
Water hyssop (*Bacopa monnieri*)	5	⅜	B,BF,FW	Apr–Nov	mat-like
LAVENDER					
Bull thistle (*Cirsium horridulum*)	many	3	BF	Mar–May	prickly leaves
Louisiana vetch (*Vicia ludoviciana*)	5	¼	BF	Feb–May	trailing
Sea lavender (*Limonium nashii*)	5	¼	TF	May–Nov	large basal leaves
Silver-leaf nightshade (*Solanum eleagnifolium*)	5	1	BF	May–Oct	joined petals
Stiff-leaf gerardia (*Agalinis strictifolia*)	5	¾	BF,SD	Sep–Nov	5-lobed flower
Texas palafoxia (*Palafoxia texana*)	none	1	BF	Apr–Dec	many thin, disk petals
Texas vervain (*Verbena halei*)	5	¼	BF	Mar–Dec	flowers in slender spikes
Toadflax (*Linaria texana*)	5	⅜	BF,SD	Mar–Apr	flower with spur
BLUE					
Blue-eyed grass (*Sisyrinchium biforme*)	6	¾	BF,SD	Mar–May	yellow eye
Bluebell (*Eustoma exaltatum*)	5	2½	BF,SD	May–Oct	tulip-like flower
Erect dayflower (*Commelina erecta*)	3	⅞	BF,SD	Mar–Dec	2 petals blue, 1 white
BLUE-VIOLET					
Coast mistflower (*Eupatorium betonicifolium*)	none	⅜	BF,SD	Apr–Dec	flowers fuzzy
VIOLET					
Butterfly pea (*Centrosema virginianum*)	5	⅞	BF	Mar–Nov	twining
Wild iris (*Alophia drummondii*)	6	1½	BF	Apr–May	3 large, 3 small petals

Species (grouped by color)	# Petals	Width*	Community**	Bloom	Comments
PURPLE					
California loosestrife (*Lythrum californicum*)	4–6	½	BF,SD	Apr–Oct	weedy
Goat-foot morning glory (*Ipomoea pes-capre*)	5	3	B,SD	May–Dec	petals in trumpet
Purple pleatleaf (*Eustylis purpurea*)	6	1¾	BF,SD	Apr–May	specked yellow center
Skullcap (*Scutellaria muriculata*)	5	⅜	BF,SD,SR	Feb–Nov	cap below petals
Stemless spiderwort (*Tradescantia subacaulis*)	3	1	BF,SD	Mar–May	hairy stamens
PINK-PURPLE					
Marsh fleabane (*Pluchea purpurascens*)	none	¼	BF,FW	May–Dec	odorous leaves
PINK					
Pink evening primrose (*Oenothera speciosa*)	4	2¼	BF	Mar–Apr	red-veined petals
Powder puff (*Mimosa strigillosa*)	none	¾	BF,SR	Apr–Nov	flowers fuzzy globes
Salt-marsh mallow (*Kosteletzyka virginica*)	5	3	BF	Sep–Nov	hibiscus-like flower
Sand pink (*Sabatia arenicola*)	5	¾	B,BF	Apr–Jun	styles twisted
Sea purslane (*Sesuvium portulacastrum*)	5	¾	B	Apr–Dec	leaves opposite, succulent
Sensitive briar (*Schrankia latidens*)	none	¾	BF,SR	Apr–Oct	leaves sensitive to touch
Wild bean (*Strophostyles leiosperma*)	5	½	BF	May–Oct	twining, keel-curved
PINK-WHITE					
Wild onion (*Allium canadense*)	6	½	BF	Apr–May	onion odor
ROSE					
Salt-marsh morning glory (*Ipomoea sagittata*)	5	3	BF,FW	May–Sep	arrowhead leaves
RED					
Coral bean (*Erythrina herbacea*)	5	1½	SR	Mar–May	tubular flowers
SALMON-RED					
Scarlet pea (*Indigofera miniata*)	5	½	BF,SR	Apr–Oct	upper petal largest

YELLOW/RED					
Indian blanket (*Gaillardia pulchella*)	8–10	2	BF,SD	Feb–Dec	disk brown
ORANGE					
Wooly globe mallow (*Sphaeralcea lindheimeri*)	5	1¼	BF	Mar–Apr	leaves downy
GOLD					
Plains coreopsis (*Coreopsis tinctoria*)	5–7	1¼	BF	Mar–Sep	petals with dark base
YELLOW					
American snoutbean (*Rhynchosia americana*)	5	½	BF,SD	Mar–Nov	heavy-veined leaves
Beach evening primrose (*Oenothera drummondii*)	4	3¼	B,SD	Mar–Nov	downy leaves
Broom groundsel (*Senecio riddellii*)	8–12	1	SD	Oct–Nov	shrubby
Broomweed (*Xanthocephalum dracunculoides*)	7–15	½	BF	Sep–Dec	weedy, dense stands
Brown-eyed susan (*Rudbeckia hirta*)	8–20	2	BF	Apr–Jun	rough, hairy leaves
Bur clover (*Medicago polymorpha*)	5	⅛	BF	Feb–Jun	3-part leaves
Bushy sea oxeye (*Borrichia frutescens*)	12–30	1¼	TF	Mar–Dec	shrub, flowers spiny below
Camphor daisy (*Machaeranthera phyllocephala*)	20–35	1¼	SD,TF	Feb–Dec	toothed leaves
Camphorweed (*Heterotheca subaxillaris*)	15–30	1	BF,SD,SR	Sep–Dec	camphor odor
Cut-leaf primrose (*Oenothera laciniata*)	4	½	BF	Mar–Jun	toothed leaves
False dandelion (*Pyrrhopappus carolinianus*)	many	1½	BF	Mar–May	petals in sunburst
Greenthread (*Thelesperma filifolium*)	8	1½	BF	Feb–Dec	leaves thin, opposite
Mexican hat (*Ratibida columnaris*)	4–10	1¼	BF	Apr–May	tall disk
Partridge pea (*Cassia fasciculata*)	5	1	SD,BF	Aug–Dec	purple stamens
Plains prickly pear (*Opuntia macrorhiza*)	many	2½	BF,SR,TF	Apr–Jun	white spines
Plains wild indigo (*Baptisia leucophaea*)	5	¾	BF	Mar–Apr	shrubby
Prairie goldenrod (*Euthamia leptocephala*)	2–3	¼	BF	Sep–Dec	weedy
Silverleaf sunflower (*Helianthus argophyllus*)	15–20	3	BF,SD	Jun–Nov	downy leaves
Stiff-stem flax (*Linum rigidum*)	5	1	B,SD,BF	Mar–May	petals copper at base

Species (grouped by color)	# Petals	Width*	Community**	Bloom	Comments
Texas prickly pear (*Opuntia engelmannii*)	many	3	BF,SD,SR	Apr–May	yellow spines
Yellow primrose (*Calylophus australis*)	4	1½	BF,SR	Mar–Jun	thin leaves
Yellow puff (*Neptunia pubescens*)	none	½	BF	Apr–Nov	leaves sensitive to touch
Yellowstems (*Flaveria brownii*)	1	⅛	BF	Oct–Dec	yellow stems
Yellow wood sorrel (*Oxalis dillenii*)	5	⅝	BF	Mar–Jun	3-part leaves
YELLOW-GREEN					
Beach ground-cherry (*Physalis viscosa*)	5	⅝	B,SD,BF	Mar–Oct	dark eye
Spotted horsemint (*Monarda punctata*)	5	¾	BF	Apr–Jul	2-lipped flower
GREEN-WHITE					
Milkweed (*Asclepias oenotheroides*)	5	⅝	BF	Mar–Nov	petal tips folded back

* In inches

** B = Beach, SD = Sand Dune, BF = Barrier Flat, TF = Tidal Flat, SR = Shell Ridge, FW = Fresh Water

Audubon Christmas Bird Count
(Matagorda Island Unit,
Aransas National Wildlife Refuge)

Species	1988	1989	1990	Total	Average
GREBES					
Least grebe	0	0	2	2	1
Pied-billed grebe	14	6	6	26	9
Eared grebe	1	0	0	1	—
PELICANS & CORMORANTS					
American white pelican	35	121	120	276	92
Brown pelican	0	7	0	7	2
Double-crested cormorant	332	74	26	432	144
HERONS & EGRETS					
Great blue heron	36	35	51	122	41
Great egret	11	25	44	80	27
Snowy egret	38	17	25	80	27
Little blue heron	20	12	17	49	16
Tricolored heron	14	16	5	35	12
Reddish egret	12	133	22	167	56
Black-crowned night heron	1	0	0	1	—
Yellow-crowned night heron	0	0	3	3	1
IBISES & SPOONBILLS					
White ibis	37	55	85	177	59
Roseate spoonbill	17	5	4	26	9
DUCKS & GEESE					
Snow goose	62	85	188	335	112
Canada goose	21	27	7	55	18
Green-winged teal	7	12	11	30	10
Mottled duck	28	36	27	91	30
Mallard	0	8	0	8	3
Northern pintail	40	125	90	255	85
Northern shoveler	20	77	29	126	42
Gadwall	3	12	2	17	6
American wigeon	0	6	7	13	4

Species	1988	1989	1990	Total	Average
Redhead	0	32	2	34	11
Lesser scaup	0	77	0	77	26
Common goldeneye	3	2	2	7	2
Bufflehead	14	4	2	20	7
Hooded merganser	30	4	2	36	12
Red-breasted merganser	62	3	4	69	23
VULTURES					
Turkey vulture	11	6	6	23	8
DIURNAL RAPTORS					
Black-shouldered kite	3	2	4	9	3
Northern harrier	6	5	10	21	7
Cooper's hawk	1	0	0	1	—
Crested caracara	0	0	1	1	—
American kestrel	2	0	1	3	1
Merlin	1	0	0	1	—
TURKEY & QUAIL					
Northern bobwhite	8	0	0	8	3
CRANES					
Sandhill crane	12	3	9	24	8
Whooping crane	4	4	5	13	4
PLOVERS					
Black-bellied plover	37	66	55	158	53
Killdeer	5	4	0	9	3
STILTS & AVOCETS					
American avocet	0	42	212	254	85
SANDPIPERS					
Greater yellowlegs	52	36	9	97	32
Lesser yellowlegs	13	2	2	17	6
Willet	10	25	9	44	15
Long-billed curlew	9	6	10	25	8
Ruddy turnstone	1	0	0	1	—
Red knot	0	0	4	4	1
Sanderling	0	0	26	26	9
Western sandpiper	78	47	24	149	50
Least sandpiper	11	0	1	12	4
Dunlin	42	577	61	680	227
Long-billed dowitcher	260	489	25	774	258
GULLS, TERNS, & SKIMMERS					
Laughing gull	0	4	5	9	3
Bonaparte's gull	0	14	0	14	5

Species	1988	1989	1990	Total	Average
Ring-billed gull	35	112	6	153	51
Herring gull	8	7	28	43	14
Caspian tern	12	0	4	16	5
Royal tern	5	0	7	12	4
Sandwich tern	0	1	21	22	7
Forster's tern	13	25	1	39	13
OWLS					
Barn owl	1	0	0	1	—
Great horned owl	1	1	0	2	1
KINGFISHERS					
Belted kingfisher	2	1	1	4	1
LARKS					
Horned lark	3	2	5	10	3
WRENS					
Sedge wren	4	0	0	4	1
KINGLETS					
Ruby-crowned kinglet	2	0	0	2	1
THRASHERS					
Brown thrasher	1	0	0	1	—
PIPITS					
Sprague's pipit	1	0	0	1	—
SHRIKES					
Loggerhead shrike	9	0	2	11	4
VIREOS					
Solitary vireo	1	0	0	1	—
TANAGERS & GROSBEAKS					
Northern cardinal	3	2	1	6	2
SPARROWS					
Vesper sparrow	0	2	1	3	1
Savannah sparrow	29	13	4	46	15
Seaside sparrow	0	0	1	1	—
Song sparrow	0	2	0	2	1
BLACKBIRDS & ORIOLES					
Eastern meadowlark	43	38	34	115	38
TOTALS	1,597	2,554	1,378	5,529	

Invertebrates Mentioned in Text

Common Name	Latin Name
Alternate tellin	*Tellina alternata*
Angel wing (clam)	*Cyrtopleura costata*
Ant lion	*Myrmeleon sp.*
Arabesque orb weaver spider	*Neoscona arabesca*
Assassin bug	*Apionerus sp.*
Atlantic moon snail	*Polinices duplicatus*
Atlantic surf clam	*Spisula solidissima*
Backswimmer	*Notonecta sp.*
Banded orb weaver spider	*Neoscona pratensis*
Bay scallop	*Argopecten irradians*
Bay tellin (clam)	*Tellina tampaensis*
Beach dragonfly	*Anax junius*
Beach flea	*Orchestia sp.*
Beach fly	*Canaceidae*
Beach hermit crab	*Isocheles wurdemanni*
Bee fly	*Anthrax analis*
Bent mussel	*Ischadium recurvum*
Bird grasshopper	*Schistocerca americana*
Blackfly	*Simuliidae*
Black salt-marsh mosquito	*Aedes taeniorhynchus*
Black widow	*Latrodectus mactans*
Blood ark (clam)	*Anadara ovalis*
Blue crab	*Callinectes sapidus*
Bombardier beetle	*Brachinus sp.*
Brackish-water dragonfly	*Erythrodiplax commata*
Brown centipede	*Lithobius sp.*
Brown rangia	*Rangia flexuosa*
Brown shrimp	*Penaeus aztecus*
Buckeye butterfly	*Junonia coenia*
Bumblebee	*Bombus sp.*
Burrowing wolf spider	*Geolycosa sp.*
Carpet moth	*Trichophaga tapetzella*
Carrion fly	*Ephydridae*
Channeled duck clam	*Raeta plicatella*

Common Name	Latin Name
Checkerspot butterfly	*Physiodes sp.*
Chigger	*Trombicula spp.*
Cicada killer (wasp)	*Sphecius speciosus*
Clench's chione (clam)	*Chione clenchi*
Cloudless sulphur butterfly	*Phoebis sennae*
Common baby's ear (snail)	*Sinum perspectivum*
Common slipper shell (snail)	*Crepidula fornicata*
Common sundial (snail)	*Architectonica granulata*
Coquina clam	*Donax variabilis*
Cordgrass bug	*Ischnodemus falicus*
Crackle-wing grasshopper	*Acrididae*
Crane fly	*Tipulidae*
Cross-barred venus (clam)	*Chione cancellata*
Dance fly	*Empididae*
Deerfly	*Chrysops sp.*
Disk (clam)	*Dosinia discus*
Dog-faced sulphur butterfly	*Zerene cesonia*
Dunes cicada	*Tibicen sp.*
Dunes grasshopper	*Trimerotropis citrina*
Dunes spider	*Lycosa spp.*
Dwarf cerith (snail)	*Cerithium variable*
Dwarf surf clam	*Mulinia lateralis*
Earthworm	*Lumbricidae*
Earwig	*Dermaptera*
Eastern murex (snail)	*Muricanthus fulvescens*
Eastern oyster	*Crassostrea virginica*
Elongate stilt spider	*Tetragnatha straminea*
Emerald-jawed jumping spider	*Phidippus audax*
Field cricket	*Gryllus pennsylvanicus*
Flatworm	*Gnesioceros sargassicola*
Flesh fly	*Sarcophagidae*
Flower spider	*Misumenops asperatus*
Fulvous wood cockroach	*Parcoblatta fulvescens*
Funnelweb spider	*Agelenopsis sp.*
German cockroach	*Blatella germanica*
Ghost crab	*Ocypode quadrata*
Ghost shrimp	*Callichirus islagrande*
Giant Atlantic cockle (clam)	*Dinocardium robustum*
Golden salt-marsh mosquito	*Aedes sollicitans*
Grass cerith (snail)	*Bittium varium*
Grass shrimp	*Palaemonetes spp.*
Grass spider	*Agelenopsis sp.*
Gray hairstreak butterfly	*Strymon melinus*

Common Name	Latin Name
Great southern white butterfly	*Ascia monuste*
Gulf Coast tick	*Amblyomma maculatum*
Gulf fritillary butterfly	*Agraulis vanillae*
Halictid bee	*Augochlora sp.*
Harvestmen	*Leiobunum spp.*
Heart urchin	*Moira atropos*
Horsefly	*Tabanus sp.*
Housefly	*Musca domestica*
Hover fly	*Syrphidae*
Humpbacked orb weaver (spider)	*Eustala anastera*
Imported red fire ant	*Solenopsis invicta*
Incongruous ark (clam)	*Anadara brasiliana*
Jackknife clam	*Ensis minor*
June beetle	*Phyllophaga sp.*
Keyhole urchin	*Mellita quinquiesperforata*
Lady-in-waiting venus (clam)	*Chione intapurpurea*
Leafhopper	*Cicadellidae*
Lettered olive snail	*Oliva sayana*
Lightning whelk (snail)	*Busycon contrarium*
Liver fluke	*Trematoda*
Long-legged fly	*Dolichopodidae*
Mantis fly	*Climaciella brunnea*
Marsh periwinkle (snail)	*Littorina irrorata*
Midge	*Tendipedidae*
Millipede	*Diplopoda*
Minuscule fire ant	*Solenopsis globularia*
Mole crab	*Emerita portoricensis*
Mole cricket	*Gryllotalpa hexadactyla*
Monarch butterfly	*Danaus plexippus*
Mossy ark (clam)	*Arca imbricata*
Mud fiddler crab	*Uca rapax*
Nudibranch	*Scyllaea pelagica*
Oriental cockroach	*Blatta orientalis*
Ostracod	*Ostracoda*
Palp worm	*Scolelepis squamata*
Paper bubble (snail)	*Haminoea antillarum*
Pear whelk (snail)	*Busycon spiratum*
Pipevine swallowtail butterfly	*Battus philenor*
Pistol shrimp	*Alpheus heterochaelis*
Plicate horn (snail)	*Cerithidea pliculosa*
Plume worm	*Diopatra cuprea*
Ponderous ark (clam)	*Noetia ponderosa*
Praying mantis	*Stagmomantis limbata*

Common Name	Latin Name
Pseudoscorpion	*Pseudoscorpionida*
Purple marsh crab	*Sesarma reticulatum*
Purple rain mosquito	*Psorophora cyanescens*
Purple storm snail	*Janthina janthina*
Pyramid ant	*Conomyrma flava*
Razor clam	*Tagelus plebius*
Red harvester ant	*Pogonomyrmyx barbatus*
Red paper wasp	*Polistes rubiginosus*
Ribbed mussel	*Geukensia demissus*
Robber fly	*Efferia pogonias*
Rock shell (snail)	*Stramonita haemostoma*
Roundworm	*Nematoda*
Salle's auger (snail)	*Hastula salleana*
Salt-marsh caterpillar	*Estigmene acraea*
Salt-marsh grasshopper	*Conocephalus spp.*
Salt-marsh plant hopper	*Prokelisia marginata*
Salt-marsh snail	*Melampus bidentatus*
Sand digger amphipod	*Pseudohaustorius americanus*
Sand fiddler crab	*Uca panacea*
Sand roach	*Arenivaga bolliana*
Sand wasp	*Bembix sp.*
Sawtooth pen shell (clam)	*Atrina serrata*
Scorpion	*Centruroides vittatus*
Scotch bonnet (snail)	*Phalium granulatum*
Seaweed fly	*Coelopidae*
Seed shrimp	*Ostracoda*
Shimmy worm	*Nephtys bucera*
Shorebug	*Pentacora sp.*
Shore fly	*Ephydridae*
Shore spider	*Pardosa lapidicina*
Southern fire ant	*Solenopsis xyloni*
Speckled crab	*Arenaeus cribrarius*
Spiny-legged rove beetle	*Bledius sp.*
Spoon clam	*Periploma inequale*
Starbellied spider	*Acanthepeira stellata*
Stone crab	*Menippe adina*
Striate bubble (snail)	*Bulla striata*
Striped hermit crab	*Clibanarius vittatus*
Sunflower seed beetle	*Eleodes sp.*
Surf crab	*Lepidopa websteri*
Swallowtail butterfly	*Papilio spp.*
Tapeworm	*Cestoda*
Tarantula	*Dugesiella hentzi*

Common Name	Latin Name
Termite	*Isoptera*
Terrestrial isopod	*Porcellio laevis*
Texas leafcutting ant	*Atta texana*
Thick lucine (clam)	*Phacoides pectinatus*
Thistledown velvet ant (wasp)	*Dasymutilla gloriosa*
Thread worm	*Lumbrineris sp.*
Tiger beetle	*Cicindela dorsalis*
Transverse ark (clam)	*Anadara transversa*
Tropical fire ant	*Solenopsis geminata*
Tulip mussel	*Modiolus americanus*
Valentine ant	*Crematogaster laeviuscula*
Variegated fritillary butterfly	*Euptoieta claudia*
Walking stick	*Anisomorpha ferruginea*
Water boatmen	*Trichocorixa sp.*
Water flea	*Cliadocera*
Wolf spider	*Lycosa spp.*
Yellow cockle (clam)	*Trachycardium muricatum*
Yellow jacket (wasp)	*Polistes exclamans*

Bibliography

1. Introduction

Phelan, R. 1976. *Texas Wild: the Land, Plants, and Animals of the Lone Star State.* New York: E. P. Dutton & Co. Inc.

Tveten, J. L. 1982. *Coastal Texas: Water, Land and Wildlife.* College Station: Texas A & M University Press.

2. Geology

McGowen, J. H., et al. 1976. *Environmental Geologic Atlas of the Texas Coastal Zone–Port Lavaca Area.* Austin: Bureau of Economic Geology.

Spearing, D. 1991. *Roadside Geology of Texas.* Missoula, Mo.: Mountain Press Publishing Company.

Weise, B. R., and W. A. White. 1980. *Padre Island National Seashore.* Austin, Tex.: Bureau of Economic Geology.

Wilkinson, B. H. 1975. Matagorda Island, Texas: The Evolution of a Gulf Coast Barrier Complex. *Bull. Geol. Soc. Amer.* 86: 959–967.

3. History

Baker, T. L. 1991. *Lighthouses of Texas.* College Station: Texas A & M University Press.

Calhoun County Historical Commission. 1967. *Calhoun County Travel Trails.* Port Lavaca, Tex.: Calhoun County Historical Commission.

———. 1981. *The Shifting Sands of Calhoun County, Texas.* Port Lavaca: Calhoun County Historical Commission.

Freier, P. 1979. *A 'Looking Back' Scrapbook for Calhoun County and Matagorda Bay, Texas.* Port Lavaca.

Grimes, R., ed. 1968. *300 Years in Victoria County.* Victoria, Tex.: Victoria Advocate Publishing Co.

Gutherie, K. 1988. *Forgotten Texas Ports.* Austin: Eakin Publications.

Historical Survey Commission, Calhoun County. 1968. *Footsteps of the Pioneers. Calhoun County, Texas. 1519–1865.* Port Lavaca, Tex.

Huson, H. 1953. *Refugio, A Comprehensive History of Refugio County.* Woodsboro, Tex.: Rooke Foundation.

Kingston, M., ed., 1988. *A Concise History of Texas.* Austin: Texas Monthly Press.

Malsch, B. 1988. *Indianola: The Mother of Western Texas.* Austin: State House Press.

Oberste, W. H. 1953. *Texas Irish Empresarios and their Colonies.* Austin: Von Boeckmann-Jones Co.

Weddle, R. S. 1987. *La Salle, the Mississippi, and the Gulf.* College Station: Texas A & M University Press.

Weniger, D. 1984. *The Explorers' Texas: The Lands and Waters.* Austin: Eakin Publications.

Wolfe, J. 1989. *The Murchisons: The Rise and Fall of a Texas Dynasty.* New York: St. Martin's Press.

4. Ecology

Amos, W. H., and S. H. Amos. 1985. *Atlantic and Gulf Coasts.* New York: Alfred A. Knopf, Inc.

Britton, J. C., and B. Morton. 1989. *Shore Ecology of the Gulf of Mexico.* Austin: University of Texas Press.

Carson, R. 1955. *The Edge of the Sea.* New York: New American Library, Inc.

Kaplan, E. H. 1988. *A Field Guide to Southeastern and Caribbean Seashores.* Boston: Houghton Mifflin Co.

McAlister, W. H., and M. K. McAlister. 1987. *Guidebook to the Aransas National Wildlife Refuge.* Victoria, Tex.: Mince Country Press.

Teal, J., and M. Teal. 1969. *Life and Death of the Salt Marsh.* New York: Random House, Inc.

5. Vegetation

Ajilvsgi, G. 1984. *Wildflowers of Texas.* Bryan: Shearer Publishers.

Cannatella, M. M., and R. E. Arnold. 1985. *Plants of the Texas Shore.* College Station: Texas A & M University Press.

Duncan, W. H., and M. B. Duncan. 1987. *The Smithsonian Guide to Seaside Plants of the Gulf and Atlantic Coasts.* Washington, D.C.: Smithsonian Institution Press.

Gould, F. W., and T. Box. 1965. *Grasses of the Texas Coastal Bend.* College Station: Texas A & M University Press.

Gunn, C. R., and J. V. Dennis. 1976. *World Guide to Tropical Drift Seeds and Fruits.* New York: New York Times Book Co.

Jones, F. B. 1982. *Flora of the Texas Coastal Bend.* Corpus Christi: Mission Press.

Kaplan, E. H. 1988. *A Field Guide to Southeastern and Caribbean Seashores.* Boston: Houghton Mifflin Co.

Metzler, S., and V. Metzler. 1992. *Texas Mushrooms: A Field Guide.* Austin: University of Texas Press.

6. Mammals

Davis, W. B. 1960. *The Mammals of Texas.* Austin: Texas Game and Fish Commission.

Schmidly, D. J. 1983. *Texas Mammals East of the Balcones Fault Zone.* College Station: Texas A & M University Press.

7. Birds

Chandler, R. J. 1987. *The Facts on File Guide to North Atlantic Shorebirds.* New York: Facts on File.

Ehrlich, P. R., et al. 1988. *The Birder's Handbook.* New York: Simon & Schuster, Inc.

National Geographic Society. 1983. *Field Guide to the Birds of North America.* Washington, D.C.: National Geographic Society.

Peterson, R. T. 1963. *A Field Guide to the Birds of Texas and Adjacent States.* Boston: Houghton Mifflin Co.

Rappole, J. H. and G. W. Blacklock. 1985. *Birds of the Texas Coastal Bend: Abundance and Distribution.* College Station: Texas A & M University Press.

8. Herptiles

Conant, R. 1975. *A Field Guide to Reptiles and Amphibians of Eastern and Central North America.* Boston: Houghton Mifflin Co.

Raun, G. G. 1965. *A Guide to Texas Snakes.* Austin: Texas Memorial Museum.

9. Fish

Robins, C. R., et al. 1986. *A Field Guide to Atlantic Coast Fishes of North America.* Boston: Houghton Mifflin Co.

Simmons, E. G., and H. D. Hoese. 1959. Studies on the hydrography and fish migrations of Cedar Bayou, a natural tidal inlet on the central Texas coast. *Pub. Inst. Mar. Sci.* 6:56–80.

10. Invertebrates

Andrews, J. 1971. *Sea Shells of the Texas Coast.* Austin: University of Texas Press.

Britton, J. C., and B. Morton. 1989. *Shore Ecology of the Gulf of Mexico.* Austin: University of Texas Press.

Fotheringham, N. 1980. *Beachcomber's Guide to Gulf Coast Marine Life.* Houston: Gulf Pub. Co.

Gosner, K. L. 1978. *A Field Guide to the Atlantic Seashore from the Bay of Fundy to Cape Hatteras.* Boston: Houghton Mifflin Co.

Kaplan, E. H. 1988. *A Field Guide to Southeastern and Caribbean Seashores.* Boston: Houghton Mifflin Co.

Lippson, A. J., and R. L. Lippson. 1984. *Life in the Chesapeake Bay.* Baltimore: Johns Hopkins University Press.

Ruppert, E. E., and R. S. Fox. 1988. *Seashore Animals of the Southeast.* Columbia: University of South Carolina Press.

Index